INTELLECTUAL PROPERTY AND THE NEW INTERNATIONAL ECONOMIC ORDER

In economic sectors crucial to human welfare – agriculture, education, and medicine – a small number of firms control global markets, primarily by enforcing intellectual property (IP) rights incorporated into trade agreements made in the 1980s onward. Such rights include patents on seeds and medicines, copyrights for educational texts, and trademarks in consumer products. According to conventional wisdom, these agreements likewise ended hopes for a New International Economic Order, under which wealth would be redistributed from rich countries to poor. Sam F. Halabi turns this conventional wisdom on its head by demonstrating that the New International Economic Order never faded, but rather was redirected by other treaties, formed outside the nominally economic sphere, that protected poor countries' interests in education, health, and nutrition and resulted in redistribution and regulation. This illuminating work should be read by anyone seeking a nuanced view of how IP is shaping the global knowledge economy.

SAM F. HALABI is the 2017–18 Fulbright Canada Research Chair in Health Law, Policy, and Ethics at the University of Ottawa, Ontario, as well as an Associate Professor of Law at the University of Missouri–Columbia and a Scholar at the O'Neill Institute for National and Global Health Law at Georgetown University. He (with Lawrence O. Gostin and Jeffrey A. Crowley) co-edited *Global Management of Infectious Disease Threats after Ebola* (2017) as well as the Co-Chair of the Ethical, Legal, and Social Implications Working Group of the Global Virome Project. Professor Halabi holds a JD from Harvard Law School, an MPhil in International Relations from the University of Oxford (St. Antony's College), and both a BA and BS from Kansas State University. At Harvard, he was a Teaching Fellow for Stanley Hoffmann's *Ethics and International Relations* as well as Larry Summers's, Michael Sandel's, and Thomas Friedman's *Globalization and Its Critics*.

Intellectual Property and the New International Economic Order

OLIGOPOLY, REGULATION, AND WEALTH REDISTRIBUTION IN THE GLOBAL KNOWLEDGE ECONOMY

SAM F. HALABI
University of Missouri

CAMBRIDGE
UNIVERSITY PRESS

CAMBRIDGE
UNIVERSITY PRESS

University Printing House, Cambridge CB2 8BS, United Kingdom

One Liberty Plaza, 20th Floor, New York, NY 10006, USA

477 Williamstown Road, Port Melbourne, VIC 3207, Australia

314-321, 3rd Floor, Plot 3, Splendor Forum, Jasola District Centre, New Delhi - 110025, India

79 Anson Road, #06-04/06, Singapore 079906

Cambridge University Press is part of the University of Cambridge.

It furthers the University's mission by disseminating knowledge in the pursuit of education, learning and research at the highest international levels of excellence.

www.cambridge.org
Information on this title: www.cambridge.org/9781107177802
DOI: 10.1017/9781316823088

First published 2018

A catalogue record for this publication is available from the British Library

ISBN 978-1-107-17780-2 Hardback
ISBN 978-1-316-62916-1 Paperback

Contents

Preface

This is a book about the nature and distribution of global wealth as it has been shaped by the changing dynamics of international political and economic relations over the last 150 years. The end of the ages of formal colonization and empire, accompanied by rapid technological change, have altered the balance between tangible and intangible sources of wealth, the division between public and private spheres in which wealth is created and managed, and the use of international versus national tools of policy to shape the flow of wealth. As the twentieth century neared its end, intangible forms of wealth in the form of intellectual property such as patents, trademarks, and copyrights assumed an unprecedented place in the wealth hierarchy. Derivative and related legal protections such as trade secrets and exclusivity for data submitted for regulatory approvals expanded the potential value of proprietary knowledge traditionally embodied in intellectual property rights. As a result of these trends, international disputes over intellectual property – as with other forms of wealth that preceded them – are now common, increasing, and high-stakes. This book explores those disputes and situates them within the much longer human history of the creation, distribution, and conflict over wealth.

While historically relevant primarily around "technology transfer" debates during most of the twentieth-century discussions about global wealth disparity, intellectual property protection is now at the core of wealth distribution controversies. Intellectual property protection has dominated international trade and investment negotiations for the last thirty years, playing a critical role in the success, delay, controversy, or termination of agreements such as the World Trade Organization (WTO), the Trans-Pacific Partnership Agreement, and the Anti-Counterfeiting Trade Agreement, to name only the broadest multilateral agreements.[1] Industrialized states successfully tied intellectual property protections they

[1] Sam Foster Halabi, *Multipolarity, Intellectual Property, and the Internationalization of Public Health Law*, 35 Mich. J. Int'l. L. 715 (2014).

desired to the reductions in tariffs and other barriers to imports of foreign agricultural, clothing, and textile goods sought by many developing countries, formalized in the WTO's Agreement on Trade-Related Aspects of Intellectual Property (TRIPS).[2] Thousands of bilateral investment treaties, largely forged between developed states and developing states in negotiations where conditions strongly favored the former, include strong protections for intellectual property rights that frequently exceed those in existing international agreements, and certainly beyond those typically found in local and national laws that developed in most countries over time.[3] This network of agreements has generated a wide range of enforcement mechanisms that reach beyond the slow diplomatic methods that characterized international intellectual property protection from the 1880s onward.[4] Proprietary, intangible knowledge has now become one of the most important sources of wealth – and conflict – in the world.

This project has two origins, one theoretical, one practical. Between 2003 and 2005, I served as a Teaching Fellow at Harvard University for two popular courses – Globalization and Its Critics (led by Thomas Friedman, Michael Sandel, and Larry Summers) and Ethics and International Relations (led by Stanley Hoffmann). Those courses – which together analyzed globalizing forces from the time of St. Thomas Aquinas to the aftermath of the post–September 11, 2001 attacks on the World Trade Center in New York City – demonstrated, for me, the persistent, inevitable confrontation between the security of human beings within their communities and the insecurity caused by communities' interactions with one another. Those interactions, over history, were rarely equal. Conquest and subjugation were far more typical. The most interesting questions were how subordinated communities, peoples, nations, and tribes emerged after conquest: diaspora, dispersion, extinction, integration, resistance, and rebellion.

Five years later, I found myself an international lawyer working within a research and advocacy institute housed at Georgetown University Law Center. While providing legal assistance to low- and middle-income countries, we received a request for assistance on behalf of the South American republic of Uruguay – which, under the leadership of a cardiologist president, had adopted some of the strongest tobacco control measures in the world. The Uruguayan government faced a demand for arbitration from two Swiss corporate entities controlled by Philip Morris

2 Agreement on Trade-Related Aspects of Intellectual Property Rights, art. 8, Apr. 15, 1994, Marrakesh Agreement Establishing the World Trade Organization, Annex 1C, 1869 U.N.T.S. 299 [hereinafter TRIPS].

3 Burton Ong, *The Trademark Law Provisions of Bilateral Free Trade Agreements*, in Graeme B. Dinwoodie & Mark D. Janis (eds), TRADEMARK LAW AND THEORY: A HANDBOOK OF CONTEMPORARY RESEARCH 230 (2008).

4 Benedict Kingsbury, *The Concept of Compliance as a Function of Competing Conceptions of International Law*, 19 MICH. J. INT'L. L. 345 (1998).

International, which, in turn, held local trademarks through a local Uruguayan subsidiary. The measures at issue – precluding tobacco manufacturers from marketing more than one variant of cigarette per brand family and requiring that graphic warnings cover 80 percent of tobacco packaging – brought into conflict the firms' asserted rights to use their trademarks to market their products for the benefit of a distant European parent company and the massive costs tobacco consumption imposed on the Uruguayan state and people.[5] That the claimants were Swiss nationals (even if intangibly so), and that the claims themselves were a legal fiction, was what made the lawsuit possible: a treaty concluded twenty years before had given Swiss nationals rights to protect investments in Uruguay, inclusive of intellectual property rights such as patents, copyrights, and trademarks. Uruguay eventually won the suit, in substantial part because its measures were determined to be sound public health policies supported by an international treaty, the World Health Organization's Framework Convention on Tobacco Control, which had authorized tight restrictions on trademarks appearing on tobacco packaging and labeling.

The episode followed a wave of intellectual property disputes that had pitted European and North American firms (and in many cases their sponsoring governments) against low- and middle-income countries seeking to protect their citizens' health and welfare: patent monopolies that had caused high prices for medicines and disrupted traditional forms of agriculture; copyrights that had limited access to books, films, and literature; and robust protections for trademarks that had favored rights to market over regulatory interests in safeguarding illiterate or semiliterate consumers from misleading or confusing images. The dynamics behind those disputes were similar: bilateral, regional, or multilateral trade and investment agreements gave firms legal claims against governments that had been negotiated between governments with unequal bargaining capacity. Moreover, the agreements appeared to reflect historical strategies adopted decades before over more familiar forms of property and investment. They also reflected the geopolitical dynamics behind those strategies. The overwhelming majority of bilateral investment treaties – the kind that allowed Philip Morris International to sue Uruguay – are between one rich country and one poor one.

The dispute between Philip Morris International and Uruguay prompted me to undertake a broad, historical examination of the ways in which countries had worked with each other and with their major corporations (which until the mid-nineteenth century had been established to carry out specific functions relevant to the state) to ensure favorable economic environments abroad over time: the commerce-promoting underpinnings of nineteenth-century international law;

[5] This is a simplification of both the corporate character and identity of Philip Morris International. It is formally incorporated under the laws of Virginia in the United States and maintains regional operational headquarters in Hong Kong, Lausanne, and New York City. Its brands and trademarks are licensed to subsidiaries and affiliates across the world.

investment agreements between European and North American firms and host governments in Africa, Asia, and South America; the influence of multilateral lending institutions on regulatory approaches in low- and middle-income countries; and the change over time between Friendship, Commerce, and Navigation treaties and their more contemporary manifestations as bilateral investment treaties, which included broader protections for intellectual property assets mostly held by multinational firms. What became clear through the analysis were certain continuities in the creation, expansion, and maintenance of markets abroad by formerly European colonial powers and some non-European ones that nevertheless regarded the international economic climate for their firms as primary geopolitical interests. Similarly, *resistance* to the policies behind those continuities in formerly colonized states or states formed out of former colonial spheres of influence showed signs of similarity and continuity over time. These trends fundamentally revolved around the European-inspired nation-state as the unit of measurement for wealth and its distribution. From the Spanish colonization of North and South America to the present, the flow of wealth has been overwhelmingly *from* what are now characterized as low- and middle-income countries *to* the wealthier countries of Europe and North America, with occasional interruptions mostly in the form of nationalizations undertaken in unpredictable and sometimes revolutionary waves from the period of the South American decolonization forward.[6]

In 1974, formerly colonized states and states within colonial spheres of influence called for a global plan to redistribute wealth and transfer technology to remedy in part the effects of "colonial and alien domination" – a New International Economic Order.[7] This New International Economic Order is slowly materializing. As analyzed through gross domestic product (GDP) change over time, growth in mean incomes within individual countries, and global distribution of income, global wealth inequality as measured by the unit of the European-inspired nation-state has in fact *decreased* in the past decade or so, even if it will remain large for the foreseeable future.[8] Within societies, of course, inequality continues to grow and, in fact, appears to be accelerating [Figure P.1].[9] Because the overwhelming scholarly consensus had determined that the call for a New International Economic Order by low- and middle-income states had achieved little of its stated agenda, the question was: *Why* had inequality between wealthier and poorer states narrowed?

6 Amy Chua, *The Privatization-Nationalization Cycle: The Link between Markets and Ethnicity in Developing Countries*, 95 Colum. L. Rev. 223 (1995).

7 Declaration on the Establishment of a New International Economic Order, Gen. Ass. Res. 3201 (S-VI), May 1, 1974; International Development Strategy for the Second United Nations Development Decade, Gen. Ass. Res. 2626 (XXV), Oct. 24, 1970.

8 Max Roser, *Global Economic Inequality* (2017) available at https://ourworldindata.org/global-economic-inequality.

9 Thomas Piketty, Capital in the Twenty-First Century (2013); Economist, *For Richer, For Poorer* (Oct. 13, 2012) available at http://www.economist.com/node/21564414.

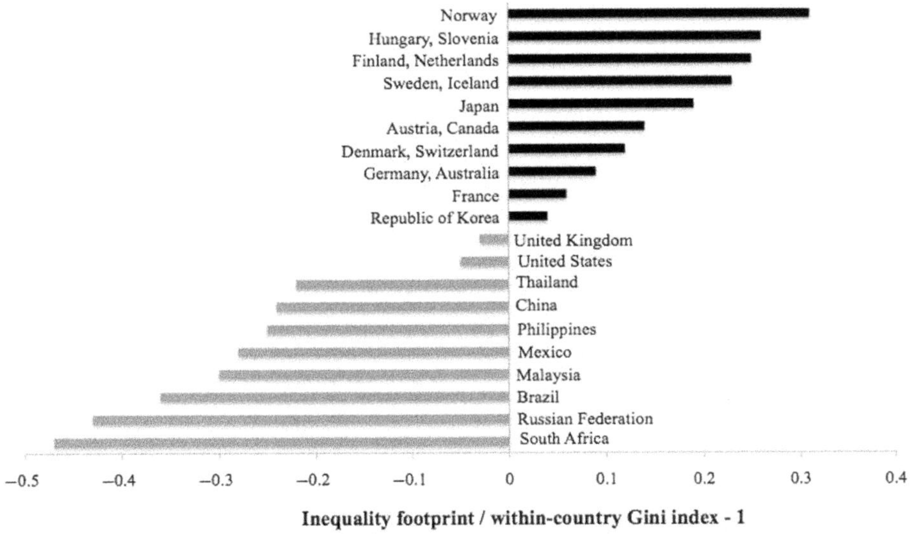

FIGURE P.1 The world's top and bottom countries in terms of the disparity between their inequality footprint and within-country inequality[10]

The answer lies in both how the conception of wealth has changed, especially since the close of the twentieth century, and how low- and middle-income states have resisted and altered their approaches to the global redistribution of wealth. With respect to the latter, the historically wealthy and developed states of Europe, North America, and Asia have not diminished their commitment to growing their national wealth through promotion of friendly economic and political environments abroad. Low- and middle-income countries have, rather, turned their priorities from explicit calls for redistribution of wealth to the establishment and promotion of international institutions and policies that reach effectively the same result. In some contexts this shift in emphasis has been subtle and latent – like calls for access and benefit sharing under the 1992 Convention on Biological Diversity – and in others explicit and pronounced, like Chinese and Indian objections to hard caps on carbon emissions for the reason that such caps would effectively threaten their own growth agendas.[11]

With respect to the former, sources of wealth are increasingly tied to human thought and creative effort, for which intellectual property rights are regularly asserted. Intellectual property-intensive industries contribute more than $6 trillion

[10] Ali Alsamawi, Joy Murray, Manfred Lenzen, Daniel Moran, & Keiichiro Kanemoto, *The Inequality Footprints of Nations: A Novel Approach to Quantitative Accounting of Income Inequality*, 9(10) PLoS One (Oct. 29, 2014) available at http://journals.plos.org/plosone/article?id=10.1371/journal.pone.0110881.

[11] John Lewis Gaddis, Strategies of Containment: A Critical Appraisal of Postwar American National Security Policy 27 (1982).

to the US GDP alone.[12] "Across a broad range of industries and geographies, intellectual property rights now constitute a significant fraction of enterprise value."[13] Approximately 70–80 percent of firms' market capitalization is in the form of intangible assets, which include "patents, trademarks, copyrights, and other business knowledge and know-how."[14] The increasing relevance of intellectual property to firm value has resulted in a corresponding effort by those firms to strengthen intellectual property protections in bilateral, regional, and multilateral trade and investment agreements.

While there is a large and growing body of mostly disputed and inconclusive evidence that strong intellectual property protections benefit low- and middle-income countries as well, their overall position toward stronger intellectual property protections has been to a significant extent antagonistic. Strong intellectual property protections for products and processes relevant to agricultural production, access to medicines, and public health measures have generated acrimonious disputes from the beginning of the modern free trade regime that, from 1995, has incorporated strong intellectual property protections. In 1998, pharmaceutical firms holding patents for HIV/AIDS medications brought suit against the South African government for its efforts to use parallel imports and price controls to expand access to treatment for its exploding HIV/AIDS population.[15] Their suit was based in significant part on the failure of the government to duly regard intellectual property provisions of the new international trade law.[16] Agriculture and seed companies based in the United States and Europe have regularly clashed with both farmers in developing countries and their governments over attempts to interrupt agricultural practices with patent infringement claims. In 2007, Indonesia withheld samples of a highly infectious avian influenza strain from the World Health Organization on the basis that it was the practice of developing countries to share their biological resources only to have them exploited, patented, and generated into commercial products priced out of the reach of consumers in the originating country, a particular problem in the context of medicines and vaccines.[17] Activist Vandana Shiva

[12] U.S. Patent and Trademark Office, *Intellectual Property and the U.S. Economy: 2016 Update ii* (2016) available at https://www.uspto.gov/sites/default/files/documents/IPandtheUSEconomySept2016.pdf.

[13] William W. Fisher III and Felix Oberholzer-Gee, *Strategic Management of Intellectual Property*, 55 Calif. Management Rev. 157 (2013).

[14] Joseph G. Hadzima, Jr, *How to Tell What Patents Are Worth*, Forbes (June 25, 2013) available at https://www.forbes.com/sites/forbesleadershipforum/2013/06/25/how-to-tell-what-patents-are-worth/#5be044fa6e5b.

[15] Ellen F. M. 't Hoen, *TRIPS, Pharmaceutical Patents and Access to Essential Medicines*, 3 Chi. J. Int'l. L. 27–46 (2002).

[16] William Fisher & Cyrill Rigamonti, *The South Africa AIDS Controversy: A Case Study in Patent Law and Policy* (Feb. 10, 2005) available at http://cyber.law.harvard.edu/people/tfisher/South%20Africa.pdf

[17] David Fidler, *Influenza Virus Samples, International Law, and Global Health Diplomacy*, 14(1) Emerg. Infect. Dis. 88–94 (2008).

declared of the international intellectual property protection regime that "the seed wars, trade wars, patent protection, and intellectual property rights [at the World Trade Organization] are claims to ownership through separation and fragmentation. If the regime of rights being demanded ... is implemented, the transfer of funds from poor to rich countries will exacerbate the Third World crisis ten times over."[18]

While a wide range of activists, advocates, scholars, and critics have analyzed the bilateral and multilateral trade and investment treaties responsible for the expansion of international intellectual property rights worldwide, they have neglected to fully appreciate the strength and form that opposition to international intellectual property expansion has taken. This book argues that while low- and middle-income countries have mounted resistance from within the agreements that expanded and strengthened intellectual property rights worldwide, they have also adopted a parallel effort to redistribute intellectual property-related gains through international agreements ostensibly aimed at expanding access to medicines, preserving biodiversity, protecting the rights of indigenous peoples, establishing evidence in support of public health policies, and facilitating access to nutritious food. This book is the first to argue that these international agreements – what are herein described as "International Intellectual Property Shelters," often couched within the language of biodiversity, public health, and food security – represent a body of international economic law that should be understood as a single, cohesive phenomenon that has emerged in response to intellectual property protections expanding through trade and investment agreements. More specifically, that body of law has developed in order to regulate the firms that promoted the incorporation of intellectual property rights into investment and trade agreements and now aggressively assert claims under them.

Within the context of international economic history, the latter agreements are the newest wave of developed countries' efforts to establish, expand, and protect the flow of wealth from poorer countries to richer ones while international public interest agreements aim to reduce or even reverse their impact. From the Doha Declaration on TRIPS and Public Health to the World Health Organization's Pandemic Influenza Preparedness Standard Material Transfer Agreements, to the Framework Convention on Tobacco Control, to the Nagoya Protocol on Access to Genetic Resources and the Fair and Equitable Sharing of Benefits Arising from Their Utilization, international intellectual property shelters put at their core the fundamental distributive questions strong intellectual property rights raise. These agreements fundamentally restructure the relationship between innovation, intellectual property, and access otherwise envisioned in international trade and investment agreements. They effectively call for the redistribution of wealth from richer countries to poorer ones.

Their redistributive objectives are only half their purpose. While low- and middle-income countries have successfully advocated establishment of international

[18] Vandana Shiva, Biopiracy: The Plunder of Nature and Knowledge 56 (1999).

intellectual property shelters in the food security and population health fields, they have also done so through mechanisms that target sectors where a small number of knowledge-intensive firms dominate global markets. The WHO Pandemic Influenza Preparedness Framework, for example, is directly supported by the dominant manufacturers of seasonal influenza vaccines who must also promise to make either intellectual property or end-use products available to poor countries. The Framework Convention on Tobacco Control implicitly authorizes the invalidation of certain classes of trademarks – tobacco firms' overwhelmingly most important asset – and explicitly authorizes measures that curtail the others held by five firms that control global markets outside China. The UNICEF-WHO International Code of Marketing of Breastmilk Substitutes similarly restricts the trademarks of the world's five major infant formula producers and in particular its leader, Nestlé.

International intellectual property shelters are not, therefore, only redistributive efforts led by low- and middle-income countries; they are a nascent and increasingly effective form of supranational regulation over firms that dominate markets closely tied to key redistributive objectives such as improvement of population health. In the class of approaches identified and analyzed in this book, negotiators from developed and low- and middle-income countries target areas of overreach or defectiveness in existing intellectual property protections and draft entirely new agreements that aim to curtail expansive intellectual property rights or impose more rigid regimes to force sharing of innovations and other benefits.

This book endeavors to identify a cycle in the political-economic movements behind global wealth creation, flow, and redistribution, rather than build a normative case for any particular analytical or even policy approach to national or global growth and redistribution questions. That cycle is fundamentally shaped by the primacy of the European-style nation-state as the unit by which global wealth is measured. As of this writing, populist waves across the globe suggest the model remains robust: British voters demanded the reprioritization of state prerogatives over those issued by the EU (so-called Brexit), while US voters similarly (at least under the archaic rules of its presidential election system) installed Donald J. Trump in substantial measure for his promises to reconstruct the relationship between patriotism and economic policy.

The analysis elaborated herein is aimed at enriching the academic debate in two overlapping disciplines: international relations and economics. With respect to the former, the book demonstrates that popular and scholarly declarations that the New International Economic Order failed or disappeared are wrong.[19] Relatedly, the conflict over distribution of global wealth remains a critical factor explaining international diplomatic and economic relations. Multinational firms (which broadly share capital and governance features no matter where established), for

19 Vinod K. Aggarwal & Steve Webber, *The New New International Economic Order*, HARV. BUS. REV., 2 (Apr. 18, 2012).

decades at the center of a wide range of disputes between wealthy and poor countries, remain so.[20] While the relationship between those firms and their supporting governments has been made more complicated by the rise of intellectual property's role in firm value (the manipulation of intellectual property assets' domicile and transfer pricing for tax minimization purposes has pitted many firms against both their own and foreign governments), the relationship between the formal, public sphere attributed to "the state" and the commercial, enterprising drive of the "firm" in the private sphere has, at least since the time of the chartered company, ebbed and flowed. Assertions or implications that at some point in time (the 1950s, the 1970s, the 1990s, etc.) either the "state" or the "firm" retreated were only inflection points in a more complex system of agents that endeavor to write, influence, or revoke international rules for their own benefit. The international competitive states' system means that states and firms will always work as agents for each other under circumstances that may change rapidly.

With respect to economics, at least since Schumpeter, there has been a robust if unresolved debate as to the relationship between research-and-development-intensive industries and market concentration.[21] While that debate has largely centered on the conditions most likely to promote innovation, it has inevitably implicated the reach and importance of competition (or antitrust) law to regulate markets. This book suggests two possibilities for enriching the analysis of this question. First, the variable of the competitive states' system has been infrequently factored into analyses of the innovation-concentration question. As this book explains, international competition between states may need to be a central, starting point of analysis rather than a marginal, infrequently considered variable. Concentration in global markets for broad classes of agrochemical products and seeds and narrower product categories of pharmaceuticals and consumer goods discussed in this book began with efforts by state foreign policy and commerce bureaucracies endeavoring to secure markets against one another (even if influenced by firms). Second, the structure of regulatory regime likely to emerge as a result of conclusions about this question (even if made under conditions of uncertainty) is too narrow both as to the source of regulatory regime and to its scope. As markets concentrate at the global level in research-and-development-intensive industries, the source of regulation is as likely to be supranational as national and involve redistribution of noncompetitively produced products as much or more than market-shaping management.

[20] Reinier Kraakman, John Armour, Paul Davies, Luca Enriques, Henry Hansmann, Gerard Hertig, Klaus Hopt, Hideki Kanda, Mariana Pargendler, Wolf-Georg Ringe, & Edward Rock, The Anatomy of Corporate Law 5 (2004).

[21] Joseph Schumpeter, Capitalism, Socialism, and Democracy 89 (1942).

Acknowledgements

As a book dedicated to changes in international political and economic history, especially as understood with reference to individual and population health, it would not have been possible without a global support network of scholars, students, and researchers who contributed both time and expertise to the final volume. Oscar Cabrera, Larry Gostin, and Nan Hunter at the O'Neill Institute for National and Global Health Law at Georgetown University invited me as a Visiting Researcher for the summer of 2011, which provided both the library resources and collegial atmosphere of Georgetown University Law Center to research the early chapters dedicated to nineteenth-century developments in early South American decolonization as well as the European colonial races in Africa and Asia. Cheng-Feng Wu at the Institutum Iurisprudentiae of Academia Sinica in Taipei, China (Taiwan), graciously invited me to its annual Workshop on Global Health: Normative Foundations and Challenges at which I was able to explore with a group of eight distinguished experts some of the ideas of the book relevant to the relationship between intellectual property and international agreements dedicated to plant genetic resources for agriculture. Peter Yu at Texas A&M University generously supported my participation in three workshops there, including the "Intellectual Property and Global Development: 50 Years After Stockholm" Symposium that brought together some of the leading scholars in the field from across the world to exchange views on the progress of international intellectual property law since 1967. Colleen Flood and Chidi Oguamanam at the University of Ottawa's Centre for Health Law, Policy, and Ethics made possible the presentation of the book's contents during my tenure as the Fulbright Canada Research Chair in Health Law, Policy, and Ethics. The University of Tulsa and the University of Missouri–Columbia supported the research through their respective Summer Research and Faculty Development grant programs.

I presented the work at various stages at the American Society of International Law's Biennial International Economic Law Workshop, the American Society for

Law, Medicine, and Ethics' Health Law Professors Conference, Arizona State University's Sandra Day O'Connor College of Law, the University of Oklahoma College of Law, Texas A&M School of Law, Washburn University Law School, the Washington University (St. Louis) Faculty Workshop, and the University of Arkansas School of Law. Thanks go to Paula Avila-Guillen, Raj Bhala, Sarah Burstein, Anna Carpenter, Carli Conklin, Dennis Crouch, Deborah Dinner, Eric Friedman, Kevin Fandl, Paolo Farah, Roger Ford, Bryan Frye, Stephen Galoob, Yaniv Heled, Laurence Helfer, Virginia Harper Ho, John Inazu, Eric Johnson, Kit Johnson, Ali Khan, Susan Kim, Matt Lamkin, Rhett Larson, Erika Lietzan, Ching-Fu Lin, Jake Linford, Han-Hsi "Indy" Liu, Lois Sheng Liu, Doris Long, Benn McGrady, Craig Martin, John Monahan, Daniel Morales, Melissa Mortazavi, Sarah Roache, Guy Rub, Ana Santos Rutschman, Laurent Sacharoff, Susan Schneider, Mike Schuster, Liz Sepper, Ganesh Sitaraman, Frederic Sourgens, Bryan Thomas, Elizabeth Trujillo, Janewa Osei Tutu, Ryan Vacca, Kristen Van De Biezenbos, Saurabh Vishnubakhat, and Amy Westbrook for helpful comments and suggestions during those presentations.

Anupam Chander, Shubha Ghosh, Paul Gugliuzza, John Head, Patricia Judd, and Megan Shaner provided extensive feedback and valuable editing advice. Special thanks go to Allyn Taylor and Sean Murphy for providing materials used by the World Health Organization's Consultation Committee on Potential Liability and Compensation Provisions for the FCTC. Larry Helfer provided invaluable materials related to the implementation of the Marrakesh Treaty to Facilitate Access to Published Works by Visually Impaired Persons and Persons with Print Disabilities. Zack Brandwein, Catie Coulter, Chris Garner, Habib Hassan, Kyoungho Moon, Dimitrios Panagopolous, Katy Spraberry, and Kelley Sweeney provided excellent research assistance. Shaye Guilfoyle provided superb editorial assistance.

I thank Matt Gallaway and Meera Seth at Cambridge University Press for shepherding the project through the publication process and three anonymous reviewers for providing helpful comments. Finally, I thank my wife and children for their patience and support throughout the publication process.

Introduction

Global Wealth and the Rise of Intellectual Property

Sources, conceptions, and disputes over wealth pervade and define world history. Ancient sources equate "wealth" with precious metals, "property" in the form of fertile land, garments, tools, spices, weapons, animal hides, ivory, precious woods such as ebony, as well as human possessions like slaves, concubines, and captives.[1] For many centuries, rice in Japan served as a source of tax, currency, and capital as well as a sacred grain.[2] Wealth-in-people anthropologists argue that wealth may be assessed in terms of numbers of dependents, followers, or social affiliations.[3]

However framed, conceptions of wealth fundamentally and essentially structure societies and influence the conditions under which societies interact with one another. "Wealth" at its conceptual core divides society into those with relatively less and those with relatively more, tying distribution to other factors that generate or shape marriage, family, caste, class, hierarchy, patriarchy, empire, and, more generally, power.[4] Aristotle associated wealth, especially landed property, with other characteristics such as responsibility, prudence, and steadfastness, although he acknowledged its pernicious tendency to lead to unvirtuous excess.[5] In the modern industrial context, Thorstein Veblen argued that the drive to make wealth *conspicuous* both reflected and steepened class divisions.[6]

1 Victor A. Hurwitz, *Two Terms for Wealth in Proverbs VIII in Light of Akkadian*, 50 Vetus Testamentum 252, 256 (2000); Geoffrey Kron, *The Distribution of Wealth at Athens in Comparative Perspective*, 179 Zeitschrift für Papyrologie und Epigraphik 129, 132 (2011); Euripides, The Trojan Women.

2 Donald Denoon et al., Multicultural Japan from Paleolithic to Postmodern 242 (2001).

3 Jane Guyer & Samuel M. Eno Belinga, *Wealth in People as Wealth in Knowledge: Accumulation and Composition in Equatorial Africa* 36 J. Afr. Hist. 91–120 (1995).

4 David Graeber, *Beads and Money: Notes toward a Theory of Wealth and Power*, 23 Amer. Ethnologist, 4, 5 (1996).

5 Aristotle, The Politics, trans. C. Reeve (1998), 14, 17 [1256b27–33, 1257b16–25].

6 Thorstein Veblen, A Theory of the Leisure Class: A Study of Economic Institutions (1899).

Wealth not only structures societies internally; it also structures the relationship between them. The acquisition of wealth through expedition and conquest was, until quite recently in human history, a legally valid justification for war. The result was garrison societies, conscription, feudalism, and the general obligation of societies to prepare to attack or defend. Wealth could be grown through trade, and while barter was an ancient form of human interaction, the increasing movement of goods through the expansion of the Islamic Empire and Silk Road networks between the eighth and twelfth centuries prompted the multiplication of legal mechanisms of wealth exchange and transfer that took modern shape in fourteenth- and fifteenth-century European city-states.

These political and economic institutions of wealth, which over time vacillated between and within public and private spheres, forcefully merged as the European arrival in the Americas (and growing commerce across Asia) promised barely imaginable riches from the indigenous civilizations of North and South America and the abundant natural resources that they oversaw. European sovereigns formed royal charter companies with the ability to trade and agree to terms with indigenous rulers; own, manage, and acquire territory; hold monopolies; form banks; and, in several cases, raise and direct armies and navies.[7] The British East India Company, for example, formed in 1600 as an entity to facilitate trade with populations in the Indian subcontinent but gradually added direct acquisition of territory, the formation of alliances with local rulers for purposes of competition with other European chartered companies, and then eventually direct rule over much of the subcontinent until the British Crown assumed control in 1858.[8]

The acquisition and transfer of wealth was established as a fundamental principle shaping the relationship between societies that had, theretofore, never interacted or created either norms or understandings for interaction. The Spanish Requierimento, an oath administered to indigenous peoples in the Americas, read in relevant part that God, through the Pope, had "made donation of these isles and Terra Firma to the aforesaid King and Queen (of Spain) and to their successors, our lords, with all that there are in these territories," and that failing to acknowledge or obey the legal assertion would result in the Spaniards taking "you, and your wives, and your children, [to] make slaves of them, and ... your goods, and shall do you all the mischief and damage that we can."[9] Even theologians who argued for more humane treatment of American indigenous populations accepted Spanish access to the new wealth as an essential principle of their interaction. Francisco de Vitoria argued that the "Indians" were made by the same God, and therefore the taking of

7 Louis H. Roper & Bertrand van Ruymbeke, eds., Constructing Early Modern Empires: Proprietary Ventures in the Atlantic World, 1500–1750 (2007).

8 John Keay, The Honourable Company: A History of the English East India Company (1991).

9 Council of Castile (Spain), Requerimiento, 1510 available at https://nationalhumanitiescenter.org/pds/amerbegin/contact/text7/requirement.pdf.

their property was prohibited unless the Indians had violated the Spaniards' lawful rights that included rights to travel, dwell, establish missions, trade, and exert ownership over common resources such as gold mined from rivers.[10] Violation of these rights justified militarized measures to protect them and, ultimately, resort to war against the "barbarians." Silver, sugar, gold, cacao, cochineal, and indigo flowed in vast quantities to the Iberian Peninsula and from there into Europe.[11]

Coincident with the rise of overseas possessions, the European nation-state became the crucial political unit by which to measure and assess wealth.[12] Mercantilism, an approach to economic policy that emphasized measurable increases in the precious metal holdings (especially gold and silver) of monarchs' treasuries, discouraged free trade between colonies and foreign merchants, prejudiced imports generally, limited exports of precious metals, and encouraged domestic manufacturing, exports, and colonial expansion.[13] Adam Smith's *Wealth of Nations* fundamentally challenged this conception of "national wealth," emphasizing the aggregate output of the nation, "the annual produce of the land and labour of the society," a measure that called for different policies toward imports, exports, and investments in agriculture and manufacturing.[14] To be sure, Smith's arguments were not separable from what he viewed as optimal for British success in international trade, commerce, and strategic supremacy, but his argument caused a major reevaluation of the nature of national wealth and the conditions under which it would flourish.[15]

The eighteenth and nineteenth centuries observed the growing tension between the European nation-state as the fundamental unit of the measure of wealth and the cultural characteristics of the beneficiaries of that wealth. The break of the American colonies from the British Crown was fundamentally caused by the development of a distinctive colonial identity that demanded acknowledgment of that identity in the process of regulating wealth transfer – tax – between the colonies and London.[16] As linguistic, merchant, and administrative classes in the Caribbean and South America began to form an essential but nevertheless marginalized link between

10 Francisco de Vitoria, *De Indis*, in Anthony Pagden and Jeremy Lawrance, eds., FRANCISCO DE VITORIA: POLITICAL WRITINGS 231 (1991).

11 Peter C. Emmer, *The First Global War: The Dutch versus Iberia in Asia, Africa and the New World, 1590–1609*, 1 E-JOURNAL OF PORTUGUESE HISTORY 2 (2003).

12 Historians, legal scholars, and political scientists justifiably designate 1648 as the crucial date for the establishment of the sovereign nation-state as the fundamental unit of the international system, but the predicate features long predated that year. Leo Gross, *The Peace of Westphalia 1648–1948*, 42 AM. J. INT'L L. 20, 20–41 (1948).

13 JOHN J. MCCUSKER, MERCANTILISM AND THE ECONOMIC HISTORY OF THE EARLY MODERN ATLANTIC WORLD (2001).

14 ADAM SMITH, AN INQUIRY INTO THE NATURE AND CAUSES OF THE WEALTH OF NATIONS, Edwin Cannan ed., I.I.9, 248 (1776, 1904).

15 Andrew Wyatt Walter, *Adam Smith and the Liberal Tradition in International Relations*, in Ian Clark and Iver B. Neumann (eds), CLASSICAL THEORIES OF INTERNATIONAL RELATIONS 142–72 (1996).

16 Grover Norquist, *Tea, Taxes, and the Revolution*, FOREIGN POLICY (July 3, 2012) available at http://foreignpolicy.com/2012/07/03/tea-taxes-and-the-revolution/

ruling classes with closer ties to Europe and lower laboring classes that produced the wealth ultimately destined for Europe, the justifications for creation of wealth for increasingly "foreign" beneficiaries and the growing cohesion of local cultural identities came under substantial pressure, resulting in the formation of new decolonized states in the Western Hemisphere from the early 1800s forward.[17] As colonization waned in North and South America, it accelerated in Africa and Asia.

To that point, the beginning of the industrial revolution, wealth – at least so far as the European states increasingly colonizing the world were concerned – was fundamentally material and tangible: gold, silver, gems, agricultural goods and raw materials, along with the weapons, armies, and navies to ensure their continued flow.[18] But the industrial revolution also elevated the relevance to wealth of creative works, inventions, and the associated monopolies that could be ordered by public authorities first for the benefit of national wealth and second for "rights holders" as they came to be understood.[19] The award of patents, it was argued, would provide an incentive for inventors to create new products or processes or improve upon existing ones while disclosing important information on which additional work could be undertaken by others, all of which dovetailed with broader policies aimed at increasing national wealth.[20] Copyrights allowed artists, musicians, writers, and other creators to control the copying, distribution, and adaptation of their works providing an incentive for these constituencies to produce works that would increase the education and understanding of participants in the economy – workers, managers, investors – while also constructing and edifying the cultural fabric in which those participants operated.[21]

These were the explicit purposes behind intellectual property laws adopted toward the beginning of the industrial revolution and the strengthening competition for overseas colonies. Historian Seaborne Davies noted of English patent law (which, like its counterparts in other countries, had covered a broad class of economic monopolies granted by the monarch) that "practically every patent refers in its recitals to the benefit which is expected to accrue to the nation – the commodity of the realm – from the invention."[22] Over the course of the 1780s, the French "royal administration facilitated the issuance of privileges in inventions, while easing procedures of prior expertise. In return, it required of privileges holders

17 BENEDICT ANDERSON, IMAGINED COMMUNITIES (1983).

18 PAUL KENNEDY, RISE AND FALL OF THE GREAT POWERS (1987).

19 CHRISTINE MACLEOD, INVENTING THE INDUSTRIAL REVOLUTION: THE ENGLISH PATENT SYSTEM 1660–1800 (1988).

20 Parliamentary Papers (UK), Report from the Select Committee on the Law Relative to Patents for Inventions (1829) 332, vol III, 415 at 681. The level of specification has increased over time and is now a feature of all patent laws.

21 Jane Ginsburg, *A Tale of Two Copyrights: Literary Property in Revolutionary France and America*, 64 TUL. L. REV. 991, 995, 1006 (1990).

22 D. Seaborne Davies, *Early History of the Patent Specification* (pts. 1–2), 50 L.Q.R. 88–109, 260–74 (1934).

the deposit of their inventions in order to promote the development of industrial knowledge."[23] In 1814, the British Literary Copyright Act provided that where a book was first published in Britain, the owner of copyright was able to bring an action against "any Bookseller or Printer, or other Person whatsoever, in any Part of the United Kingdom of Great Britain and Ireland, in the Isles of Man, Jersey or Guernsey, or in any other part of the British Dominions, [who] shall ... print, reprint, or import ... any such Book or Books."[24]

The actual relationship between intellectual property rights and wealth – individual and social – is poorly understood, acrimoniously disputed, and capable of multiple, mutually exclusive interpretations.[25] Monopolies over ideas, creative works, and inventions may be justified by the idea of a social contract type of reward system: that a creator or inventor should receive compensation for making something useful for society.[26] The result of creative pursuits and innovation would thereby enrich both the creator and society. Extending a temporary monopoly to the creator or inventor is an administrable way (with long historical precedents) to tailor the benefit.[27] Monopolies given to certain images, combinations of words, logos, sounds, or color schemes – trademarks – are mutually beneficial because they lower the cost to consumers of identifying qualities and characteristics of goods and services they prefer.

Another theory suggests that profits from intellectual property monopolies extend incentives for optimal levels of creation and invention.[28] According to this view, whatever level of creative or inventive activity might occur in society would be far less than what could be achieved through the disproportionate profits given to creators and inventors who enjoyed monopolies. Joseph Schumpeter famously argued that innovation was far more likely to progress under conditions of monopoly, which provides conditions for "long-range planning," "superior methods" – such as experience and financial resources – and that are not available to competitive firms. It also provides for the "insuring or hedging" activities needed for investment.[29]

A third theory applicable to patents is compensation for revealing the secret. Without some kind of incentive, the argument goes, inventors would hoard knowledge or at least not share it as readily. "Patents are said to be the price that must be

[23] Gabriel Galvez-Behar, *Was the French Patent System Democratic? France, 19th Century* (2008), available at https://hal.archives-ouvertes.fr/halshs-00544730/document.

[24] Lionel Bently, *The "Extraordinary Multiplicity" of Intellectual Property Laws in the British Colonies in the Nineteenth Century*, 12 THEOR. INQ. LAW 161, 172 (2011).

[25] Rachel Brewster, *The Surprising Benefits to Developing Countries of Linking International Trade and Intellectual Property*, 12 CHI. J. INT'L. L. 1, 6 (2011).

[26] Bently, *supra* note 24.

[27] Adam Karbowski & Jacek Prokop, *Controversy over the Economic Justifications for Patent Protection*, 5 PROCEDIA ECONOMICS AND FINANCE 393 (2013).

[28] *Id.*

[29] Michael Carrier, *Two Puzzles Resolved: Of the Schumpeter–Arrow Stalemate and Pharmaceutical Innovation Markets*, 93 IOWA L. REV. 394 (2008).

paid to induce the innovator to disclose the workings of the patented product or process, thus allowing for a more rapid diffusion of the underlying knowledge."[30]

Each of these arguments is rebutted by similarly persuasive evidence and logic. Many of the most important works and inventions that have contributed to human culture, health, and welfare materialized without intellectual property monopolies behind them.[31] As Boldrin and Levine argue,

> The list of industries that were born and grew in the absence of intellectual property protection is almost boundless. In Italy, pharmaceutical products and processes were not covered by patents until 1978; the same was true in Switzerland for processes until 1954, and for products until 1977. Agricultural seeds and plant varieties could not be patented in the United States until 1970, and they still cannot be in most of the world. All kinds of "basic science" from mathematics to physics (and even economics, but no longer finance) cannot be patented. Simultaneously, the copyright on scientific articles enriches a handful of encroached and inefficient publishers instead of the scholars who wrote the articles.[32]

Creative works and inventions are inevitably the result of witting and unwitting collaboration, learning, and influence, rarely an individual author's or inventor's exclusive conception or idea.[33] Intellectual property rights, therefore, limit and cordon off wealth-creating relationships and interactions, perhaps ultimately *reducing* social welfare.[34] Large rewards through monopoly can and do give some creators and inventors disproportionate gains for low-cost creations that may also play a critical role for entire industries.[35] Innovators (now more commonly the firms who employ them) may then become wealthy while slowing innovation to society as a whole.

The level of disclosure communicated by patents may also fail to reach a socially optimal level while still providing a monopoly to a claimant.[36] This occurs when a

30 Alex Tabarrok, *Patent Theory versus Patent Law*, 1(1) Contributions to Economic Analysis and Policy 1, 20 (2002).

31 *Id.*

32 Michele Boldrin & David Levine, Against Intellectual Monopoly (2005).

33 Mark Lemley, *The Myth of the Sole Inventor*, 110 Mich. L. Rev. 709 (2012); Hyejin Youn, Deborah Strumsky, Luis M. A. Bettencourt, & José Lobo, *Invention as a Combinatorial Process: Evidence from US Patents*, 12 J. Royal Soc. Interface (2015); John M. Golden, *Biotechnology, Technology Policy, and Patentability: Natural Products and Invention in the American System*, 50 Emory L. J. 101, 110–11 (2001).

34 Michael Heller & Rebecca Eisenberg, *Can Patents Deter Innovation? The Anticommons in Biomedical Research*." 280 (5364) Science 698–701 (1998); James Bessen & Eric Maskin, *Sequential Innovation, Patents, and Imitation*, 40(4) RAND Journal of Economics 611–35 (2009).

35 Alex Tabarrok, *Patent Theory versus Patent Law*, 1(1) Contributions to Economic Analysis and Policy 1, 3 (2002).

36 Over the course of history studied in this book, countries maintained different systems for claims related to a patent – some were "first to file," others were "first to invent," and still others were "first to disclose."

patent application fails to reveal, or reveals in an obscured way, adequate information for the patented claims to be used by others.[37] Because challenging patent validity on the basis of disclosure is costly, it creates an opportunity for firms to secure a monopoly while at the same time limiting the ability of others to use the invention for other socially beneficial purposes.

In between or perhaps outside disagreements as to the usefulness and abuse of intellectual property rights are theories that suggest that the orthodox arguments made for or against the intellectual property–monopoly relationship overemphasize the mutual benefit promised and neglect the structural economic game behind the relationship. These theories suggest that the system of monopolies for intellectual property claims works for *society* precisely because it *does not* really work for authors and inventors. Copyrights and patents are costly to enforce, patent infringement claims especially are frequently defeated, and so the huge monopoly profits promised to entrepreneurs are rarely realized while society benefits from knockoffs and proliferation of inventions that fail to obtain patent protection.[38]

Whether or not intellectual property protections *actually* promote aggregate wealth creation for society is (somewhat curiously) beside the point. As Albert Hu and I. P. L. Png pithily phrased it, "while empirical support for the hypothesis that stronger IP rights lead to greater innovation is sparse, pressure to strengthen IP rights has been unrelenting."[39] That pressure has largely been mounted by "transnational firms in knowledge-intensive sectors" that can move into and exploit new markets with greater ease than firms in other industries.[40] Those firms in knowledge-intensive sectors lobby for changes to strengthen intellectual property laws in most countries as part of the normal legislative process, as well as their home or sponsor governments through trade and investment agreements those countries negotiate with others.[41] To be sure, the latter governments are fundamentally convinced as to the relationship between *national wealth* and strong intellectual property protection. As Daniel Marti, the US Intellectual Property Enforcement Coordinator, declared, "the protection of intellectual property rights is about promoting economic prosperity and supporting jobs; opening new markets for U.S. goods and services; and fostering innovation and investments in research and development," notwithstanding the possibility that

37 Nathaniel B Lipkus, Jocelyn E Mackie, & Peter A Singer, *Guidance for Reconciling Patent Rights and Disclosure of Findings at Scientific Meetings*, 8 Health Res. Pol. Syst. 15 (2010).

38 Kal Raustiala & Chris Sprigman, The Knockoff Economy: How Imitation Sparks Innovation (2012); Mariano Zukerfeld, *On the Link between the English Patent System and the Industrial Revolution: Economic, Legal, and Sociological Issues*, 8(1) Intersect (2014).

39 Albert G. Z. Hu & I. P. L. Png, *Patent Rights and Economic Growth: Evidence from Cross-Country Panels of Manufacturing Industries*, 65(3) Oxford Econ. Papers 675–98 (2013).

40 Susan Sell, Private Power, Public Law: The Globalization of Intellectual Property Rights 19 (2003).

41 Margot Kaminski, *The Capture of International Intellectual Property Law through the U.S. Trade Regime*, 87 S. Cal. L. Rev. 977 (2014).

expanding intellectual property rights may actually do none of those or only some combination of them depending on the industry involved.[42]

For the countries that emerged from European colonization, by contrast, the relationship between intellectual property and wealth was and is fundamentally different.[43] Intellectual property laws in Europe and North America adapted as those economies developed. For example, the United States was largely hostile to extending copyright protections to foreign works for much of the nineteenth century, based in significant part on the desire to have its growing population enjoy access to literature and educational materials. Yet, as this book emphasizes (in line with earlier scholars), the current global pressure to strengthen intellectual property rights applies regardless of the effect on economies in which stronger intellectual property protections may be, and likely are, at best benign and at worst wealth destroying.

In a 1997 study, Walter Park and Juan Carlos Ginarte examined the effects of intellectual property rights on growth in both wealthy and poor countries.[44] Their study analyzed intellectual property index values (comprised of coverage of specific intellectual property rights membership in international patent agreements, provisions for loss of protection, enforcement mechanisms, and the duration of rights protection) in sixty countries between 1960 and 1990.[45] They determined that intellectual property rights do not appear to have a direct impact on growing national wealth but may, under certain circumstances, encourage investment and risk taking within the research sector.[46]

Their study found that a 1 percent increase in a country's intellectual property rights index raised the capital investment rate by 0.26 percent and the research investment rate by 0.77 percent.[47] But this impact was *much larger* in the wealthier thirty countries in their study. *Non–intellectual property market liberalization measures* had a much larger impact in poorer countries. Comparably, physical capital was less significant in the richer nations while human capital was found to be more valuable and impactful in poorer ones. Ultimately, intellectual property rights "explained only the physical and research capital investment behavior of the top 30 economies."[48]

Indeed, to the extent developing countries must cultivate human capital in order to grow, robust enforcement of intellectual property may harm more than help.

42 Daniel Marti, *Supporting, Innovation, Creativity, and Enterprise: Charting a Path Ahead* 5 (2016), available at https://www.whitehouse.gov/sites/whitehouse.gov/files/omb/IPEC/2016jointstrategicplan.pdf.

43 Kal Raustiala, *International Rights Approaches to Intellectual Property* 40 U.C. Davis L. Rev. 1021, 1032–33 (2007).

44 Walter Park & Juan Carlos, *Intellectual Property Rights and Economic Growth*, 15 Contemporary Economic Policy 51 (1997).

45 *Id.* at 52.

46 *Id.* at 51.

47 *Id.* at 59.

48 The authors explain this by noting that richer nations have "accumulated larger stocks of tangible capital," resulting in "greater diminishing returns to physical capital." *Id.* at 59.

Because intellectual property protections authorize monopolies to their proprietors, they undermine many of the policies that are necessary for the development of human capital in developing countries, especially healthy and literate working populations. For example, before 1995, intellectual property rights on drugs were generally recognized in wealthier countries, but developing countries viewed such rights as antithetical to development objectives. A study undertaken by World Intellectual Property Organization (WIPO) in 1988 for the negotiating group that was dealing with TRIPS in the Uruguay Round revealed that of the ninety-eight Members of the Paris Convention for the Protection of Industrial Property (Paris Convention), forty-nine excluded pharmaceutical products from protection, forty-five excluded animal varieties, forty-four excluded methods of treatment, forty-four excluded plant varieties, forty-two excluded biological processes for producing animal or plant varieties, thirty-five excluded food products, thirty-two excluded computer programs, and twenty-two excluded chemical products.[49]

Some developing countries that had inherited European and North American intellectual property laws through colonization and empire revisited and revised those laws to fit their economic circumstances:

> After World War II, many developing countries became independent States. Some of them began to review the operation of the intellectual property systems that had been left to them by their colonizers. So, for example, after India's independence, two expert committees conducted a review of the Indian patent system. They concluded that the Indian system had failed "to stimulate inventions among Indians and to encourage the development and exploitation of new inventions". Interestingly, India did not choose to abandon patent law as a tool of regulatory policy but instead to redesign it to suit her own national circumstances-a country with a low research-and-development (R&D) base, a large population of poor people and some of the highest drug prices in the world. Passed in 1970, India's new patent law followed the German system of allowing the patenting of methods or processes that led to drugs but not allowing the patenting of the drugs themselves. Patent protection for pharmaceuticals was only granted for seven years, as opposed to fourteen years for other inventions. This law became the foundation stone for a highly successful Indian generics industry.[50]

While limited to a relatively few developing countries, the decisions to selectively advantage certain intellectual property sectors appears prudent given subsequent analyses. Economists Yongmin Chen and Thitima Puttitanun have hypothesized that there may exist an optimal level of intellectual property rights protection that balances incentives for domestic innovation with "imitation of northern advanced

[49] World Intellectual Property Organization, *Existence, Scope and Form of Generally Internationally Accepted and Applied Standards/Norms for the Protection of Intellectual Property*, wo/INF/ Sep. 29, 1988, issued as GATT Document MTN.GNG/NG~ 1/W/ 24/REV. 1.

[50] Peter Drahos, *Developing Countries and International Intellectual Property Standard-Setting* 5 (5) J. WIPO 765–89 (2002).

technologies."[51] Examining sixty-four developing countries between 1975 and 2000, their study utilized a model for a small developing country with an import sector and a domestic sector.[52] Using Park and Ginarte's index, they found that strengthened intellectual property rights protection made imitation more difficult in both sectors but increased the incentive to innovate in the domestic firms of both the local and import sectors.[53] They concluded that a developing country's ideal level of intellectual property protection "exhibits a U-shaped curve with respect to its level of economic development."[54] As a country's technological capabilities exceed a specific threshold, innovation overtakes imitation, and the optimal intellectual property protection strength increases in correlation with the levels of development. Thus strong intellectual property protection regimes make sense after a certain point in economic development.[55] This demonstrated that increasing intellectual property rights protection had "a greater impact on innovations in countries with higher levels of economic development."[56]

Indeed, that is precisely the experience of now middle- or high-income countries that achieved substantial growth in relatively short time periods. Yee Kim, Kuen Lee, Walter Park, and Kineung Choo studied South Korea's experience with intellectual property protections tailored to given points in development.[57] They sought to establish "not only the *strength* of [intellectual property rights] but also the different *types* of [intellectual property rights] that would be appropriate for countries at different stages of economic development."[58] Their study analyzed a large data set of more than seventy nations in addition to a focused case study on the impact of varied forms of intellectual property protections to South Korea's economic development and growth.

They observed that patent protection contributes to innovation and growth in developed nations, but not necessarily in the developing world. Conversely, utility model protection – which encourages local modifications of patented inventions by requiring less stringent criteria, imposing simpler procedures, and offering shorter term of protection – affords developing countries opportunities to "build up their indigenous innovative capacities."[59] They concluded that "different types of

51 Yongmin Chen & Thitima Puttitanun, *Intellectual Property Rights and Innovation in Developing Countries*, 78 J. Dev. Econ. 474 (2005).

52 The import sector is comprised of a northern foreign firm and a domestic firm, while the local sector consists of two domestic firms. *Id.* at 476.

53 *Id.*

54 *Id.*

55 *Id.* at 488.

56 *Id.*

57 Yee Kyoung Kim, Keun Lee, Walter G. Park & Kineung Choo, *Appropriate Intellectual Property Protection and Economic Growth in Countries at Different Levels of Development*, 41 Research Policy 358 (2012).

58 *Id.*

59 Stephen Ladas, National and International Protection of Patents, Trademarks and Related Rights (1975). At the time of his writing, only Brazil, Germany, Italy, Japan, the

intellectual property rights are more appropriate for countries at different stages of economic development."[60] They highlighted that what matters in innovation and growth is not simply the strength of intellectual property protection, but also the types of protection employed.

With its focus on protection of innovation with relatively low inventiveness, few developed countries feature the utility model in their intellectual property framework, but many developing economies use it to encourage domestic technological capacity.[61] Utility model adoption is, however, tied primarily to the historical legal traditions of a country, rather than conscientious planning.[62]

Their analysis explains why South Korea, which shared many characteristics with poor developing countries in the 1950s (its per capita GDP in 1960 was lower than several sub-Saharan countries), became the eleventh largest economy in the world by 2017.[63] Before the mid-1980s, South Korea was a nation of "limited technological capability" that relied primarily on "reverse engineering, importation of technology, and imitation" to innovate and satisfy its technological needs.[64] By the late 1990s, the country had become "one of the leading patenting nations," increasing the number of US patents granted to Koreans from 14 in 1982 to 3,562 in 1999.[65] Similarly, the number of utility model applications in the country exceeded the number of patent applications until the early 1990s, the period immediately after South Korea strengthened its intellectual property laws.[66] By 1995, the number of patent applications had exceeded the number of utility model applications. This demonstrated that utility model innovation is more appropriate for "companies that are resource-poor or below the technological frontier."[67] Patents, on the other hand, are "more conducive to innovation" in companies that have "reached some critical technological capability" that allows them to "produce innovations with sufficient inventive steps to qualify for patent protection."[68]

Philippines, Poland, Portugal, South Korea, Spain, and Taiwan had official protections for utility models.

60 Kim, Lee, Park & Choo, *supra* note 57, at 368.

61 For example, South Korea, Taiwan, China, and Malaysia. *Id.*

62 Daron Acemoglu, Simon Johnson & James A. Robinson, *The Colonial Origins of Comparative Development: An Empirical Investigation*, 91 Am. Econ. Rev. 1369 (2001); Rafael La Porta, Florencio Lopez-de-Silanes & Andrei Shleifer, *The Economic Consequences of Legal Origins*, 46 J. Econ. Lit. 285 (2008).

63 OECD, Korea, available at http://www.oecd.org/korea/.

64 Kim, Lee, Park & Choo, *supra* note 57, at 359.

65 The share of US patents granted to Koreans increased from 0.01% to 2.32%. *Id.*

66 The aggregate R&D/GDP ratio went from less than 1% to more than 2.5%, and the share of private R&D in the national R&D grew from less than 50% in the early 1980s to 80% by the end of the same decade. The number of corporate R&D centers by the mid-1980s was five times greater than the forty-five that existed in 1981. *Id.*

67 *Id.*

68 *Id.*

Moreover, the strength of patent protection has a "significant, positive association" with innovations in high-income countries, but a "statistically insignificant coefficient" in middle and low-income nations.[69] The study further indicated that patenting intensity in middle- to low-income countries had a "negative but statistically insignificant association with GDP per capita growth" in all economic models, unlike the "much larger" impact that patenting intensity had for high-income countries.[70] Patents raise business costs in middle- to low-income countries via royalties and fees, which in turn increase the production cost of technological innovation. Regarding utility models in the developing world, however, their results demonstrated a positive and statistically significant association with growth in all economic models, indicating innovative value "specific to middle and low income countries."[71]

Some evidence even suggests that stronger intellectual property protections in poorer countries not only make firms in those countries worse off but firms in wealthy countries as well. In a 1999 study, Amy Glass and Kamal Saggi sought to determine the effect that stronger intellectual property rights in developing countries exerted on innovation, imitation, and foreign direct investment (FDI).[72] They hypothesized that multinational corporations in wealthy countries tended to develop high-value products through innovation while poorer countries tended to develop high-value products through imitation.[73] They determined that not only did stronger intellectual property rights in poorer countries make firms "no more secure from imitation"; they also raised the cost of imitation, such that poorer countries simply had to expend more resources to achieve the same level of imitation.[74] This, in turn, left fewer resources for production, negatively impacting foreign direct investment in those countries.[75] The adverse impact on foreign direct investment, in turn, raised costs for innovation for firms in wealthy countries.[76] The reduced imitation efficiency created by stronger intellectual property rights was "equivalent to a tax on imitation combined with a reduction in [poorer countries'] resources."[77] Regardless of the model employed, "stronger [intellectual property protection in poor countries] reduces FDI and innovation."[78] Conversely, when intellectual property

[69] *Id.* at 365.
[70] *Id.*
[71] *Id.* at 368.
[72] Amy Jocelyn Glass & Kamal Saggi, *Intellectual Property and Foreign Direct Investment*, 56 J. Int'l Econ. 387, 387 (2002).
[73] *Id.* at 389.
[74] *Id.*
[75] The authors termed this a "resources wasting effect" that served to reduce the Southern labor supply. *Id.*
[76] As more labor is expended on imitation in the South, FDI is "crowd[ed] out" of these nations, reducing innovations in Northern countries as they must employ resources to account for the reduction in FDI. *Id.*
[77] *Id.* at 399.
[78] *Id.*

protection was weakest "all products [were] produced by multinationals in [poorer countries]."[79]

Moreover, most evidence suggests that the impact of patent protection "varies from industry to industry," and that the pharmaceutical and chemical industries benefit the most from the protection patents afford.[80] Sixty-five percent of pharmaceutical inventions and 30 percent of chemical industry inventions "would not have taken place but for patent protection."[81] In other industries, however, such strong intellectual property protection "was not found to be essential."[82] For many high technology industries, like the aerospace industry, the complexity of inventions and innovations make any attempts at reverse engineering particularly challenging and costly, even without the obstacle of intellectual property protection.[83] Another study exploring the effect of strengthened pharmaceutical patent protection in 1970s Italy concluded that the changes "had little or no impact" on research and development expenditures or the "introduction of new chemical entities."[84] Overall, evidence that intellectual property rights can correlate with development and innovative activity "is quite weak."[85] In fact, the World Bank has noted that stronger intellectual property protections may instead instead limit "follow-up innovations" in both the developed and developing world, since so many of these innovations "draw on inventions whose patents have not yet expired."[86]

The competing perspectives, evidence, and intellectual property policies adopted along the global rich–poor fault line are the subject of the following chapters. Over the course of the 1960s, 1970s, and 1980s, the relationship between wealth, intellectual property, and development began to foment tensions in bilateral and multilateral fora.[87] Over the course of the 1960s and especially the 1970s, global firms became influential intermediaries between rich and poor countries, increasingly powerful in national and international bodies traditionally comprised of nation-states, and ultimately the subject of direct regulation in international legal areas where poor countries held sway.[88] More importantly, multinational firms – which

79 *Id.* at 408.

80 Nagesh Kumar, *Intellectual Property Rights, Technology and Economic Development: Experiences of Asian Countries*, 38 Econ. Pol. Weekly 209, 210 (2003).

81 *Id.*

82 *Id.*

83 *Id.*

84 *Id.*

85 *Id.* at 212.

86 *Id.* at 212.

87 D. M. Mills, *Patents and the Exploitation of Technology Transferred to Developing Countries (in particular those of Africa)* 24 Industrial Property (1985); Pfizer, *Protecting Intellectual Property in a Global Marketplace*, Harvard Business School (1992); J. Braithwaite & P. Drahos, Global Business Regulation (2000).

88 S. K. Sell, *Intellectual Property Protection and Antitrust in the Developing World: Crisis, Coercion, and Choice*, 49 Int'l Org. 315 (1995); C. F. Johnson, *The Origins of the Stockholm Protocol*, 18 Bulletin of the Copyright Society of the U.S.A. 91 (1970–71).

became gradually more dependent on intangible intellectual property assets for their value – transformed in the eyes of developing countries from recalcitrant and sometimes disloyal partners on the path to wealth to the chief enemy of their human development goals.[89] Intellectual property became metaphorically and to some extent literally an extension of policies originally adopted during the period of global colonization and implemented through firms largely established during that period.

Developing countries from the 1960s began to advocate and construct global mechanisms by which multinational firms' behavior might be constrained. In contrast to laws used in Europe and North America, which focused on competition and, in the utilities context, price regulation, developing countries began to focus on access to firms' knowledge and products. The model of regulation they developed deeply influenced international agreements formed around the mid-1990s.

[89] P. Drahos, *Global Property Rights in Information: The Story TRIPS at the GATT*, 13 PROMETHEUS 6 (1995).

PART I

Movements in Global Wealth Creation and Redistribution

1

Economic Development in Low- and Middle-Income Countries after Decolonization

"Decolonization" – and the economic and social features decolonized states generally shared – is a figurative reconstruction of complex geopolitical phenomena that, most importantly, created new gravitational centers in international economics and politics.[1] While the Cold War overshadowed the creation of new states from former, primarily European, empires, and dictated certain realities for them, the gap between wealthy and poor countries became one of the major fault lines of international relations then and now.[2] Between 1945 and 1960, at least three-dozen new states in Asia and Africa emerged from former European colonial projects [Figure 1.1.].[3] Some of these states achieved independence or autonomy through violent struggle while others broke peacefully and with terms established for relations thereafter. In 1946, there were 35 member states in the United Nations; as the newly independent nations of the "third world" joined the organization, membership grew to 127 by 1970.[4] The size, location, and administrative sophistication of the new states mattered. Egypt, India, and Indonesia, for example, became major regional and in some ways global powers within quite short time periods while countries in much of Africa and Asia struggled to establish and maintain cohesive states.[5] In 1955, Indonesia hosted the most important early conference of newly decolonized states – at that time "new emerging forces" – who articulated a unified vision based on resistance to Western neocolonialism whether or not veiled through Cold War machinations.[6]

1 David Strang, *Global Patterns of Decolonization, 1500–1987*, 35 International Studies Quarterly 429–54 (1991).

2 Roger Hansen, Beyond the North-South Stalemate 245–78 (1979).

3 U.S. Department of State, *Decolonization of Asia and Africa*, 1945–60 available at https://2001-2009.state.gov/r/pa/ho/time/cwr/98782.htm

4 United Nations, *Growth in United Nations Membership, 1945–Present*, available at http://www.un.org/en/sections/member-states/growth-united-nations-membership-1945-present/index.html.

5 Mohamad Heykal, Sphinx and Commissar: The Rise and Fall of Soviet Influence in the Arab World (1978); Greg Fealy & Hugh White, *Indonesia's "Great Power" Aspirations: A Critical View*, 3(1) Asia and the Pacific Policy Studies 92–100 (2016); Henry Kissinger, Diplomacy (1997).

6 Richard Wright, The Color Curtain: A Report on the Bandung Conference (1956).

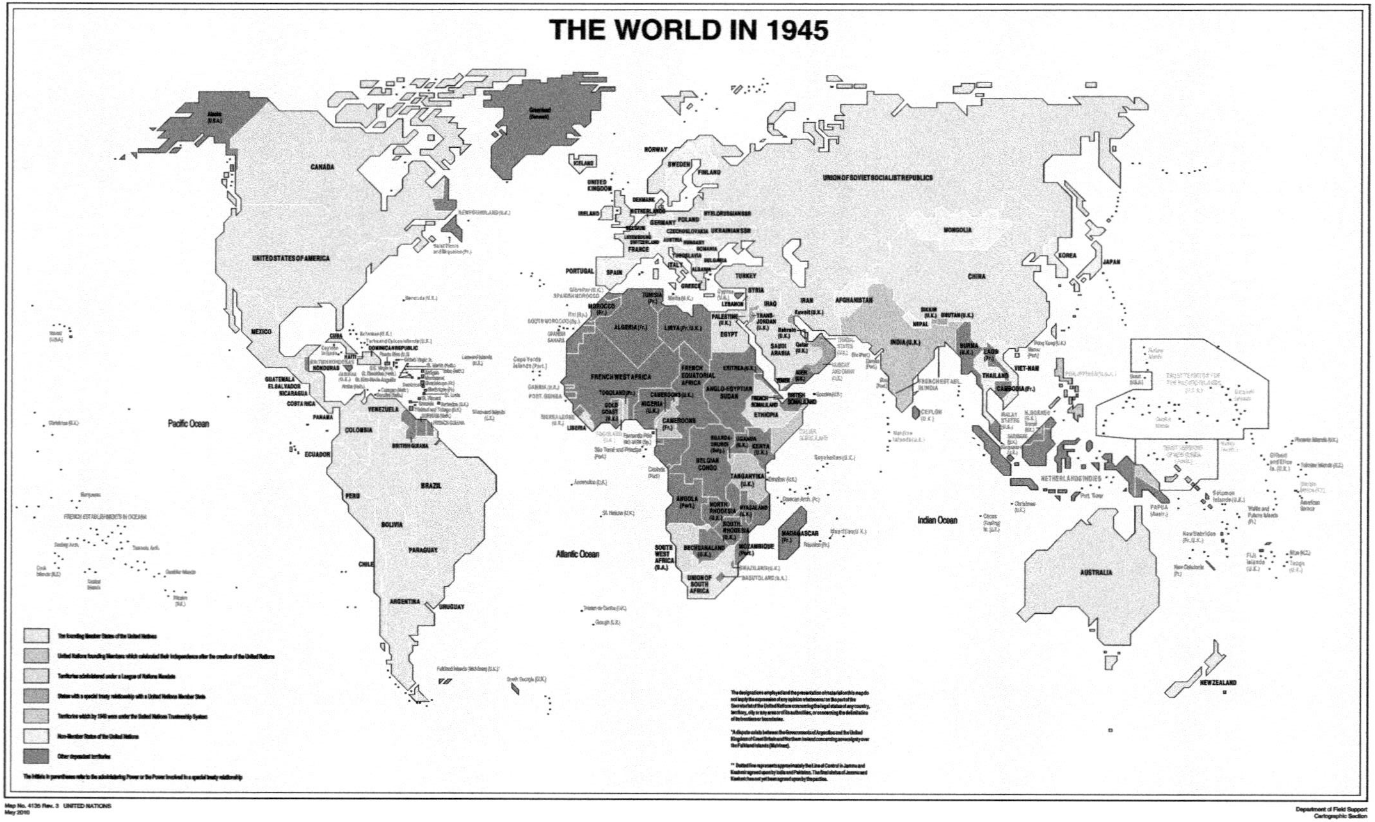

FIGURE 1.1 European Colonial Empires circa 1945. Based on Map No. 4135 Rev. 3, United Nations, May 2010.[7]

7 https://commons.wikimedia.org/wiki/Atlas_of_colonialism#/media/File:Colonization_1945.png

Most new states were desperately poor or struggled with large impoverished populations. High rates of illiteracy, traditional agrarian economies, and inchoate telecommunications and infrastructure networks exposed vast gaps between the conditions of living for those in low-income countries and the significantly wealthier countries of Europe and North America. In 1955, 148 out of every 1,000 children under the age of five in developing countries died largely from preventable or treatable conditions such as pneumonia, measles, and malnutrition.[8] At the point of its first census – four years after independence from Britain - India's literacy rate was only 16%.[9] By 1972, most of the world's population still lived in countries with a per capita income below $200.[10] Of the eighty or so "underdeveloped countries of the world" in 1966, more than thirty depended for more than half their foreign-exchange earnings on exports of a single crop or commodity, and many others depended on just two.[11]

Sources of industrial and financial wealth were (and largely remain) in already wealthy countries. In 1960, only four developing countries were significant exporters of manufactured goods, and by 1968, only thirty.[12] By 1974, in terms of ownership and management, all global corporations were American, British, Dutch, German, French, Swiss, Italian, Canadian, Swedish, or Japanese.[13]

Development – the right or claim of poor countries to become like wealthier ones – spawned an overwhelming academic literature and corresponding policy approaches. Scholars argued whether the economic problems of developing countries differed so drastically from those of developed countries that different types of assumptions about behaviors and related models must be used.[14] Developing economies were hypothesized to be dysfunctional combinations of subsistence economies with inchoate potential for capital-intensive agriculture, manufacturing, and diversified labor; corrupt quasi-states with inadequate institutions to attract and protect foreign investment (both industry-specific and generally) of capital that they desperately needed; inhospitable to entrepreneurs; mired in one of the lower stages of development through which all countries must pass on their way to mass consumption; or sustained cultural or religious norms – including ethnic pluralism and conflict – that thwarted the progress demonstrated by developed countries.[15]

8 Mark Cameron Edberg, Essential Readings in Health Behavior 214 (2010).

9 Preetika Rana & Joanna Sugden, *India's Record since Independence*, Wall Street Journal (Apr. 15, 2013) available at https://blogs.wsj.com/indiarealtime/2013/08/15/indias-record-since-independence/

10 Barrie Ireton, Britain's International Development Policies: A History of DFID and Overseas Aid 41 (2013).

11 George Woods, *The Development Decade in the Balance*, 44(2) Foreign Affairs 208 (1966).

12 Richard J. Barnet & Ronald E. Muller, Global Reach: The Power of the Multinational Corporations 196 (1974).

13 *Id.* at 16.

14 Albert O. Hirschman, The Strategy of Economic Development (1958).

15 J. H. Boeke, Economics and Economic Policy of Dual Societies (1953); W. W. Rostow, *The Stages of Economic Growth*, 12(1) Econ History Review 1–16 (1959); David McCellland, The Achieving Society (1961); Everitt E. Hagen, On the Theory of Social Change (1962).

Some went so far as to argue that most developing countries were not states capable at all of doing what wealthier states had done and existed primarily as an indulgence of the international system that depended on the sovereign state to facilitate commerce and diplomacy.[16]

Theorists from, or sympathetic to, the conditions in poorer countries argued that, rather than endogenous dysfunction in those countries that explained why they were impoverished, the situation was explained by a continuous if modified process by which wealthy countries, through and with their firms, enriched themselves at the expense of poor ones.[17] Disadvantageous trade terms caused prices for raw materials produced by less developed countries to decrease while the finished manufactured goods – which generally maintain a more elastic price – remained under the control of advanced economies. Jagdish Bhagwati argued that this cycle led to so-called immiserizing growth, under which pressure to increase exports led to ever-deteriorating terms of trade for poorer countries.[18] Marxist theorists such as Rosa Luxemburg and Vladimir Lenin hypothesized (in a slightly earlier epoch) that the search for new capital and markets was by nature relentless, and therefore wealthy states would adopt policies toward poorer countries that served their economic interests, necessarily to the detriment of poorer countries.[19] Immanuel Wallerstein famously interpreted many of the latter theories to comprehensively form his classification of the world into core, semi-peripheral, and peripheral states, all ordered by agents (sometimes, but not always states) competing for capital.[20]

There is likely no resolution to these competing views, and, broadly speaking, "macro" theories will inevitably fail to account for important, explanatory economic, historical, and geopolitical variables. Consider three examples of decolonized countries. India became influential because of its size, location, and historical ties to Britain, including the prevalence of English-language speech and press.[21] The Hashemite Kingdom of Jordan – its existence, foreign, and domestic policy – is almost entirely explained by the relationship between the British government and Sharif Hussein (and his descendants) as well as the successes of Wahhabism in the Arabian peninsula and Zionism in Palestine.[22] The Democratic Republic of Congo's brutal

16 Robert Jackson, Quasi-States: Sovereignty, International Relations, and the Third World (1990).

17 Paul Baran, The Political Economy of Growth (1957).

18 Jagdish Bhagwati, *Immiserizing Growth: A Geometrical Note*, 25 Review of Economic Studies 201–05 (1958).

19 Rosa Luxemburg, The Accumulation of Capital, translated by Agnes Schwarzschild in 1951 (2003). Originally published as Die Akkumulation des Kapitals in 1913; Vladimir Lenin, Imperialism: The Highest Stage of Capitalism (1916).

20 Immanuel Wallerstein, The Modern World System (1974).

21 The Economist, India as a Great Power (Mar. 30, 2013).

22 Peter Mansfield, A History of the Middle East (1991).

colonial history is different in relevant, continuously influential ways than that of several countries that border it that experienced British, French, or German control.[23]

Each view, however, justified policies adopted by poor and wealthy countries as well as the new international organizations that had been born alongside decolonization. To the extent US aid and development support decisions could be disentangled from Cold War objectives, they emphasized support for domestic protections for foreign investors, prioritized constitutional and legal protections for contracts and private property, and focused on technical support.[24] The "law and development" movement advocated the diffusion of legal structures and concepts to poorer countries so as to aid in their modernization.[25] "Modern" law was believed to be the "functional prerequisite of an industrial economy."[26] John F. Kennedy's "Decade of Development" speech at the United Nations was explicit in its support of narrow, technical support in furtherance of these principles:

> That is why my nation, which has freely shared its capital and its technology to help others help themselves, now proposes officially designating this decade of the 1960s as the United Nations Decade of Development. Under the framework of that Resolution, the United Nations' existing efforts in promoting economic growth can be expanded and coordinated. Regional surveys and training institutes can now pool the talents of many. New research, technical assistance and pilot projects can unlock the wealth of less developed lands and untapped waters. And development can become a cooperative and not a competitive enterprise – to enable all nations, however diverse in their systems and beliefs, to become in fact as well as in law free and equal nations.[27]

Contemporaneously with the reorganization of US development support according to these objectives under the 1961 Foreign Assistance Act, Canada, the Netherlands, Sweden, and the United Kingdom similarly adapted their aid programs.[28]

Developing countries similarly justified growth policies – where possible – based on rectifying what was regarded as past and continuing exploitation by former powers or their corporate instrumentalities.[29] Egypt nationalized the Suez Canal in 1956; Chile and Zambia began nationalizing their copper mines toward the end of the 1960s; and Brazil, Bolivia, Burma, Iran, Iraq, Indonesia, and Peru

[23] ADAM HOCHSCHILD, KING LEOPOLD'S GHOST (1998).

[24] Dennis Merrill, *The Truman Doctrine: Containing Communism and Modernity*, 36(1) PRES. STUD. Q. 27–37 (2006).

[25] David M. Trubek, *Toward A Social Theory of Law: An Essay on the Study of Law and Development*, 82 YALE L. J. 44 (1972).

[26] David Trubek & Mark Galanter, *Scholars in Self-Estrangement: Some Reflections on the Crisis in Law and Development Studies in the United States*, 4 WISC. L. REV. 1062 (1974)

[27] John F. Kennedy, *Address at U.N. General Assembly, 25 September* 1961 available at https://www.jfklibrary.org/Asset-Viewer/DOPIN64xJUGRKgdHJ9NfgQ.aspx

[28] George Woods, *The Development Decade in the Balance* 44(2) FOREIGN AFFAIRS 208 (1966).

[29] DANIEL YERGIN & JOSEPH STANISLAW, THE COMMANDING HEIGHTS: THE BATTLE BETWEEN GOVERNMENT AND THE MARKETPLACE THAT IS REMAKING THE MODERN WORLD 88–90 (1998).

nationalized their petroleum industries over the course of the 1950s and 1960s.[30] Between 1970 and 1974, thirty-four countries in Latin America, Asia, and Africa adopted measures to "take over or to force out U.S. controlled operations in their territory" worth $1.2 billion, mostly in transportation, communications, and banking.[31] These efforts understandably provoked conflict with sponsor governments. In some cases, the United States and European countries resorted to force or sponsored rebellion to reclaim nationalized industries or corporate assets.[32]

These dynamics played out in international organizations as well. The International Bank for Reconstruction and Development (IBRD) – the anchor entity of the World Bank – intended to make long-term capital available to countries struggling economically in the aftermath of the Second World War.[33] The major disagreement among delegates at the time of its establishment was whether the focus of IBRD should be on reconstruction or development.[34] Europe advocated for reconstruction while developing countries such as Mexico stressed development; ultimately, IBRD served both purposes.[35]

Even at that, the IBRD's development activities became a separately charged issue between the developed countries which held (and hold) most of its shares and poorer countries which receive most of its support. The IBRD "does not just lend money and produce ideas: it packages the ideas and money together."[36] Over its life, the IBRD moved from lending exclusively to tangible investment projects such as infrastructure like bridges and roads to "policy-based or program lending for policy reforms."[37] Conditions attached to structural assistance loans required "reform of the government's budget or taxes, improvement of financial performance of public enterprises, revision of agricultural prices, and strengthening of the state's capacity to formulate and implement public investment programmes" in ways that poor countries asserted were ultimately for the benefit of wealthy countries.[38]

30 Guiliano Garavini, *Completing Decolonization: The 1973 "Oil Shock" and the Struggle for Economic Rights*, 33(3) International History Review 473–87 (2011).

31 Richard J. Barnet & Ronald E. Muller, Global Reach: The Power of the Multinational Corporations 188 (1974).

32 C. F. Amerasinghe, *The New International Economic Order: Some Aspects of the Quantum of Compensations Payable upon Expropriation*, 87 Am. Soc'y Int'l L. Proc. 459, 477 (1993).

33 Eric Toussaint, The World Bank: A Critical Primer (2008).

34 Sandra Blanco & Enrique Carrasco, *The Functions of the IMF and the World Bank*, 9 Transnat'l L. & Contemp. Probs. 67, 72 (1999).

35 *Id.* at 73.

36 Carlos Santiso, *Good Governance and Aid Effectiveness: The World Bank and Conditionality*, 7 Geo. Pub. Pol'y Rev. 1, 3 (2001).

37 Sarah L. Babb & Bruce G. Carruthers, *Conditionality: Forms, Function, and History*, 4 Ann. Rev. L. & Soc. Sci. 13, 18 (2008).

38 Namita Wahi, *Human Rights Accountability of the IMF and the World Bank: A Critique of Existing Mechanisms and Articulation of a Theory of Horizontal Accountability*, 12 U.C. Davis J. Int'l L. & Pol'y 331, 340 (2006).

These tensions in turn unfolded between international organizations. At the United Nations, developing countries used the forum in which they held the most influence – the General Assembly – to press for declarations about the respective rights of developing countries versus wealthier ones (and their firms abroad). A "Resolution on Permanent Sovereignty over Natural Resources" adopted in 1962 recited strongly worded clauses as to the rights of sovereignty and self-determination for formerly colonized states.[39]

At the World Bank, where wealthier states held more influence over governance and process, the International Centre for the Settlement of Investment Disputes (ICSID) was established in 1965 to create a forum in which multinational corporations could bring disputes with expropriating governments and subject those disputes to binding arbitration.[40] ICSID has become the primary "international venue to resolve foreign direct investment ... disputes around the world, which on a global scale amount to $1.66 trillion annually," and conducts conciliation and arbitration proceedings directly to contracting states or nationals of contracting states.[41] The primary criticism leveled at ICSID is that it favors the interests of foreign investors over those of the (mostly developing) states in which they invest.[42]

After the failure of the International Trade Organization to materialize along with the International Bank for Reconstruction and Development and the International Monetary Fund, the less centralized General Agreement on Tariffs and Trade (GATT) became the organizing treaty under which primarily wealthy states reduced tariff and regulatory barriers to trade.[43] Over eight rounds of negotiations lasting more than forty years, trading states lowered tariffs as well as "non-tariff barriers" to trade, such as customs procedures, import licensing requirements, and export subsidies.[44] Prior to 1986, the trade liberalization negotiation process had been driven by the trade priorities of developed states; they largely excluded agriculture, and the key bargains were achieved between industrialized countries.[45]

In 1964, developing countries formed the United Nations Conference on Trade and Development in order to pursue trade-related development policies marginalized by GATT.[46] UNCTAD was established to "maximize the trade, investment and development opportunities of developing countries and assist them in their efforts to

39 G.A. Res. 1803 (XVII), U.N. Doc. A/5217/Supp. No. 17 (Dec. 14, 1962).

40 Yaraslau Kryvoi, International Center for Settlement of Investment Disputes 26–27 (2010).

41 Tai-Heng Cheng, *The Role of Justice in Annulling Investor-State Arbitration Awards*, 31 Berkeley J. Int'l L. 236, 243 (2013).

42 Bruno Simma, *Foreign Investment Arbitration: A Place for Human Rights?*, 60(3) Int'l and Comp. L. Q. 573–96 (2011).

43 John Head, *Throwing Eggs at Windows: Legal and Institutional Globalization in the 21st-Century Economy*, 50 U. Kan. L. Rev. 731, 734 (2002).

44 Alan Oxley, *The Achievements of the GATT Uruguay Round*, 1 Agenda 45–53 (1994).

45 Alex F. McCalla, *Liberalizing Agricultural Trade: Will It Ever Become a Reality?*, 28(3) Journal of Agricultural Economics 419–34 (2003).

46 John Toye, UNCTAD at 50: A Short History 3 (2014).

integrate into the world economy on an equitable basis."[47] The organization's primary material achievement was the agreement on a Generalized System of Preferences under which GATT members would offer special tariff concessions to exports from developing countries, although it also facilitates technical assistance and lobbies other international organizations such as the IMF for policies to benefit developing countries.[48] UNCTAD also played a substantial role in generating research analyses surrounding technology transfer issues between wealthy and poor countries, which has ultimately had a much more significant and long-lasting impact.

In the immediate post-decolonization years, intellectual property – or, as it was understood for much of this period, industrial property – played a peripheral role in the most visible disputes between wealthy and poor countries.[49] To be sure, control of and access to patents, copyrights, trademarks, trade secrets, and the data generated for regulatory approvals of pharmaceutical and agricultural products fit within the theoretical analyses generated by scholars and policy-makers studying development. The technology identified as crucial for development was invariably shaped by intellectual property assets, which were controlled by wealthy foreign parties as were the tangible assets at risk of nationalization or expropriation. A 1972 study by Constantine Vaitsos found that between 1957 and 1961, more than 89 percent of patents granted in India, Turkey, Egypt, Syria, Trinidad & Tobago, and Pakistan were granted to foreign firms.[50] Between 1937 and 1967, foreign ownership of patents in Chile grew from 65 percent to 95 percent.[51] In Colombia, by 1970, fewer than 10 percent of firms holding pharmaceutical patents controlled more than 60 percent of those patents.[52] While it is possible that patents make foreign direct investment more likely (i.e., a firm with a patent is more likely to build a facility that manufactures the invention in the host state), there was (and is) little evidence to suggest that relationship actually results in – and, indeed, a great deal of evidence to suggest that the patent is rather used to quash – domestic and international competition.[53]

The relevance of intellectual property to development was not entirely overlooked. India adopted a patent law in 1970 that created incentives for the development of its now strong generic pharmaceutical sector.[54] In 1971, Brazil revised its patent law to exclude substances obtained by chemical processes as well as

[47] D. N. Dwiveldi, International Economics: Theory and Practice 464 (2013).

[48] *Id.* at 465.

[49] John Hughes, *A Short History of "Intellectual Property" in Relation to Copyright*, 33 Cardozo L. Rev. 1293, 1299 (2012).

[50] Constantine Vaitsos, *Patents Revisited*, 9 J. Development Studies 73 (1972).

[51] *Id.* at 74.

[52] *Id.*

[53] Edwin L.-C. Lai, *International Intellectual Property Rights Protection and the Rate of Product Innovation*, 55 J.Dev. Econ. 133 (1998).

[54] Government of India, The Patents Act, 1970, Ministry of Commerce and Industry, Department of Industrial Policy and Promotion, Controller General of Patents Designs and Trade Marks.

pharmaceutical processes and products; institute a mandatory registration of assignments and licenses of patent rights; eliminate restrictions on exports; and improve inventions belonging to the licensee rather than the licensor.[55] These aspects of the law more tightly regulated conditions of technology transfer and created conditions for local innovation and improvement.[56] From the 1970s, biotechnology has been one of the most important drivers of innovations for agriculture and medicine; recombinant DNA technologies for plants, animals, and microorganisms began to enjoy legal protection under varieties of patent and plant innovation policies.[57] By the 1980s, only the United States, Japan, Switzerland, and a few European countries extended such protections. The aforementioned changes in Brazilian and Indian patent laws allowed them to be more competitive in developing peripheral biotechnology industries than other developing countries that did not.

Between the 1964 session of UNCTAD and its next session in 1968, the issue of industrial property generally had grown from a brief discussion as to the relationship between patents and technology transfer to the abusive uses of industrial property by corporations headquartered in wealthy states.[58] But, as Peter Drahos has documented, for the most part, developing countries neglected intellectual property as part of their development objectives. Patent offices in poor countries were likely to cooperate with the patent offices of Europe, Japan, and the United States even while their negotiators elsewhere were trying to advance development agendas at multilateral trade fora or even, after 1967, the World Intellectual Property Organization.[59]

By the early 1970s, despite UNCTAD, nationalizations, and the declared interest of wealthy countries in improvement in poor ones, the relative situation of developing countries vis-á-vis developed countries had barely improved, and for many their absolute position had worsened.[60] As a result, developing countries became more aggressive in their calls for policies aimed at redistribution. On April 19, 1972, Mexican President Luis Echeverria urged the adoption of a Charter of Economic Rights and Duties of States aimed at

> freedom to dispose of natural resources; the right of every nation to adopt the economic structure it considered most suitable and to treat private property as the public interest required; renunciation of the use of economic pressures; subjection of foreign capital to domestic laws; prohibition of interference by supranational

[55] PETER DRAHOS, GLOBAL GOVERNANCE OF KNOWLEDGE: PATENT OFFICES AND THEIR CLIENTS 247 (2010).

[56] *Id.*

[57] *Id.* at 66.

[58] UNCTAD SECOND SESSION OF THE UNITED NATIONS CONFERENCE ON TRADE AND DEVELOPMENT, SECOND SESSION (UNCTAD II). JAN. 31–MAR. 29, 1968. NEW DELHI (INDIA) 272 available at http://unctad.org/en/Docs/td97vol1_en.pdf.

[59] PETER DRAHOS, GLOBAL GOVERNANCE OF KNOWLEDGE: PATENT OFFICES AND THEIR Clients xiv (2010).

[60] Charles N. Brower & John B. Tepe Jr. *The Charter of Economic Rights and Duties of States: A Reflection or Rejection of International Law?* 9 INT'L. LAWYER 295 (1975).

corporations in the internal affairs of States; abolition of trade practices that discriminated against the exports of non-industrial nations; economic advantages proportionate to levels of development; treaties guaranteeing stable and fair prices for basic products; transfer of technology; and greater economic resources for long-term untied aid.[61]

Following the oil crisis of 1973, the UN General Assembly adopted the Declaration for the Establishment of a New International Economic Order, which was to embody many of the principles laid out by Echeverria. The UN declaration urged change in the global economic system, particularly in management regarding emerging or developing nations.[62] The developing nation-states called for: (1) management of volatile commodity markets, (2) most-favored-nation status for developing nations, (3) increased exchange rate stability, (4) regulation of capital flowing across borders, (5) heightened aid to least developed countries, (6) more favorable debt rescheduling, and (7) stricter regulation of multinational corporations' compliance with national laws and transfer of technology.[63]

As most historical analyses have concluded, the New International Economic Order (NIEO) represented quite different policy alternatives to different constituencies. UN Ambassador Andrew Young called the New International Economic Order "a broad framework for dialogue and progress" as opposed to a formal "order."[64] Jagdish Bhagwati argued that the NIEO adopted a form of geopolitical "trade union militancy" aimed at redistributing a "fair share" of the world's wealth to poorer countries.[65] The World Bank's Director of Policy Planning, Mahbub ul Haq, insisted that the NIEO was ultimately about creating conditions for equal opportunity for growth under international legal rules as they then existed.[66] Robert Cox concluded that there were many answers to the question, "What is the New International Economic Order?" – all of them in some measure correct.[67]

What is relevant for purposes of the argument developed in this book is that there seems to be fairly wide agreement that, whatever the NIEO was, it ended, mostly without accomplishing many if any of its stated objectives.

61 Summary of Address, UNCTAD Proceedings, Third Session, U.N. Doc. TD/180, Vol. 1A, Part I at 184, 186 (1972).

62 Harold Hongju Koh, *The* New *New International Economic Order*, 87 AM. SOC'Y INT'L L. PROC. 459, 460 (Mar./Apr. 1993).

63 Vinod K. Aggarwal & Steve Webber, *The* New *New International Economic Order*, HARV. BUS. REV., 2 (Apr. 18, 2012).

64 Johan Kaufmann, *Decision Making in the New International Economic Order* in Antony Dolman & Jan Van Ettinger (eds), PARTNERS IN TOMORROW: STRATEGIES FOR A NEW INTERNATIONAL ORDER PLUS RESHAPING THE INTERNATIONAL ORDER 177 (1978).

65 JAGDISH BHAGWHATI (ed), THE NEW INTERNATIONAL ECONOMIC ORDER: THE NORTH SOUTH DEBATE 6 (1977).

66 Mahbub ul Haq, *The Third World and the International Economic Order*, ODIC 11 (Sept. 22, 1976).

67 Robert W. Cox, *Ideologies and the New International Economic Order: Reflections on Some Recent Literature*, 33(2) INT'L ORG. 257–302 (1979).

> So, what choices were made and what did happen to the NIEO demands of the 1970s? In retrospect, not very much. Some efforts were made to provide developing countries with additional trade preferences. The IMF created a trust fund to help developing countries by selling off a third of its gold holdings, particularly by the Europeans. A few commodity agreements were signed, for example in sugar and rubber. But for the most part, the general strategy of the rich countries was to reject the NIEO broadly. This meant rejecting the idea that the problems of the developing countries were the responsibility of the rich countries, brushing off the idea that developing countries had meaningfully shared interests, and more or less dismissing the notion that any good would come from having these countries participate at a higher level in international institutions. The rich countries were confident they could win the argument because they believed the developing countries had little or no power to push their position – and that what power they did have as a result of control of oil supplies could be countered and would fade.[68]

Since the 1970s, developing countries have emerged as substantial players in world markets.[69] Developing countries have significantly grown in terms of GDP, exports volume, outflows of investments, and other indicators of economic influence.[70] Many of these shares in the global market have doubled for emerging economic players. For example, the most significant gain is the increased percentage of foreign exchange reserves owned by the developing states – from less than 13 percent in 1975 to 47 percent in 2010.[71] Developing countries now lead successful challenges against disadvantageous trade practices at the World Trade Organization, earn fairer terms in trade deals, and negotiate more effectively with potential foreign investors.[72]

Certainly, some of the NIEO agenda seems obsolete. There are far fewer calls for global coordination of commodity prices, most countries have now achieved at least some level of most favored nation status through the establishment of the World Trade Organization, and sovereign debt has receded as a crisis issue in global politics even if there are, indeed, current crises and the specter of sovereign default plays continuously relevant (and interrelated) roles for richer and poorer countries alike.[73] Yet the core components of the New International Economic Order – most importantly global redistribution of wealth and the regulation of multinational corporations – remain as influential today as when the NIEO was declared nearly 45 years ago.

68 Vinod K. Aggarwal & Steve Webber, *The* New *New International Economic Order*, HARV. BUS. REV., 2 (Apr. 18, 2012).

69 Robert Zoellick, *The End of the Third World?* (address to Woodrow Wilson Center for International Scholars, Washington, DC, Apr. 14, 2010).

70 Daniel Price, *The* New *New International Economic Order*, 87 AM. SOC'Y INT'L L. PROC. 459, 460 (Mar./Apr. 1993).

71 International Monetary Fund, ANNUAL REPORT, APPENDIX I, INTERNATIONAL RESERVES 1–4 (2014).

72 Sam Foster Halabi, *Efficient Contracting between Foreign Investors and Host States: Evidence from Stabilization Clauses* 31 NW. J. INT'L L. & BUS. 261, 263 (201).

73 Juan Carlos Hatchondo and Leonardo Martinez, *The Politics of Sovereign Defaults*, 96(3) ECONOMIC QUARTERLY 291–317 (2010).

The calls for redistribution and regulation have changed in form and substance, not intensity. First, developing countries altered their own development priorities in two principal ways. Rather than focus on mimicry of North American and European models as they then existed – including borrowing their technology and law - countries in Africa, Asia, and South America focused on population health, education, and basic human indicators as the priorities for development of human capital.[74] This shift in strategy manifested in the U.N. General Assembly as well, where resolutions increasingly focused on children, nutrition, human rights, and women.[75] Those resolutions were less likely to meet resistance from the traditional NIEO antagonists. Indeed, the United States' primary development agency, USAID, refocused its aid program in the 1970s to align with many of these objectives as did the development agencies of other wealthy countries. By the 1990s, addressing problems like poverty, maternal mortality, and literacy became the major focus of the international community, culminating in the Millennium Development Goals – a set of benchmarks the world community was charged with meeting by 2015.[76]

Second, the subject of intellectual property, as a component of developing countries' agenda, transitioned from a broadly understood barrier to technology transfer to a weapon wielded chiefly by multinational corporations. The most beneficial results of intellectual property – new technology, and other innovative activity – is (and has been since decolonization) concentrated in a handful of developed countries.[77] Ten countries account for a majority of all technological activity around the world.[78] These same top ten countries represent at least 84 percent of worldwide resources annually spent on research and development, 94 percent of patents taken out in the US, and 91 percent of international royalties and technology licensing fees received.[79] Over the course of the 1960s and early 1970s, developing countries demanded that wealthy countries' governments, more than their firms, take action on technology transfer.

After the mid-1970s, developing countries targeted firms more directly while adopting a more nuanced position with respect to the technology they demanded. The ability to use the inventions and processes disclosed in patent applications (submitted in developing countries overwhelmingly by North American, European, and Japanese firms) was of little aid to development in countries that lacked human

74 International Labour Organisation, Employment, Growth, and Basic Needs (1976).

75 Declaration on Social Progress and Development, G.A. Resolution 2543(XXIV) (Dec. 11, 1969); Question of a Convention on the Rights of the Child: Report of the Working Group, U.N. Comm'n on Hum. Rts., 35th Sess., Agenda Item 13, at 1, U.N. Doc. E/CN.4/L.1468 (1979); World Plan of Action and related resolutions from the International Women's Year Conference United Nations General Assembly Resolution 30/3520 (XXX) (1975).

76 Sakika Fukuda-Parr, *Millennium Development Goals: Why They Matter*, 10(4) Global Governance 395–402 (2004).

77 Nagesh Kumar, *Intellectual Property Rights, Technology and Economic Development: Experiences of Asian Countries*, 38 Econ. Pol. Weekly 209, 210 (2003).

78 Japan, Germany, France, United Kingdom, Canada, Italy, Netherlands, Sweden, Switzerland, and United States.

79 *Id.*

capital and technological capacity. Control over copyright by another set of firms based in the aforementioned countries limited access to creative and practical knowledge which might be ultimately crucial for developing countries to build their human capital and technological capacity. Large foreign firms aggressively policed the availability of intellectual property assets and the conditions under which those assets could be accessed by those outside the boundary of the firm. Firms' practices aimed at limiting access stifled sources of local competition and erected barriers to entry by foreign competitors.[80] Even in the 1970s, the tension between intellectual property assets held by foreign firms and the new orientation of developing countries' priorities toward health and education outcomes began to boil over.[81] Those flash-points occurred in the context of century-old agreements protecting industrial property and copyright; agreements developing countries sought to radically change.

[80] Peter Drahos, *Global Property Rights in Information: The Story of TRIPS at the GATT*, 13 PROMETHEUS 6, 7 (1995).

[81] Susan Sell, *Intellectual Property Protection and Antitrust in the Developing World: Crisis, Coercion, and Choice*, 49(2) INT'L ORG. 315–49 (1995).

2

The Expansion of International Intellectual Property Protection

Few observers of international politics or international law would have placed intellectual property as a defining issue of the late nineteenth or early twentieth century.[1] Yet the history of the international expansion of intellectual property protections occurred at roughly the same time as the Scramble for Africa and the beginning of what Eric Hobsbawm declared as the "Age of Empire."

> The economic and military supremacy of the capitalist countries had long been beyond serious challenge, but no systematic attempt to translate it into formal conquest, annexation and administration had been made between the end of the eighteenth and the last quarter of the nineteenth century. Between 1880 and 1914 it was made, and most of the world outside Europe and the Americas was formally partitioned into territories under the formal rule or informal political domination of one or other of a handful of states: mainly Great Britain, France, Germany, Italy, the Netherlands, Belgium, the USA and Japan.[2]

The development of international intellectual property norms and laws moved in tandem with these developments.[3] Over its history – from the international intellectual property regime's inception in 1883 through the formalization of the World Intellectual Property Organization as a specialized UN agency in 1974 – the same calls for redistribution of wealth from low- and middle-income countries through the New International Economic Order pervaded changes to the international intellectual property protection regime.[4]

1 Amy Kapczynski, *The Access to Knowledge Mobilization and the New Politics of Intellectual Property*, 117 Yale L.J. 804, 806 (2008).
2 Eric Hobsbawm, The Age of Empire 1875–1914 57 (1987).
3 Sam Halabi, *Multipolarity, Intellectual Property, and the Internationalization of Public Health Law*, 35(4) Mich. J. Int'l. L. 715, 741 (2014).
4 Christopher May, *The World Intellectual Property Organization and the Development Agenda*, 13(2) Global Governance 161–70 (2007).

With late nineteenth-century efforts to establish colonies and open overseas markets, the movement and protection of creative works, inventions, and associated trademarks took on increasing importance for publishing houses, manufacturers, and governments. These interests were not always aligned. The United States, for example, maintained laws that made enforcing foreign copyrights difficult as part of its effort to ensure the flow of literature, art, and music to its growing and expanding population.[5] In the second half of the nineteenth century, many countries introduced national systems for protection of patents, industrial designs, and trademarks.[6] Countries protected these laws internationally by either unilaterally codifying the protection of foreign industrial property or entering into bilateral agreements.[7]

The development of international intellectual property law toward the end of the nineteenth century coincided with the development of global agricultural, industrial, and financial firms in Britain, France, Germany, and the United States. The American Tobacco Company, Philip Morris, Bayer, Siemens, Anglo-Swiss Milk Co. (Nestlé), Schering, PriceWaterhouse, Deloitte, General Electric, Poulenc Brothers, Ciba, Sandoz, Dow Chemical Company, Glaxo, Beecham (together with others GlaxoSmithKline), HSBC, Thomson McClintock (now KPMG), DuPont, Merck KGaA (the latter two were founded much earlier but grew through acquisition during the same period), Dunlop Rubber, Rio Tinto, United Fruit Company, to name only several prominent firms, emerged during this period as both national and international entities.[8] These firms (and many others tied to imperial expansion of the late nineteenth century) remain, in some form or another, present today, and their trajectories have crossed product sectors even as they have consolidated.[9] Bayer started as firm producing synthetic dyes but moved over time into medicines, agrochemicals and seeds, and a broader portfolio of chemical products.[10] General Electric was formed through the 1892 merger of Edison General Electric Company and Thomson-Houston Electric Company and eventually developed into a global diversified firm offering products and services across aviation, banking, entertainment, health care, home appliances and electronics, and telecommunications, in addition to its original electrical device–related services and products.[11]

5 Robert Spoo, Without Copyrights: Piracy, Publishing, and the Public Domain 21 (2016).

6 J. Duffy, *Harmony and Diversity in Global Patent Law*, 17 Berkeley J. L. & Tech. 685 (2002).

7 Stephen Ladas, Patents, Trademarks, and Related Rights 45–46 (1979).

8 John Dunning & Sarianna Lundan, Multinational Enterprises and the Global Economy 78 (1992)

9 Raymond Vernon, Sovereignty at Bay: The Multinational Spread of United States Enterprises (1971).

10 Bayer, *A Journey through the History of Bayer*, available at https://www.bayer.com/en/history.aspx

11 GE, *Management's Discussion and Analysis. Summary of Operating Segments*, available at https://www.ge.com/sites/default/files/GE_AR13_Operating_Segments.pdf

These firms used foreign production as a strategic tool, especially in consolidated sectors with potentially large foreign markets such as pharmaceuticals, rubber products, and electrical equipment.[12] Those strategies were, in turn, affected by governmental policies such as tariffs, currency regulation, and intellectual property laws. Selectively imposed tariffs shaped the markets and locations for firms active in these products, with the United States using high tariffs in certain sectors to attract foreign manufacturers to its much larger internal market, firms investing in Britain to take advantage of access to its possessions, as well as many intra-European movements in specific sectors such as chemicals, medicines, textiles, and tobacco.[13] Governments also used patent policy. "Local working requirements," for example, required that foreign inventors locally exploit their inventions, encouraging them to establish manufacturing facilities in jurisdictions that maintained such a requirement, like France and Germany.[14]

As a tool of industrial policy, intellectual property law introduced problems for firms seeking to arbitrage production and market access advantages gained by introducing products into foreign markets.[15] Intellectual property law was essentially national in nature. Without some sort of international agreement in place (or, more rarely, a domestic law protecting foreigners), an invention or, in the case of authors, a creative work may not be protected from imitation, reproduction, and exploitation by local competitors.[16] Disparate national patent and trademark regimes meant that rights holders in one state might lose patent or trademark protection in another if they did not simultaneously file for protection in all relevant states.[17] Copyright protections were similarly fragile.

Belgian, French, and German publishing houses began printing translated copies of British works as early as the 1820s, threatening both the continental market for the British publishers as well as the decline of prices as continental reprints were imported into Britain.[18] By 1842, the *Publishers' Circular* was "loudly calling" the attention of the British Parliament to the "foreign invasion of British Copyright" by French and Belgian "pirates."[19] Although popular authors like G. P. R. James and Charles Dickens were active on the issue, the greatest pressure both within Britain and toward international copyright protection were the major publishing houses:

12 Dunning & Lundan, *supra* note 8, at 158.

13 *Id.*

14 Marketa Trimble, *Patent Working Requirements: Historical and Comparative Perspectives* 6 U.C. Irvine L. Rev. 483, 491 (2016).

15 Louise Joan Duncan, From Privileges to the Paris Convention: The Role of Theoretical Debate in the Evolution of National and International Patent Protection 223 (1997).

16 *Id.*

17 Seth M. Reiss, Commentary on The Paris Convention for the Protection of Industrial Property 1 available at http://www.lex-ip.com/Paris.pdf.

18 Catherine Seville, The Internationalisation of Copyright Law 41 (2006).

19 *Id.* at 42–43.

Longman, Colburn, Blackwood, and Spottiswoode. Related firms in industries such as papermaking pressed the British government for tighter laws and greater diplomatic pressure.[20] A series of bilateral agreements were stitched together between primarily European countries in the mid-1800s, but they proved relatively ineffective within participating states and never included such important players as Holland, Russia, or the United States.[21] In 1858, the Belgian government convened a meeting of approximately 300 representatives of states, universities, booksellers, publishers, and printers to discuss international and uniform copyright possibilities between "civilised nations."[22]

Related, if somewhat more complex, problems drove firms to advocate for greater international protections for industrial property.[23] For patents, trademarks, and industrial designs, each country maintained its own criteria for the protection (if any) of those kinds of property.[24] An invention patented in the United States, for example, if brought into Germany, may not receive protection – at least not for the US patentee. Many countries' industrial policy rewarded those who were the first to import an invention, rather than the inventor.[25] Moreover, countries maintained idiosyncratic rules that jeopardized the validity of the patent, even if the original patentee filed in all the jurisdictions in which it sought protection.[26] For example, many countries required the invention to be manufactured within the country before a specified time – a problem exacerbated by the delay bureaucratic approvals might cause. For international expositions held in London in 1851 and 1862 and Paris in 1855 and 1867, special laws were adopted that excepted inventions brought for purpose of demonstration at the exposition.[27]

Publishing houses, industrialists, and firms played key organizing roles behind the movement to expand intellectual property protections domestically and internationally: national protection for foreign inventions and creative works and uniformity in the intellectual property protection offered. The idea for an international congress devoted to international patent protection originated in the United States in 1872, although it was convened at the invitation of the Austro-Hungarian government

20 *Id.* at 44.
21 Stephen Ladas, The International Protection of Literary and Artistic Property 66 (1938).
22 Peter Yu, *The Copyright Divide*, 25 Cardozo L. Rev. 331, 348 (2003).
23 Jorge M. Katz, *Patents, The Paris Convention and Less Developed Countries*, 9 (Yale Univ. Econ. Growth Center, Discussion Paper No. 190, Nov. 1973).
24 Eric Schiff, Industrialization without National Patents: The Netherlands, 1869–1912; Switzerland, 1850–1907 25–41 (1971).
25 Steven Webb, *Tariffs, Cartels, Technology, and Growth in the German Steel Industry, 1879 to 1914* (1980) 40(2) Journal of Economic History 309–30 (1980).
26 Teruo Doi, *The Territoriality Principle of Patent Protection and Conflict of Laws*, 26 Fordham Int'l. L.J. 377, 380 (2002).
27 *Scientific American* dated Dec. 23, 1871, reproduced in USA, Congressional Papers, *Papers Relating to the Foreign Relations of the United States*, 1872, 42nd Cong., 3rd Sess., H of R, Ex Docs VI, part 1 a 48–49.

toward the end of the 1873 World's Fair in Vienna.[28] "Manufacturers, scientific artisans, political economists, and other experts" participated alongside government representatives, including in decision-making, to "afford complete protection" to the rights of inventors and to move toward uniform patent legislation in all countries.[29] Most participants came from industrial property backgrounds. The congress ended with a declaration of four resolutions, the first of which established that the rights of inventors were a part of natural law that "should be protected by the laws of all civilized nations." These resolutions were supported by seven reasons, the first of which acknowledged that "the sense of right among civilized nations demands the legal protection of intellectual work."[30]

In 1878, the French Minister of Commerce convened a similar congress during the World's Fair in Paris to discuss a wider range of industrial property – patents, trademarks, industrial designs, photographic works, and trade names – where, again, approximately 500 mostly industrial representatives adopted resolutions to hold an official, diplomatic conference to "determine the bases of uniform legislation" and to establish a Permanent Committee "to give effect to the propositions adopted by the Congress of Industrial Property."[31] This Committee developed a draft treaty in 1880 in Paris, which was to become the 1883 Paris Convention for the Protection of Industrial Property.

Meanwhile, states in Europe were becoming frustrated with the numerous bilateral treaties regarding treatment of foreign authors' works, feeling that these agreements were often uneven.[32] In 1878, French author Victor Hugo started the International Literary and Artistic Association (ALAI), holding meetings leading to the 1883 Congress in Berne.[33] The objective of this congress was to follow the example of the Paris Convention and forge a multilateral copyright agreement. This led to the 1886 Berne Convention for the Protection of Literary and Artistic Works.[34] Remaining outside the Berne Convention, the United States continued to require

28 Heinrich Kronstein & Irene Till, A *Reevaluation of the International Patent Convention*, 12(4) LAW AND CONTEMPORARY PROBLEMS 765–81 (1947).

29 U.S. Centennial Commission, Reports on the Vienna Universal Exhibition, 1873 available at https://archive.org/stream/reportsonviennauooblak/reportsonviennauooblak_djvu.txt.

30 T. Webster, *Vienna Universal Exhibition 1873: Report on the International Patent Congress*, UK, Parliamentary Papers, 1874, 399 at 342.

31 LOUISE JOAN DUNCAN, FROM PRIVILEGES TO THE PARIS CONVENTION: THE ROLE OF THEORETICAL DEBATE IN THE EVOLUTION OF NATIONAL AND INTERNATIONAL PATENT PROTECTION 482, 493 (1997).

32 CHRISTOPHER MAY, THE WORLD INTELLECTUAL PROPERTY ORGANIZATION RESURGENCE AND THE DEVELOPMENT AGENDA 15–35 (2007).

33 Anna Balakian, *The International Character of Symbolism*, 2(4) MOSAIC 1–8 (1969)

34 BERNE CONVENTION FOR THE PROTECTION OF LITERARY AND ARTISTIC WORKS of Sept. 9, 1886, completed at Paris on May 4, 1896, revised at Berlin on Nov. 13, 1908, completed at Berne on Mar. 20,1914, revised at Rome on June 2, 1928, revised at Brussels on June 26, 1948, and revised at Stockholm on July 14, 1967 (with Protocol regarding developing countries). Done at Stockholm on July 14, 1967.

authors to register in Washington and send a copy of the work to the Library of Congress, and later through the Chace Act imposed other restrictions on foreign authors.[35] It was not until after 1986, when the Chace Act expired, that the United States joined the Berne Convention.[36]

The Paris Convention for the Protection of Industrial Property created a legal union between participating states in which foreign industrial design, patent, and trademark applications received the same treatment as did national applications; established that covered intellectual property first protected in one state received priority in other participating states; and codified some common substantive protections.[37] The treaty also specifically addressed forms of unfair competition not related to patents or trademarks, provisions that were subsequently strengthened when the parties revised the treaty in several conferences from 1886 to 1967. Of the eleven countries that formed the initial union in 1883, six were major colonial powers and a seventh, Britain, joined in 1884.[38]

As colonial powers, this small group of states sought to protect their citizens' and firms' industrial assets as they moved across borders.[39] The Paris and Berne Conventions were part and parcel of imperial control over intellectual property within expanding empires. Lionel Bently has noted how British participation in the Paris and Berne processes served to consolidate its position with respect to colonies:

> International norms would, after all, not be British norms imposed at the behest of British publishing interests, but rather would reflect an "international consensus," indeed, a consensus amongst "civilized" nations. On the other hand, effective negotiation of any treaty by the British government would be significantly enhanced by authority to negotiate for the whole Empire. Britain wanted to negotiate for the colonies, recognizing that to do so would increase its bargaining power significantly (while at the same time highlighting that Britain did not really need to join a convention of non-English speaking states). International negotiation made a single Imperial position attractive. As Australian Senator McGregor explained,
>
> [t]he first principle laid down by the British Act is that copyright is an Imperial matter ... The majority of the countries of Europe ... are in the Berne Convention, and the protection of this Act would extend to our authors and artists in all of the countries which are in the Convention ... we have the power of the British

35 James West, *The Chace Act and Anglo-American Literary Relations*, 45 Studies in Bibliography 303–11 (1992).

36 *Id.*

37 Paul Reinsch, *International Unions and Their Administration*, 1(3) AJIL 579, 583 (1907); Otto Sommerich, *Austria: German Trademarks and the 1883 Paris Convention*, 5(2) Am. J. Comp. L. 281–83 (1956).

38 World Intellectual Property Organization, International Treaties and Conventions on Intellectual Property 5 available at http://www.wipo.int/export/sites/www/about-ip/en/iprm/pdf/ch5.pdf

39 GHC Bodenhausen, Guide to the Application of the Paris Convention for the Protection of Industrial Property 9 (1968) (Belgium, Brazil, France, Guatemala, Italy, Netherlands, Portugal, Salvador, Serbia, Spain, and Switzerland).

> Empire behind us when we ask for anything which is just and fair from another country.[40]

Doris Long has written more broadly about the imperial powers:

> The countries that signed the agreement did so with the power to bind their colonies even though such colonies played virtually no role in the negotiations. While Tunisia was one of the signatories to the Berne Convention and at the time was a protectorate of France, it is doubtful that it had an independent role in the negotiation of the Convention because its interests were represented by the same individual that represented France."[41]

"[D]ependent" colonies were those to whom the laws of the colonizing countries extended.[42] Autonomous colonies, by contrast, could become Members of the Union, but only by applying for membership.[43]

In 1897 a group of manufacturers, businessmen, engineers, and lawyers met in Brussels and established the Association Internationale pour la Protection de la Propriété Industrielle (AIPPI), to conduct research and to advocate for expanded industrial property protections both nationally and internationally.[44] The association was modeled upon the ALAI.[45] The first congress of AIPPI, held in Vienna in October 1897, pressed for the introduction of uniform industrial property laws in all countries.

The relationship between industrial representation in the congresses and treaty processes decisively affected the outcome of patent debates under way even in industrialized countries such as England and Germany at the time. The *Economist*, the Vice-President of the Board of Trade, some outstanding inventors of the time, members of Parliament, and representatives of manufacturing districts such as Manchester and Liverpool advocated abolition of patents as pernicious monopolies that stifled rather than promoted innovation.[46] In Holland, the anti-patent movement was even more than elsewhere linked with Dutch interests in free trade.[47] German scholars argued that limited monopolies were generally disproportionate to the value of inventions and paralyzed the industry of others.[48] As early as 1868

[40] Lionel Bently, Intellectual Property Laws in the British Colonies 192–93 (2011).

[41] Sam Ricketson & Jane Ginsburg, International Copyright and Neighboring Rights: The Berne Convention and Beyond (2006).

[42] Bodenhausen, *supra* note 39, at 18.

[43] *Id.*

[44] Carolyn Deere Birkbeck, The World Intellectual Property Organization: A Reference Guide 7 (2016).

[45] Sara Bannerman, International Copyright and Access to Knowledge 167 (2016).

[46] Fritz Machlup & Edith Penrose, *The Patent Controversy in the 19th Century*, 10(1) J. Econ. History 1–29 (1950).

[47] Eric Schiff, Industrialization without National Patents: The Netherlands, 1869–1912; Switzerland, 1850–1907 25–41 (1971).

[48] Machlup & Penrose, *supra* note 46, at 20.

Bismarck, then Chancellor of the North German Federation, had gone on record as hostile to any form of patent protection.[49]

It was the availability of an international forum that allowed these arguments to be resolved in favor of strong industrial property rights to then be leveraged within national debates on the issue. The invitation to the 1873 Vienna Congress read in part:

> The present condition of Patent legislation in the most enlightened and progressive countries shows on which side the majority stands; with the exception of Switzerland and with her, Holland, which recently abolished her Patent law, the legislation of all the other Industrial States today recognizes the protection of Patents as a necessity.[50]

The conference endorsed the "English, American, and Belgian patent laws, and the draft of a patent law prepared for Germany by the society of German engineers" (those opposing Bismarck on the issue). Kronstein and Till summarize the strength the international negotiations provided for pro-patent constituencies:

> Bismarck immediately found himself confronted with a combined attack from within and without Germany. The Society of German Engineers was already hard at work; and now it had the added prestige of powerful support from abroad. Bismarck was forced to retreat. In 1876 he called a committee of experts to study the patent situation. In February 1877, he submitted a patent bill to Parliament.[51]

Similar pressures applied in England and Switzerland and eventually in Holland as well. In Switzerland, "strong external pressures had attached to the lack of a patent system the stigma of 'piracy' and threatened the pirate nation with discrimination in commercial policy."[52]

Indeed, the determination to use the language of what "civilised" nations did with respect to intellectual property (despite the existence of intra-European disagreement) was intimately tied to nomenclatures and paradigms adopted across a range of human activity that involved colonialism and imperialism.[53] According to Lorimer, writing in 1883,

> As a political phenomenon, humanity, in its present condition, divides itself into three concentric zones or spheres – that of civilised humanity, that of barbarous humanity, and that of savage humanity. To these, whether arising from peculiarities of race or from various stages of development in the same race, belong, of right, at the hands of civilised nations, three stages of recognition-plenary political

[49] Thomas Curson Hansard, Hansard's Parliamentary Debates 609–10 (1881).

[50] Heinrich Kronstein & Irene Till, A *Reevaluation of the International Patent Convention*, 12(4) Law and Contemporary Problems 765–81 (1947).

[51] *Id.*

[52] Malchup & Penrose, *supra* note 46, at 6.

[53] Anthony Anghie, *Finding the Peripheries: Sovereignty and Colonialism in 19th Century International Law*, 40 Harv. Int'l. L.J. 31 (1999).

> recognition, partial political recognition, and natural or mere human recognition. Intensively, the first of these forms of recognition embraces the two latter; extensively, the third embraces the two former. The sphere of plenary political recognition extends to the existing States of Europe, with their colonial dependencies, insofar as these are peopled by persons of European birth or descent; and to the States of North and South America which have vindicated their independence of the European States of which they were colonies. The sphere of partial political recognition extends to Turkey in Europe and in Asia and to the old historical states of Asia which have not become European dependencies-yiz. to Persia and the other separate States of Central Asia, to China, Siam, and Japan. The sphere of natural, or mere human recognition, extends to the residue of mankind; though here we ought, perhaps, to distinguish between the progressive and non-progressive races.[54]

Thus arguments made even by Switzerland or Holland – that patents were not natural rights of the kind acknowledged by "civilized" peoples, but specific tools of national economic policy that must balance interests – ran afoul of declarations made through the international negotiation process. Protection of intellectual property became over the course of the nineteenth century something that more "advanced" peoples acknowledged.

The major treaties were to play a significant role in the intellectual property laws that operated in states as they broke from European or North American control. With respect to Berne, "colonial past served to extend individual state membership, as newly independent countries would usually choose to continue the Berne membership of their metropolitan state."[55] Lionel Bently has detailed the ways by which British colonial possessions and later independent states internalized intellectual property laws adopted "at Home."[56] Indeed, as Sara Brannerman explains, the development of international intellectual property protections and those adopted by colonial states are related.[57] With respect to the Berne Convention, its initial membership of nine included six powers with vast territorial possessions; as these possessions became independent states, many of them chose to retain Berne membership.[58]

Even with the success of the Berne and Paris Conventions at establishing a specific international consensus on the general desirability of intellectual property protections, in both letter and practice, their effect was limited until the 1980s.[59] The most important principle was that of national treatment– that domestic regulatory

[54] James Lorimer, The Institutes of the Law of Nations ([1883] 2005), 101–03, 113–25.

[55] Sam Ricketson & Jane Ginsburg, *The Berne Convention Historical and Institutional Aspects*, in Daniel Gervais (ed), Intellectual Property: A Handbook of Contemporary Research 15 (2013).

[56] Lionel Bently, Intellectual Property Laws in the British Colonies 185 (2011).

[57] Sara Brannerman, International Copyright and Access to Knowledge 5 (2016).

[58] Ricketson &*supra* note 55.

[59] Sam F. Halabi, *Multipolarity, Intellectual Property, and the Internationalization of Public Health Law*, 35 Mich. J. Int'l L. 715, 729–30 (2014).

criteria would apply equally to domestic as well as foreign protected inventions and works. The treaties reflected differences in national intellectual property policies – including broad exceptions to their applicability – that were later to serve as pressure points for developing countries' resistance to their implementation through the World Trade Organization's Trade-Related Aspects of Intellectual Property (TRIPS) Agreement (indeed, the United States did not join the Berne Convention until 1989 because of some of these differences). Compulsory licenses under the Paris Convention were always contemplated for public health reasons, while the addition of Article 6quinquies(B)(iii) to the Paris Convention allowed the denial of registration or the invalidation of trademarks for regulatory reasons.[60] In short, the Paris Convention, later incorporated into TRIPS, provided broad limitations to intellectual property rights so as to balance them with other national policy priorities.[61]

Even were more protective provisions to be adopted (the Convention was updated intermittently between 1886 and 1967 – in some cases in ways that *weakened* protections), the Berne and Paris Conventions tended to suffer from underenforcement as well as the absence of a specific forum to which an aggrieved intellectual property rights holder might resort. Compliance and complaint were largely diplomatic matters.[62] For example, the international organization created to administer the Paris Convention and, later, the Berne Convention for the Protection of Literary and Artistic Works – the United International Bureaux for the Protection of Intellectual Property (BIRPI) – its French acronym) – never enjoyed more than a formal coordinating role and was, strictly speaking, an arm of the Swiss government.[63]

Between 1900 and 1958, the number of developing nations who were members of the Paris Convention/Union grew from three to fifteen.[64] By 1973, this number had increased to forty-four nations.[65] Various other larger developing nations demonstrated initial reluctance to adhere to the intellectual property conventions.[66] Governments of countries in the Americas were initially "skeptical of the merits of international IP agreements."[67] By 1970, only eight developing nations from the

60 Paris Convention Art. 5; Paris Convention Art. 6 *quinquies(B)(iii)*.

61 John Walker Baxter, John P. Sinnot, & William Cotreau, World Patent Law and Practice § 8 (2007).

62 J.H. Reichman, *Universal Minimum Standards of Intellectual Property Protection under the TRIPS Component of the WTO Agreement*, 29 Int'l Lawyer 345, 362 (1995); Benedict Kingsbury, *The Concept of Compliance as a Function of Competing Conceptions of International Law*, 19 Mich. J. Int'l. L. 345 (1998); Abram & Antonia Chayes, The New Sovereignty: Compliance with International Regulatory Agreements 135 (1995).

63 Bodenhausen, *supra* note 39, at 9.

64 Carolyn Deere Birbeck, Developing Country Perspectives on Intellectual Property in the WTO, Setting the Pre-TRIPS Context 5 (2009).

65 African nations lead this push to join the international IP system, with Egypt, Morocco, and Tunisia becoming members in 1960 and an additional twenty African nations joining by 1975. *Id.*

66 *Id.*

67 *Id.* at 6.

Americas were members of the Paris Union. Most of the Americas' developing nations did not begin to adhere to the Paris Convention until after the 1990s, following the adoption of TRIPS. Likewise, countries such as Bangladesh, China, Malaysia, Korea, Sudan, and Thailand did not join the Paris Convention until the 1980s.[68] India did not ultimately become a member until 1998, with Pakistan following in 2004.

From 1893 to 1967, BIRPI oversaw revisions to the major treaties, including the ways in which the agreements would govern new technologies, entry by newly independent former colonies, and increasing efforts to include substantive law in the treaties.[69] In 1967, the parties agreed to transform BIRPI into an international organization, the World Intellectual Property Organization (WIPO), which operated formally from 1970 and as a specialized agency of the United Nations from 1974. WIPO has largely overseen the growing body of intellectual property law harmonization and substantive law treaties such as the Patent Cooperation Treaty, the Trademark Law Treaty, and the (slowly forming) Substantive Patent Law Treaty. Indeed, it is funded largley through the fees paid by private users of the treaties it develops.[70] Because WIPO became a specialized agency of the United Nations in the same period that developing and newly independent states were pressing for a New International Economic Order, it never fully served the interests of strong international intellectual property protections.[71] The debates over compulsory education and development licenses almost brought an end to the Convention in the late 1960s.[72]

68 *Id.*
69 Christopher May, *The Pre-History and Establishment of WIPO*, 2009 WIPO J. 16, 20–21 (2009).
70 *Id.* at 24.
71 John Hughes, A *Short History of "Intellectual Property" in Relation to Copyright*, 33 CARDOZO L. REV. 1293, 1299 (2012).
72 Ricketson &*supra note* 55, *at* 29.

3

The Merger between International Intellectual Property, Investment, and Trade Law

Toward the mid-1960s and over the course of the 1970s, three of the afore-analyzed trends in international politics and international law began to conflict. First, technology and knowledge transfer became a priority for developing states as part of their demand for a restructuring of the global economic order, implicating the content, reach, and aims of the Berne and Paris Conventions. Second, global, knowledge-intensive firms increasingly sought protections for copyrights, patents, and trademarks as part of opening and maintaining markets abroad. Third, GATT (the trading club for wealthier countries) and UNCTAD (the trade lobbying group for poorer ones) clashed over the role of developing country exports as part of the international trade agenda.

In general, technology may be transferred through patent licensing, joint ventures, research cooperation, technology servicing, foreign direct investment, technology sharing agreements, and training.[1] It may also be transferred through reverse engineering and imitation. A series of reports commissioned by UNCTAD over the course of the 1960s and 1970s identified multinational corporations as the principal channel through which technology flowed from wealthier countries to poorer ones; criticized the means by which those firms used their technology to stifle competition and limit access for local capacity building; and called for wealthy countries to take unilateral action (against their firms) as well as to revise intellectual property agreements in light of technology transfer priorities.[2] Firms' restrictive business practices included, among others, prohibiting the use of technology for the purpose of producing exports;

[1] Hiroko Yamane, Interpreting TRIPS: Globalization of Intellectual Property Rights and Access to Medicines 52 (2011).

[2] G. Oldham, C. Freeman, & E. Turkman, The Transfer of Technology to Developing Countries, with Special Reference to Licensing and Know-How Agreements, TD/28/Supp.1 (1967); Major Issues Arising from the Transfer of Technology to Developing Countries, TD /B /AC. 11 / 10Rev.2 (1975); An International Code of Conduct on the Transfer of Technology, TD/B/C.6/AC.1/ 2/ Supp. 1 / Rev. 1 (1975); A. F. Ewing, *UNCTAD and the Transfer of Technology*, 10 J. World Trade L. 197 (1976); S. J. Patel, *The Technological Dependence of Developing Countries*, 12 J. Mod. Afr. St., 1 (1974).

furnishing only final, end-use technology in a given developing market; transferring obsolete technology at high prices; manipulating transfer pricing; use of licensing arrangements to extend intellectual property rights that would otherwise have expired or terminated; restrictions on original research or adaptive research; and patent pooling arrangements that effectively created market cartels.[3] UNCTAD found that 84 percent of patents in developing countries were owned by nationals of Britain, France, Germany, Switzerland, and the U.S. while only one percent of patents issued by developing countries were to their own citizens.[4] Thus the control of patents allowed firms to steeply regulate the terms of technology transfer and use.[5]

From 1975, UNCTAD began to develop an International Code of Conduct on the Transfer of Technology. The Code aimed to "eliminate those clauses in transfer of technology contracts which [were] harmful to the economic development of developing countries". Firms in the importing developing country were required to hire employees of the contracting transnational technology firm.[6] In November 1961, "Brazil and many other developing nations demanded for the first time – within the UN system – rules on the protection of intellectual property ... favourable to their economic development, including proper controls against abuse, thereby putting 'development' issues and 'public interest concerns' on the international [intellectual property] agenda".[7] The push for such an international instrument further accelerated in the wake of the oil crisis and OPEC's success in the early 1970s, when developing countries gained unprecedented momentum in their negotiations with developed countries. As Susan Sell recounted,

> In 1963 the United Nations held a Conference on the Application of Science and Technology for Development in Geneva. This conference affirmed the developing countries' belief that the United Nations could help them in their quest for greater access to technology ... [T]he conference's most important outcome was the conviction that the United Nations had a central role to play 'to facilitate the transfer of science and technology to developing countries and to help developing countries overcome obstacles in their access to necessary knowledge and its effective application.[8]

3 Amy Jocelyn Glass & Kamal Saggi, *International Technology Transfer and the Technology Gap*, 55 J. DEV. ECON. 369, 369 (1998); Michiko Ariga, *Restrictive Business Practices and International Controls on Transfer of Technology*, in Tagi Sagafi-Nejad, Richard W. Moxon & Harold Perimutter (eds), CONTROLLING INTERNATIONAL TECHNOLOGY TRANSFER (1981).

4 U.N. Dep't of Economic & Social Affairs, UNCTAD Secretariat, and Int'l Bureau of the WIPO, *The Role of the Patent System in the Transfer of Technology to Developing Countries* at 92, U.N. Doc. TD/B/AC.11/19 (1974).

5 R. P. Merges & R. R. Nelson, *On the Complex Economics of Patent Scope* 90 COLUM. L. REV. 839, 840 (1990).

6 SUSAN K. SELL, POWER AND IDEAS: NORTH–SOUTH POLITICS OF INTELLECTUAL PROPERTY AND ANTITRUST 93 (1998). For other practices that developing countries proposed but failed to include, see MICHAEL BLAKENEY, LEGAL ASPECTS OF THE TRANSFER OF TECHNOLOGY TO DEVELOPING COUNTRIES 149–50 (1989).

7 Andrea Koury Menescal, *Changing WIPO's Ways? The 2004 Development Agenda in Historical Perspective*" 8 J. WORLD INTEL. PROP. 761–62 (2005).

8 Sell, *supra* note 6, at 67.

Ton Zuijdwijk provided a concise summary of the major developments in the early UNCTAD sessions relating to the technology transfer debate:

> At [UNCTAD's first session], the Conference recommended that "[c]ompetent international bodies ... should explore possibilities for adaptation of legislation concerning the transfer of industrial technology to developing countries, including the possibility of concluding appropriate international agreements in this field." The idea was raised again in 1972 at UNCTAD III in Santiago, Chile when the Conference requested a joint study by the UNCTAD and WIPO Secretariats of "possible bases for new international legislation regulating the transfer of technology from developed to developing countries of patented and non-patented technology." The idea became more pronounced when, in 1973, the Trade and Development Board of UNCTAD requested the Intergovernmental Group on Transfer of Technology (the predecessor of the UNCTAD Transfer of Technology Committee) "to study the possibility and feasibility of an international code of conduct in the field of transfer of technology." ... In the summer of 1974, the concept of a Code was boosted by the General Assembly in its important Programme of Action on the Establishment of a New International Economic Order in which the Assembly specifically decided that '[a]ll efforts should be made: "[t]o formulate an international code of conduct for the transfer of technology corresponding to needs and conditions prevalent in developing countries."[9]

For example, Article 7 of the Charter of Algiers, which the group adopted in its first ministerial meeting in 1967, declared:

> (a) The developed countries should encourage the transfer of knowledge and technology to developing countries by permitting the use of industrial patents on the best possible terms which will enable products manufactured in developing countries to compete effectively in world markets;
> (b) They should also promote the elimination of restrictive practices, relating to market distribution and price-fixing, which are imposed by enterprises in developed countries in granting licences for the use of patents and trade-marks in developing countries;
> (c) The developed countries should provide guidance to their industrial entrepreneurs regarding investment opportunities in the export industries of the developing countries and familiarize them with legal, political, economic and other relevant information on the situation in the developing countries.[10]

The 1971 Lima Declaration "stated that the international community should promote the massive transfer of operative technology to developing countries on favorable

[9] Ton J. M. Zuijdwijk, *The UNCTAD Code of Conduct on the Transfer of Technology*, 24 McGill L. J. 563–65 (1978).

[10] First Ministerial Meeting of the Group of 77: The Charter of Algiers available at http://www.g77.org/doc/algier~1.htm (1967).

terms to contribute to their industrialization".[11] The 1975 Manila Declaration also "addressed the issues of technology transfer, strengthening the technological capacity of developing countries, ... and called for a code of conduct for the transfer of technology and the revision of the international patents system".[12] To put into practice the abstract ideas contained in these ministerial declarations, "a number of developing countries introduced legislative measures to increase state intervention in the screening and control of technology transactions [and to reduce their dependence on foreign suppliers] ... In the late 1960s and early 1970s Argentina, Brazil, India, Mexico, and the Andean Pact countries each enacted laws that codified their dissatisfaction with market principles governing technology transactions."[13]

Countries such as Argentina and Brazil pioneered "the assertion of a distinct developing country voice on international IP regulation" in the 1960s and beyond.[14] Brazil's 1961 proposal at the UN General Assembly on patents and developing countries was the first of its kind and resulted in a General Assembly Resolution seeking a study on the effects of patents on developing country economies.[15] Brazil had been initially concerned with the "progressive strengthening of the Paris Convention" and sought to use this Resolution, and further UN action, to encourage revisions to the convention "that would better address the special needs of developing countries.[16] The resolution even sought consideration for an international conference "to examine problems related to patents and the special needs of developing countries."[17]

India would also lead developing nations in promoting reforms to international copyright treaties following the 1960s. These countries argued that improvements to their respective mass educations systems were hindered by "publishing cartels" coupled with the "high royalties and licensing fees" expected by copyright holders in developed nations.[18] Their efforts ultimately led to a campaign to revise the Berne Convention in order to "increase [] access to information, literature, and artistic works."[19]

[11] Lima Group of 77 Declaration, 1971, 10 ILM 207 (1971).
[12] Peter K. Yu, *International Technology Contracts, Restrictive Covenants and the UNCTAD Code* in Christopher Heath and Anselm Kamperman Sanders (eds), EMPLOYEES, TRADE SECRETS AND RESTRICTIVE COVENANTS 41–57 (2017).
[13] Sell, *supra* note 6, at 69.
[14] *Id.*
[15] UNCTAD, THE CHANNELS AND MECHANISMS FOR THE TRANSFER OF TECHNOLOGY FROM DEVELOPED TO DEVELOPING COUNTRIES (a study by Charles Cooper with the collaboration of F. Sercovitch), TD/B/AC.11/5 (1971).
[16] CAROLYN DEERE, THE IMPLEMENTATION GAME: THE TRIPS AGREEMENT AND THE GLOBAL POLITICS OF INTELLECTUAL PROPERTY REFORM IN DEVELOPING COUNTRIES 42 (2009).
[17] U.N.G.A. Resolution 1713 (XVI) (1961).
[18] Deere, *supra* note 16.
[19] *Id.*

Developing nations began to contend that the international patent conventions and rules "were intrinsically unbalanced in favor of developed countries."[20] Developing countries questioned the correlation between stronger intellectual property protections and increases in domestic innovations, particularly since only a small number of the patents granted in their countries were actually used in domestic production. In 1972, Latin American nations arranged the Organization of American States (OAS) regional conference in Brazil to seek reform to international conventions on patents; the conference reached the consensus that international intellectual property regimes were "inadequate and ha[d] been exploited by technology exporters to impose consumption patterns and obtain production, distribution, and trade privileges."[21] In 1975, UNCTAD concluded in a report regarding the role of the international patent system on developing nations that there existed a "need for revision of international conventions."[22] Developing nations would again utilize the 1975 UN General Assembly to "advance a resolution calling for the reform of the Paris Convention to ensure that it addressed the needs of developing countries."[23] This led to WIPO's creation of an Ad Hoc Croup of Governmental Experts on the Revision of the Paris Convention.[24] The Paris Convention would become a "'battleground' between developed and developing countries" by 1980.[25]

Developing countries sought three major modifications of the major international treaties through WIPO: the use of reward mechanisms that operated differently than patents (typically without a right to exclude others); a requirement that patents be worked locally; and, upon failure to do so, compulsory licenses to issue (some alternatives included adding "public interest" reasons for compulsory licenses as well).[26] Additionally, the UNCTAD Secretariat suggested changes to priority rights – that is, when a patent claim would be determined to be the first to enjoy legal recognition – propagated by the Paris Convention.[27] First, the Secretariat argued that the priority period be reduced to account for developments in modern communication that did not exist at the time the Convention was adopted.[28] Second, the Secretariat recommended that the priority period be made inapplicable to "third

20 *Id.* at 43.
21 *Id.* at 90.
22 *WIPO: Revision of the Paris Convention*, 13 J. WORLD TRADE L. 564, 575–77 (1979).
23 TONYA PUTNAM, COURTS WITHOUT BORDERS: LAW, POLITICS, AND U.S. EXTRATERRITORIALITY 174 (2016).
24 HIROKO YAMANE, INTERPRETING TRIPS: GLOBALIZATION OF INTELLECTUAL PROPERTY RIGHTS AND ACCESS TO MEDICINES 47 (2011).
25 Peter Drahos, *Negotiating Intellectual Property Rights: Between Coercion and Dialogue*, in Peter Drahos & Ruth Mayne (eds), GLOBAL INTELLECTUAL PROPERTY RIGHTS: KNOWLEDGE, ACCESS AND DEVELOPMENT 161–82 (2002).
26 DUNCAN MATTHEWS, GLOBALISING INTELLECTUAL PROPERTY RIGHTS: THE TRIPS AGREEMENT (2002).
27 Regina A. Loughran, *The United States Position on Revising the Paris Convention: Quid Pro Quo or Denunciation*, 5 FORDHAM INT. L. J. 411, 426 (1981).
28 *Id.*

parties who in good faith ... [begin] exploitation of an invention ... identical to the one for which priority is claimed," when the claimed invention has not been published or disclosed.[29] The Secretariat also suggested changes to preferential treatment under the Convention, proposing that such treatment be granted to inventors from developing countries when they applied for patents during priority period of a developed nation's applicant.[30] Developed states led by Britain, France, and the United States resisted these changes. Meetings were held in Geneva twice (1980, 1982) and in Nairobi (1981) in order to resolve the impasse.

Paradoxically, the growth in liberalized trade through GATT made firms in North America, Europe, and Japan more sensitive to the potential threat posed by competitive products produced elsewhere sometimes but not always using technology adapted from their proprietary claims.[31] As WIPO negotiations proceeded, developed nations, urged by international firms, began to fret "waning competitiveness" and an increased emphasis on value that "the strategic role of technology and the protection of intangible assets" brought to their economic growth and trade prospects.[32] European and North American companies highlighted the challenges created by weaker intellectual property protection inside and outside national borders, arguing that "stronger [intellectual property] rights were central to their business model both at home and abroad."[33] Competitors were enjoying a "free ride" on their research and development efforts, and so they sought governmental intervention to impose limits or entirely quash imitation and reverse-engineering occurring abroad. The leaders of various US corporations soon united to effect a US agenda for trade-based understanding of intellectual property rights that integrated intellectual property protections into international trade policies.[34]

Until the early 1980s, these efforts were not particularly organized: pharmaceutical and industrial firms and audio-visual interests initially attempted to amend the obvious treaties, such as Paris and Berne, while trademark proprietors (which included the latter interests as well as other firms such as beverages and tobacco, whose value was almost entirely in their trademarks) endeavored to influence GATT. The UK Publishers Association requested the Office of the U.S. Trade Representative in 1978 to take action against infringement worldwide.[35] In 1979 the

[29] The Secretariat argued that it would be unjust to require a third party to stop use of an invention in such circumstances. *Id.*

[30] *Id.*

[31] Simon Walker, The TRIPS Agreement, Sustainable Development, and the Public Interest 7 (2001).

[32] Carolyn Deere, The Implementation Game: The TRIPS Agreement and the Global Politics of Intellectual Property Reform in Developing Countries 46 (2009).

[33] *Id.*

[34] Key actors were the International Intellectual Property Alliance, the Pharmaceutical Manufacturers Association, the Chemical Manufacturers Association, the Agricultural Chemicals Association, the Motor Equipment Manufacturers Association, the Auto Exports Council, the International Anti-counterfeiting Coalition, and the Semiconductor Industry Association.

[35] *Id.* at 46.

United States and the European Community reached agreement on a draft "Agreement on Measures to Discourage the Importation of Counterfeit Goods".[36] Between 1980 and 1982 informal meetings with a number of industrialized countries resulted in a revised draft Anti-Counterfeiting Code.[37]

Through the 1980s, intellectual property lobby, especially within the United States, began to shape trade policy toward intellectual property promoting objectives. IBM CEO John Opel and Pfizer CEO Edmund Pratt "pursued parallel efforts" to advance the intellectual property concerns of their respective companies and industries to the US government.[38] Both men were involved in the International Anti-Counterfeiting Coalition at the GATT negotiations in Tokyo, and Pratt would become chair of the Advisory Committee for Trade Negotiations (ACTN), providing private-sector input on trade policy to the US administration.[39] Pharmaceutical companies, fearing cheaper generic competitors, complained of the narrow scope and short term of patent protection afforded by many developing countries, and adopted the rhetorical approaches emphasizing "crimes" and "theft" of intellectual property.[40] A priority of large multinational corporations was to ensure that efforts to adopt strategic intellectual property approaches like those in Argentina, Brazil, India, and Mexico did not become the norm for developing nations.[41] Eventually, Hewlett-Packard CEO John Young would become the chair of the Commission on Industrial Competitiveness and overseeing its 1984 report highlighting the negative impact of weak IP protection on American competitiveness.[42]

Before it became clear that WIPO was not going to serve as the major engine for advancing intellectual property rights, firms also lobbied for changes aimed at increasing protections. Beginning in the late 1970s, the US research pharmaceutical industry began to petition WIPO on the issue of national treatment – only the changes it sought were to use WIPO to target countries that offered little or no protection to pharmaceutical patents.[43] After the renegotiation process over the Paris Convention failed, Lou Clemente, then general counsel of Pfizer, declared that

36 GATT Doc. No. L/4817 (July 31, 1979).

37 *Agreement on Measures to Discourage the Importation of Counterfeit Goods*, GATT Doc. No. L/5382 (Oct. 18, 1982).

38 Susan K. Sell, Private Power, Public Law: The Globalization of Intellectual Property Rights 38 (2003).

39 *Id.*

40 Christopher Harrison, The Politics of the International Pricing of Prescription Drugs 80–81 (2004).

41 *Id.* at 77–78.

42 United States Senate Finance Committee, *Review of Findings of the President's Commission on Industrial Competitiveness* (Mar. 29, 1985) available at https://www.finance.senate.gov/imo/media/doc/HRG99-75.pdf

43 Valbona Muzaka, The Politics of Intellectual Property Rights and Access to Medicines 43 (2011).

"our experience at WIPO was the last straw in our attempt to operate by persuasion."[44] Indeed, shortly after the failure of the last negotiation at Geneva, the United States added intellectual property specifically to Section 301 of its 1974 Trade Act.[45] Fred Abbott phrased the situation this way:

> A collection of like-minded industries ... led by the pharmaceutical and agricultural chemical sector, the software and audiovisual sector, and the high-fashion trademark sector – used their political influence in the Trade Representative's office and elsewhere to put protection of [Intellectual Property Rights] high on the US trade negotiation agenda. In the early 1970s, there was very little empirical research, or even theoretical research on the role of IPRs in international trade, or the effect of developing country intellectual property practices on the interests of OECD country producers.[46]

What evidence did exist was largely gathered through questionnaires sent to firms with obvious interests in depicting a "pirating" crisis.[47] The measures eventually adopted by the United States created widespread disaffection with its trade policy. Yet behind United States' policy was a belief, shared by other wealthy countries, that as intellectual property has become an increasingly important component of national wealth and international trade, it is was properly the subject of trade protection, regardless of whether that was originally contemplated by the international trade regime under GATT.[48] Intellectual property became the new focus of debates over national wealth.[49]

There was, in fact, not much in GATT through which to develop an entire international legal approach to intellectual property. One provision of the agreement permitted the adoption by individual GATT member states of domestic legislation necessary to protect intellectual property (as long as the legislation was consistent with GATT), and to a provision aimed at preventing the use of trade names to misrepresent origin.[50]

44 *Id.*

45 The Trade Act of 1974 (Pub.L. 93–618, 88 Stat. 1978, enacted Jan. 3, 1975, codified at 19 U.S.C. ch. 12)

46 Fred Abbott, *The TRIPS-Legality of Measures Taken to Address Public Health Crises: Responding to USTR-State-Industry Positions That Undermine the WTO* in Daniel Kennedy and James Southwick (eds), THE POLITICAL ECONOMY OF INTERNATIONAL TRADE LAW 313 (2002).

47 U.S. Int'l Trade Commission, Pub. No. 2065, Foreign Protection of Intellectual Property Rights and the Effect on U.S. Industry and Trade (1988).

48 Fred Abbott, *Protecting First World Assets in the Third World: Intellectual Property Negotiations in the GATT Multilateral Framework*, 22 VAND. J. TRANSNAT'L. L. 689, 692 (1989).

49 Scholars such as Professor Walter Hamilton, who wrote on the subject of patents for the Temporary National Economic Committee in 1941, emphasized the role of technology as a component of national wealth. SENATE TEMPORARY NATIONAL ECONOMIC COMM., 76TH CONG., 3D SESS., INVESTIGATION OF CONCENTRATION OF ECONOMIC POWER: PATENTS AND FREE ENTERPRISE 164 (Comm. Print 1941) (W. Hamilton, Monograph No. 31)

50 GATT art. XX(d).

Yet the Anti-Counterfeiting Code became a priority for developed countries as they entered the 1982 ministerial for the preparations for the forthcoming GATT Round.[51] When the issue was raised, developing countries, led by Brazil and India, argued that intellectual property issues belonged exclusively to the World Intellectual Property Organization (WIPO) and that, in any event, GATT was concerned with trade in tangible goods, and therefore the issue of counterfeit in trademark lay outside is authority.[52] The resulting Ministerial Declaration requested the Director General of GATT to hold consultations with his counterpart at WIPO in order to clarify the appropriateness of joint action in relation to counterfeiting.[53] A GATT Expert Group produced a report on the effects of counterfeit on international trade.[54] Similar discussions occurred in the national lawmaking bodies of developed countries.[55]

Between 1982 and 1986 a Preparatory Committee of the GATT identified the issues that would be the concern of the forthcoming GATT Round.[56] The United States proposed that the Round consider all intellectual property rights, implying that GATT was an appropriate forum to consider and legislate over intellectual property issues. Subsequent negotiations led by the Swiss and Colombian trade representatives sought a compromise between the opposing views on the jurisdiction of GATT and produced a proposal that served as the basis for the Ministerial Declaration of September 20, 1986, which launched the Uruguay Round.[57]

The Advisory Committee for Trade Negotiations (ACTN) was "designed to provide direct input by the US business sector into US trade policy" and acted as a line of communication between American businesses and the bureaucratic [center] of trade policy.[58] The strategy created a long-term goal for the United States of "placing intellectual property into the GATT" through the use of trade tools in bilateral and unilateral efforts.[59] The United States dispatched intellectual property advocates to developing countries to promote stronger intellectual property rights while also pressuring countries' access the Generalized System of Preferences (GSP)

[51] Jane Bradley, *Intellectual Property Rights, Investment and Trade in Services in the Uruguay Round: Laying the Foundations*, 23 Stanford J. Int'l Law 57 (1987).

[52] *Id.* at 66–67.

[53] GATT, Ministerial Declaration (Nov. 29, 1982) available at https://www.wto.org/gatt_docs/English/SULPDF/91000208.pdf

[54] *Trade in Counterfeit Goods*, GATT Doc. No. L/5758 (1982).

[55] *Possible Renewal of the Generalised System of Preferences-Hearing Before the Subcommittee on Trade of the U.S. House of Rep. Comm. on Ways and Means* , 98th Cong., 1st Sess. (1983); *Unfair Foreign Trade Practices, Stealing American Intellectual Property: Imitation Is Not Flattery*, 98th Cong., 2d Sess.1–3 (1984).

[56] Terence P. Stewart (ed) The GATT Uruguay Round. A Negotiating History (1986–1992), vols I–III (1993).

[57] *Id* (vol. II) 2263–64.

[58] Carolyn Deere, The Implementation Game: The TRIPS Agreement and the Global Politics of Intellectual Property Reform in Developing Countries 42 (2009).

[59] *Id.*

developed by UNCTAD. Intellectual property–intensive firms maintained a "continuous[] and intimate[]" presence in the development of US policy.[60]

There is a rich history explaining how developed countries successfully folded intellectual property into the international trade regime between 1986 and 1994, when the treaty establishing the World Trade Organization was finalized.[61] From 1984, the United States and European countries added intellectual property protection explicitly to domestic trade laws and applied them to the Generalized System of Preferences negotiated by UNCTAD – effectively using unilateral policy to leverage negotiations over intellectual property during the Uruguay Round of GATT.[62] Section 301 of the 1974 Trade Act "authorizes the President to take all appropriate action, including retaliation, to obtain the removal of any act, policy, or practice of a foreign government that violates an international trade agreement or is unjustified, unreasonable, or discriminatory, and that burdens or restricts U.S. commerce."[63] In 1988, Congress enhanced Section 301 by requiring the Office of the US Trade Representative to compile "Special 301" Reports, which identified countries that do not provide "adequate and effective" protection of intellectual property rights or "fair and equitable market access to United States persons that rely upon intellectual property rights."[64] The United States used Section 301 as a negotiating "stick" during GATT negotiations. Individual firms used these legislative changes to threaten governments that adopted intellectual property policies they viewed as hostile – even using draft texts of the future TRIPS agreement as representative of binding law.[65]

The European Union (then European Economic Community) also enhanced its ability to leverage its trade preferences against developing countries during the negotiations. In 1984, the EEC adopted Regulation 2641/84 to "engage in trade retaliation against 'illicit commercial practices'" that were found to affect European economic interests.[66] While the United States used its own intellectual property standards for purposes of Section 301 sanctions, Europeans focused on violations of obligations in international treaties, such as the Berne and Paris Conventions.

[60] *Id.*

[61] Peter Drahos, *Global Property Rights in Information: The Story of TRIPS at the GATT*, 13 Prometheus 6, 7 (1995); Susan Sell, Private Power, Public Law: The Globalization of Intellectual Property Rights 19 (2003).

[62] Carolyn Deere, The Implementation Game: The TRIPS Agreement and the Global Politics of Intellectual Property Reform in Developing Countries 48 (2009). At a November 1985 GATT committee meeting, some developing nations criticized the approach of the United States as being "quite alien to the spirit and purpose of the Generalized System of Preferences (GPS).

[63] U.S. Trade Act of 1974, (Pub.L. 93–618, 19 U.S.C. § 2411).

[64] Office of the U.S. Trade Representative, 2009 Special 301 Report 3, 8–9, 17, 20, 25, 31 (2009).

[65] Sam F. Halabi, *Multipolarity, Intellectual Property, and the Internationalization of Public Health Law*, 35 Mich. J. Int'l L. 715, 754 (2014).

[66] Michael Buton Devine, *The Adoption of EEC Regulation 2641/84 on Illicit Commercial Practices with Special Reference to the USA*, 22 Int'l. Lawyer 1091 (1988).

In 1987, the EEC suspended trade privileges to South Korea.[67] The EEC's subtler approach allowed it to mimic US action. The EEC would occasionally send negotiators to "conclude a bilateral agreement on intellectual property with a developing country" that had initially been motivated to negotiate by the United States' use of the 301 process.[68] The GATT negotiating period marked the beginning of US and European efforts to include intellectual property provisions in their respective bilateral and regional agreements. Some of the first bilateral trade agreements to feature intellectual property commitments were the US trade agreements with Israel and Vietnam. The United States would go on to negotiate intellectual property–specific bilateral agreements with Ecuador, China, Korea, the Philippines, Taiwan, and Sri Lanka.

Coordination between Canada, Europe, Japan, and the United States was achieved in substantial part through the influence of the Intellectual Property Committee (IPC) (Bristol-Myers, Du Pont, FMC Corporation, General Electric, General Motors, Hewlett-Packard, IBM, Johnson & Johnson, Merck, Monsanto, Pfizer, Rockwell International, and Warner Communications, although these members changed somewhat over the negotiating period), which created consensus between the business communities in the four regions.[69] That consensus, in turn, was used to shape the joint negotiating position of wealthier countries (perfect consensus was never achieved – even at the end of the negotiations, the United States, Europe, and Japan disagreed on some aspects of TRIPS).[70] Certainly, the group was influential in persuading governments that GATT was an appropriate home for intellectual property disputes. In the process, the IPC developed close relationships with the US administration and Congress, allowing it to shape many of the United States' proposals and positions during the GATT negotiations.[71] Any resistance from developing countries was met with the 301 process by the United States.[72] Ultimately, the 301 process became crucial to the United States' success on intellectual property at the GATT, and by the final stages of negotiations, developing countries began acquiescing to the various intellectual property proposals advanced by wealthier countries.

67 Council Regulation EEC No 3912/87 of Dec. 18, 1987 suspending the generalized tariff preferences for 1988 for products originating in the Republic of Korea.

68 Peter Drahos, *Developing Countries and International Intellectual Property Standard-Setting* 5 (5) J. WIPO 765–89 (2002) available at https://www.anu.edu.au/fellows/pdrahos/articles/pdfs/2002devcountriesandipstandards.pdf.

69 Peter Drahos, *Global Law Reform and Rent-Seeking: The Case of Intellectual Property* in Benedict Atkinson and Brian Fitzgerald (eds), Copyright Law Volume III: Copyright and the 21st Century 52 (2016).

70 *Id.*

71 *Id.*

72 Peter Drahos, *Global Property Rights in Information: The Story TRIPS at the GATT*, 13 Prometheus 6 (1995)

Significantly, the United States was one of the few countries to send negotiators who possessed "strong intellectual property expertise."[73] This provided a notable advantage to the United States during the negotiation process where they worked with negotiators from other countries who had no experience with intellectual property. Even the GATT Secretariat was "dealing with intellectual property for the first time."[74] The combination of negotiating power and expertise explains the overwhelming success the United States and, to a significant extent, Canada, Europe, and Japan enjoyed at the conclusion of negotiations.

The Agreement – which established the WTO – was signed by 111 countries on April 15, 1994.[75] The Agreement "embodie[d] the outcomes of Uruguay Round of Multilateral trade negotiations" and contained separate agreements dealing with trade-related aspects of intellectual property rights (TRIPS).[76] TRIPS grants patent, copyright, and trademark holders rights to certain minimal statutory protections as well as resort to administrative and judicial processes to enforce those rights.[77] Member states may pass protections greater than those detailed in TRIPS, but additional protections must be extended to nationals of other member states.[78] In addition to substantive provisions, TRIPS also outlines a comprehensive framework for civil adjudication of intellectual property rights.[79] Member States must create private causes of action as well as remedies including injunctions, money damages, and the use of border restrictions.[80] States must also give intellectual property rights holders access to judicial review of all administrative decisions concerning their intellectual property laws.[81]

[73] US negotiators had already been involved in intellectual property–related negotiations through the bilateral process as well as NAFTA negotiations. *Id.*at 14.

[74] *Id.*

[75] Agreement on Trade-Related Aspects of Intellectual Property Rights art. 8, Apr. 15, 1994, Marrakesh Agreement Establishing the World Trade Organization, Annex 1C, 1869 U.N.T.S. 299.

[76] The agreement required signatories to increase the duration of protection for some intellectual property rights, as well as enact new rights. Countries were also required to take a greater role in enforcement of monopoly privileges and established a Council for TRIPS that monitored its operation and members' compliance. Drahos, *supra* note 72, at 6, 7.

[77] Nuno Pires De Carvalho, The TRIPS Regime of Patent Rights (3d ed. 2010); Global Intellectual Property Rights, Knowledge, Access and Development (Peter Drahos & Ruth Mayne eds., 2002).

[78] TRIPS art. 1(1) and art. 3 (providing the caveat that this provision is subject to any Paris Convention exceptions).

[79] TRIPS art. 41.

[80] TRIPS arts. 44–45, 57.

[81] TRIPS, art 61. See also TRIPS, arts 44 (injunctive relief), 45 (damages); 41(4) (requiring that [p] arties to a proceeding shall have an opportunity for review by a judicial authority of final administrative decisions and, subject to jurisdictional provisions in the Member's law concerning the importance of a case, of at least the legal aspects of initial judicial decisions on the merits of the case").

The success of the United States and US businesses in achieving their international intellectual property objectives reflected their relentless push "at all possible levels, in all possible fora, using all possible agents."[82] This effort was motivated in the United States by both the influence of US corporations seeking to protect their IP portfolios and profits from piracy and political fears about the country's loss of wealth to developing countries, which corresponded to a loss of competitiveness vis-á-vis other wealthy nations.[83]

The global distribution of wealth was at the core of the commencement, conclusion, and unaddressed aspects of TRIPS. The United States and, to a lesser extent, Canada, Europe, and Japan maintained that "as the net importers of technological and cultural information, [developing nations] should pay more for the importation of that information."[84] Developing countries, by contrast, were generally "culturally predisposed" to rejecting intellectual property regimes and saw intellectual property protection efforts as "a form of recolonization or economic imperialism."[85] Prior to the Uruguay Round, the trade liberalization negotiation process had been largely driven by the trade agenda of developed states; agriculture was for the most part excluded, and the important bargains were struck between the industrialized countries. The Uruguay Round, by contrast, involved a greater range of issues, many of which were long-standing priorities of developing states. Their interests in lowering barriers to trade in agricultural goods, clothes, and textiles resulted in a "grand bargain" in which they agreed to impose strong monopoly protections for copyrights, trademarks, and, most importantly from the North American, Japanese, and European perspective, copyrights and patents.[86]

According to Susan Sell, IPC members got 95 percent of what they wanted, but the remaining 5 percent mattered and, as Part III of this book explains, it has redirected the global wealth redistribution debate toward issues that TRIPS left incomplete.[87] It is toward those issues that the New International Economic Order is now directed. Developing states won flexibilities with respect to implementation of TRIPS obligations, including Articles 7 and 8, which, respectively, emphasized

[82] Drahos, *supra* note 61.

[83] Better protection was expected to produce more jobs and allow IP based industries to "restore the US to a positive trade balance with the world." Peter Drahos, *Global Property Rights in Information: The Story of TRIPS at the GATT*, 13 PROMETHEUS 6, 7 (1995).

[84] *Id.*

[85] *Id.* at 9.

[86] Laurence Helfer, *Regime Shifting: The TRIPS Agreement and New Dynamics of International Intellectual Property Lawmaking*, 29 YALE J. INT'L. L. 1 (2004).

[87] SUSAN SELL, PRIVATE POWER, PUBLIC LAW: THE GLOBALIZATION OF INTELLECTUAL PROPERTY RIGHTS 48 (2003) (quoting Interview with Jacques Gorlin, Aanser, IPC in Washington, DC (Jan. 22, 1996)).

the need for intellectual property rules to allow for development, technology transfer, and measures necessary to protect public health and nutrition.[88] Article 8 did not provide a general public health exemption from TRIPS implementation, but rather conditioned those measures on TRIPS compliance.[89] Article 31 of TRIPS allows for the nonconsensual authorizations of patents – a provision whose importance was elevated by the Doha Declaration on the TRIPS Agreement and Public Health.[90]

States parties are not required to allocate more resources toward enforcement of intellectual property rights than "law in general," so many individual intellectual property rights-holders may not see a sufficient payoff to invest resources in pursuing individual civil actions to vindicate property rights.[91] The economic sectors closely tied to TRIPS Articles 7 and 8 – food, tobacco, alcohol, and pharmaceuticals – are precisely those in which firms, although not necessarily governments, are likely to try and preserve substantial investments in advertising, research, and development.[92] As a result, TRIPS effectively created a situation where developing countries would grapple directly with firms in specific sectors.

The "5 percent" mattered for firms as well, not only developing countries.[93] TRIPS and other WTO agreements that regulated intellectual property rights became a floor for both bilateral and multilateral agreements born at the time and since developed.[94] The Anti-Counterfeiting Trade Agreement represents the codification of principles advanced in a number of initiatives undertaken by developed states to enhance protections for intellectual property holders beyond what TRIPS achieved.[95] According to the US Trade Representative, "the goal [of ACTA is to set a new, higher benchmark for enforcement that countries can join on a voluntary basis ... ACTA will include commitments in three areas: (1) strengthening international cooperation, (2) improving enforcement practices, and (3) providing a

88 A. Blackett, *Whither Social Change? Human Rights, Trade Theory and Treaty Interpretation*, 31 Colum. Hum. Rts. L. Rev. 1 (1999).

89 United Nations Conference on Trade and Development & Int'l Ctr. for Trade and Sustainable Dev., Resource Book on TRIPS and Development 739, 748 (2005), available at http://www.iprsonline.org/ unctadictsd/docs/6.3TRIPS_COUNCIL_UPDATE.pdf.

90 TRIPS art. 41(5); Peter Drahos, *Intellectual Property and Pharmaceutical Markets: A Nodal Governance Approach*, 77 Temple Law Review 401–24 (2004).

91 Patricia Judd, *Towards a TRIPS Truce*, 32 Mich. J. Int'l. L. 613, 622 (2011).

92 Rachel Brewster, *The Surprising Benefits to Developing Countries of Linking International Trade and Intellectual Property*, 12 Chi. J. Int'l. L. 1, 32 (2011).

93 Susan Sell, *TRIPS Was Never Enough: Vertical Forum Shifting, FTAS, ACTA and TPP*, 18(2) J. Intell. Prop. 447, 448 (2011).

94 For example, the Anti-Counterfeiting Trade Agreement § 1, art. 1, *opened for signature* (Oct. 1, 2011), available at http://www.ustr.gov/acta.

95 Peter K. Yu, *Six Secret (and Now Open) Fears of ACTA*, 64 SMU L. Rev. 975, 977–81 (2011).

strong legal framework for IPR enforcement."[96] After eleven rounds of negotiations, the final ACTA text was adopted[97] in May 2011.[98]

ACTA contains increased criminal sanctions for intellectual property rights infringement and stronger border measures to target illegal trafficking in infringing goods through customs processes.[99] While commentators have detailed criticisms of those measures specifically (especially border controls), this section will focus on ACTA's civil enforcement provisions.[100] Among those procedures are injunctions, damages, other remedies, and the collection and preservation of evidence.[101] These civil enforcement provisions are not limited to first-party infringers. "Each Party shall provide that, in civil judicial proceedings concerning the enforcement of intellectual property rights, its judicial authorities shall have the authority to order against a party to desist from infringement an order to that party or where appropriate to a third party . . . to prevent infringing good from entering the channels of commerce."

This latter provision implicates the movement of medicines, among other goods.[102] For example, because ACTA requires that judicial authorities have the power to issue injunctions against third parties, any intermediary provider of generic medicines to developing countries potentially faces liability under the ACTA regime.[103]

> In the context of access to medicines, the concept "intermediary services" may be quite ominous. Services are obviously provided by ISPs allowing supplier to market medicines online and in the pharmaceutical context by shipping agents . . . Perhaps

[96] Press Release, Office of the U.S. Trade Rep. [USTR], Ambassador Schwab Announces U.S. Will Seek New Trade Agreement to Fight Fakes (Oct. 23, 2007), available at http://www.ustr .gov/ambassador-schwab-announces- us-will-seek-new-trade-agreement-fight-fakes.

[97] Eight parties have signed ACTA: Australia, Canada, Japan, Korea, Morocco, New Zealand, Singapore, and the United States. *Anti-Counterfeiting Trade Agreement (ACTA)*, Office of the United States Trade Representative, available at http://www.ustr.gov/acta. The EU signed ACTA on January 26, 2012, but still needs to be signed and ratified by all twenty-seven member states because ACTA contains "criminal enforcement provisions, an area that is considered 'shared' competence between the EU and its Member States." European Commission, *Fact Sheet*, ACTA-Anti-Counterfeiting Trade Agreement, (May 4, 2012, 5:00 PM), *available at* http://trade.ec.europa.eu/doclib/docs/2012/january/tradoc_149003.pdf.

[98] http://www.ustr.gov/acta/

[99] Margot Kaminski, *The Origins and Potential Impact of the Anti-Counterfeiting Trade Agreement*, 34 Yale J. Int'l L. 247, 250 (2009).

[100] Eddan Katz & Gwen Hinze, *The Impact of the Anti-Counterfeiting Trade Agreement on the Knowledge Economy: The Accountability of the Office of the U.S. Trade Representative for the Creation of IP Enforcement Norms Through Executive Trade Agreements*, 35 Yale J. Int'l L. Online 24–25 (2009).

[101] ACTA art. 8–11. Parties' competent authorities have the power to order a party to "desist from an infringement . . . and . . . prevent goods that involve the infringement of an [IPR] from entering into the channels of commerce."

[102] Sean Flynn, *ACTA's Constitutional Problem: The Treaty Is Not a Treaty*, 26 Am. U. Int'l. L. Rev. 903, 905 (2012).

[103] Cynthia M. Ho, *Global Access to Medicine: The Influence of Competing Patent Perspectives*, 35 Fordham Int'l. L. J. 1, 94–95 (2011).

> more ominously, many others who helped fund or facilitate purchases of generic drugs, as they moved through the stream of international commerce from producer to consumer could face intermediary liability. For example, the Global Fund [one of the two major purchasers of HIV/AIDS drugs] solicits and funds country-led proposals for funding priority disease prevention, treatment and care.[104]

The force of the agreement extends beyond its power to shape domestic law, as it will inevitably also form the template for future bilateral agreements between ACTA and non-ACTA states. The Trans-Pacific Strategic Economic Partnership Agreement, or TPP, mimicks many of ACTA's intellectual property provisions, although the Trump administration has ended, for now, US participation.[105]

More common than broad, multilateral trade instruments such as TRIPS and ACTA bilateral and regional investment and trade agreements contain some of the strongest protections for intellectual property.[106] Bilateral investment and trade treaties (BITs), for example, take a number of forms and include provisions authorizing intellectual property rights-holders to vindicate claims in national or international courts or dispute resolution fora. At the end of the 1980s, records at the UN Conference on Trade and Development showed 385 BITs; a decade later, the number reached 1,857; current estimates show approximately 3,000 BITs in force.[107] Generally, BITs are negotiated between one wealthy country and one poorer country.[108] BITs contain provisions guaranteeing investors from one state protections for their "investments" in the other state which are often to define intellectual property in broad terms.[109] These guarantees may include fair and equitable or nondiscriminatory treatment, free transfer of profits and currency, and, in many cases, payment of compensation should a host state adopt measures having the effect of direct or indirect expropriation.[110]

BITs do not, typically, include enumerated rights for contracting states outside their ability to prohibit certain economic activities altogether, exempt certain

104 Brook Baker, *ACTA-Risks of Third-Party Enforcement for Access to Medicines*, 26 Am. U. Int'l L. Rev. 579, 588–89 (2011).

105 Robert Stumberg, *Safeguards for Tobacco Control: Options for the TPPA*, 39 Am. J. L. & Med. 382 (2013); Jane Kelsey, *The Trans-Pacific Partnership Agreement: A Gold-Plated Gift to the Global Tobacco Industry?* 39 Am. J. L. & Med. 237, 264 (2013).

106 United Nations Conference on Trade & Dev. (UNCTAD), Intellectual Property Provisions in International Investment Arrangements 5 (2007).

107 U.N. Conf. on Trade and Dev. (UNCTAD) Bilateral Investment Treaties 1959–1999, at 1, U.N. Doc. UNCTAD/ITE/IIA/2 (2000); Jose E. Alvarez, *A Bit on Custom*, 42 N.Y.U. J. Int'l L. & Pol. 17, 23 (2009); Robert E. Greig, Claudia Annacker & Roland Ziade, *How Bilateral Investment Treaties Can Protect Foreign Investors in the Arab World or Arab Investors Abroad*, 25 J. Int'l Arb. 257, 259 (2008)

108 Sam Foster Halabi, *Efficient Contracting between Foreign Investors and Host States: Evidence from Stabilization Clauses* 31 Nw. J. Int'l L. & Bus. 261, 263 (2011).

109 Kojo Yelpaala, *Fundamentalism in Public Health and Safety in Bilateral Investment Treaties [Part I]*, 3 Asian J. WTO & Int'l Health L. & Pol'y 235, 236, 239 (2008).

110 Graham Mayeda, *Playing Fair: The Meaning of Fair and Equitable Treatment in Bilateral Investment Treaties*, 41 J. World Trade 273, 274 (2007).

economic sectors from the treaty's applicability, or to take normal regulatory action in the interest of national security, public order, public health, or public morality – so-called "non-precluded measures."[111] Contracting states are still potentially obligated to compensate investors for these "regulatory takings." Public health exceptions, for example, are often phrased in vague ways in the preamble, undermining their use as a defense to an investor claim.[112] Most of these treaties provide investors access to one of the major international arbitral tribunals identified in Chapter 1.[113]

These treaties often give much stronger protection, with fewer standard exceptions, to intellectual property rights than international intellectual property agreements, TRIPS, or domestic law. For example, the standard Swiss BIT protects as investments "copyrights, industrial property rights (such as patents, utility models, industrial drawings or models, manufacturer's or commercial marks, trade names, indications of provenance or *appellations d'origine contrôlées* (AOC, or "controlled terms of origin"), know-how and clientele" and requires the counterparty to compensate an investor for "measures, [taken] directly or indirectly, of expropriation, nationalization, or any other measure having the same character or same effect."[114] Under the 2012 US Model BIT, an "investment means every asset that an investor owns or controls, directly or indirectly ... include[ing] ... intellectual property rights," which are accorded similar rights to arbitration, although the US Model BIT creates an explicit nexus between rights to compensation and measures consistent with TRIPS.[115]

The aforementioned TRIPS "wins" for developing countries are diminished, sometimes drastically, in bilateral investment and trade treaties.[116] For example, the US–Jordan Free Trade Agreement includes limitations on compulsory licenses and parallel imports. The costliest TRIPS-plus terms are those that impose "data exclusivity" separate from patent protection. Under "data exclusivity" regimes, a firm that submits clinical or other safety trial data in connection with initial regulatory approvals may prohibit follow-on manufacturers from using that data, even after the

111 Bill Burke-White & Andreas von Staden, *Investment Protection in Extraordinary Times: The Interpretation and Application of Non-Precluded Measures Provisions in Bilateral Investment Treaties*, 48 VA. J. INT'L L. 307 (2008).

112 Julien Chaisse, *Exploring the Confines of International Investment and Domestic Health Protections – Is a General Exceptions Clause a Forced Perspective*, 39 AM. J. L & MED. 332, 341 (2013).

113 Jason Webb Yackee, *Pacta Sunt Servanda and State Promises to Foreign Investors Before Bilateral Investment Treaties: Myth and Reality*, 32 FORDHAM INT'L L.J. 1550, 1555 (2009).

114 Agreement between the Swiss Confederation and the Oriental Republic of Uruguay on the Reciprocal Promotion and Protection of Investments, Switz.-Uru., art. 5, Apr. 22, 1991, 575 U.N.T.S. 159, available at http://untreaty.un.org/unts/120001_144071/26/2/00021341.pdf.

115 2012 U.S. Model Bilateral Investment Treaty, available at http://www.ustr.gov/sites/default/files/BIT%20text%20for%20ACIEP%20Meeting.pdf

116 Lee Petherbridge, *Intelligent TRIPS Implementation Strategy for Countries on the Cusp of Development*, 22 U. PA. J. INT'L ECON. L. 1029, 1048 (arguing for the use of interpretative devices).

patent has expired. The effect is to make other market participants undertake prohibitively expensive clinical trials and reimposing the cost to the government or end-user that off-patent manufacturing saves.

> These expenditures have required that both public health system and individuals pay higher prices for many new medicines that are needed to treat serious non-communicable diseases (NCDs), such as hypertension, asthma, diabetes, and mental illness. For example, new medicines to treat diabetes and heart disease cost anywhere from two to six times more in Jordan than in Egypt, where there are no TRIPS-plus barriers.[117]

Philippe Baechtold, Tomoko Miyamoto, and Thomas Henninger provide examples of how these agreements expand intellectual property protections:

> *Patentability*: Article 14.8 of the US–Bahrain FTA states that each party shall make patents available for plant inventions.
>
> *Grace period:* Article 15.8 of the US–Oman FTA provides for a 12-month grace period for the public disclosure made or authorized by, or derived from, the applicant with respect to the determination of novelty and inventive step.
>
> *Patent-term extension:* Article 2(b) in Annex XIII of the European Free Trade Association (EFTA)–Republic of Korea FTA provides for a compensatory term of protection for pharmaceuticals of up to five years for curtailment of the term of patent protection as a result of the delay caused by the marketing approval process.
>
> *Exhaustion* :Article 15.9 of the US–Morocco FTA states that each Party shall provide that the exclusive right of the patent owner to prevent importation of a patented product, or a product that results from a patented process, without the consent of the patent owner shall not be limited by the sale or distribution of that product outside its territory . . .[118]

European countries and the EU broadly mimic these kinds of expansive terms in their bilateral treaties as well.[119]

To be certain, low- and middle-income countries have responded to the pressures imposed by wealthy countries to expand intellectual property protections through international legal mechanisms, although the full extent of that response has not been understood or analyzed. Not only have they undertaken a concerted effort to redistribute the wealth channeled to rich countries through international intellectual property protections; they have slowly forged international regimes that target

[117] Oxfam, All Costs, No Benefits: How TRIPS-Plus Intellectual Property Rules in the US–Jordan FTA Affect Access to Medicines, Oxfam Briefing Paper (Mar. 2007) available at http://www.oxfam.org/sites/www.oxfam.org/files/all%20costs,%20no%20benefits.pdf

[118] Philippe Baechtold, Tomoko Miyamoto, & Thomas Henninger *International Patent Law: Principles, Major Instruments, and Institutional Aspects* in Daniel Gervais (ed), Intellectual Property: A Handbook of Contemporary Research 67–68 (2013).

[119] Sam Foster Halabi, *International Trademark Protection and Global Public Health, a Just Compensation Regime for Expropriations and Regulatory Takings*, 61 Cath. U. L. Rev. 321, 344 (2012).

the global firms behind those agreements. As the next chapter details, over the course of the negotiating period for TRIPS, and before, developing countries had adopted alternative strategies for development. Those strategies – focusing on basic human needs – gathered a wider consensus and, in fact, proved more advantageous with respect to regulating global firms than had efforts through UNCTAD and at WIPO to persuade wealthy governments to do so themselves.

PART II

Rethinking Wealth

Firms, Basic Human Needs, and Technology

4

The Pivot to Basic Human Needs

The story summarized in Chapter 3 – the story behind TRIPS and the aftermath – forms by far the most robust area of advocacy and scholarly exploration since 1995. Carlos Correa, Peter Drahos, Graham Dutfield, Daniel Gervais, Laurence Helfer, Chidi Oguamanam, Ruth Okediji, Kal Raustiala, Jerome Reichman, Susan Sell, Vandana Shiva, and Peter Yu – several of whom participated directly or indirectly in the process – along with dozens and perhaps hundreds of others, have told it within the context of other arguments: developing countries pressed for access to proprietary knowledge as part of their demand for a restructured global economy; the developed states (and more specifically their client firms) resisted first within the context of WIPO and then, when that proved impossible, within the WTO where they secured the TRIPS regime that has since been ratcheted up through other multilateral and bilateral agreements.[1] The result, by almost all accounts, has been at best adverse and at worst catastrophic for developing countries – a part of the story elaborated more completely in this chapter.[2]

Yet it is not the whole story – neither with respect to the ways in which developing countries sought to build wealth, how they resisted the expansion of unfavorable intellectual property protections, nor the actors they deemed the correct targets for resistance activities. From the 1960s, developing countries saw multinational corporations as the chief agent for technology transfer and argued as much to their governments.[3] Those governments responded, more or less, that they had little or

[1] Indeed, the body of work from each of these activists and scholars is too lengthy to be cataloged here. Noteworthy and influential works include Carlos Correa, Intellectual Property Rights, the WTO and Developing Countries: The TRIPS Agreement and Policy Options (2000); Susan Sell, Private Power, Public Law: The Globalization of Intellectual Property Rights (2003); and Vandana Shiva, Biopiracy: The Plunder of Nature and Knowledge (1999).

[2] David Bigman, Globalization and the Developing Countries 188, 205 (2002).

[3] Debra Lynn Miller, *Panacea or Problem? The Proposed International Code of Conduct for Technology Transfer*, 33(1) J. Int'l. Aff. 43, 44–45 (1979).

no power to force private corporations to share their assets (tangible or intangible), or impose terms for sharing, with anyone else (even in the unlikely circumstance they were inclined to do so).[4] While the story of nationalizations is part of the response mounted by developing countries to the presence of North American and European firms post-decolonization, movements were also undertaken at international bodies like the OECD, GATT, UNCTAD, and WIPO as well as the UN.[5]

At the same time that multinational firms became, themselves, priorities for developing countries' efforts to restructure the global economy, the conceptions of societal wealth and approaches to development also shifted. Technology transfer – on the terms that it had been conveyed throughout the 1960s and 1970s – had exacerbated development problems generally and, just as importantly, had contributed to steep inequalities even within quite poor countries.[6] Technology – expensive to acquire and costly to maintain – ended up privileging a relative few when simpler, inexpensive interventions like plows, heifers, vaccines, and access to primary health care could create a wealthier society by having more healthy people able to work and build the infrastructure for the progression of human capital.[7]

The "basic human needs" approach to development – in contrast to emphasis on measures of economic growth built on capital flows, legal structures, technology, entrepreneurial skills, export stimulation, and savings – emphasized the achievement of "providing all persons with a certain minimum standard of these basic needs as a central priority of development. A basic needs strategy is the deliberate adoption of a set of policies designed to provide, or help people provide for themselves, these basic needs."[8] The precise origins of the basic human needs alternative are not clear. Pitambar Pant, head of India's Perspective Planning Division, introduced the idea of "minimum needs" at an informal Indian planning conference in 1962 (it was developed before then) emphasizing minimum income and state expenditures for education and health. It was evidently redistributive in nature.[9]

[4] David Gisselquist, John Nash, & Carl Pray, *Deregulating the Transfer of Agricultural Technology: Lessons from Bangladesh, India, Turkey, and Zimbabwe*, 17(2) World Bank Research Observer 237, 238 (2002).

[5] John Toye, UNCTAD at 50: A Short History (2014); Christopher May, *The World Intellectual Property Organization and the Development Agenda*, 13(2) Global Governance 161–70 (2007).

[6] Jean Jacques Salomon & André Lebeau, Mirages of Development: Science and Technology for the Third Worlds 45–48 (1993).

[7] Bai Kanu, *Farm-Level Economic Benefits of Using Oxen for Plowing and Weeding in Sierra Leone* in P. Starkey & T Simalenga (eds) , Animal Power for Weed Control 262 (2000); Albert O. Hirschman, *The Changing Tolerance for Income Inequality in the Course of Development* in Essays in Trespassing: Economics to Politics and Beyond (1981).

[8] J. Stephen Hoadley, *The Rise and Fall of the Basic Needs Approach*, 16 Conflict and Cooperation 149, 150 (1981).

[9] A. Vaidyanathan, *Poverty and Development Policy* in Raj Kapila & Uma Kapila (eds) India's Economy: A Journey in Time and Space 82, 100 (2006).

Over the course of the 1960s, the growth model of development did appear to register successes:

> South Korea, Taiwan, Hong Kong, Singapore, Israel, most of Latin America, and to some extent in Egypt, Nigeria, Kenya, Uganda, India and, it seemed in early 1970, Pakistan. In South Asia the advent of the Green Revolution promised to ease the agricultural production bottleneck.[10]

But those modest successes appeared offset by the steep inequality and resulting political autocracy required to contain their negative consequences:

> The Latin American successes turned out to harbour festering urban slums, landless agricultural labourers, dispossessed ethnic minorities, downtrodden women, and malnourished children in the interstices of prosperity. Political strife and partition shattered the illusion of Pakistan's industrial growth. And throughout the Third World economic growth seemed to rely increasingly upon a combination of foreign borrowing and rapid natural resource exploitation, stabilized by political authoritarianism.[11]

Thus the growth model appeared vulnerable at the same time that a promising alternative appeared. In 1972, Robert McNamara, then President of the World Bank, argued that governments in developing countries should redesign their economic growth and spending plans so as to meet the needs of the poorest 40 percent of their people – those largely illiterate "absolute poor" who lived with or succumbed to preventable diseases, suffered from persistent hunger and malnutrition, and created generational cycles of poverty and exclusion.[12] Similarly, McNamara's concern was primarily "moral" and redistributive – the necessity to address the problems of the absolute poor sounded in respect for human dignity rather than in arguments about human capital or domestic consumption that would otherwise work in support of the growth model.[13] Indeed, McNamara was clear that such redistribution should not go so far as to threaten otherwise growth-promoting policies (although even with these, he broke with past World Bank conventions).[14]

The "basic human needs" approach, while always elusive in terms of its specific components, implicated symbiotic relationships between needs: healthier children were better able to learn even in fairly rudimentary schools; investments in vaccines, sanitation, women's literacy, and primary health care facilities were necessary for

[10] Hoadley, *supra* note 8.

[11] *Id.*at 151.

[12] John L. Maddux, The Development Philosophy of Robert S. McNamara 18 (1981).

[13] Robert S. McNamara, Address to the Board of Governors, Nairobi, Kenya (Sept. 24, 1873), available at http://www.juerg-buergi.ch/resources/Archiv/Entwicklungspolitik-Archiv/Dokumente-zur-Entwicklungspolitik/McNamara_Nairobi_speech.pdf.

[14] *Id.*

healthier children; and the integrity of the biological and physical environment was necessary for all of these other investments to yield improvement.[15] Some models of these approaches – China, Cuba, Sri Lanka, Tanzania – had demonstrated measurable effectiveness but had also implicitly suggested that commitments to basic human needs traded off with higher rates of economic growth.

Basic human needs became a larger part of the planning in developing countries; the foreign aid budgets of developed countries, especially the United States; the agendas of international organizations such as WHO and UNICEF; and prompted a series of UN conferences individually devoted to components of the approach.[16] Some countries, such as China and India, with its "minimum needs" program, adopted basic needs strategies before the term became popular.[17] Some countries adopted the basic human needs approach and implemented it quickly; others at least paid lip service to its principles.[18] Over the course of the late 1960s to late 1970s, Burma, Brazil, China, Colombia, Costa Rica, Cuba, Egypt, India, Indonesia, Jamaica, Kenya, Malaysia, Mali, Panama, Paraguay, the Philippines, South Korea, Sri Lanka, Taiwan, Tanzania, and Uruguay all adopted at least minor and in some cases major investments aimed at "basic human needs" even if those investments varied significantly as to the need (e.g., education, health, nutrition) and kind of intervention (e.g., direct services, economic subsidy).[19]

"Basic human needs" also grew as a priority for wealthier countries' aid and development programs, especially following McNamara's elevation of it as a World Bank priority between 1968 and 1972.[20] Rolf Sartorius and Vernon Ruttan argued that a mix of influences from official development aid agencies, congressional resistance to failed policies in Vietnam, new insights from academic research, and even public opinion helped shape the "New Directions" US development assistance took from the 1970s, reorienting toward "encompass[ing] minimum human needs of man for food, health, and education, and for a job which can give him both the means to acquire these basic needs as well as a psychological sense of participating usefully in the world."[21] One of the leading

[15] Dokun Ayeshola, *Development and Poverty: A Symbiotic Relationship and Its Implication in Africa*, 4(4) Afr. J. Tradit. Complement. Med. 553–58 (2007).

[16] Ariel Pablos-Mendez & Lesley Stone, *Health Development as Nation Strengthening*, in José M. Zuniga, Stephen P. Marks, & Lawrence O. Gostin (eds), Advancing the Human Right to Health 56 (2013).

[17] Victor H. Li, *Politics and Healthcare in China: The Barefoot Doctors*, 27(3) Stan. L. Rev. 827–40 (1975).

[18] Paul Streeten, Shahid Javed Burki, Mahbub ul Haq, Norman Hicks, & Francis Stewart, Meeting Basic Human Needs in Developing Countries 26 (1981), available at http://documents.worldbank.org/curated/en/882331468179936655/pdf/997710english.pdf

[19] *Id.* at 98–99.

[20] Neil Dias Karunaratne, *Foreign Aid, New Economic Order, and Basic Human Needs*, 14(4) Intereconomics 18–84 (1979).

[21] Rolf Sartorius & Vernon Ruttan, *The Sources of the Basic Human Needs Mandate*, 23(3) J. Dev. Areas 331, 349 (1989).

contributors to "New Directions" – James P. Grant – moved to UNICEF in 1980 where he undertook the same reorientation toward deploying basic, measurable, inexpensive interventions to reduce child morbidity and mortality in poor countries.[22] Agriculture, rural development, health, nutrition, and family planning received increased emphasis in the development assistance budget.[23] The basic needs orientation of USAID was complemented by the efforts of the World Bank and a number of bilateral donors including Canada, Britain, the Netherlands, and the Nordic countries.[24] Indeed, over the course of the 1970s, an increasing number of OECD countries prioritized basic human needs as part of their assistance programs.[25]

Because of the nebulous nature of "basic human needs"–type approaches, it is difficult to trace the influence between the adoption of those types of approaches and major UN-sponsored conferences that explored individual components of basic human needs. The first of these major conferences was that on the Human Environment at Stockholm in 1972 (led by Maurice Strong who was to resurrect that role during the 1992 Rio Summit).[26] The 1968 General Assembly resolution calling for the conference explicitly linked the human environment to "essential for sound economic and social development."[27] According to Louis Sohn's extensive analysis of the Stockholm Declaration that resulted from the conference, the relationship between development generally and basic human needs specifically (including the role of firms) was recurrently raised in amendments to the text by developing countries.[28] To be sure, the declaration reemphasized the importance of development generally and of technology transfer specifically to realize the aims of the conference.[29]

The World Conference on Food in 1974 was held in response to disastrous global food harvests in 1972 and 1974 but also aimed at studying global patterns in grain cultivation, export, consumption, and specialization that caused the margin between abundance and scarcity to be so narrow.[30] The conference was notable for its acknowledgment of historical biases in favor of large farmers and landowners to the detriment of small subsistence cultivators and landless laborers.[31] The

22 Richard Jolly, *The Man behind the Vision*, in Richard Jolly (ed), JIM GRANT: UNICEF VISIONARY 45–46 (2002)
23 USAID, *USAID History*, available at https://www.usaid.gov/who-we-are/usaid-history.
24 Sartorius & Ruttan, *supra* note 21.
25 ROGER HANSEN, BEYOND THE NORTH-SOUTH STALEMATE 245–78 (1979).
26 Roger Coate, *Civil Society as a Force for Peace*, 9(2) INT'L. J. PEACE STUDIES 57–86 (2004).
27 U.N. General Assembly Resolution 2398 (XXIII) (Dec. 3, 1968).
28 Louis B. Sohn, *The Stockholm Declaration on the Human Environment*, 14 HARV. INT'L L.J. 423 (1973).
29 Declaration of the United Nations Conference on the Human Environment (Stockholm Declaration, 1972) (Principle 9).
30 W. Klatt, *Asia After the World Food Conference*, 51 INT'L. AFF. 344–357 (1975).
31 *Id.* at 355

outcomes of the Stockholm Conference and the Rome Conference were remarkably similar.[32] Kissinger's declaration that in ten years' time no child would go hungry was, even if rhetoric, consistent with changes in US policy toward basic human needs.[33]

The Conference was, of course, also politicized along developing and developed country lines.[34] Wealthier countries blamed the 1973 Arab oil embargo for raising the costs of fertilizers, petrochemical inputs, and transportation as well as for contributing to inflation generally. The developing countries in turn blamed wealthy countries for the distorting effect their domestic, "luxurious" consumption (reflected in foreign policies) had on agricultural planning in poorer countries, as well as their intellectual property policies that raised the cost of "machinery, fertilizers and chemical pesticides," all of which "contributed to the shortage of foodstuffs now suffered by the countries of Asia and Africa."[35]

The 1975 UN Conference on Women marked, at the very least, international recognition that neither the growth model – which assumed that growth alone would lift all boats, including socially marginalized groups – nor the basic human needs approach could succeed without rethinking the social position, empowerment, opportunity, and equality of women.[36] Women comprised 70 percent of the world's poor and a similar share of illiterate adults. Core elements of basic human needs – nutrition, health, and education – depended on massive investments in women's education and access to primary health care.[37] The latter relationship drove, along with a growing body of literature analyzing the ties between decreasing poverty and access to primary health care, the world's first major conference dedicated to primary health (as part of the New International Economic Order) at Alma-Ata, Kazakhstan, where 3,000 delegates convened from 134 governments and 67 international organizations including WHO, the International Labor Organization (ILO), and the Food and Agriculture Organization.[38]

In 1968, the ILO adopted its "World Employment Programme," which aimed to focus its efforts on developing countries, especially the most marginalized groups in those countries, for whom employment was pitched as both a means and an end.[39]

32 Thomas G. Weiss & Robert S. Jordan, *Bureaucratic Politics and the World Food Conference: The International Policy Process*, 28 World Politics 422, 434 (1976).
33 D. John Shaw, World Food Security: A History since 1945 139 (2007).
34 Mark W. Charlton, *Innovation and Inter-Organizational Politics: The Case of the World Food Programme*, 47(3) Int'l. J. 630 (Summer 1992).
35 Gerald W. Thomas, *The World Food Conference: A Frustrating First Step*, 25(2) BioScience 131–33 (1975).
36 Esther Dufflo, *Women Empowerment and Economic Development*, 50(4) J. Econ. Lit. 1051–79 (2012).
37 UNDP, Human Development Report iii (1995).
38 Marcos Cueto, *The Origins of Primary Healthcare and Selective Primary Healthcare*, 94(11) Am. J. Public Health 1864–74 (2004); Sam Halabi, *Participation and the Right to Health: Lessons from Indonesia*, 11 Health and Human Rights 43 (2009).
39 David A. Morse, *The World Employment Programme*, 97 Int'l. Labour Rev. 517 (1968).

Over the course of the 1970s, the ILO increasingly couched the World Employment Programme work in terms of basic human needs and, at the 1976 World Conference on Employment in Geneva, adopted a Programme of Action based on:

> (1) basic needs; (2) international manpower movements and employment; (3) technologies for productive employment creation; (4) active manpower policies and adjustment assistance in developed counitries; (5) the role of multinational enterprises in employment creation in the developing countries.[40]

The ILO defined basic needs in terms of food, clothing, housing, education, and public transportation as well as the participation in decision-making as part of those needs.[41] Louis Emmerij has given the ILO decisive credit for basic human needs:

> The basic needs development strategy grew out of the work of the ILO World Employment Program (WEP) of the 1970s. It brought employment – and people and human needs – back to the center of development strategy. This was directly in line with the centrality of employment in the early days of the UN and of the IMF as well. But ILO work in the 1970s enriched and elaborated the earlier concept of employment and policies to deal with it by relating both directly to the situation and needs of developing countries.[42]

These conferences, in turn, paved the way for the later, often more significant conferences (e.g., the 1992 Earth Summit, the 1995 Fourth World Conference on Women, and the Millennium Summit), which led to binding international agreements and better-developed measures for meeting basic human needs as part of development strategy.

As John McArthur has explained, the basic needs conferences led directly to the consensus and declaration of the Millennium Development Goals, "the world's central reference point for development cooperation."[43] The Millennium Development Goals established broad development objectives, many of which were supported by quantitative targets: eradicating extreme poverty and hunger; achieving universal primary education; promoting gender equality and empowering women; reducing child mortality; improving maternal health; combating HIV/AIDS, malaria, and other diseases; ensuring environmental sustainability; and developing a global partnership for development.[44]

[40] DH, *Population and the World Employment Conference*, 2(3) POPUL. DEV. REV., 502–05 (1976).

[41] NOZILAKHON MUKHAMEDOVA & KAI WEGERICH, LAND REFORMS AND FEMINIZATION OF LABOR IN SUGHD PROVINCE, TAJIKISTAN 3–4 (2014).

[42] Louis Emmerij, *The Basic Needs Development Strategy* (2010), available at http://www.un.org/en/development/desa/policy/wess/wess_bg_papers/bp_wess2010_emmerij.pdf

[43] John A. McArthur, *The Origins of the Millennium Development Goals*, 34(2) SAIS REV. 5 (2014).

[44] United Nations, The Millennium Development Goals Report 4–7 (2015), available at http://www.un.org/millenniumgoals/2015_MDGReport/pdf/MDG%202015%20rev%20(July%201).pdf.

> The MDGs were a product of iterated distillation, extracted from a wide array of global processes, with many actors involved over several years. During the 1990s, many international goals and targets were established through a series of major subject-specific conferences. The agendas spanned priorities like education (Jomtien 1990), children (New York 1990), the environment (Rio 1992), population (Cairo 1994), social development (Copenhagen 1995), and the status of women (Beijing 1995).[45]

It is virtually impossible to overstate the influence of the Millennium Development Goals. The Goals have mobilized governments and businesses to contribute tens of billions of dollars to obtaining targets such as antiretroviral drugs and mosquito nets.[46] The goals have structured partnerships between public, private, and non-governmental organizations. In some cases, such as the Global Fund to Fight AIDS, Tuberculosis, and Malaria and GAVI, the Vaccine Alliance, those public–private partnerships have mobilized billions in resources toward specific Goals. In his 2008 address to the UN General Assembly, Bill Gates called the goals "the best idea for focusing the world on fighting global poverty that I have ever seen."[47]

Both the development and implementation of the Millennium Development Goals (with basic human needs as antecedents) depended on specialized agencies of the United Nations, which were structured in such a way as to make more active approaches to basic human needs straightforward.[48] The ILO – in many ways the world's first modern international organization - became the UN's first specialized agency. The ILO had adopted a governance structure that included workers and firms as well as governments.[49] UNESCO– the UN Educational, Scientific, and Cultural Organization – developed programs and recommendations with respect to basic education as well as helped develop scientific research and development capacity.[50] While WIPO quickly became politicized along the global rich/poor divide, it nevertheless played an important role in facilitating access to copyrighted materials for the blind and visually impaired, who lived in disproportionate numbers in developing countries.

45 McArthur, *supra* note 43, at 6.

46 John McArthur, Own the Goals: What the Millennium Development Goals Have Accomplished (2013), available at https://www.brookings.edu/articles/own-the-goals-what-the-millennium-development-goals-have-accomplished/

47 Bill Gates, U.N. General Assembly (Sept. 25, 2008) available at https://www.gatesfoundation.org/media-center/speeches/2008/09/bill-gates-speaks-at-the-united-nations.

48 ILO Activities in the Post-War World: Key Documents, International Labour Organization, available at http://www.ilo.org/public/english/support/lib/century/sources/sources 1946.htm.

49 Resolution Concerning the Relationship between the International Labour Organization and the United Nations, International Labour Office, available at http://www.ilo.org/public/libdoc/ILO_Chronology/09734(1945–27)1–3.pdf.

50 Raymond Wanner, *UNESCO: An Introduction to its Education Program*, 26(3) Comp. Ed. Rev. 420–34 (1982).

Three UN specialized agencies played particularly important roles in both promoting the realization of basic human needs as well as establishing the global structures through which developing countries addressed intellectual property protections that most significantly affected them: the World Health Organization, UNICEF, and FAO. Each of these international organizations oversees at least one international agreement that now limits intellectual property rights or redirects the benefits derived from intellectual property sources.

When international lawmakers established the World Health Organization (WHO) they intended to give it strong lawmaking and regulatory authority.[51] Article 19 of the WHO Constitution authorized it to conclude treaties within its broadly worded mandate, while Article 21 gave the World Health Assembly (WHO's governing body) the authority to adopt legally binding recommendations in five discrete areas: sanitary and quarantine regulations; nomenclatures on diseases, causes of death, and public health practices; standards for diagnostic procedures for international use; standards for safety, purity, and potency of biological, pharmaceutical, and similar products moving in international commerce; and advertising and labeling of biological, pharmaceutical, and similar products moving in international commerce.[52] Article 22 established the binding legal effect of these regulations unless states opted out of them within the notification period, an innovation that collapsed the usual drawn-out ratification process historically experienced in the international lawmaking process.[53] WHO first exercised that authority in 1952 (the International Sanitary Regulations) before taking a leading global role in disease monitoring and epidemiological research.[54] Beginning in 1959, it undertook the first of what were to be several campaigns to eradicate vaccine-preventable illnesses.[55] The World Health Assembly updated the International Sanitary Regulations in 1969 and again in 2005.[56] WHO's epidemiological and technocratic expertise gave it an influential coordinating role among other international and nongovernmental organizations.[57]

[51] George Codding, Jr. *Contributions of the World Health Organization and the International Civil Aviation Organization to the Development of International Law*, 59 PROC. ASIL 147 (1965).

[52] WHO Constitution Art. 19, 21, available at http://www.who.int/governance/eb/who_constitution_en.pdf.

[53] WHO Constitution Art. 19, 21, 22.

[54] Editorial Board, *International Sanitary Regulations*, 147(1) JAMA 62–64 (1951).

[55] Colette Flight, *Smallpox: Eradicating the Scourge*, BBC (Apr. 20, 2014), available at http://www.bbc.co.uk/history/british_seapower/smallpox_01.shtml#three; F. FENNER, D. A. HENDERSON, I. ARITA, Z. JEŽEK & I. D. LADNYI, SMALLPOX AND ITS ERADICATION (1988).

[56] Rebecca Katz & Julie Fischer, *The Revised International Health Regulations: A Framework for Global Pandemic Response*, 3 GLOBAL HEALTH GOVERNANCE, 1, 2 (2010), available at http://blogs.shu.edu/ghg/files/2011/11/Katz-and-Fischer_The-Revised-International-Health-Regulations_Spring-2010.pdf.

[57] Ilona Kickbush, Wolfgang Hein, & Gaudenz Silberschmidt, *Addressing Global Health Governance Challenges through a new Mechanism: The Proposal for a Committee C of the World Health Assembly*, 38 J. L. MED. & ETHICS 550, 558 (2010).

President Franklin D. Roosevelt proclaimed the importance of food security in his famous January 6, 1941 State of the Union Address in which he discussed the "four freedoms," one of which – the freedom from want – involved the idea that people have a right to maintain an adequate standard of living and have a right to food.[58] Ultimately, these ideas caused President Roosevelt to invite allied countries to Hot Springs, Virginia to discuss emerging issues in food and agriculture.[59] These nations met from May 18 to June 3, 1943, and established an interim commission that would create a permanent organization – the FAO – for food and agriculture.

Established in 1946, the United Nations International Children's Emergency Fund ("UNICEF") had as its purpose the goal of "respond[ing] to the needs of children affected by war and its creation raised the world's hopes that children would never again face the tragedies of war."[60] As UNICEF evolved, it broadened its focus beyond solely providing humanitarian and emergency relief and began involving itself in the more common problems such as disease eradication and infant and maternal health.[61] Eventually, its mission came to include such things as the elimination of poverty and early childhood development, among others.[62] As with WHO, its regional structure allows it to work directly and consistently with other organizations and local authorities.[63]

Indeed, WHO FAO and UNICEF frequently coordinated with each other on basic human needs issues. The FAO and WHO coordinated as early as 1950 on international nutrition issues and still jointly administer the most important global food safety authority, the Codex Alimentarius Commission.[64] Over the course of the 1970s, WHO and UNICEF coordinated responses to the major declines in breastfeeding among women in developing nations. WHO and UNICEF held joint meetings with numerous actors, eventually resulting in a regulatory code for

58 Mark S. Shulman, *The Four Freedoms: Good Neighbors Make Good Law & Good Policy in a Time of Insecurity*, 77 FORDHAM L. REV. 555, 557 (2008).

59 RALPH W. PHILLIPS, FAO: ITS ORIGINS, FORMATION AND EVOLUTION 1945–1981 5 (1981).

60 The official name of the organization "was later changed to the United Nation's Children Fund after being officially adopted as a permanent branch of the UN in 1954." Farahnaz Mohammed, *The History of UNICEF*, THE BORGEN PROJECT (June 17, 2013), available at http://borgenproject.org/the-history-of-unicef/. Rebeca Rios-Kohn, *The Impact of the United Nations Convention on the Rights of the Child on UNICEF's Mission*, 6 TRANSNAT'L L. & CONTEMP. PROBS. 287, 291 (1996). *See also* Richard Horton, *UNICEF Leadership 2005–2015: A Call for Strategic Change*, THE LANCET, Vol. 364 No. 9451, 2071–72 (2004), available at http://www.thelancet.com/pdfs/journals/lancet/PIIS0140-6736%2804%2917560-0.pdf.

61 Rios-Kohn, *supra* note 60, at 292.

62 Horton, *supra* note 60, at 2071.

63 Chiara Giorgetti, *International Health Emergencies in Failed and Failing States*, 44 GEO. J. INT'L L. 1347, 1353 (2013).

64 Sam Halabi, *The Codex Alimentarius Commission, Corporate Influence and International Trade*, 41 AM. J. LAW & MED. 406–21 (2015).

breast-milk substitutes generally and a growing ability to negotiate with firms directly over practices that affected basic human needs.[65]

The emergence of basic human needs as the prevailing priority and paradigm toward developing countries had at least two significant effects on global trends in intellectual property protection. First, it brought multinational firms with practices that substantially affected basic human needs – medicine, food, and education – into direct participation with the international entities that sought to advance the basic human needs agenda. In previous decades, those entities, such as UNCTAD, and their constituent countries had theretofore made demands primarily on governments in North America, Europe, and Japan. This had the ultimate effect of facilitating regulatory efforts over firms within the legal authority and reach of such international entities as WHO, FAO, and UNICEF.

Second, basic human needs altered the substance and focus of intellectual property demands made by developing countries. Those demands in the 1960s and 1970s focused on technology transfer (emphasizing both patent and copyright), with significantly less attention paid to trademark.[66] This explains in some measure why developing countries looked to wealthy governments more than firms to facilitate transfer.[67] From the mid-1970s through the present, developing countries' focus has been on the limitations intellectual property protections have imposed on access to basic health interventions, practices in the agricultural sector with adverse employment and nutrition effects, and growing attention to the ways in which trademarks imply or manipulate vulnerable (e.g., illiterate) consumers.[68] These two phenomena – supranational regulation of firms and the growing effect of intellectual property protections on basic human needs – explain how the New International Economic Order became redirected at firms and channeled through international organizations.

65 Benjamin Mason Meier & Miriam Lobbok, *From Bottle to the Grave: Realizing a Human Rights to Breastfeeding Through Global Health Policy*, 60 Case W. Res. L. Rev. 1073, 1088 (2010).

66 Irwin Olian, *International Copyright and the Needs of Developing Countries: The Awakening at Stockholm and Paris*, 7(2) Cornell Int'l. L.J. 94–96 (1974).

67 Debra Lynn Miller, *Panacea or Problem? The Proposed International Code of Conduct for Technology Transfer*, 33(1) J. Int'l Affairs 43, 49 (1979).

68 Sam Halabi, *International Intellectual Property Shelters*, 90(4) Tulane L. Rev. 903 (2016).

5

The Rise of Supranational Regulation of Global Firms

For the most part, colonizing European governments accomplished the division of large tracts of Africa and Asia with the use of specialized investment and risk vehicles: companies given certain rights and privileges under a charter issued by the sovereign.[1] The charter usually gave the company a nationally recognized trading monopoly for a defined geographic area and for specific trade items, and the right to use force to open and maintain trade.[2] Indeed, the "charter" and the "patent" played similar roles in carrying out sovereign grants until the thirteenth century.[3] The use of the chartered company peaked in the seventeenth and eighteenth centuries and then again from 1880 to 1900: the eras of mercantilism and of the "Scramble for Africa."[4]

The chartered company was useful for undertaking overseas colonial ventures for the same reasons firms (used here interchangeably with corporations) are useful today: legal personality (which allows them to enter into agreements and use courts); limited liability (which limits risk); transferable shares (which allowed investors to manage their overall risk); and centralized management under a board structure (which gave them political and legal forbearance from the sovereign).[5] The use of capital from investors limited costs to the sovereign treasury of often high-risk/high-reward colonial

1 Julia Adams, *Principals and Agents: Colonialists and Company Men: The Decay of Colonial Control in the Dutch East Indies*, 61 AM. SOC. REV. 12–28 (1996).

2 Linden A. Mander, *The British Commonwealth and Colonial Rivalry in Southeast Asia*, 11(1) PACIFIC HIST. REV. 19 (1942).

3 Herbert L. Osgood, *The Corporation as a Form of Colonial Government*, 11(2) POL. SCI. Q. 259–77 (1896).

4 Peter Slinn, *Commercial Concessions and Politics during the Colonial Period: The Role of the British South Africa Company in Northern Rhodesia 1890–1964*, 70 AFR. AFF. 365–84 (1971).

5 REINIER KRAAKMAN ET AL., THE ANATOMY OF CORPORATE LAW 5 (2009). To this might be added "ownership" by contributors of capital, although in both the colonial period and nowadays this "ownership" is highly attenuated.

activity. The sovereign provided political support and authorization to trade overseas, but the risks and (especially) military expense was borne by investors and unsecured creditors. After 1600, chartered companies like the Dutch West India Company, the Royal African Company, and the Portuguese Guinea Company established permanent, secure territory on African coasts.[6] After 1870, the British South Africa Company, the German West African Company, the Companhia de Moçambique, and the Royal Niger Company facilitated colonization of most of the African continent.[7] The British East India Company maintained control of the Indian subcontinent until 1858.[8]

The end of the formal era of colonization corresponded to the liberalization of the limited liability, joint-stock, incorporated firm. Rather than issue purpose-by-purpose charters, wealthy states began to adopt generalized incorporation laws that allowed business organizers to use this form for nearly any potentially profitable activity (in some sectors like accounting, banking, insurance, law, and those affecting national security, special rules might affect accessibility to the corporate form or structures adopted thereafter).[9] In Britain, Germany, Japan, and the United States, for example, the growth of large corporations followed the adoption of liberalized corporation laws around the middle of the nineteenth century.[10]

The liberalization of access to the corporate form loosened the relationship between the interests of the state and the interest of the firm, but only to a certain extent. Firms, especially those with significant foreign operations or interests, frequently relied on governments to advocate their interests diplomatically and sometimes militarily.[11] This is why, among others, the United Fruit Co. lobbied the United States to intervene in Guatemala after Jacobo Arbenz seized its plantations as part of a broader effort to redistribute wealth from large landowners to landless farmers; French shareholders of the Suez Canal Company pushed for military intervention after Gamal Abdel Nasser nationalized it; and the Anglo-Iranian Oil Company successfully urged the British government to intervene after Iran

6 Van Cleaf Bachman, Peltries or Plantations: The Economic Policies of the Dutch West India Company in New Netherland, 1623–39 (1970).

7 Allen Isaacman & Barbara Isaacman, *Resistance and Collaboration in Southern and Central Africa, c. 1850–1920*, 10(1) Int'l J. Afr. Hist. St. 31–62 (1977); G. L. Baker, *Research Notes on the Royal Niger Company, Its Predecessors and Successors*, 2 J. Hist. Soc. of Nigeria 151–61 (1960).

8 P. J. Marshall, *British Society in India under the East India Company*, 31(1) Modern Asian Studies 89–108 (1997).

9 Erik Gerding, Law, Bubbles, and Financial Regulation (2014).

10 P. Wardley, *The Emergence of Big Business: The Largest Corporate Employers of Labour in the United Kingdom, Germany and the United States, c. 1907*, 41 Bus. Hist. 88–114 (1999); M. G. Blackford, The Rise of Modern Business in Great Britain, the United States and Japan (1998); Y. Cassis, Big Business: The European Experience in the Twentieth Century (1997).

11 Peter T. Muchlinski, Multinational Enterprises and the Law (2007); David Ijalaye, The Extension of International Personality in International Law 221–37 (1978).

nationalized its fields (although in the latter case, the government was a decisive stakeholder).[12]

While most episodes of disputes between firms and developing country governments did not involve military force, the influence of the former did lead to acknowledgment at the international level that firms increasingly played roles as influential as governments'.[13] In 1974, the UN Economic and Social Council adopted Resolution 1908(LVII), which led to the establishment of the Commission on Transnational Corporations. Wealthy countries acknowledged the issue as well, drafting their own set of guidelines for multinational enterprises (which were precatory, voluntary, and without significant effect), while developing countries endeavored to address the influence of multinational firms through arms of the UN system.[14]

Wealthy and developing states reached intermediate, if somewhat limited, compromises. The establishment of the International Centre for the Settlement of Investment Disputes (ICSID) in 1965 created a mechanism through which firms could bring grievances against nationalizing governments instead of encouraging them to interfere through their governments in domestic politics.[15] ICSID saw few disputes over the first three decades of its history.[16] For the most part, multinational firms remained almost exclusively regulated by their national governments and in some cases industry-generated guidelines or codes of conduct that they had drafted in efforts to ward off more formal measures.

The influence of multinational firms on basic human needs as they came to be understood over the course of the 1970s created conditions for firms to be regulated at the supranational level with far more specificity than they had previously. Firms' activities with respect to labor practices, marketing, and environmental impact became subject to the argument that – because of global reach – regulatory mechanisms must correspondingly expand. In the intellectual property context,

[12] Gordon L. Bowen, *U.S. Foreign Policy toward Radical Change: Covert Operations in Guatemala 1950–54*, 10 LATIN AMERICAN PERSPECTIVES 88, 90 (1983); MARTIN THOMAS & RICHARD TOYE, ARGUING ABOUT EMPIRE: IMPERIAL RHETORIC IN BRITAIN AND FRANCE 1882–1956 39 (2017).

[13] Sotirios Mousouris, *Transnationals in the UN Spotlight: The Beginning* in Khalil Hamdani and Lorraine Ruffing (eds), THE UNITED NATIONS CENTRE ON TRANSNATIONAL CORPORATIONS: CORPORATE CONDUCT AND THE PUBLIC INTEREST (2015); Stephen Kobrin, *Expropriation as an Attempt to Control Foreign Firms in LDCs: Trends from 1960 to 1979*, 28 ISQ 329–34 (1984).

[14] Jill Murray, *A New Phase in the Regulation of Multinational Enterprises: The Role of the OECD*, 30(3) IND'L L. J. 255–270 (2001); Karl P. Sauvant, *The Negotiations of the United Nations Code of Conduct on Transnational Corporations Experience and Lessons Learned*, 16 J. WORLD INVESTMENT & TRADE 11 (2016); Debra Lynn Miller, *Panacea or Problem? The Proposed International Code of Conduct for Technology Transfer*, 33(1) J. INT'L AFFAIRS 43, 49 (1979).

[15] Leon Trakman, *The ICSID under Siege*, 45 CORNELL INT'L. L. J. (2012); John Blum, *Reshaping the Global legal Structures of public health*, 12 MICH. ST. J. INT'L. L. 207, 218 (2004).

[16] ANTONIO PARRA, THE HISTORY OF ICSID 235 (2012).

developing nations pushed for the development of a Code of Conduct on the Transfer of Technology under the auspices of UNCTAD that would "promote technology transfer under more advantageous terms."[17] Developing nations also sought a UN Code of Conduct on Transnational Corporations in order to regulate the monopoly powers enjoyed by transnational companies as well as the impact of their practices on development generally.[18]

In 1975, UNCTAD released a report on the role of the international patent system on technology transfer to the developing world.[19] Unlike earlier studies, the report "advanced more assertive conclusions" regarding the relationship between firms' practices and technology transfer as it might improve development.[20] The report led to a series of demands for "substantial changes" to the traditional means of technology transfer.[21] In some Latin American countries, those demands were codified into laws that banned restrictive business practices: terms in licenses that limited access to additional technology, imposed territorial or quantitative limits for exports, and/or designated personnel to be employed by the licensee.[22] Some laws also required licenses to be registered and reviewed with a national authority.[23] Many of those laws were explicitly based on competition and antitrust laws found in Europe and North America and the regulation of foreign investment and licensing in Japan.[24]

There were multiple difficulties in solving what developing countries saw as the technology transfer problem through a state-by-state approach. First, even though a handful of countries had adopted technology transfer controls, only five – which collectively purchased 75 percent of all technology transferred – could effectively enforce the laws they had adopted.[25] Second, with respect to those five, there was a relationship between the promise of the market and firms' tolerance of technology transfer restrictions. Large, promising markets such as Argentina, Brazil, and Mexico found enforcement generally straightforward while smaller states found that adopting and enforcement of new laws would result in firms moving their operations

17 Carolyn Deere, The Implementation Game: The TRIPS Agreement and the Global Politics of Intellectual Property Reform in Developing Countries 45 (2009).

18 Karl P. Sauvant, *The Negotiations of the United Nations Code of Conduct on Transnational Corporations Experience and Lessons Learned*, 16 J. World Investment & Trade 11 (2016).

19 UNCTAD, The Role of the Patent System in the Transfer of Technology to Developing Countries (1975).

20 Deere, *supra* note 17.

21 Pease Jefferies, *Regulation of Transfer of Technology An Evaluation of the UNCTAD Code of Conduct*, 18 Harv. Int. L. J. 309, 310 (1977).

22 Eduardo White, Control of Restrictive Business Practice in Latin America 86–103 (1975).

23 *Id.*

24 Debra Lynn Miller, *Panacea or Problem? The Proposed International Code of Conduct for Technology Transfer*, 33(1) J. Int'l Affairs 43, 50 (1979).

25 *Id.* at 49.

elsewhere.[26] Third, investment and trade rules in other international agreements such as Friendship, Commerce, and Navigation treaties obstructed effective enforcement of technology transfer laws, even where efficient bureaucratic infrastructures existed to do so.[27]

Developing countries viewed a binding international agreement that effectively created an "international law of prohibited business practices" as a solution to these coordination and implementation problems. UNCTAD developed a Code of Conduct on Transfer of Technology that was aimed at "balancing the economic well being of the [developing world] against the TNCs' profit motives."[28] Developed governments negotiated on behalf of their firms, and generally took the position that genuinely anticompetitive practices in technology transfer agreements might be legitimate issues for the code, but always rejected efforts to impose on firms obligations to eliminate practices that were "injurious" but not anticompetitive. They also rejected the possibility of making the Code legally binding.[29]

The Code focused on using regulation of firms' activities and changes to contemporary technology transfer to help developing nations achieve increased technology flow.[30] For developing nations, the Code created "a stable environment" that allowed for "the protection of technology suppliers' property rights" while still eliminating "risks of expropriation or infringement of contractual rights."[31] The Code "eliminate[ed] restrictive business practices" by regulating the prices and payments for technology as well as necessitating that "technology be appropriate to the needs of the recipient."[32] Significantly, the Code recognized the right of source and recipient governments to develop their own respective legislation, policies, and regulations regarding transfer of technology agreements, allowing for countries to regulate terms, conditions, and prices in these contracts.[33]

The draft Code prohibited clauses within transfer agreements that "directly or indirectly ... have adverse effects on the national economy of the recipient country."[34] By eliminating "a long list of clauses and practices," the Code sought

[26] Sam Foster Halabi, *Efficient Contracting between Foreign Investors and Host States: Evidence from Stabilization Clauses*, 31 Nw. J. Int'l L. & Bus. 261, 304 (2011).

[27] Jason Webb Yackee, *Pacta Sunt Servanda and State Promises to Foreign Investors before Bilateral Investment Treaties: Myth and Reality*, 32 Fordham Int'l L. J. 1550, 1555 (2009).

[28] Jefferies, *supra* note 21, at 311.

[29] Besides seeking the protection of the industrial rights of TNCs, the representatives of developed nations were "relatively silent" regarding their concerns on technology transfer. *Id.* at 315.

[30] *Id.* at 317.

[31] *Id.*

[32] Two drafts were developed, one prepared by developing nations, and one prepared by developed countries. *Id.* at 331.

[33] Paragraph 3.2(x) of the Code allows governments to define modalities and prices for payments as well as payment duration and aspects related to the screening and registration of technology transaction. *Id.* at 332.

[34] Ton J. M. Zuijdwijk, *The UNCTAD Code of Conduct on the Transfer of Technology*, 24 McGill L. J. 563, 596–97 (1978).

to "encourage utilization and absorption of technology by the recipient enterprise."[35] Additionally, the draft Code provided a list of mandatory guarantees that technology suppliers would have to include in their agreements. These included guarantees as to the suitability and appropriateness of technology to the needs and capabilities of its recipients, as well as "minimal level[s] of production" and the use of "consulting organizations."[36]

UNCTAD also recognized that developing nations also dealt with "institutional deficiencies" and suggested development of "Transfer Technology [Centers]" at the regional and national levels.[37] Such Centers were intended to strengthen the technological capabilities of developing countries by identifying specific technological needs while collecting, storing, and distributing information on alternative technology sources. Centers could also engage in evaluation and selection of technology that appropriately met the needs of respective developing countries.[38] In conjunction with these Centers, the United Nations Commission on Transnational Corporations would provide developing nations with technical assistance in a variety of crucial fields along with training services and workshops.[39] These efforts were anticipated to operate concurrently with the work of other international organizations to create various other "codes of conduct and systems of international research and development cooperation."[40]

These early attempts at the development of international codes failed.[41] The Code of Conduct on the Transfer of Technology never went into effect (after a decade of negotiations), and the Code of Conduct on TNCs became the far more circumscribed Draft Norms on the Responsibilities of Transnational Corporations and Other Business Enterprises with Regard to Human Rights.[42] However, developing countries took advantage of the corresponding negotiations to address issues relating to the scope of rights, including intellectual property rights, extended to foreign individuals and companies within their borders.[43] Moreover, the episodes with technology transfer introduced, at least in its most pronounced way, the possibility of regulating firms at the supranational level. For example, during the

[35] This included, for example, a provision that prohibited clauses that obligated recipients to use specific trademarks or names along with technology acquired. Jefferies, *supra* note 21, at 315.

[36] Consulting organizations could be employed to determine which technology and engineering to transfer to specific countries. *Id.*

[37] UNCTAD, *Draft Outline of an International Code of Conduct on Transfer of Technology*, 7 Development and Change 175–93 (1976).

[38] *Id.*

[39] Workshops would focus on issues like negotiations and regulating technology agreements. This included advice on TNC activity in addition to economic, legal, and financial expertise.

[40] Jefferies, *supra* note 21, at 339.

[41] Padmashree Gehl Sampath & Pedro Roffe, Unpacking the International Technology Transfer Debate: Fifty Years and Beyond 7 (2012).

[42] Jennifer Bair, *Corporations at the United Nations: Echoes of the New International Economic Order?* 6(1) Humanity 159–71 (2015).

[43] *Id.*

1982 negotiations for the UN Convention on the Law of the Sea, these same countries were able to "push[] for commitment to technology transfer on fair and reasonable terms and conditions."[44]

The reasons for failure have never been adequately analyzed and understood. To be sure, fundamental reasons included the intractable differences between developing countries that saw the Code as an instrument of the New International Economic Order (and in the NIEO declaration called for technology transfer explicitly) – part of their right to develop – and wealthy countries who viewed it as an infeasible and imprudent way to constrain their global firms. But it was also the case that a broadly worded agreement on "technology" inevitably created problems of definition and application. There were hundreds or thousands of businesses based in Europe, Japan, the United States, and, increasingly, developing countries that might be affected by an international agreement affecting "technology" and without some idea of its ultimate effect could cause unanticipated and adverse consequences even for its intended beneficiaries.[45] Under circumstances where there were fewer firms, with wider reach, controlling larger portions of markets, regulation could be, and eventually was, more selectively applied.

Together with industry concentration in key sectors, the possibility for supranational regulation of global firms has grown stronger as intellectual property has increased its absolute and relative role in the value of companies as well as more significantly affecting the basic human needs of those in developing countries. Medicines, for example, are valuable not only for the patents that secure exclusive rights to their chemical structure but also for the clinical trial and safety data that support their regulatory approval as well as the trademarks and trade dress that protect their marketing and physical appearance.[46] Trademarks on consumer products, especially food products, help sell specific firms' brands but also may distort or impliedly mislead consumers about the nutritional content or effect of those products.[47]

The history behind the 1981 World Health Organization/UNICEF International Code of Marketing of Breastmilk Substitutes provides an early and foretelling example of how supranational regulation of firms – especially in concentrated industries – may occur.[48] While the health outcomes between infants fed exclusively by breast for the first six months of life and those fed with formula are negligible or nonexistent in wealthy countries, exclusive breastfeeding for the first six months of

44 Deere, *supra* note 17.

45 Sampath & Roffe, *supra* note 41.

46 Jeremy Greene & Aaron Kesselheim, *Why Do the Same Drugs Look Different? Pills, Trade Dress, and Public Health* 365(1) New Eng. J. Med. 83 (2011).

47 Sam Halabi, *International Trademark Protection and Global Public Health: A Just Compensation Regime for Expropriations and Regulatory Takings*, 61 Cath. U. L. Rev. 325 (2012).

48 WHO, *International Code of Marketing of Breast Milk Substitutes* 1 (1981), available at http://www.who.int/nutrition/publications/code_english.pdf.

life in poor countries is a critical practice for a number of basic human needs.[49] Because substantial populations in developing countries lack access to clean drinking water, breastfeeding "reduces or eliminates exposure to food and waterborne pathogens."[50] Breastmilk also contains several compounds that can improve the infant's ability to resist infection.[51] The expense of formula creates an incentive in poorer countries to dilute the content of formula containers, increasing the risk of malnutrition, illness, and death. The late US Senator Ted Kennedy phrased the problem this way:

> Can a product which requires clean water, good sanitation, adequate family income and a literate parent to follow printed instructions be properly and safely used in areas where water is contaminated, sewage runs in the street, poverty is severe and illiteracy high?[52]

But the market for infant formula, especially in developing countries, was also potentially enormous. European and US firms adopted aggressive sales practices including nursing attire for salespeople, images on formula containers that explicitly stated or implicitly suggested the superiority of formula over breastmilk, and the wide distribution of free samples to encourage women, often with little or no education, to use formula instead of breastfeeding.[53] Over the 1970s, the developing country market was estimated to run into the billions of dollars.[54] Nestlé controlled approximately 50 percent of the market during that period (more now) along with well-known US pharmaceutical companies Abbott Laboratories, Bristol-Myers Squibb, and American Home Products (later Wyeth and now Pfizer) and food firms such as Gerber (acquired by Sandoz in 1994, which later became Novartis – its baby food unit was sold to Nestlé in 2007), which still controls 61 percent of the market in

[49] Bonnie Worthington-Roberts, *Lactation and Human Milk: Nutritional Consideration* in SR Williams (ed), NUTRITION IN PREGNANCY AND LACTATION 244–322(1989); C. Garza et al., *Special Properties of Human Milk*, 14 CLINICS IN PERINATOLOGY 11–32 (1987).

[50] J. Van Derslice, B. Popkin, & J. Briscoe, *Drinking-Water Quality, Sanitation, and Breastfeeding: Their Interactive Effects on Infant Health*, 72(4) BULL. WHO 589–601 (1994), available at https://www.ncbi.nlm.nih.gov/pmc/articles/PMC2486614/pdf/bullwh00415-0057.pdf

[51] J. K. Welsh & J. T. May, *Anti-Infective Properties of Breast Milk*, 94 J. PEDIATRICS 1–9 (1979).

[52] Marketing and Promotion of Infant Formula in the Developing Nations, 1978: Hearings Before the Subcommittee on Health and Scientific Research of the Comm. on Human Resources, 95th Cong., 2nd Sess. 1–2 (1978) (statement of Sen. Kennedy).

[53] Kenneth D. Rosenberg et al., *Marketing Infant Formula through Hospitals: The Impact of Commercial Hospital Discharge Packs on Breastfeeding*, 98(2) AM. J. PUB. HEALTH 290–95 (2008).

[54] Pierre Borgoltz, *Economic and Business Aspects of Infant Formula Promotion: Implications for Health Professionals* in D. B. Jelliffe and E. P. C. Jelliffe, ADVANCES IN INTERNATIONAL MATERNAL-CHILD HEALTH 158–202 (1982).

the United States.[55] Nestlé bought Pfizer's baby food division for $11.9 billion in 2012.[56] Acquiring the Pfizer product line expanded Nestlé's already substantial reach into developing countries, as 85 percent of Pfizer's baby food division sales were in developing countries.[57]

The advertising and promotion of breast-milk substitutes had already led to a decline in breastfeeding rates in wealthy countries, from more than 70 percent in the 1930s to 14 percent in the 1970s.[58] Aggressive marketing tactics in poorer countries suggesting that formula was "modern" and superior to breast milk depressed breastfeeding rates across the globe.[59] Breastfeeding declined rapidly in the 1960s. In Mexico in 1960, almost 100 percent of six-month-old babies were breastfed; by 1966, it was only 40 percent.[60] In Chile in 1960, more than 90 percent of thirteen-month-old babies were breastfed; in 1968, only 5 percent. In Singapore in 1951, more than 80 percent of three-month-old babies were breastfed; by 1971, it was only 5 percent.[61] As a result, infant mortality from malnutrition, pneumonia, and diarrhea increased.[62]

The mobilization of constituencies within developed and developing countries as well as the World Health Organization and UNICEF led the WHO Director-General Halfdan Mahler to convene a WHO/UNICEF Meeting on Infant and Young Child in October 1979.[63] The conference included representatives from constituencies that had mobilized against industry practices, including health professionals and charities as well as industry representatives. The International Code of Marketing of Breastmilk Substitutes was adopted by the World Health Assembly in 1981 under a resolution that set out guidelines for both firms and governments.[64] The Code's text included details for the content of product labels, the appropriate relationships between firms health workers and the general public, and even firms' compensation systems (no relationship between volume of sales and compensation).

55 Stephen Solomon, *The Controversy over Infant Formula*, N.Y. Times (Dec. 6, 1981), available at http://www.nytimes.com/1981/12/06/magazine/the-controversy-over-infant-formula.html?pagewanted=all

56 The Henry Fund, *Infant Formula* 3 (Mar. 17, 2016) available at https://www.biz.uiowa.edu/henry/download/research/Infant_Nutrition.pdf

57 *Id.*

58 D. B. Jelliffe & E. P. C. Jelliffe, *Feeding Young Infants in Developing Countries: Comments on the Current Situation and Future Needs*, 11 Studies in Family Planning 72–75 (1978); L. Hambraeus, *Proprietary Milk versus Human Breast Milk in Infant Feeding: A Critical Appraisal from the Nutritional Point of View*, 24 Pediatric Clinician of North America 17–36 (1977).

59 Solomon, *supra* note 503.

60 A. Berg, The Nutrition Factor (1973).

61 *Id.*

62 D. P. Jellife, *Commerciogenic Malnutrition?* 30 Nutrition Reviews 199–205 (1972).

63 David Bornstein, How to Change the World: Social Entrepreneurs and the Power of New Ideas 246–48 (2007); Population Council, *Halfdan Mahler on Women's Control of Their Reproductive Lives*, 21 Population and Development Review 696–68 (1995).

64 WHO, *International Code of Marketing of Breast Milk Substitutes* 1 (1981), available at http://www.who.int/nutrition/publications/code_english.pdf.

The Code was adopted under Article 23 of the WHO Constitution and has enjoyed robust enforcement primarily in large developing countries.[65] Nevertheless, the Code included prohibitions on specific images and messaging – trademarks – and was effectively addressed to a small number of firms such that it represented an important change in how developing countries approached the regulation of global enterprise.

Similarly, the 1983 FAO International Undertaking on Plant Genetic Resources was aimed at regulating the conduct of a relatively small number of firms that consolidated around seed, pesticide, and herbicide markets in the early 1980s.[66] Until then, chemical and pharmaceutical firms, mostly in North America and Europe, focused on pesticides and herbicides, rather than seeds, the patent protection of which was uncertain in many countries.[67] Seed companies tended to be small and specialized.[68] In the 1970s, new protections for hybrid seeds led to the entrance of these firms, particularly for corn.[69] By the 1980s, patents on major pesticides were expiring, patents on living organisms became more secure, especially in the United States, and larger firms moved into seed markets more robustly than before.[70] As Philip Howard notes,

> What were once 30 separate firms in the 1970s became just Monsanto, DuPont, Syngenta, Bayer, Dow, and BASF by 2001. Estimates from 2011 indicate that these Big Six agrochemical companies controlled 60% of global proprietary seed market, with the top three (Monsanto, DuPont, and Syngenta) controlling more than 53%; in addition, the Big Six firms controlled 76% of the global agricultural chemical market. Their domination of seed patents in the U.S. is even higher, with the top three owning 85% of corn patents and 69.6% of non-corn patents.[71]

Many of these firms overlapped with those in the aforementioned infant formula industry. Pfizer acquired the second-largest U.S. corn market participant, DeKalb, in 1982.[72] Ceiba-Geigy, the maker of blockbuster pesticide atrazine, controlled 10 percent of the global pesticide market before it merged with Sandoz to become

65 Sam Foster Halabi, *Multipolarity, Intellectual Property, and the Internationalization of Public Health Law*, 35 MICH. J. INT'L. L. 715 (2014).

66 John Walsh, *Seeds of Dissension Grow at FAO*, 223 SCIENCE 147–48 (1984).

67 CARY FOWLER & PATRICK MOONEY, SHATTERING: FOOD, POLITICS, AND THE LOSS OF GENETIC DIVERSITY 128–29 (1996).

68 KATHRYN RUDIE HARRIGAN, VERTICAL INTEGRATION, OUTSOURCING, AND CORPORATE STRATEGY 216 (1983).

69 Philip Howard, *Intellectual Property and Consolidation in the Seed Industry*, 55 CROP SCI. 1–7 (2015).

70 Paul Robbins & Julie Sharp, *Turfgrass Subjects: The Political Economy of Urban Monoculture* in Nik Heynen, Maria Kaika, & Erik Swyngedovw (eds), IN THE NATURE OF CITIES: URBAN POLITICAL ECOLOGY AND THE POLITICS OF URBAN METABOLISM 118 (2006).

71 Howard, *supra* note 69.

72 Economic Research Service/USDA, MERGERS AND ACQUISITIONS ROSE IN THE PAST THREE DECADES 31, available at https://www.ers.usda.gov/webdocs/publications/42517/13606_aib786h_1_.pdf?v=41055

Novartis, which spun off seed giant Syngenta.[73] There were 167 mergers, acquisitions, and other strategic alliances in the agricultural biotechnology industry between 1981 and 1985.[74]

In the case of seeds, the relationship between the International Undertaking and the New International Economic Order – whether framed in terms of growth or basic human needs – was direct and salient. The major food crops of the world originated in Latin America, Asia, and Africa, so protected seeds and related agrochemical products were necessarily dependent on plant genetic resources taken from what had become the developing world.[75] "The concern within developing countries that their genetic resources were being exploited resonated with the then-recent effort to establish a New International Economic Order aimed at a redistributing global wealth through new international institutions and reigning in the powers of multinational corporations."[76]

The International Undertaking was a response not only to consolidation in the agrochemical industries based in Europe, North America, and Japan but also to the strength of wealthy countries' organized efforts to enhance patent protection over genetic sources of food after recombinant DNA discoveries in the 1970s. That technology was overwhelmingly developed and owned by firms in those countries. The principal coordinating organization was the International Convention for the Protection of New Varieties of Plants, or UPOV, as it is most commonly known, a Geneva-based international organization focused on providing intellectual property protection for plant breeders' rights.[77] This international organization was formed by treaty on December 2, 1961 when five European countries – the Netherlands, Germany, France, Italy, and Belgium - seeking to provide greater protections to their respective plant breeders signed the Convention.[78] Other countries soon followed, including Denmark, Switzerland, and the United Kingdom in 1962.[79] Amendments to the original Convention were made in 1972, 1978, and 1991. After the 1978 revision, the United States became party to the Convention.[80]

[73] Federal Trade Commission, *In the Matter of Ciba-Geigy Ltd.*, available at https://www.ftc.gov/system/files/documents/cases/961217cibacmpt.pdf

[74] Robin Shoemaker et al. Economic Issues in Agricultural Biotechnology (2001), available at http://www.ers.usda.gov/publications/aib762/aib762.pdf.

[75] John Walsh, *Seeds of Dissension Sprout at FAO*, 223 Science 147–48 (1984).

[76] Kal Raustiala & David Victor, *The Regime Complex for Plant Genetic Resources*, 58 Int'l Org. 277–310 (2004).

[77] International Convention for the Protection of New Varieties of Plants, Act of 1991, art. 24(3), Dec. 02, 1961, 815 U.N.T.S. 89.

[78] UPOV is the French acronym for the Union Internationale pour la Protection des Obtentions Végétales. Juliana Santilli, Agrobiodiversity and the Law: Regulating Genetic Resources, Food Security and Cultural Diversity 77 (2012).

[79] *Id.*

[80] The United States ratification of the UPOV Convention contains reservations to Article 35(2) of the 1991 Act. *Id.* Article 35(2) contains provisions pertains to an exception for signatories of the 1978 Convention to continue to provide protection by an industrial property title other than a

For centuries, the protections the UPOV Convention aimed at securing were nonexistent. Traditionally, farmers were responsible for propagation of seeds and plants.[81] "Although 'scientific' plant breeding did not emerge until relatively recently – particularly at the beginning of the twentieth century, after the rediscovery of Mendel's principles of genetics and heredity – plant improvements made by farmers have taken place throughout past millennia."[82] Farmers historically accomplished improvements through saving, exchanging, and/or selling seed of their own harvest. Until the UPOV's major revisions (in 1978 but also 1991), this process was aided by an open system of sampling, sharing, and redistribution supported by both wealthy and developing nations as well as major charitable foundations such as Rockefeller and Ford.[83]

The UPOV agreement requires the authorization of plant breeder firms for production or reproduction of covered seeds; offering seeds for sale; selling or other marketing; exporting; importing; and stocking (under most circumstances). If a farmer undertakes any of the seed-related actions by which he or she has traditionally bred resilient or improved crops, such as saving, using, exchanging or selling farm-saved seed or propagating material, the right of the owner of the protected plant variety is infringed.[84]

The International Undertaking did not go so far as the WHO/UNICEF International Code of Marketing of Breastmilk Substitutes with respect to the detail of regulating firms' practices.[85] It nevertheless created a pathway by which developing countries could later assert rights over both plant genetic resources and the rights of farmers. The Undertaking adopted a definition of plant genetic resources (both in nature and as adapted by firms and researchers) as the "common heritage" of humanity.[86] As such, those resources "should be available without restriction;" and "free of charge . . . or on the most favorable terms."[87]

The Undertaking applied the common heritage principle to the "special genetic stocks," varieties that the breeder uses to produce the variety sold on the market.[88]

breeder's right without having to apply to the UPOV Convention for protection over varieties covered by the industrial property title.

81 Denis Murphy, Plant Breeding and Biotechnology: Societal Context and the Future of Agriculture 16 (2007).

82 Julianna Santilli, supra note 78, at 78.

83 German Federal Ministry for Economic Cooperation and Development, The UPOV Convention, Farmers' Rights and Human Rights: An Integrated Assessment of Potentially Conflicting Legal Frameworks 24 (2015), available at https://www.giz.de/fachexpertise/downloads/giz2015-en-upov-convention.pdf.

84 *Id.*

85 FAO Resolution C 9/83, Report of the 22nd Session of the FAO Conference (FAO, Rome, 1983).

86 *Id.*

87 *Id.*

88 Harold Bordwin, *The Legal and Political Implications of the International Undertaking on Plant Genetic Resources*, 12(4) Ecology L. Quarterly 1053, 1063 (1985).

In the case of hybrids, for example, the seed produced by the crop grown by farmers is not suitable for planting.[89] Thus, farmers must buy seed annually rather than plant seed saved from their own harvest. If farmers had access to the parents of the hybrids, then they would be able to produce the hybrid themselves.[90] The American Seed Trade Association protested that adopting such required sharing would "strike at the very heart of free enterprise and intellectual property rights."[91] Despite its nonbinding character, the United States and a number of other developed countries refused to sign the Undertaking.

Unsuccessful at regulating agrochemical firms through the Undertaking, developing countries – which by virtue of geological history possess the overwhelming majority of plant genetic resources for food and agriculture – erected their own proprietary claims to germplasm taken from their territories. In 1989, the Undertaking was amended to state that "plant breeders rights as provided for under UPOV ... are not incompatible with the International Undertaking" and, through Resolution 5/89, adopted the concept of "farmers' rights": "rights arising from the past, present and future contributions of farmers in conserving, improving, and making available plant genetic resources, particularly those in the centers of origin/diversity."[92] In 1991, the Undertaking was amended again to recognize the sovereign rights of states over their genetic resources, providing the pathway by which developing countries would regulate firms through diluting property rights and sharing the results of research on resources taken from developing countries' territories. That shift played an important role in the negotiations leading to the 1992 Convention on Biological Diversity, which has become one of the most important agreements by which developing countries have achieved redistribution of global wealth and regulation of increasingly concentrated life sciences firms.

From 1980, the United Nations General Assembly began considering the next steps following its first major conference on the environment and human sustainability in 1972.[93] The Governing Council of the UN Environmental Programme (UNEP) had commissioned a "report of the high-level group of experts on the interrelationships between population, resources, environment and development" which led to the establishment of the "Environmental Perspective," a special commission to propose long-term environmental strategies for achieving sustainable development to the year 2000 and beyond.[94] That commission, ultimately named the World Commission on Environment and Development, began its work in May

89 *Id.*
90 *Id.*
91 The American Seed Trade Assoc., Position Paper on FAO International Undertaking on Plant Genetic Resources 2 (1984).
92 Shawn Sullivan, *Plant Genetic Resources and the Law: Past, Present, and Future*, 135(1) Plant Physiology 10–15 (1994).
93 Lynton Caldwell, International Environmental Policy (1984).
94 United Nations, Rio Declaration on Environment and Development 1 (2012), available at http://legal.un.org/avl/pdf/ha/dunche/rio_ph_e.pdf.

1984. Over the next three years – which overlapped with the commencement of the Uruguay Round of GATT negotiations detailed in Chapter 2 – the Commission reached the conclusion that there should be a legally binding instrument to guide the world toward sustainability and meaningful development after 2000.

Contemporaneously with movements to revisit the 1972 environmental conference, scientists and nongovernmental organizations had elevated the issue of biodiversity loss as a pressing environmental issue.[95] The visceral threats to the rainforests in the Amazon basin – logging, extraction, agriculture – highlighted the potentially rapid loss of crucial environmental resources and the role private enterprise played in those threats.[96] As with coordination problems encountered in the health and agriculture contexts, an international agreement seemed a promising solution not only for managing common resources but also for adopting a more comprehensive approach than previous international agreements that had focused only on particular named species and habitats.[97] In 1987, the governing council of UNEP resolved to create a working group to explore such a convention.[98] In 1991 – contemporaneous with the negotiations on the UN Framework Convention on Climate Change (FCCC) – formal multilateral negotiations began on a Convention on Biological Diversity.[99]

During the forty-third session of the General Assembly, in 1988, Canada, Finland, and the Scandinavian countries submitted a draft resolution proposing a United Nations Conference on Environment and Development be convened in 1992, twenty years after the 1972 Stockholm Conference on the Human Environment.[100] In 1989, the General Assembly formally named the convening the United Nations Conference on Environment and Development (UNCED) as well as its location – Brazil – and established a preparatory committee.[101] UNEP imposed a sixteen-month deadline for finishing its work related to the Convention on Biological Diversity so that the treaty would be complete in time for UNCED.[102]

95 D. H. Janzen, *The Future of Tropical Ecology*, 17 Ann. Rev. Ecology and Systematics 305 (1986).
96 Michael J. Heckenberger, J. Christian Russell, Joshua R. Toney & Morgan J. Schmidt, *The Legacy of Cultural Landscapes in the Brazilian Amazon: Implications for Biodiversity*, 362 Philosophical Transactions: Biological Scis. 197, 197 (2007).
97 Elizabeth Hope, *A Lack of International Agreement over the Protection of Forests: How Nations Have Risen to the Challenge of Forest Management*, 29 J. Envtl. L. & Litig. 247 (2014).
98 The Reports of the INC Negotiating Sessions are contained in documents UNEP/Bio.Div/INC.3/11, UNEP/Bio.Div/N4-INC.2/5, UNEP/Bio.Div/N5-INC.3/5, UNEP/Bio.Div/N6-INC.4/4, UNEP/Bio.Div/N7-INC.5/L1.
99 Raustiala and Victor, *supra* note 76.
100 U.N. General Assembly Resolution (A/C.2/43/L.36).
101 U.N. General Assembly Resolution (A/Res/44/28).
102 Raustiala and Victor, *supra* note 76.

Influences from the New International Economic Order declaration pervaded the preparatory process for UNCED.[103] In 1991, the UN preparatory committee established a separate working group for examining the feasibility of elaborating principles on general rights and obligations of states and regional economic integration organizations in the fields of environment and development, and incorporating those principles into an appropriate instrument.[104] Ghana introduced, on behalf of developing countries, a draft set of principles on general rights and obligations of states to be considered at the Conference.[105] Eventually, these preparatory meetings led to the 1992 UN Conference on Environmental and Development (or "Earth Summit") held in June 1992 in Rio De Janeiro, the result of which included the Rio Declaration, the Convention on Biological Diversity, the UN Framework Convention on Climate Change, the UN Convention to Combat Desertification, and Agenda 21 (a nonbinding action plan for sustainable development).

As with negotiations that proceeded under the WHO/UNICEF International Code, global firms operated as direct negotiators in the formation of international agreements considered at UNCED. Maurice Strong, a Canadian businessman with extensive experience in the extractive and energy sectors, who had served as Secretary-General of the 1972 Stockholm Conference, was selected as Secretary-General of UNCED. In his opening speech to an UNCED preparatory conference in New York, Strong called for UNCED to reach outcomes compatible with the Uruguay Round of GATT negotiations.[106] He was also instrumental in including direct access to negotiations for global firms.

Strong appointed Stephan Schmidheiny, a Swiss industrialist, as Principal Adviser for Business and Industry.[107] At the time of the appointment, Schmidheiny sat on the boards of Nestlé and UBS as well as serving as a Vice-Chairman of the International Chamber of Commerce Commission and a member of the Board of the ICC's International Environmental Bureau.[108] He created a Business Council on Sustainable Development (BCSD) comprised of forty-eight chief executives from large multinational firms such as Du Pont, Shell, Dow, Ciba-Geiby, and Mitsubishi.[109] The BCSD gave firms special access to Strong not enjoyed by NGOs,

[103] Ileana Porras, *Binge Development in the Age of Fear: Scarcity, Consumption, Inequality, and the Environmental Crisis* in Barbara Stark (ed), International Law and Its Discontents: Confronting Crises 51 (2015).

[104] Report of the Preparatory Committee for the United Nations Conference on Environment and Development to the General Assembly, A/46/48 (1991).

[105] Rio de Janeiro Charter/Declaration on Environment and Development (A/CONF.151/PC/WG.III/L.6).

[106] Tom Athanasiou, Divided Planet: The Ecology of Rich and Poor 167–68 (1998).

[107] Stephan Schmidheiny, Changing Courses: A Global Business Perspective on Development and the Environment xix (1992).

[108] Memorandum from Ms. H. Honour to D. Bacon, et al., *Environment*, available at https://www.industrydocumentslibrary.ucsf.edu/tobacco/docs/hgll0192

[109] Dyan Machan, *Saving the Planet with Maurice Strong*, Forbes (Jan. 12, 1998), available at http://www.forbes.com/forbes/1998/0112/6101046a.html.

trade unions, or representatives of women, children, indigenous peoples, and farmers' groups.[110] The upshot of BCSD involvement in the Rio process was the minimization or omission of multinational firms' practices from the resulting Rio Declaration and the Agenda 21 statement.[111]

The Rio Declaration is a set of twenty-seven principles meant to govern states in their activities with respect to the environment and their usage of natural, domestic resources through international cooperation.[112] Most of these principles are hortatory and broad. Principle 12, for example, declares:

> States should cooperate to promote a supportive and open international economic system that would lead to development *in all countries* [emphasis added], to better address the problems of environmental degradation. ... Environmental measures addressing transboundary or global environmental problems should, ... be based on an international consensus.[113]

Principle 3 notes the need for development to "equitably" meet the "environmental needs of present and future generations."[114] The Rio Declaration calls for reducing disparities in the standard of living throughout the world (Principle 5) and the "needs of developing countries ... shall be given special priority" (Principle 6). Agenda 21 similarly exhorted all stakeholders that

> Integration of environment and development concerns and greater attention to them [in order to] lead to the fulfilment of basic needs, improved living standards for all, better protected and managed ecosystems and a safer, more prosperous future.[115]

Agenda 21 requests funds from developed countries to be used in support of developing economies or "economies in transition," and gives "full respect of all the principles contained in the Rio Declaration.[116]

What developing countries did not implement with respect to the New International Economic Order (especially firms) in the Rio Declaration and Agenda 21

[110] RICHARD WELFORD, HIJACKING ENVIRONMENTALISM: CORPORATE RESPONSES TO SUSTAINABLE DEVELOPMENT 73–74 (1997).

[111] KENNY BRUNO & JOSH KARLINER, THE CORPORATE TAKEOVER OF SUSTAINABLE DEVELOPMENT 26–29 (2002).

[112] United Nations, "Earth Summit," *UN Conference on Environment and Development (1992)* 2, http://www.unep.org/documents.multilingual/default.asp?documentid=78&articleid=1163

[113] "Principle 12," *Rio Declaration on Environment and Development* 1992, http://www.jus.uio.no/lm/environmental.development.rio.delcaration.1992/12/html (last visited June 7, 2016).

[114] United Nations Environment Programme. "Principle 3," *Rio Declaration on Environment and Development*, http://www.unep.org/documents.multilingual/default.asp?documentid=78&articleid=1163 (1992).

[115] Agenda 21, Preamble 1.1, 3 https://sustainabledevelopment.un.org/content/documents/Agenda21.pdf (June 14, 1992).

[116] *Id.*

they *did* accomplish in the legally binding Convention on Biological Diversity.[117] In the Preamble to the CBD, the NIEO manifested in requests for technology access as well as the acknowledgment that benefits derived from genetic resources should be equitably shared.[118] Article 15 of the CBD acknowledged "the sovereign rights of States over their natural resources, the authority to determine access to genetic resources" and to impose conditions for prior informed consent to access those resources as well as to establish systems for the sharing of benefits resulting from use of those resources.[119] While Article 16 repeated calls for technology transfer, Article 15 and its implementing guidelines and later protocol provided a substantial platform by which developing countries could demand facilitated access to medicines and vaccines, shared agricultural resources, and more specific regulation over global firms.

[117] Joel Paul, *The* New *New International Economic Order: The Effect of Economic Integration on Environmental Standards*, 87 AM. SOC'Y INT'L L. PROC. 459, 473 (1993).

[118] United Nations, Convention on Biological Diversity, Preamble, Dec. 29, 1993; Robert Blomquist, *Ratification Resisted: Understanding America's Response to the Convention on Biological Diversity*, 1989–2002, 32 GOLDEN GATE U. L. REV. 493, 497 (2002); Robert F. Blomquist, *Protecting Nature "Down Under": An American Law Professor's View of Australia's Implementation of the Convention on Biological Diversity Laws, Policies, Programs, Institutions and Plans*, 1992–2002, 9 DICK J. ENVTL. L & POL'Y 227 (2000).

[119] Convention on Biological Diversity, Art. I, Dec. 29, 1993.

6

Access to Medicines and Vaccines

Between 1981, when the members of the World Health Assembly adopted the International Code on the Marketing of Breast-milk Substitutes, and 1994, when the World Trade Organization (and the TRIPS Agreement) was finalized, intellectual property had become one of, if not the, most important sources of wealth: for firms as a matter of establishing and controlling market share; for developing countries as a matter of meeting basic human needs as well as growth; and for wealthy countries seeking to preserve and expand markets for their goods and services, mostly in competition with one another. Medicine became one of the most important issues illustrating the conflict between these trends. According to a Credit Suisse report issued around the time the WTO was formed, "the pharmaceutical industry is the greatest beneficiary of the [TRIPS] agreements."[1] But just as the United States, Japan, and European countries had increasingly tied intellectual property protections to trade preferences and then TRIPS as part of their competition, basic human needs policy interventions implicating intellectual property rights became crucial for developing countries. Access to medicines arose as a crucial component of poorer countries' efforts to fight HIV/AIDS, non-communicable diseases, and novel viral threats, especially influenza.[2] Addressing non-communicable diseases also implicated other interventions like the regulation of misleading trademarks on alcohol and tobacco containers.[3]

[1] OXFAM, DARE TO LEAD: PUBLIC HEALTH AND COMPANY WEALTH 20 (2000).

[2] UN MILLENNIUM PROJECT, REPORT OF THE TASK FORCE ON HIV/AIDS, MALARIA, TB, AND ACCESS TO ESSENTIAL MEDICINES, WORKING GROUP ON ACCESS TO ESSENTIAL MEDICINES (2005).

[3] Sam Foster Halabi, *International Trademark Protection and Global Public Health, a Just Compensation Regime for Expropriations and Regulatory Takings*, 61 CATH. U. L. REV. 321, 344 (2012).

Developing countries' need for patented medicines is vividly illustrated by the HIV/AIDS crisis.[4] Scientists discovered the virus that caused AIDS in 1983, largely because of increasing reports of rare types of pneumonia, cancer, and other illnesses in specific populations such as gay men, Haitians returning from the Democratic Republic of Congo, and intravenous drug users.[5] By the end of 1986, 85 countries had reported 38,401 cases of AIDS to the World Health Organization. By region these were: Africa 2,323, Americas 31,741, Asia 84, Europe 3,858, and Oceania 395.[6] The numbers for Asia and Africa clearly reflected surveillance inadequacies, as those regions even by that time produced exponentially more infections than anywhere else in the world.[7]

By the early 1990s, the population of people living with HIV/AIDS exploded in sub-Saharan Africa, quickly comprising the large majority of the HIV/AIDS-afflicted population worldwide.[8] At the same time, populations living in Africa tended to have the least access to relatively rapidly developed (and patented) antiretroviral treatments. By 2001, approximately 20 million people had died from AIDS, and another 40 million people were infected and/or dying.[9] Africa accounted for two-thirds of the people living with HIV/AIDS, despite holding a relatively small percentage of the global population.[10] While antiretroviral drug treatments – which work by inhibiting the various viral enzymes critical to the HIV replication cycle – had been developed, patented, and approved as early as 1987, they ran approximately $1,000 per month when the HIV/AIDS problem in South Africa became clear in scope.[11] It was an unimaginable sum given the severity of the problem.

As noted in Chapter 2, before the establishment of TRIPS, many low- and middle-income countries refused to allow pharmaceutical patents whatsoever on the basis that doing so would erect barriers to access to medicines for their often large and poor populations.[12] TRIPS introduced a twenty-year minimum floor for patents, including

4 Paul Hunt, *Human Rights Guidelines for Pharmaceutical Companies in Relation to Access to Medicines*, ¶ A (Draft for consultation Mar. 1, 2008).

5 Robert Gallo & Luc Montagnier, *The Discovery of HIV as the Cause of AIDS*, 349 New. Engl. J. Med. 2283–85 (2003).

6 Bureau of Hygiene and Tropical Diseases (Jan. 15, 1986) "AIDS newsletter" 2(1).

7 Jonathan Mann, AIDS in the World II: Global Dimensions, Social Roots and Responses Vol 2 (2000).

8 *Id.*

9 World Health Organization, AIDS Epidemic Update 1 (2005).

10 World Health Organization, HIV/AIDS (2017), available at http://www.who.int/gho/hiv/en/.

11 Rachel Swarns, *Drug Makers Drop South Africa Suit over AIDS Medicine*, N.Y.Times (Apr. 20, 2001), available at http://www.nytimes.com/2001/04/20/world/drug-makers-drop-south-africa-suit-over-aids-medicine.html.

12 N. Nanda & R. Lodha, *Access to Essential Medicines and Affordable Drugs: Making Essential Medicines Affordable to the Poor – with Special Reference to India*, 20 Wisc. Int'l. L. J. 581 (2002); Vikas Bajaj & Andrew Pollack, *India's Supreme Court to Hear Dispute on Drug Patents*, N.Y. Times (Mar. 7, 2012), available at http://www.nytimes.com/2012/03/07/business/global/indias-supreme-court-to-hear-long-simmering-dispute-on-drug-patents.html?pagewanted=all&_r=0

pharmaceuticals, and required that "undisclosed test or other data" be protected from "unfair commercial use."[13] Subsequent international agreements not only reinforced that floor but also included protections for other aspects of drug development and approval including marketing exclusion based on animal and clinical testing data used as part of a regulatory approval. In short, pharmaceutical patents had caused high global prices for drugs at precisely the point that the world needed less expensive drugs to address a crisis that disproportionately affected people in developing countries.

Before analyzing the steps developing countries' governments took with respect to the relationship between patents and antiretroviral medicines, it is worth understanding some of the special features of pharmaceutical patents that distinguish them from other product and process patents.[14] There are basically two categories of drugs available to patients: patented or "brand name" drugs, which are more expensive because the patent holder may exclude others; and off-patent or "generic" drugs, which are less expensive because the manufacturer as a general matter did not spend money to research, develop, or market the original drug – it used the formula disclosed in the patent.[15] In addition to the research and development of new (small- and large-molecule) drugs, firms must also generate scientific evidence supporting the safety and efficacy of drugs for use in specific patient populations.[16] The clinical trial process typically involves both animal and human trials.[17] This process is costly and risky (among other possibilities, clinical trials may show special risks to patients or failure to show efficacy against current approved treatments).[18] That evidence is used by national regulatory authorities to determine whether a medicine may be licensed, for which populations, and to inform the labeling information to instruct providers.[19]

There are, therefore, two related types of intellectual property claims made by pharmaceutical manufacturers: first, patents covering the discovery of new drugs; second, the data generated for purposes of regulatory approval.[20] Generics manufacturers use both the information disclosed in patents and on the safety and efficacy data generated by the patent-holding pharmaceutical firms; as a result, prices for generic drugs are lower, in some cases 90-95 percent lower.[21] This has caused

13 TRIPS art. 39.

14 David Taylor, *The Pharmaceutical Industry and the Future of Drug Development*, in R. E. Hester & R. M. Harrison (eds), PHARMACEUTICALS IN THE ENVIRONMENT 1–33 (2016).

15 Cynthia M. Ho, *Drugged Out: How Cognitive Bias Hurts Drug Innovation*, 51 SAN DIEGO L. REV. 419, 430 (2014).

16 *Id.* at 432.

17 Sam Halabi, *The Drug Repurposing Ecosystem*, 20 YALE J. LAW & TECH. (2018).

18 *Id.*

19 Jesse Goodman, *Addressing Emerging Challenges in the Pharmaceutical Product Development Ecosystem*, in Sam Halabi (ed), FOOD AND DRUG REGULATION IN AN ERA OF GLOBALIZED MARKETS 4–5 (2015).

20 Halabi, *supra* note 17.

21 Beth Levine, *The Truth about Generic versus Brand Name Medications*, HUFF. POST (Feb. 22, 2015), available at http://www.huffingtonpost.com/2015/02/22/generic-prescriptions_n_6730194.html

considerable controversy surrounding pharmaceutical patents.[22] "Of all the goods and services traded in the market economy, pharmaceuticals are perhaps the most contentious. Though produced by private companies, they constitute a public good, both because they can prevent epidemics and because healthy people function better as members of society than sick ones do."[23] "The high price of patented drugs lies at the heart of a major global public health crisis."[24]

Moreover, pharmaceutical patents are subject to a unique and idiosyncratic set of disputes that overlap, but are not coextensive, with the academic disagreements surrounding patents detailed in the Introduction. Certainly, pharmaceutical patent apologists repeat the general justification for patents: "they provide the necessary incentive or reward for research that ultimately benefits society by promoting innovation that is shared with the public rather than kept secret."[25] According to Benjamin Roin, "pharmaceuticals have long been considered the one area where patents function in reality as they do in theory because drugs are expensive to develop but easy to copy."[26] Further, scholars claim that the current system works as it is designed, in that it encourages socially valuable investments, by firms that would not otherwise invest.[27] Firms must invest hundreds of millions or billions of dollars in order to bring a drug to market.[28] Without incentives to make profits or recoup their costs, many companies would not invest in new research and development.[29] Proponents for stronger patent protection argue that pharmaceutical prices are necessarily high because innovation requires it.[30] Whatever exclusion is caused by high prices is justified by the necessity those prices meet in supporting the discovery of new drugs.[31] These scholars tend to focus on abstract arguments about patent utility and claim the pharmaceutical industry is a prime example of how patents are supposed to work.

22 Cynthia M. Ho, *Should All Drugs Be Patentable?: A Comparative Perspective*, 17 VAND J. ENT. & TECH. L. 295 (2014–2015).

23 *Pharmaceutical pricing The New Drugs War*, ECONOMIST, available at http://www.economist.com/news/leaders/21592619-patents-drugs-are-interests-sick-well-industry-protection-should-notf.

24 Kevin Outterson & Donald W. Light, *Global Pharmaceutical Markets*, A COMPANION TO BIOETHICS (Helga Kuhse & Peter Singer, eds. 2nd ed, 2009); Jean O. Lanjouw, A *Patent Policy Proposal for Global Diseases*, BROOKINGS, (June 2001), http://www.brookings.edu/research/papers/2001/06/globaleconomics-lanjouw.

25 Cynthia M. Ho, *Patent Breaking or Balancing? Separating Strands of Fact from Fiction under TRIPS*, 34 N.C.J. INT'L L. & COM. REG. 371, 381 (2009).

26 Ho *supra* note 25, at 433.

27 Benjamin N. Roin, *Unpatentable Drugs and the Standards of Patentability*, 87 TEX. L. REV. 503, 507 (2009).

28 The cost to bring a new drug to market is acrimoniously disputed. Jerry Avorn, *The $2.6 Billion Pill – Methodologic and Policy Considerations*, 372 NEW ENGL. J. MED. 1877–79 (2015).

29 Roin, *supra* note 27.

30 Harvey Bale, *Industry, Innovation, and Social Values*, 11(1) SCIENCE AND ENGINEERING ETHICS 31–40 (2005).

31 Roin *supra* note 27, at 511.

Pharmaceutical companies further claim that "innovation accounts for most of the cost of production, so the price of drugs is much higher than their cost of manufacture."[32] Litigation is often the only means by which to prevent imitation and the deterioration of profit necessary to reinvest.[33] Further, "most inventions build upon prior inventions, encouraging inventors to share their knowledge can be socially valuable, even if there is a temporary cost of higher prices during the period of patent protect."[34]

Critical scholars argue that strong pharmaceutical patents "fail to incentivize drugs for unprofitable treatments as well as overincentivizing development of minimally innovative drugs."[35] These scholars point to evidence that pharmaceutical firms spend far more on marketing and promotion than on research and development.[36] Research and development in any case is focused on "evergreening" strategies by which firms adapt the modality or other characteristic of an approved drug to extend its patentable life even though there is marginal therapeutic benefit to patients.[37]

Innovative work is done by others, critics argue, often with public support. The distribution of pharmaceutical company investments is borne out by some data on new approvals. A study of 252 new drugs approved by the US FDA between 1998 and 2007 found that drugs initially discovered in biotechnology companies or universities accounted for approximately half of the drugs that responded to unmet medical needs and represented innovative rather than "me-too" (drugs that add marginal benefit to existing therapies) approvals.[38] This theory is supported by a study that found "of the 1,284 new drug approvals from 1990 to 2004, only 289 ... were for 'priority' reviews, defined as a product that presents a 'significant improvement compared to marked products in the treat, diagnosis, or prevention of a disease.'"[39] The largest cost of development is clinical trials.[40] Many companies

[32] Economist, *supra* note 23.
[33] *Id.*
[34] Cynthia M. Ho, *Should All Drugs Be Patentable?: A Comparative Perspective*, 17 Vand J. Ent. & Tech. L. 295, 304 (2014–2015).
[35] Ho *supra* note 25, at 422.
[36] Ana Swanson, *Pharmaceutical Companies Are Spending Far More on Marketing than Research*, Wash. Post (Feb. 2015), available at https://www.washingtonpost.com/news/wonk/wp/2015/02/11/big-pharmaceutical-companies-are-spending-far-more-on-marketing-than-research/?utm_term=.70c66e904f8f
[37] Roger Collier, Drug Patents: The Evergreening Problem, 185(9) CMAJ E385–86 (2013).
[38] Robert Kneller, *The Importance of New Companies for Drug Discovery: Origins of a Decade of New Drugs*, 9 Nature Reviews Drug Discovery 867 (2010).
[39] James Love & Tim Hubbard, *The Big Idea: Prizes to Stimulate R&D for New Medicines*, 82 Chi.- Kent L. Rev. 1519, 1528–34 (2007).
[40] *Id.*

admit that they "invest in clinical trials that have little scientific value, largely for marketing purposes."[41]

As with the patent debate more broadly, there is little hope of any near-term resolution to these disputes.[42] What is clear is that once the *global* market for pharmaceuticals is considered, these two kinds of intellectual property (research and development for new molecules and clinical data for licensing) become more complex and their value becomes more volatile.[43] Under the doctrine of patent independence – which survived TRIPS even if it has waned under bilateral and multilateral investment and trade agreements – a patent is a right granted by a specific country and is valid only within that jurisdiction's borders.[44] Patentability criteria, therefore, such as novelty, nonobviousness, and utility (under TRIPS, "inventive step" and "industrial application"), may be narrower or wider depending on the country's laws.[45] Certain peripheral features of drugs such as their coating or normal metabolites may enjoy patent protection in some countries but not in others.[46] There is, therefore, no global patent system even if some standards have been harmonized or made more uniform through international agreements.[47]

Moreover, under the doctrine of patent exhaustion, the economic exploitation of intellectual property rights is limited to first sale.[48] Therefore, if a party in one country makes a valid purchase of pharmaceuticals, there would not be, under this doctrine alone, any barrier to then selling those pharmaceuticals in a second country. For Type I diseases (i.e., those diseases incident in both rich and poor countries, with large numbers of vulnerable populations in each), which is where global pharmaceutical research and development is focused, this creates an incentive for poorer countries to import cheaper drugs instead of negotiating with pharmaceutical companies over pricing – so-called "parallel imports."[49] Type II diseases (such as tuberculosis, which is incident in both rich and poor countries, but with a substantial proportion of the cases in poor countries) and Type III diseases (such as malaria, which overwhelmingly affects poorer countries) present special

41 *Id.*

42 Roin *supra* note 27, at 512.

43 Janice M. Mueller, *The Tiger Awakens: The Tumultuous Transformation of India's Patent System and the Rise of Indian Pharmaceutical Innovation*, 68 U. PITT. L. REV. 491, 491 (2007).

44 Paris Convention, art. 4, cl. 1. Art. 4, cl. I.

45 RALPH FOLSOM, MICHAEL GORDON, MICHAEL VAN ALSTINE & MICHAEL RAMSEY, PRINCIPLES OF INTERNATIONAL BUSINESS TRANSACTIONS § 19.5 (2005).

46 James Love & Tim Hubbard, *The Big Idea: Prizes to Stimulate R&D for New* Medicines, 82 CHI-KENT L. REV. 1519, 1542 (2007).

47 JOHN R. THOMAS, PHARMACEUTICAL PATENT LAW 782 (2015).

48 Impression Products, Inc. v. Lexmark Inc., 581 U.S. ___ (2017).

49 Gene M. Grossman & Edwin L.-C. Lai, *Parallel Imports and Price Controls*, 39(2) RAND J. ECON. 378–402 (2008).

problems addressed later in Part III.[50] These types of diseases "have more than [ninety-nine] (99) percent of their disease burden in low-income countries.[51]

Global diseases that affect both rich and poor countries are important causes of disability and mortality among the poor.[52] A 1999 World Health Organization report showed that "disability adjusted life years" statistic was four times higher for cancer and heart disease than malaria.[53] Further, a significant share of a developing country's drug expenditures go toward treatment of global diseases.[54]

However, this only accounts for a small part of worldwide expenditures on global diseases.[55] Poor countries with 46 percent of the world's population account for approximately 2 percent of the spending on cardiovascular drugs.[56] Roughly 15 percent of the world's population consume 90 percent of the world's pharmaceuticals.[57]

TRIPS allowed no country to exempt any class of inventions from protection, so countries that became members of the World Trade Organization had to adopt twenty-year patent terms for pharmaceuticals under Article 33 of the agreement, as well as provide less certain protection for data submitted in support of regulatory approval under Article 39. TRIPS did allow patent law to be shaped by public health and nutrition priorities and also provided for a mechanism by which patents could be involuntarily licensed (i.e., compulsory licenses).[58] A compulsory license permits a nation to use (or authorizes a third party to use) a patented invention without the permission of the patent owner at a government-imposed royalty rate that is likely below what the patent owner would freely negotiate.[59] The South African government's effort to navigate post-TRIPS legal complexity to address its HIV/AIDS crisis demonstrated new tensions between global firms and developing countries as intellectual property rights assertions obstructed efforts to address basic human needs.

[50] World Health Organization, Defining Disease Types I, II, and III (2012) available at http://www.who.int/phi/3-background_cewg_agenda_item5_disease_types_final.pdf

[51] *Id.*

[52] Jean O. Lanjouw, A *Patent Policy Proposal for Global Diseases*, Brookings 2 (2001), available at http://www.brookings.edu/research/papers/2001/06/globaleconomics-lanjouw.

[53] *Id.*

[54] Susan Foster, Richard Laing, Bjørn Melgaard, & Michel Zaffran, *Ensuring Supplies of Appropriate Drugs and Vaccines* in D. T. Jamison, J. G. Breman, A. R. Measham, et al. (eds), Disease Control Priorities in Developing Countries 1323–37 (2006).

[55] Lanjouw, *supra* note 52.

[56] *Id.*

[57] *Id.*

[58] Outterson & Light, *supra* note 24, at 3.

[59] Read Beall & Randall Kuhn, *Trends in Compulsory Licensing of Pharmaceuticals since the Doha Declaration: A Database Analysis* (Jan. 2012) available at http://www.plosmedicine.org/article/info%3Adoi%2F10.1371%2Fjournal.pmed.1001154

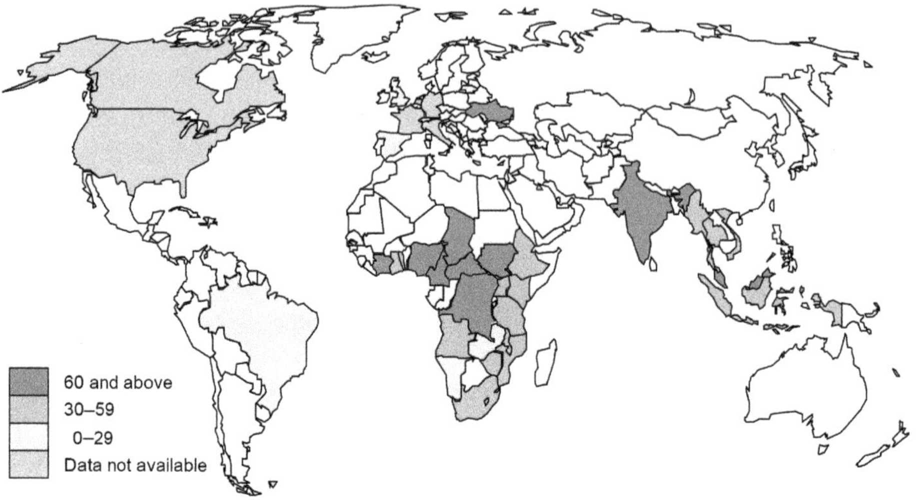

FIGURE 6.1 Map of AIDS death rate per 1,000 people living with HIV for 2013 for thirty high AIDS mortality burden countries and eight high-income countries.[60]

ANTIRETROVIRAL MEDICATIONS

By the early 1990s, the population of people living with HIV/AIDS exploded in sub-Saharan Africa, quickly comprising the large majority of the HIV/AIDS afflicted population worldwide [Figure 6.1].[61] Between 1994 and 2001, South Africa became home to the world's largest population of people living with HIV/AIDS.[62] The South African government regarded expanding access to patented medications as part of its responsibility under its constitution and announced that pharmaceutical firms' pricing strategies made it unable to do so.[63] It adopted legislation amending its patent act to authorize parallel imports and to more steeply regulate available medicines notwithstanding existing patent rights.[64]

60 http://journals.plos.org/plosone/article?id=10.1371/journal.pone.0131353. UNAIDS AIDS-related deaths estimates for 2013 are not available for countries shown in grey. Countries in white were not included in analyses.

61 William Fisher & Cyrill Rigamonti, *The South Africa AIDS Controversy: A Case Study in Patent Law and Policy* (Feb. 10, 2005) available at http://cyber.law.harvard.edu/people/tfisher/South%20Africa.pdf.

62 UNAIDS & WHO, A History of the HIV/AIDS Epidemic with Emphasis on Africa 6 (2003), available at http://www.un.org/esa/population/publications/adultmort/UNAIDS_WHO Paper2.pdf.

63 Amir Attaran & Lee Gillespie-White, *Do Patents for Antiretroviral Drugs Constrain Access to AIDS Treatment in Africa?*, 286 (15) *JAMA* 1886, 1888 (2001).

64 Public Protector of the Republic of South Africa, Report on the Propriety of the Conduct of Members of the Ministry and Department of Health Relating to Statements in Connection with the Prices of Medicines and Utilisation of Generic Medicines in South Africa, Special

The Pharmaceutical Manufacturers' Association of South Africa as well as the major global pharmaceutical firms individually sued the government, alleging that the law violated a number of constitutional provisions including uncompensated property takings as well as constitutional commitments to honor obligations under international law generally and TRIPS specifically.[65] Under the pharmaceutical firms' theory, medicines patents relevant to HIV/AIDS drugs were no different than other pharmaceutical patents. The same intellectual property principles – exclusivity and monopoly rents in exchange for investments in innovation and disclosure of resulting inventions – would lead to the same socially optimal outcomes for HIV/AIDS drugs as for other medicines.[66]

In Ghana, GlaxoWellcome (later GSK) licensed combivir for marketing in 1999.[67] In 2000, a local Ghanaian distributor attempted to introduce Indian generics, including a copy of Combivir, into the market. GSK lobbied Ghana's medicines licensing agency and threatened suit against the distributor. The Indian generics manufacturer then offered to donate the generic directly to Ghanaian physicians. GSK again challenged the "infringing activity." A similar dynamic occurred in Uganda .In some cases, the disputes resulted in deals between so-called name brand manufacturers and generics' firms to share markets.

In 1996, Brazil adopted a "local working" requirement as part of its Industrial Property Law which enabled the Brazilian government to license patented medicines and technology to other firms for production if the patent was not "worked" in Brazil.[68] Pharmaceutical firms, which had exported patented medicines to Brazil but not produced them locally, immediately protested the measure and, unlike in the dispute with South Africa, convinced the US government to bring a formal dispute at the World Trade Organization for violating TRIPS.[69] Brazil, in return, requested consultations under the WTO Dispute Settlement Understanding (DSU), alleging that certain aspects of US patent law, particularly those obtained with federal support, violated TRIPS.[70] The United States and Brazil terminated their dispute in 2001 in the wake of the Doha Declaration on TRIPS and the Public Health that they jointly drafted, analyzed in more detail in Chapter 10. In 2007,

Report No. 6 (1997); E 't Hoen, *TRIPS, Pharmaceutical Patents and Access to Essential Medicines*, 3 CHI. J. INT'L. L. 27–46 (2002).

65 Pat Sidley, *Drug Companies Sue South African Government over Generics*, 322(7284) *BMJ* 447 (2001).

66 Maya Prabhu & Kathryn Garforth, *International Public Health and Trade Law* in Markus Gehring and Marie Claire Codonier-Singer (eds), SUSTAINABLE DEVELOPMENT IN WORLD TRADE LAW 560–61 (2005).

67 Oxfam, *supra* note 1, at 21.

68 See Article 68 of Law No. 9,279 of May 14, 1996, effective May 1997.

69 World Trade Organization, Brazil–Measures Affecting Patent Protection, Request for the Establishment of a Panel by the United States, WT/DS199/3, Jan. 9, 2001 (01–0093).

70 John S. Odell & Susan K. Sell, *Reframing the Issue: The WTO Coalition on Intellectual Property and Public Health*, 2001, in John S. Odell (ed), NEGOTIATING TRADE: DEVELOPING COUNTRIES IN THE WTO AND NAFTA 94–96 (2006).

Brazil granted a compulsory license for Merck's efavirenz after negotiations over price reductions failed. Merck filed a motion for injunctive relief, which was rejected by Brazilian courts.[71]

Between 2006 and 2007, Thailand also issued compulsory licenses for Merck's efavirenz and Abbott's liponavir/ritonavir, noting that discussions with the firms over prices had lasted more than two years.[72] After granting the compulsory licenses, the firms threatened to withdraw or not register other medicines in Thailand, complained to the Office of the U.S. Trade Representative, but ultimately agreed to lower their prices for the medications.[73]

The conflict between firms and developing country governments has also reached trade (not just licensing) channels. Indeed, for the vast majority of developing countries that lack a domestic pharmaceutical manufacturing capacity, imports are the means by which antiretroviral drugs are acquired. As recently as 2008, 80 percent of drugs used to treat HIV/AIDS in Africa were imported.[74] In November 2008, Dutch customs agents seized a shipment of HIV medications manufactured in India and destined for Nigeria.[75] The seizure in the Netherlands came at the request of GlaxoSmithKline, which claimed that the Indian drug, abacavir, violated its patent rights.[76] During 2008 and 2009, Médecins Sans Frontières found at least nineteen shipments of generic medicines from India to other countries were impounded while in transit in Europe.[77] The disputes between the parties led to formal action at the World Trade Organization both by European countries and by Brazil and India.[78]

[71] Carlos Correa, *The Use of Compulsory Licenses in Latin America*, in Reto M. Hilty & Kung-Chung Liu (eds), COMPULSORY LICENSING, PRACTICAL EXPERIENCES AND WAYS FORWARD 52 (2015).

[72] Amy Nunn et al., *Evolution of Antiviral Drug Costs in Brazil in the Context of Free and Universal AIDS Treatment* 4(11) PLoS MED. E305 (2007), available at https://www.ncbi.nlm.nih.gov/pmc/articles/PMC2071936/#pmed-0040305-b065.

[73] J. Kuanpoth, *Compulsory Licenses: Law and Practice in Thailand*, in Reto M. Hilty & Kung-Chung Liu (eds), COMPULSORY LICENSING, PRACTICAL EXPERIENCES AND WAYS FORWARD 65–68 (2015).

[74] African Union, *Progress report on the pharmaceutical manufacturing plan for Africa: business plan*. Addis Ababa: African Union Commission – UNIDO Partnership (2012), available at http://www.unido.org/fileadmin/user_media_upgrade/Resources/Publications/Pharmaceuticals/PMPA_Business_Plan_Nov2012_ebook.PDF

[75] Michael Geist, *Why Dutch Guards Holding Indian-Made Drugs Bound for Nigeria Sends a Warning to Canadian Legislators*, THE STAR (Feb. 2014), available at http://www.thestar.com/business/2014/08/29/why_dutch_guards_holding_indianmade_drugs_bound_for_nigeria_sends_a_warning_to_canadian_legislators.html

[76] *Id.*

[77] MÉDECINS SANS FRONTIÈRES, HOW THE TRANS-PACIFIC PARTNERSHIP AGREEMENT THREATENS ACCESS TO MEDICINES 4 (2011), available at https://www.msfaccess.org/sites/default/files/MSF_assets/Access/Docs/Access_Briefing_TPP_ENG_2011.pdf.

[78] KAISER FAMILY FOUNDATION, INDIA, BRAZIL LAUNCH TRADE DISPUTE AGAINST EU, NETHERLANDS OVER SEIZURES OF GENERIC DRUGS (May 2010), available at http://www.kff.org/news-summary/india-brazil-launch-trade-dispute-against-eu-netherlands-over-seizures-of-generic-drugs/

CANCER AND HEART DISEASE MEDICATIONS

Trade and investment liberalization has promoted the availability of consumer goods – such as processed foods containing high levels of fat, salt, and sugar – that contribute to poor individual health without the access to medicines and other health care infrastructure wealthier countries maintain to address noncommunicable diseases such as cancer, diabetes, and heart disease.[79] Even where these medicines are available in a given market, international agreements including and influenced by TRIPS push prices higher. For example, the U.S.-Jordan Free Trade Agreement includes limitations on compulsory licenses and parallel imports.[80] The costliest TRIPS-plus terms are those that impose constraints on a generic manufacturer's ability to use clinical and safety trial data used with the initial drug application, essentially requiring the generics applicant to undertake prohibitively expensive clinical trials and reimposing the cost to the government or end-user that generics theoretically exist to save.

These expenditures have required that both public health systems and individuals pay higher prices for many new medicines that are needed to treat diseases such as cancer, hypertension, asthma, diabetes, and mental illness. For example, new medicines to treat diabetes and heart disease cost anywhere from two to six times more in Jordan than in Egypt, where there are no agreements imposing additional intellectual property protections for pharmaceuticals.[81]

Access to these medicines has generated conflicts with strong intellectual property agreements as have medicines that prevent or treat infectious disease that disproportionately affects low- and middle-income countries. Along with compulsory licenses for HIV/AIDS drugs in 2007, Thailand also issued a compulsory license for Plavix, one of the most prescribed heart disease drugs in industrialized countries.[82] It also announced compulsory licenses for four patented cancer medications.[83] The Thai government noted that its decision was based on the relative burden each disease imposed on the Thai people. As many or more people in Thailand die from cancer as HIV/AIDS.[84] The Thai licenses prompted immediate retaliation from Abbott Laboratories (now AbbVie), which withdrew seven

79 Lee Petherbridge, *Intelligent TRIPS Implementation Strategy for Countries on the Cusp of Development*, 22 U. Pa. J. Int'l Econ. L. 1029, 1048 (2001).

80 Ryan Abbott, Rania Bader, Lina Bajjaji, et al., *The Price of Medicines in Jordan :The Cost of Trade-Based Intellectual Property*, 9(2) J. Gen. Med. 75–85 (2012).

81 Oxfam, All Costs, No Benefits: How TRIPS-Plus Intellectual Property Rules in the US-Jordan FTA Affect Access to Medicines, Oxfam Briefing Paper (Mar. 2007) available at http://www.oxfam.org/sites/www.oxfam.org/files/all%20costs,%20no%20benefits.pdf

82 Inthira Yamabhai et al., *Government Use Licenses in Thailand: An Assessment of the Health and Economic Impacts*, 7 Global Health 28 (2011).

83 B. Stirner & H. Thangaraj, *Learning from Practice: Compulsory Licensing Cases and Access to Medicines*, 2 Pharm. Pat. Anal. 195–213 (2013).

84 Toni Johnson, *The Debate Over Generic Drug Trade*, Council on Foreign Relations Backgrounder, available at http://www.cfr.org/drugs/debate-over-generic-drug-trade/p18055

medications from the Thai market as well as initiating a more concerted effort to pressure the Thai government from US and European countries.[85]

VACCINES

Historically, it is not HIV/AIDS or noncommunicable diseases such as cancer, diabetes, or heart disease that have threatened large populations in developing countries; it is primarily influenza and other vaccine-preventable diseases.[86] The development of some vaccines, notably influenza, depends on biological resources in low- and middle-income countries being made available to researchers, organizations, governments, and pharmaceutical firms in the major industrialized countries. Vaccines are one of the most important lines of defense against the emergence of pandemics.[87] Not only are vaccines typically patented but components of vaccines that make them more effective are as well.[88] Seasonal and pandemic influenza vaccines are possible in significant part because developing countries share influenza samples with the World Health Organization's Global Influenza Surveillance and Response System (GISRS), even though their populations have not historically received a proportionate benefit of resulting vaccines or other breakthroughs.[89] GISRS was created by the World Health Organization in 1957.[90] Access to viruses is crucial to the development of vaccines and other forms of treatment, and the WHO's system allows countries to effectively "coordinate surveillance efforts" for influenza outbreaks.[91] Through the GISRS, national influenza centers (NIC) submit local virus samples to WHO for monitoring and research.[92] NICs also

[85] Amy Kazmin & Andrew Jack, *Abbott Pulls HIV drug in Thai Patents Protest*, FINANCIAL TIMES (Mar. 14, 2007).

[86] Christopher Ingraham, *In 2013, Measles Killed More Kids than Car Accidents or AIDS*, WASH. POST (Feb. 25, 2015), available at at www.washingtonpost.com/blogs/wonkblog/wp/2015/02/25/in-2013-measles-killed-more-kids-than-car-accidents-or-aids/.

[87] Eileen Kane, *Achieving Clinical Equality in an Influenza Pandemic: Patent Realities*, 39 SETON HALL L. REV. 1137, 1143 (2009).

[88] *Id.* at 1158.

[89] Kumanan Wilson, Barbara von Tigerstrom & Christopher McDougall, *Protecting Global Health Security through the International Health Regulations: Requirements and Challenges*, 179(1) CMAJ 44 (2008), available at http://www.ncbi.nlm.nih.gov/pmc/articles/PMC2464486/. David P. Fidler & Lawrence O. Gostin, *The New International Health Regulations: An Historic Development for International Law and Public Health*, 34 *JLME* 85, 86–87 (2006).

[90] JEROME H. REICHMAN, PAUL UHLIR & TOM DEDEURWAERDERE, GOVERNING DIGITALLY INTEGRATED GENETIC RESOURCES, DATA, AND LITERATURE: GLOBAL INTELLECTUAL PROPERTY STRATEGIES FOR A REDESIGNED MICROBIAL RESEARCH COMMONS, 44 (2016).

[91] *Id.*

[92] Samples are often collected from hospitals, clinics, and other laboratories. *Id.*; *see also* MARIE WILKE, THE WORLD HEALTH ORGANIZATION'S PANDEMIC INFLUENZA PREPAREDNESS FRAMEWORK AS A PUBLIC HEALTH RESOURCE POOL, COMMON POOLS OF GENETIC RESOURCES: EQUITY AND INNOVATION IN INTERNATIONAL BIODIVERSITY LAW 315–43 (2013).

provide epidemiological information accessible to all participating laboratories and, in turn, may share samples to develop vaccines and other therapeutics.[93]

The infrastructure and technology for vaccine development is overwhelmingly located in a small number of firms based in wealthy states.[94] Five large firms generate approximately 80 percent of global vaccine sales across all products.[95] By product, many of the individual vaccine markets are monopolies or oligopolies.[96] This concentration renders many developing states dependent on wealthier states to manufacture and distribute vaccines in sufficient quantities to address their needs in routine and emergency circumstances.[97] Yet influenza pandemics have typically originated in low- or middle-income states such as Cambodia, China, Indonesia, Mexico, and Vietnam. These states must therefore be willing to share disease samples and biological material relevant to risk assessment, risk management, disease research, and vaccine development. When firms patent shared samples to produce unaffordable vaccines, the willingness to share is undermined.[98]

In 2007, Indonesia withheld H5N1 avian flu samples from the WHO system, compromising efforts to monitor and produce vaccines in response to an avian flu outbreak that had not only spread worldwide but threatened to become easily transmissible from birds to humans and then between humans.[99] Indonesia asserted that its decision was a response to an Australian company's development of a vaccine derived from a virus sample Indonesia provided to WHO.[100] The cycle demonstrated the inequities inherent in the global vaccine distribution system:

> Developing countries provided information and virus samples to the WHO-operated system; pharmaceutical companies in industrialized countries then

93 Reichman et al., *supra* note 90 at 44.

94 Kane, *supra* note 87, at 1148.

95 World Health Organization, *Vaccine Market* available at http://www.who.int/immunization/programmes_systems/procurement/market/global_supply/en/

96 *Id.*

97 David P. Fidler, *Negotiating Equitable Access to Influenza Vaccines: Global Health Diplomacy and the Controversies Surrounding Avian Influenza H5N1 and Pandemic Influenza H1NI*, 7(5) PLoS MED. 1 (2010), available at http://www.plosmedicine.org/article/info%3Adoi%2F10.1371%2Fjournal.pmed.1000247.

98 Kane, *supra* note 87, at 1153–55 ("In an effort to document the patent landscape of the field, the WHO has undertaken a project to map where patents have been sought on any of the relevant H5N1 viral materials. This research demonstrates that a small cluster of patent applications have been filed on various sequences and proteins of H5N1 and several patents have been issued, but the report further notes that patent landscaping must continue as the field matures. The sequence of the H5N1 and novel H1N1 influenza viruses have been determined. The WHO provided notice that genetic sequences from one novel H1N1 virus isolate were available on the GISAID database within several days of the first reports of the outbreak ... Three separate groups of international researchers filed U.S. patent applications on the DNA sequences of the virus.").

99 David Fidler, *Influenza Virus Samples, International Law, and Global Health Diplomacy*, 14(1) EMERG. INFECT. DIS. 88–94 (2008).

100 *Id.*

> obtained free access to such samples, exploited them, and patented the resulting products, which the developing countries could not afford.[101]

As David Fidler noted, "[w]ithout access to Indonesia's influenza strains, global surveillance was jeopardized, as was the refinement of diagnostic reagents and the development of intervention strategies, which depend on the information surveillance provides."[102]

In 2009, the outbreak of H1N1 influenza in Mexico demonstrated not only that the global surveillance system benefited pharmaceutical firms but that in the case of a real pandemic, those firms (and their governments) could not be relied on to equitably share vaccines:

> Canada awarded its vaccine contract to a Canadian company because it feared that foreign governments might restrict exports to Canada because of vaccine shortages within their territories. The Australian government made it clear to the Australian manufacturer CSL that it must fulfill the government's domestic needs before exporting vaccine to the United States. The United States pledged on September 17, 2009, to donate 10% of its vaccine purchases to WHO but on October 28, US Secretary of Health and Human Services Kathleen Sebelius stated that the United States would not donate H1N1 vaccine as promised until all at risk Americans had access, because production problems had created shortages in the United States.[103]

Despite clear acknowledgment that the 2009 outbreak originated in Mexico and leveled its most significant toll there, Mexico had "a terrifically difficult time getting access to the pandemic vaccine."[104]

[101] *Id.* at 88.

[102] *Id.*

[103] David P. Fidler, *Negotiating Equitable Access to Influenza Vaccines: Global Health Diplomacy and the Controversies Surrounding Avian Influenza H5N1 and Pandemic Influenza H1NI*, 7(5) PLoS MED. 1 (2010), available at http://www.plosmedicine.org/article/info%3Adoi%2F10.1371%2Fjournal.pmed.1000247.

[104] Richard Knox, *WHO Resolves Impasse Over Sharing of Flu Viruses, Access to Medicines*, NPR (Apr. 18, 2011) available at http://www.npr.org/blogs/health/2011/04/18/135519592/who-resolves-impasse-over-sharing-of-flu-viruses-access-to-vaccines

7

Food and Agriculture

Over the course of the 1970s and 1980s, access to food and agricultural technology became a similar flashpoint between intellectual property rights and basic development needs.[1] The Green Revolution – the development of high-yielding crop varieties enhanced with fertilizers and other agrochemicals – had operated more or less successfully because it was built on the open sharing of knowledge (about agricultural inputs) and the heavily subsidized transfer of agricultural technology.[2] Devastatingly poor harvests during the early 1970s prompted a reevaluation of development as approached from a purely macroeconomic perspective and strengthened the relationship between development and food security.[3] What unfolded after the late 1970s was the increasing transfer of agricultural knowledge from open sources to private ones, firms that developed proprietary seeds, fertilizers, and pesticides that, when introduced into developing countries, channeled wealth from relatively poor farmers to distant firms.[4]

Colonization itself had reorganized agricultural systems in sometimes drastic ways.[5] Commercial, export-oriented farms focused on cash crops such as tobacco,

1 Mywish Maredia, Application of Intellectual Property Rights in Developing Countries: Implications for Public Policy and Agricultural Research Institutes 17–20 (2001); Prabhu L. Pingali, *Green Revolution: Impacts, Limits, and the Path Ahead*, 109(21) *PNAS* 12303–08 (2012).

2 *Id.*

3 Amartya Sen, Poverty and Famines: An Essay on Entitlement and Deprivation 42 (1981).

4 Jean Christie, *Enclosing the Biodiversity Commons: Bioprospecting or Biopiracy?* in Richard Hindmarsh & Geoffrey Lawrence (eds), Altered Genes II 176 (2001).

5 Allen Isaacman, Michael Stephen, Yussuf Adam, Maria Joao Homen, Eugenio Macamo & Augustinho Pililao, *"Cotton Is the Mother of Poverty": Peasant Resistance to Forced Cotton Production in Mozambique, 1938–1961*, 13(4) Int'l. J. African Historical Studies 581–615 (1980).

tea, sugar, cocoa, cotton, and groundnuts while smaller farms produced mainly for subsistence.[6] During periods of drought or natural disaster, the dedication of land to cash crops exacerbated food shortages and malnutrition.[7] The efforts of British, German, French, and Portuguese colonial companies to turn large tracts of African land to cotton cultivation was not only in many cases a failure for its stated purpose, but it required large-scale coercion of peasants who suffered the loss of land that could be used for food.[8] Nevertheless, cotton became an important export for many especially Francophone countries such as Benin, Burkina Faso, Cameroon, Cote d'Ivoire, and Mali. India similarly turned into a cotton exporter by the late nineteenth century.[9]

While agricultural yields were poor before and after decolonization, the Green Revolution promised a rapid change in the food security situation of many developing countries, both newly independent and not.[10] The Green Revolution combined traditional breeding techniques, direct participation of governments, and orchestrated technology transfer. For all developing countries between 1960 and 2000, wheat yields increased 208 percent, rice 109 percent, maize 157 percent, potatoes 78 percent, and cassava 36 percent.[11] Between 1961 and 1999, overall food crop yield per unit area grew by 106 percent.[12]

Its aftereffects, however, including reduced dependence on seed exchange and more intensive fertilizer and pesticide use, laid the groundwork for more of the agricultural sector to be subject to intellectual property claims. Between 1958 and 1975, pesticide use increased 50-fold in India and petrochemical fertilizer use increased 350-fold in Mexico between 1940 and 1979.[13] In more recent decades, the trend has continued. "In the past 20 years, there have been substantial increases in pesticide use, with consumption in China growing four-fold, Argentina eight-fold, Brazil three-fold, Bangladesh five-fold, and Thailand four-fold. Countries starting

6 Anne Margaret Thomson & Manfred Metz, Implications of Economic Policy for Food Security 72–75 (1999).

7 T. A. Brun, *The Nutrition and Health Aspects of Cash Cropping in West Africa: A Historical Perspective*, 65 World Rev. Nutr. Diet 124–62 (1991).

8 Richard Roberts, Two Worlds of Cotton Colonialism: Colonialism and the Regional Economy in French Sudan 1800–1946 (1996); Thomas Bassett, The Peasant Cotton Revolution in West Africa: Cote d'Ivoire 1880–1995 (2006); Andrew Zimmerman, *A German Alabama in Africa: The Tuskegee Expedition to German Togo and the Transnational Origins of West African Cotton Growers*, 110(5) Am. Hist. Rev. 1362–98 (2005).

9 Sven Beckert, Empire of Cotton: A Global History 340–78 (2015).

10 Moritz Feichtinger, *Strategic Villages: Forced Relocation, Counter-insurgency, and Social Engineering in Kenya and Algeria* in Martin Thomas & Gareth Curless (eds), Decolonization and Conflict: Colonial Comparisons and Legacies 149 (2017).

11 FAO, The State of Food and Agriculture 2003–2004 (2004).

12 Rhys Green, Stephen Cornell, Jorn Scharlemann & Andrew Balmford, *Farming and the Fate of Wild Nature*, 307 Science 550–55 (2005).

13 Muriel Lightbourne, Food Security, Biological Diversity, and Intellectual Property Rights (2016); David Sonnenfeld, *Mexico's Green Revolution 1940–80: Toward an Environmental History*, 28(4) Env. Hist. Rev. 28–52 (1992).

from a low base have seen greater increases: Burkina Faso by 50-fold, Ethiopia 13-fold, Ghana 17-fold, and Cameroon eight-fold."[14]

> While the reporting of pesticide use and market data is patchy and irregular, it is generally clear that the use of synthetic pesticides in agriculture has grown steadily, and now amounts to 3.5 billion kg of active ingredient (a.i.) per year. The highest world market growth rates occurred in the 1960s, at 12% per year, later falling back to 2% and below during the 1980s–1990s, then rising to 3% per year to 2014. The value of the global market is now US $45 billion per year. Herbicides account for 42% of sales, insecticides 27%, fungicides 22%, and disinfectants and other agrochemicals 9%.[15]

Of three important components of farming – fertilizer, seeds, and pesticides – seeds and their hybrids enjoyed widespread intellectual property protections at a relatively later stage (irrigation, while less subject to intellectual property claims, is nevertheless affected by other intellectual property–intensive firms such as Nestlé, PepsiCo, and Coca-Cola who either dominate or substantially influence water availability in many countries).[16] "Once considered the common heritage of mankind, wild animals, plants and crops were taken without asking or freely exchanged."[17] This was true even in countries that generally favored expanded intellectual property protections like the United States. Until a 1980 US Supreme Court decision, *Diamond v. Chakrabarty*, genetically modified microorganisms were thought to be living things and therefore unpatentable. Separate legislative frameworks in the United States extended intellectual property protections to new sexually and asexually reproducing plants.[18]

The relevance of seeds to global wealth inequality is even more salient because geologically and evolutionarily, the developing countries of the world hold far more diverse sources of crops – almost all original germplasm used in modern agricultural research – but had lacked the capacity or control to commercialize those resources, which firms largely located in Europe and North America did.[19] Between 1974 and 1984, more than 125,000 duplicate samples were drawn from collecting expeditions

[14] Jules Pretty & Zareen Pervez Bharucha, *Integrated Pest Management for Sustainable Intensification of Agriculture in Asia and Africa*, 6(1) INSECTS 152–82 (2015).

[15] *Id.*

[16] Edgar Chen & Sarah A. Altschuller, *Corporate Accountability and Human Rights in the Age of Global Water Scarcity*, 24 NATURAL RESOURCES & ENVIRONMENT 3, 9 (2010); John Wilkinson, *Water and Land in Latin America: Global Strategies and Policies*, 33 REVIEW (FERNAND BRAUDEL CENTER) 153, 156 (2010).

[17] Andrew Pollack, *Biological Products Raise Genetic Ownership Issues*, N.Y. TIMES (Nov. 26, 1999), available at http://www.nytimes.com/1999/11/26/business/patenting-life-special-report-biological-products-raise-genetic-ownership-issues.html.

[18] Diamond v. Chakrabarty, 447 U.S. 303 (1980); The Plant Patent Act of 1930 (enacted on 1930–06–17 as Title III of the Smoot–Hawley Tariff, ch. 497, 46 Stat. 703; Plant Variety Protection Act of 1970 (PVPA), 7 U.S.C. §§ 2321–582.

[19] Sara Peres, *Saving the Gene Pool for the Future: Seed Banks as Archives*, 55 STUDIES IN HISTORY AND PHILOSOPHY OF BIOLOGICAL AND BIOMEDICAL SCIENCES 96–104 (2016); Sharmishta Barwa

under the International Board for Plant Genetic Resources, an international scientific organization under the auspices of the Consultative Group on International Agricultural Research (CGIAR), which is itself a cooperative group of agricultural research centers located primarily in developing countries.[20] More than 90 percent of those samples came from developing countries.[21] About 120 plant species are important as food crops worldwide, but 90 percent of human energy intake is met by twenty crops, and just three crops – maize, rice, and wheat – provide 60 percent.[22]

The main diversity in food crops has always existed at the intra-species level, manifested by the vast array of varieties of the principal crops. For example, in the Philippines, 123 rice varieties have been found on just 5 sites; in the Andes, 50 potato cultivars on one farm are typical in many areas; and in Malawi, 12 bean cultivars are used on an average farm.[23] Diversity is important for food security at global and local levels: agriculture in practically all countries is heavily dependent on a supply of plant genetic resources from other parts of the world. The agricultural systems of the developed world are particularly dependent on genetic resources from tropical and subtropical regions of developing countries.[24]

Prior to the 1930s, there were few commercial interests in plants and seeds. Farmers primarily managed seeds by either producing enough for the next year's crop, or governments distributed seeds, as did the United States.[25] "Until 1924, farmers received seed from the [U.S.] Government's extensive free seed program that distributed millions of packages of seed annually ... In 1930, seed companies were not primarily concerned with varietal protection, but were still trying to successfully commodify seeds. There was no need to protect seed breeding because there were few markets for seeds."[26]

Scientific advances in seed hybridization began to emerge in the mid-1930s.[27] Successful attempts at modification such as Norman Borlaug's famed wheat adaptation, and further advancements sparked by James Watson's and Francis Crick's

& Shirin Rai, *The Political Economy of Intellectual Property Rights: A Gender Perspective* in P. Newell et al. (eds), DEVELOPMENT AND THE CHALLENGE OF GLOBALISATION 42 (2002).

20 *IBPGR: International Board for Plant Genetic Resources*, available at https://cgspace.cgiar.org/handle/10568/45742.

21 ASHOK KUMAR, INTELLECTUAL PROPERTY RIGHTS 191 (1993).

22 FAO, *Staple Foods: What Do People Eat?*, available at http://www.fao.org/docrep/u8480e/u8480e07.htm.

23 Overseas Development Institute, *Patenting Plants: The Implications for Developing Countries* (Nov. 17, 1993), available at https://www.odi.org/sites/odi.org.uk/files/odi-assets/publications-opinion-files/6819.pdf.

24 *Id.*

25 Center for Food Safety, *History of U.S. Seed Development and Patent Regimes*, available at http://www.centerforfoodsafety.org/issues/303/seeds/history-of-us-seed-development-and-patent-regimes#.

26 J.E.M. Ag Supply, Inc. v. Pioneer Hi-Bred Int'l, Inc 534 U.S. 124, 136 (2001).

27 Donald Duvick, *Biotechnology in the 1930s: The Development of Hybrid Maize*, 2 NATURE REVIEW GENETICS 69–74 (2001); Laura Tangley, *Agricultural Biotechnology: Who's Holding the Reins?*, 36 BIOSCIENCE 652, 652 (1986).

discovery of double helix of DNA in the 1950s, prompted commercial interest in plant breeding and subsequently fueled the privatization of the seed industry.[28] Countries began to introduce *sui generis* protections and rights for commercial plant breeders in the 1950s, utilizing more flexible eligibility standards, with the purpose of stimulating and protecting the investments of professional breeders.[29]

At the international level, the growing interest in protecting the activities of plant breeding firms took shape in the International Convention for the Protection of New Varieties of Plants, or UPOV, previewed in Chapter 5.[30] Amended several times throughout its history, its two most significant changes, 1978 and 1991, applied first a "copyright-like approach" and later a "patent-like approach" to plant variety protection.[31]

The "copyright-like approach" 1978 amendment required plant materials be "novel, stable, homogenous, and distinct in at least one characteristic."[32] It afforded breeders "phenotypical" protection over the "complete living organism," as opposed to its genetic makeup.[33] Under this approach, the protected plant could be "freely accessed and used" to develop new, and also protectable, varieties that only needed to differ from the origin plant by at least one major trait.[34] This model, subsequently, only prohibited wholesale plant duplication and did not protect against farmers' use of seed, while allowing protected plants to be utilized in research and breeding.[35]

Conversely, the 1991 "patent-like approach" extended the term of protection (from fifteen to twenty years) and expanded the scope of protected plants to include the entire plant and parts of the plants, in addition to allowing countries to extend protection to products made from the materials of protected plants.[36] The 1991 Act

[28] Norman Borlaug, *The World Food Prize – Improving the Quality, Quantity and Availability of Food in the World*, available at http://www.worldfoodprize.org/index.cfm?nodeID=25304&audienceID=1.

[29] Jagjit Kaur Plahe, *TRIPS Downhill: India's Plant Variety Protection System and Implications for Small Farmers*, 41 Journal of Contemporary Asia 75–98 (2011).

[30] International Convention for the Protection of New Varieties of Plants, Act of 1991, art. 24(3), Dec. 02, 1961, 815 U.N.T.S. 89 (hereinafter UPOV Convention "UPOV is the French acronym for the Union Internationale pour la Protection des Obtentions Végétales." Juliana Santilli, Agrobiodiversity and the Law; Regulating Genetic Resources, Food Security and Cultural Diversity 77 (2012).

[31] Jerome H. Reichman, *Legal Hybrids between Patent and Copyright Paradigms*, 94 Colum. L. Rev. 2432, 2467–72 (1994).

[32] International Convention for the Protection of New Varieties of Plants, *adopted on* Dec. 2, 1961, *as revised on* Oct. 23, 1978, art. 1(4)(iv), available at http://www.upov.int/upovlex/en/conventions/1978/content.html.

[33] Jerome Reichman et al., Governing Digitally Integrated Genetic Resources, Data, and Literature: Global Intellectual Property Strategies for a Redesigned Microbial Research Commons 54 (2016).

[34] *Id.* at 54–55.

[35] *Id.*

[36] International Convention for the Protection of New Varieties of Plants, *adopted on* Dec. 2, 1961, *as revised on* Mar. 19, 1991, *available at* http://www.upov.int/upovlex/en/conventions/1991/content.html.

also protected against any "sale, selling, exporting, importing, or stocking" of plant materials.[37] Infringement under the new act also covered breeders' initial rights to derivatives of their varieties by prohibiting the reproduction or sale of any variety developed from a protected plant.[38] The act further removed de facto exemptions that allowed for the free exchange of seeds by farmers.[39] The amendment also did away with prohibitions on overlapping protection from patent rights and breeders' rights, explicitly allowing a single plant variety to be protected by both systems.[40] This protection gives the breeder the right to require authorization over the variety's "production or reproduction; conditioning for the purpose of propagation; offering for sale; selling or other marketing; exporting; importing; or stocking for any of the purposes"[41] for the production or reproduction and conditioning for the purpose of propagation of the variety. Thus, entities wishing to use the variety must obtain a license, or contract for the use of the variety, with the breeder.

UPOV foreshadowed the extent to which international agreements could reach into what would have conventionally been understood to be the sovereign, national lawmaking process (the Paris and Berne Conventions provided broad requirements but did not establish a centralized system of statutory or regulatory review).[42] States seeking admission into the Convention must develop a draft law that conforms to the 1991 Convention.[43] UPOV provides assistance in drafting laws for countries seeking to comply with the terms of the treaty.[44] The draft law must be translated into one of the four languages utilized by UPOV. After the analysis of the law is complete, UPOV creates a document analyzing the law and posts it to the UPOV website in order to allow members and observers to the treaty the opportunity to consider and comment on the law.[45] The law then moves to UPOV's Consultative Committee for examination.[46] The Committee makes recommendations for the Council – the treaty's governing body – to consider when scrutinizing the law for adherence to UPOV standards.[47]

While the farmers' exception has narrowed, the breeders' exception has remained: access to genetic material from protected plant varieties in order to develop new varieties of plants is protected.[48] In Article 15 of the Convention, the exclusive monopoly granted over plant varieties do not extend to "acts done privately

37 Reichman et al., *supra* note 34, at 55.
38 *Id.*
39 The act instead allows governments to deny famers rights to reuse seed and require royalties to the breeders for reuse. *Id.* at 56.
40 *Id.*
41 *Id.* at art. 14(1)(i)–(vii).
42 UPOV/INF/13/1 (Oct. 22, 2009).
43 *Id.* at § A(4).
44 *Id.* at § A(5).
45 *Id.* at § B(12).
46 *Id.* at § B(13). The Consultative Committee is made up of members of the Council.
47 *Id.* at § B(14).
48 Santilli, *supra* note 31, at 85.

and for non-commercial purposes and acts done for experimental purposes, and acts done for the purpose of breeding other varieties."[49] As elaborated more thoroughly in Chapter 11, individual states may grant farmers certain retention and exchange rights, and many developing countries have done so.

The establishment of UPOV as well as the laws it later influenced raised the specter of a conflict between farmers, who had developed desirable traits through retention and exchange, and plant breeders, who gained financially by making various aspects of breeding proprietary.[50] This confrontation was already well under way when TRIPS was negotiated, and it was essentially codified in Article 27.3(b), which allowed countries to exclude from patentable subject matter "plants and animals other than micro-organisms, and essentially biological processes for the production of plants or animals other than non-biological and microbiological processes," but required protection for plant varieties either through patents or through a *sui generis* system like the UPOV and left "micro-organisms" undefined.[51] Developing nations argued at the time of its adoption that Article 27.3(b) necessarily entailed matters implicated by the Convention on Biological Diversity, including prior informed consent and benefit sharing.[52] Indeed, as early as 1999 – four years after TRIPS became international law – African countries sought to revisit the scope and reach of Article 27:

> The African Group seized the opportunity of the provision and prepared a strongly worded communication during the preparations for the WTO Ministerial Meeting in Seattle [in 1999], which vehemently questioned the overall provisions of Article 27.3(b). The Group suggested that the revision of the article should take into account the Convention on Biological Diversity as well as the FAO International Undertaking. Insinuating that a review of 27.3(b) could lead to changes in its substantive nature, the Group highlighted the artificial distinctions that it made "between biological and microbiological organisms and processes."[53]

Patented seeds and tailored pesticides, insecticides, and fungicides, at a general level, interrupt or displace traditional forms of agriculture predominant in low- and middle-income countries. Philippe Cullet described the change from traditional forms of agriculture, including seed exchange and crop rotation, to dependence on patented seeds and related products in Africa:

[49] UPOV Convention, art. 15(1)(i)–(iii), *supra* note 37, at 1.

[50] Hans Morten Haugen, *The Right to Food, Farmers' Rights and Intellectual Property Rights: Can Competing Law Be Reconciled?* In Nadia C. S. Lambek, Priscilla Claeys, Adrienna Wong & Lea Brilmayer (eds), Rethinking Food Systems: Structural Challenges, New Strategies and the Law 195–218 (2014).

[51] C. Niranjan Rao, *Patents for Biotechnology Patents in TRIPS*, 37(22) Economic and Political Weekly, 2126–29 (2002).

[52] Jagjit Kaur Plahe & Chris Nyland, *The WTO and Patenting of Life Forms: Policy Options for Developing Countries*, 24(1) Third World Quarterly 29–45 (2003).

[53] *Id.*

> The introduction of plant variety protection in African countries is a novelty for all but a few states. It constitutes a significant departure from previous practice which generally emphasized the free sharing of knowledge at all levels. The challenge is further compounded by the fact that plant variety protection has until now only been introduced in countries with relatively small but highly industrialized agricultural sectors.[54]

Fertilizers and pesticides long enjoyed patent protection of the same type extended to small-molecule pharmaceutical compounds, so the growing protection of new varieties of crops created a mutually reinforcing product concentration – manufacturers tailored proprietary seed varieties to patented fertilizer and pesticides tailored to the seeds.[55] These agricultural packages are sold at relatively high prices. These laws, however, do not necessarily protect farmers from contractual constraints requiring that no harvested seed be used for replanting or resale.[56] As noted earlier, the farmer's exception was protected in the earlier versions of UPOV, but the 1991 amendment left the decision of granting the right to replant seeds to the respective members.

The arguments for made for patent and data exclusivity protections for agrochemicals and seeds are similar to those made for medicines. It has been estimated that the costs to bring a single active ingredient for a synthetic pesticide to market are $250 million, a cost that includes tests on at least 140,000 synthesized compounds to find each success.[57] While most fertilizers used in the world today were developed by the Tennessee Valley Authority between 1950 and 1970 with public funding, that program and corresponding public support ended decades ago.[58] Next-generation fertilizers are therefore being developed through patented processes resulting in patented products with correspondingly higher prices.[59]

As with medicines, "data exclusivity" provisions are being added to bilateral investment and trade treaties between developed and developing countries to allow agrochemical firms to extend the period that they may charge high prices for their products.[60] Data exclusivity serves as an alternative form of exclusive rights that

54 Philippe Cullet, *Plant Variety Protection in Africa: Toward Compliance with the TRIPS Agreement*, 45 J. African L. 97 (2001).

55 David Goodman & Michael Redclift, Refashioning Nature: Food, Ecology and Culture (2002) ("the aim is to create an agricultural package reaching from fertilizers to pesticides to the plant itself").

56 Bowman v. Monsanto, 133 S. Ct. 1761, 1763, 185 L. Ed. 2d 931 reh'g denied, 134 S. Ct. 24, 186 L. Ed. 2d 937 (2013).

57 C. Lamberth, S. Jeanmart & T. Luksch, *Current Challenges and Trends in the Discovery of Agrochemicals* 341 Science 742–46 (2013).

58 IFDC, *Fertilizer Technology Used Worldwide, but Few New Sources*, Science News (Aug. 26, 2008), available at https://www.sciencedaily.com/releases/2008/08/080825103527.htm.

59 Ashok Kumar, Intellectual Property Rights 192 (1993); Maria DeRosa, Carlos Monreal, Morris Schnitzer, Ryan Walsh & Yasir Sultan, *Nanotechnology in Fertilizers*, 5 Nat. Nanotechnol. 91 (2010).

60 Bharti Jain, *Impact of Granting Data Exclusivity in Agro-Chemical Sector*, 21 J. Intell. Prop. Rights 38–41 (2016); Jerome H. Reichman, *Rethinking the Role of Clinical Trial Data in International Intellectual Property Law: The Case for a Public Goods Approach*, 13 Marq. Int. Prop. L. Rev. 1, 2 (2009).

impede the entry of competitors into the market for as long as the exclusivity lasts.[61] Multinational firms have been seeking data exclusivity for their pharmaceuticals and agrochemicals, and while there is no data exclusivity requirement in the TRIPS agreement, it does require that governments protect such data "from unfair commercial use by competitors."[62] The introduction of data exclusivity provisions delays the introduction of more affordable generic products in poorer nations, and since they can be granted with or without a patent, these provisions afford companies additional protection after or alongside patent protection.

Relatedly, there is substantial evidence to suggest that the growing influence of intellectual property into a market traditionally characterized by more open systems of research and sharing is limiting crucial research and innovation. In 2004, 18 percent of academic requests for genetic materials were denied, while industry requests were similarly denied 33 percent of the time.[63] In fact, 93 percent of academics in the field of agricultural biology view intellectual property rights as having a negative impact on their research efforts.[64] Yet yields of such staple crops as rice and wheat have now plateaued in some intensively farmed parts of the world. The spread of existing best practices might increase yields up to these plateau levels, but to exceed them will require improved technology.[65]

Accompanying the higher prices available through intellectual property protection of seeds, fertilizers, and pesticides is substantial consolidation in the providers of all of these products.

> When an Indian farmer plants his cotton crop, there's at least a 75% chance the seeds have been bought from a company owned by Monsanto. If a Latin American farmer sprays insecticide on her genetically engineered soya beans, the chemical is more than likely to have been provided by German chemical and drugs company Bayer or by US firm DuPont. And when African farmers add chemicals to their maize fields or plant it's odds-on that they have come from Swiss company Syngenta.[66]

Robust intellectual property protections for agricultural inputs including seeds and pesticides have allowed large agrochemical firms to enter, shape, and in some cases exercise substantial control over markets in developing countries.[67] Patented or plant

[61] *Id.*

[62] TRIPS art. 39.

[63] John P. Walsh, Wesley M. Cohen & Charlene Cho, *When Exclusivity Matters: Material versus Intellectual Property in Academic Biomedical Research*, 36 Res. Pol'y 1191 (2007).

[64] Zhen Lei, Rakhi Juneja & Brian D. Wright, *Patent Versus Patenting: Impediments of Intellectual Property Protection for Biological Research*, 27 Nature Biotechnology 36, 38–39 (2009).

[65] Economist, *The Future of Agriculture* (2016), available at http://www.economist.com/technology-quarterly/2016-06-09/factory-fresh.

[66] John Vidal, *Farming Mega-Mergers Threaten Food Security, Campaigners Say*, The Guardian (Sep. 26, 2016), available at https://www.theguardian.com/global-development/2016/sep/26/farming-mega-mergers-threaten-food-security-say-campaigners.

[67] FAO, Promoting the Growth and Development of Smallholder Seed Enterprises for Food Security Crops 3 (2010).

variety protected seeds displace heirloom seeds, shifting agricultural markets from traditional save-and-exchange to annual purchase-from-firm (or intermediary) systems.[68] This shift, in turn, causes higher prices for the latter to extract greater profits from farmers.[69] Modified seeds often require more herbicide and pesticide.[70] This matters because appropriate use of protective clothes for pesticide application "is almost unknown," in many developing countries leading to common incidents of poisoning and hospitalization in some part of the region.[71] In Mali specifically, 40 percent of the cost paid by farmers for pesticides products are pesticide externalities.[72]

The risk of crop diversity erosion also increases following the growth of agricultural intellectual property protections. As more farms are cultivated with commercial seeds, a growing number of farmers will "grow the same crops, using the same improved varieties on their fields."[73] Recent efforts have focused on development and sale of "a limited number of standard, high-yielding varieties," resulting in a little over 150 species currently being cultivated.[74] Currently, most of the world is fed on "no more than twelve plant varieties."[75] An estimated 75 percent of all plant genetic diversity has been lost due to the selection of genetically uniform varieties, and their higher yields, over local varieties.[76] For example, Sri Lanka saw its 2,000 rice varieties in 1959 reduced to less than 100 varieties by 1992, 75 percent of which were descended from a common stock.[77] Similarly, 62 percent of rice varieties in Bangladesh and 74 percent of Indonesian rice varieties are currently descended from a common stock.[78] In Zimbabwe, 90 percent of all maize seeds are derived from two hybrid varieties, resulting in displacement of "many traditional varieties of millet and sorghum."[79]

[68] Michael Tortorello, *What Comes after Heirloom Seeds?*, THE NEW YORKER (Sept. 10, 2015), available at http://www.newyorker.com/tech/elements/luther-burbank-what-comes-after-heirloom-seeds; *Cherokee Nation to Disperse Rare, Traditional Seeds*, available at http://www.cherokee.org/News/Stories/123113CherokeeNationtodisperserare,traditionalseeds.aspx.

[69] Jane Ayeko-Kummeth, *Less Choice for African Farmers after Bayer's Monsanto Takeover*, DEUTSCHE WELLE (June 15, 2016), available at http://www.dw.com/en/less-choice-for-african-farmers-after-bayers-monsanto-takeover/a-19555537.

[70] Philip J. Landrigan & Charles Benbrook, *GMOs, Herbicides, and Public Health*, 373 NEW ENG. J. MED. 693–95 (2015);

[71] Jules Pretty & Zareen Pervez Bharucha, *Integrated Pest Management for Sustainable Intensification of Agriculture in Asia and Africa*, 6 INSECTS 4 (2015).

[72] *Id.*

[73] Production levels and stability of crops requires genetic diversity in order to allow crops to be "resistant to specific diseases, drought, or variations in temperature."

[74] Olivier De Schutter, *The Right of Everyone to Enjoy the Benefits of Scientific Progress and the Right to Food: From Conflict to Complementarity*, 33 HUMAN RIGHTS Q. 304, 313 (2011).

[75] The four major staple crops – wheat, rice, maize, and potato – account for "a lion share" of these varieties.

[76] FAO, *Crop Biodiversity: Use It or Lose It* (Oct. 26, 2010), available at http://www.fao.org/news/story/en/item/46803/icode/.

[77] Schutter, *supra* note 75.

[78] *Id.*

[79] Patenting Plants: The Implication for Developing Countries, Overseas Development Institute, Briefing Paper 2 (Nov. 1993).

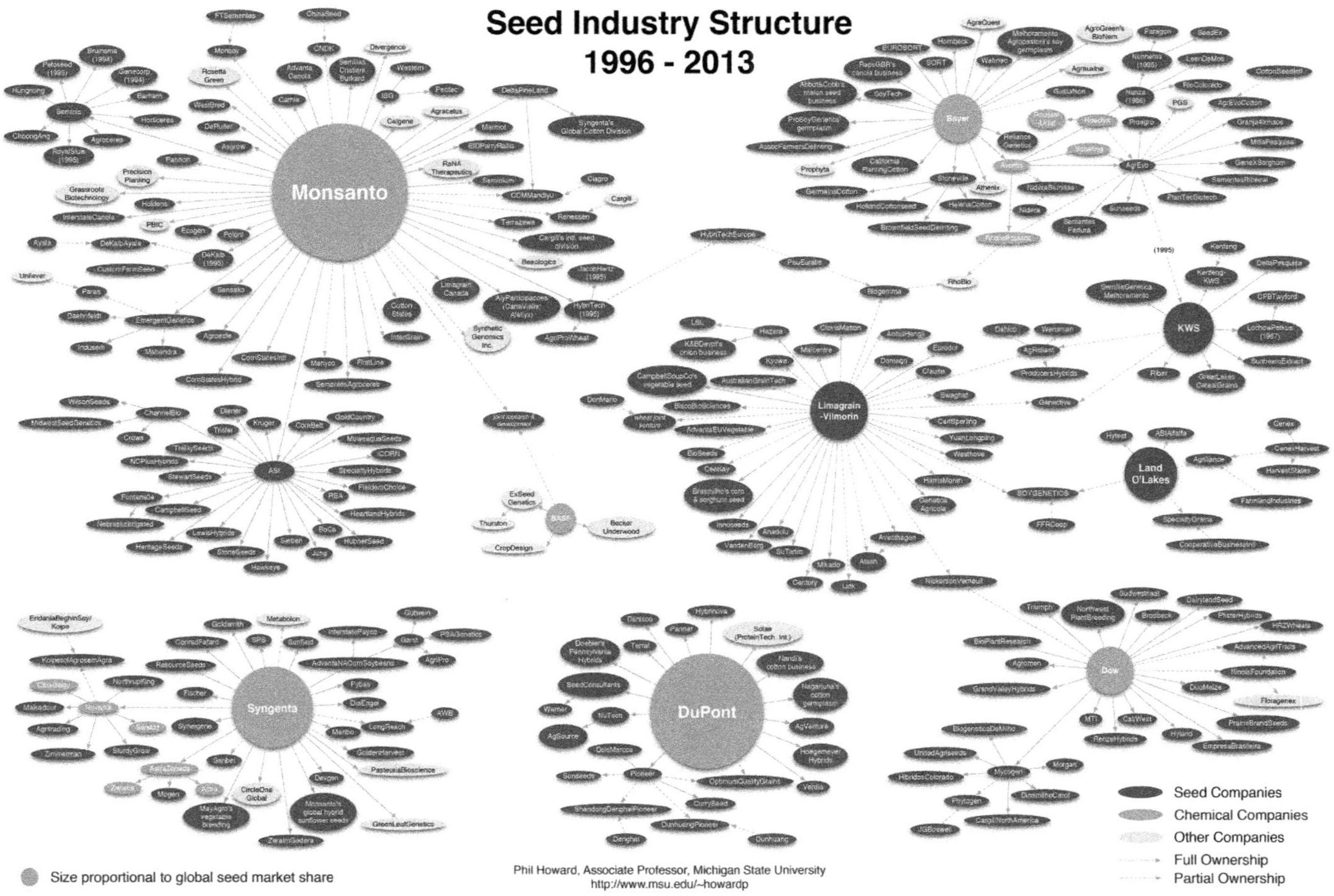

FIGURE 7.1 Concentration in the global seed sector

As with markets for infant formula and specific medicines and vaccines described in Chapters 5 and 6, the global markets for genetically modified seeds and tied chemical products have become concentrated.[80] Three corporations control nearly 50 percent of the global market.[81] Dow, DuPont, Syngenta, Monsanto, Bayer, and BASF together control 75 percent of the global pesticide market and 70 percent of the global seed market [Figure 7.1].[82]

Moreover, until recently, the division between consumer product pharmaceutical and agrochemical corporations was not so clear.[83] The Swiss pharmaceutical giant Novartis is a name adopted after a merger between Ciba-Geigy and Sandoz, which consolidated massive pharmaceutical and agrochemical units.[84] In 2000, Novartis spun off its agrochemical unit into Syngenta, the world's third-largest seed and agrochemical company that draws more than half its sales from emerging markets.[85] "Syngenta sells its products (cereals, corn, rice, soybeans, vegetables, as well as herbicides and pesticides) in more than 90 countries under such brand names as Acuron, Axial, Beacon and Callisto."[86] Syngenta merged with ChemChina to form the world's largest agrochemical company.[87] The merged entity will directly or indirectly control 75 percent of the market in Vietnam, as only one example.[88] Monsanto, formerly the largest agrochemical firm, is now in negotiations to merge with Bayer. A successful merger would create the world's largest agrichemical firm, which will control more than one-fourth of the combined global market for seeds and pesticides.[89] If EU and US regulators allow the Bayer-Monsanto "mega-merger," three firms will control of almost 60 percent of global seed production, "nearly 70 percent of the chemicals and pesticides needed to grow food," and almost all of the genetically modified crop genetic traits in

80 James MacDonald, Mergers and Competition in Seed and Agricultural Markets (2017), available at https://www.ers.usda.gov/amber-waves/2017/april/mergers-and-competition-in-seed-and-agricultural-chemical-markets/.
81 Jack Lerner, *Intellectual Property and Development at* WHO *and* WIPO, 34 Am J. L. and Med. 257, 260 (2008).
82 https://www.gmxconsulting.co.uk/single-post/2017/03/30/Impact-of-agrochemical-mega-mergers-on-developing-countries.
83 Peter Andree, Genetically Modified Diplomacy: The Global Politics of Agricultural Biotechnology and the Environment 46 (2011).
84 Novartis, *Novartis Company History*, available at https://www.novartis.com/about-us/who-we-are/novartis-company-history.
85 Reuters, *Syngenta's Earnings to Miss Expectations*, (Oct. 17, 2013), available at http://www.reuters.com/article/us-syngenta-results-idUSBRE99G06620131017.
86 Reuters, *ChemChina Clinches its $43 Billion Takeover of Syngenta*, Fortune (May 4, 2017), available at http://fortune.com/2017/05/05/chemchina-syngenta-deal-acquisition/.
87 https://www.rt.com/business/387219-chemchina-syngenta-takeover-completed/.
88 Quan Le, *Impact of Agrochemical Mega-mergers on Developing Countries* (Mar. 29, 2017), available at https://www.gmxconsulting.co.uk/single-post/2017/03/30/Impact-of-agrochemical-mega-mergers-on-developing-countries.
89 Zhai Yun Tan, *Bayer-Monsanto Merger: Concerns about a Seed-and-Pesticide Food Monopoly*, Christian Science Monitor (Sept. 15, 2016), available at https://www.csmonitor.com/Business/2016/0915/Bayer-Monsanto-merger-Concerns-about-a-seed-and-pesticide-food-monopoly.

the world.[90] Cross-licensing between these firms in specific product sectors means even tighter concentration than market share alone suggests.[91]

As with medicines, litigation or the threat of litigation is each a critical tool for enforcing intellectual property rights. In 2013, Monsanto was estimated to have collected $23.7 million from judgments against (U.S.) farmers. It collected somewhere between $85 and $160 million via out-of-court settlements through 2006.[92] While Monsanto has been the leader in these types of lawsuits, DuPont has adopted the same strategy, also hiring private detectives tasked with "polic[ing] farmers' fields for evidence of seed saving."[93] Typically, when farmers buy genetically modified seeds, they must sign an agreement that disallows seed saving or sharing.[94] In India, Monsanto uses investigators to find those who violate the agreement and vigorously prosecutes those who violate it.[95] In other developing countries with weak judicial systems, firms turn to alternative means of ensuring revenue streams.[96] For example, in Brazil, Monsanto collaborated with the top four largest grain traders in the world to begin charging "indemnity fees" as a means of collecting royalties on soybeans that had been obtained from other farmers.[97]

As with medicines, there has been significant mobilization against enhanced intellectual property rights in agriculture based on their interference with basic human needs approaches to development (as well as their exploitation of traditional knowledge discussed in Chapter 11). Farmers' rights groups have vehemently lobbied against so-called "Monsanto Laws" in their respective states against adoption of plant variety protection laws that would be meet UPOV standards.[98] After the devastating 2010 Haitian earthquake, Monsanto offered to donate 475 tons of its seeds to Haiti.[99] Haitian farmers called for the seeds to be burned.[100]

From low- and middle-income countries' perspective, implementing intellectual property–protected seeds and agricultural products to relatively undeveloped

90 John Vidal, *Farming Mega-mergers Threaten Food Security, Say Campaigners*, The Guardian (Sept. 26, 2016), available at https://www.theguardian.com/global-development/2016/sep/26/farming-mega-mergers-threaten-food-security-say-campaigners.

91 Philip Howard, *Intellectual Property and Consolidation in the Seed Industry*, 55 Crop Science 1–7 (2015).

92 D. Barker, B. Freese, & G. Kimbrell, Seed giants vs. U.S. farmers (2013).

93 Howard, *supra* note 92.

94 Muzaffar Assadi, *Seed Tribunal: Interrogating Farmers' Suicides*, Economic and Political Weekly, 35, at 3808 (2000); Phillipe Cullet, *Farmer Liability and GM Contamination: Schemeiser Judgment*, 39 Economic and Political Weekly 2551 (2004).

95 *Id.*

96 Suman Sahai, *The Seeds of Discontent*, 33 India International Centre Quarterly 162, 163 (2007).

97 *Id.*

98 David Jefferson, *Development, Farmers' Rights, and the Ley Monsanto: The Struggle Over the Ratification of UPOV 91 in Chile* 55 (1) IDEA 39 (2014).

99 *Haitian Farmers Commit to Burning Monsanto Hybrid Seeds*, huffingtonpost.com, http://www.huffingtonpost.com/beverly-bell/haitian-farmers-commit-to_b_578807.html.

100 *Id.*

agricultural markets is to essentially redistribute wealth from farmers to the small number of global seed and agribusiness firms that dominate global markets. Farmers pay high prices for seeds and products to treat the crops that grow from them while prices for the resulting commodities are pressured lower by a small number of global food firms.[101] Increased intellectual property protection "necessarily lead[s] to transfers of resources from technology users to technology producers," a phenomenon observed both within individual nations and at the international level.[102] These factors act to "reinforce the domination of a limited number of northern firms in the global food system," as these firms enjoy control over improved seed varieties and biotechnological innovation.[103] Additionally, the presence of commercial seed systems in the developing world may influence a "shift in decision making about which crops to grow and sell to men [from women]."[104] In many of these countries, women play crucial roles in determining which seed and germplasm are produced, selected, and saved, as well as controlling growth and preservation of "underutilized species that local communities use to supplement their diets."[105]

[101] Olivier De Schutter, *The Right of Everyone to Enjoy the Benefits of Scientific Progress and the Right to Food: From Conflict to Complementarity*, 33 Human Rights Q. 304, 311 (2011).
[102] *Id.* at 311–12.
[103] *Id.* at 312.
[104] *Id.*
[105] *Id.*

8

Consumer Products

Although trademarks (and the associated allegations of counterfeiting) provided the principal justification for shifting the international intellectual property regime from development to trade over the course of the 1970s, trademarks had not, until that point, played a significant role in disputes between wealthier and poorer countries. Patents and copyrights, with their clearer relationship with technology transfer and the establishment of domestic industry, had led to calls for revisions to the major international treaties as well as occupying significant efforts at UNCTAD.[1] As sources of wealth have become less tangible, however, signs, images, sounds, appearance, and display have become crucial factors distinguishing competing products in the market. This is why the movement for stronger intellectual property protections by firms over the course of the 1970s was anchored primarily in trademark (and to a lesser extent copyright): those firms asserted that goods were being manufactured and sold using misappropriated images, colors, logos, and signs.[2]

Historically, the justifications for trademark protection differed from those for patents and copyrights. Trademark law focused on the effect a mark or tradename had on consumers, providing an inexpensive source of product information that the law reasonably protected from imitators. This protection benefited both firms and consumers.[3] Over the course of the late 1970s through the establishment of TRIPS and after, trademark law in wealthy countries increasingly focused (in common with arguments for strong patent and copyright protection) on the investments made by the trademark holder and the corresponding (though speculative) goodwill

[1] Ruth L. Okediji, *Public Welfare and the Role of the WTO Reconsidering the TRIPS Agreement*, 17 Emory Int. L. Rev. 819 (2003).

[2] William Walker, *Private Initiative to Thwart the Trade in Counterfeit Goods*, 4 The World Economy 29–48 (1981).

[3] Eugene C. Lim, *Dilution, the* Section 22 *Debacle, and the Protection of Business Goodwill in Canada: Some Insights from U.S. Trademark Law and Policy*, 101 Trademark Rep. 1232, 1268 (2011).

generated by those investments.[4] The result of this "propertization" of trademark is the ability of trademark proprietors to take legal action against not only competitors but also third parties with attenuated and difficult-to-prove effects on the value of a mark as well as governments who might diminish the value of a mark through regulation.[5]

Strong trademark protections carry substantial implications for basic human needs as envisioned both before and after the establishment of the Millennium Development Goals. In product sectors such as alcohol, infant nutritional substitutes, food, nonalcoholic beverages, and tobacco, trademarks and tradenames can impliedly convey dubious health information. They may also obscure (and thus undermine) warnings intended to achieve better-informed health decisions. These effects are often intended. For example, where it is still permitted, cigarette manufacturers use the words "light" and "mild" and associated colors in their trademarks to suggest those cigarettes are less harmful than "full flavor" cigarettes.[6] Similarly, combinations of signs, colors, and adjectives shape consumers' perceptions of the nutritional value of packaged food and the inherent safety of consuming alcohol, as well as thresholds beyond which consumption is unsafe.[7] Because of the highly consolidated global structure of these industries and the nature of the products sold, consumers cannot rely on truthful, comparative advertising to expose health risks.[8] Even in sectors where products are not ingested or inhaled, trademarks may obscure relevant product information, shape consumers' perception of short- and long-term health risks, or suggest attributes that are costly or impossible to verify.[9]

These problems are magnified in the context of developing countries [Figure 8.1].[10] Consumers in those countries, even where literate, face more severe imbalances in economic terms, educational levels, and bargaining power.[11] At the global level, the adult literacy rate increased from post–World War II decolonization forward:

4 Nicholas S. Economides, *The Economics of Trademarks*, 78 TRADEMARK REP. 523 (1988); WILLIAM M. LANDES & RICHARD A. POSNER, THE ECONOMIC STRUCTURE OF INTELLECTUAL PROPERTY LAW 167–68 (2003); Laura A. Heymann, *The Birth of the Authornym: Authorship, Pseudonymity, and Trademark Law*, 80 NOTRE DAME L. REV. 1377, 1414 (2005).

5 Ruth Okediji, *The International Intellectual Property Roots of Geographical Indicators*, 82 CHICAGO-KENT L. REV. 1329, 1332 (2008).

6 *United States v. Philip Morris USA, Inc.*, 449 F. Supp. 2d 1, 26–27 (D.D.C. 2006).

7 Gill Cowburn & Lynn Stockley, *Consumer Understanding and Use of Nutrition Labelling: A Systematic Review*, 8 PUBLIC HEALTH NUTRITION 21, 21–22 (2005); David Jernigan & James O'Hara, *Alcohol Advertising and Promotion*, in Richard J. Bonnie & Mary Ellen O'Connell (eds), REDUCING UNDERAGE DRINKING: A COLLECTIVE RESPONSIBILITY (2004).

8 Mark Armstrong, *Interactions Between Competition and Consumer Policy*, 4 COMPETITION POLICY INTL 87, 103 (2008).

9 Michael R. Darby & Edi Karni, *Free Competition and the Optimal Amount of Fraud*, 16 J. L. & ECON. 67, 68–69 (1973).

10 Kojo Yelpaala, *Quo Vadis WTO? The Threat of TRIPS and the Biodiversity Convention to Human Health and Food Security*, 30 B.U. INT'L L.J. 55, 85–86 (2012).

11 U.N. General Assembly Resolution on Consumer Protection, A/RES/39/248 16 Apr. 19 1985.

from 56 percent in 1950 to 70 percent in 1980, and to 82 percent through 2006.[12] While the more developed countries had already attained more than 90 percent adult literacy rates in the 1950s, rates in developing countries then averaged lower than 50 percent but have since increased to more than 75 percent.[13] Far more women than men are illiterate. Their literacy rate has increased from 58 percent in 1960 to 64 percent today.[14] To the extent safe product consumption depends on certain consumer capabilities, like reading labels, populations in developing countries are more susceptible to advertising accomplished through the use of colors and images.

For many areas of consumer products, expanding the property protections of trademarks benefits consumers.[15] Consumers who know that a particular brand of implement or electronic, for example, offers a balance of quality and price spend less time searching for products or information about products.[16] Trademark law protects firms from imitation by competitors as well as the expectations that consumers build into those brands.[17] Advocates of broader trademark protection argue that this, in turn, encourages manufacturers to invest in advertising (cheap consumer information) and quality and, correspondingly, lowers consumer information costs across a wider range of products and services.[18] Internationally, trademark protection reduces the costs for manufacturers to do business across national boundaries; their brands facilitate entry into new markets.[19]

However, it is precisely in the economic sectors most likely to affect basic human needs (in particular, health) that the welfare-enhancing benefits of trademark protection give way to efforts to suggest false product attributes, hide health-related risks, and shape consumer perceptions about the relationship between consumption levels and health effects. A 1999 study, for example, determined that the "three most valuable brand names were Marlboro, Coca-Cola and Budweiser, in that order."[20]

12 UNESCO, MAPPING THE GLOBAL LITERACY CHALLENGE 165 (2006), available at http://www.unesco.org/education/GMR2006/full/chapt7_eng.pdf.

13 *Id.*

14 *Id.*

15 Jeremy Sheff, *Biasing Brands*, 32 CARDOZO L. REV. 1245, 1250 (2011).

16 Simon P. Anderson & Régis Renault, *Pricing, Product Diversity, and Search Costs: A Bertrand-Chamberlin-Diamond Model*, 30 RAND J. ECONOMICS 719–35 (1999).

17 George Miaoulis & Nancy D'Amato, *Consumer Protection and Trademark Infringement*, 42(2) J. MARKETING 48–55 (1978).

18 Irene Calboli, *Trademark Assignment "with Goodwill": A Concept Whose Time Has Gone*, 57 FLORIDA L. REV. 771, 773–74 (2005).

19 Keith E. Maskus, *Intellectual Property Challenges for Developing Countries: An Economic Perspective*, 2001 U. ILLINOIS L. REV. 457, 461 (2001).

20 Kevin Casey, *Problem Trademarks of the Descriptive-Misdescriptive-Deceptive Types*, 7 PENNSYLVANIA BAR ASSOCIATION INTELLECTUAL PROPERTY L. NEWSLETTER 7 (2012).

The extraordinarily competitive environment of consumer products guarantees that in certain economic sectors, firms will use trademarks to increase consumer demand in ways other than quality improvement.[21] Common tactics include minimizing or obfuscating mandatory health warnings, using descriptors likely to lead to false impressions, and shaping containers – for example, to mimic famous perfume packaging – to appeal to target populations.[22] Trademark holders can communicate certain product qualities by way of design suggestion and implication, circumventing prohibitions against explicitly deceptive representations.[23]

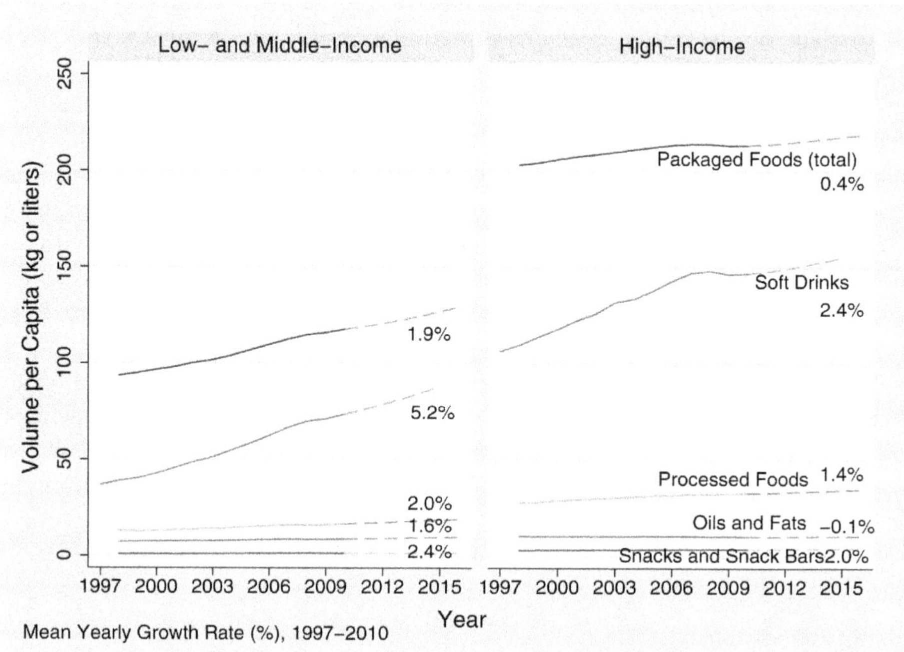

FIGURE 8.1 Global consumption trends of packaged foods, soft drinks, processed foods, and snacks.[24]

[21] Jon Hanson & Douglas Kysar, *Taking Behavioralism Seriously: Some Evidence of Market Manipulation*, 112 HARV. L REV. 1420, 1466 (1999).

[22] American Heart Association, *Deadly in Pink: Big Tobacco Steps Up its Targeting of Women and Girls*, available at http://www.lung.org/assets/documents/publications/other-reports/deadly-in-pink.pdf; WHO, GENDER, WOMEN, AND THE TOBACCO EPIDEMIC 106 (2010).

[23] Rebecca Tushnet, *Running the Gamut from A to B: Federal Trademark and False Advertising Law* 159 U PENN. L. REV. 1305, 1318–19 (2011); Mark Armstrong, *supra* note 8, at 106.

[24] http://journals.plos.org/plosmedicine/article?id=10.1371/journal.pmed.1001235.

Tobacco firms, for example, accompanied "light," "low" descriptors in cigarette trademarks with color schemes so that even after lawmakers slowly adopted bans on those marks, the implicit message remained communicated:[25]

> Even after the [EU] ban, Benson & Hedges Lights will be recognizable by their silver color, contrasting with the gold of the regular packs. White-and-gold Marlboro Lights will still suggest "lightness" just by the stark contrast to the red, full-strength Marlboros. The powder-blue Camel Lights with their pastel camel will still look milder than the ornery desert-ocher animalon the regular "Filters" pack.[26]

Strategic marketing is used for other potentially hazardous products as well. The colors and symbols on alcoholic beverage containers also obscure government-mandated warnings.[27] The image of a healthy, smiling infant or cartoon characters held in nursing positions on a formula container may lead consumers to misunderstand the nutritional superiority and risks inherent in food alternatives for infants.[28] Problems associated with the latter scenario are heightened in nations with minimal education outcomes and lack of access to potable water, where erroneously mixed formula or contamination pose a major threat to infants younger than six months of age.[29] In countries where illiteracy rates are high and symbols are a principal means to both warn and sell, trademark protections pose greater barriers to the promotion of individual and public health.[30]

In industry sectors such as soda and tobacco, a trademark's value may compose the majority of a company's worth precisely because the associated advertising, promotion, and marketing costs are indistinguishable from consumer preference for the trademark.[31] As the CEO of a major brewer noted, "A beer is a beer is a beer ... so therefore it is all about brands ... We are not selling beer, we are selling image."[32]

[25] Geoff Winestock, *"Light" Tobacco Ads Found Deceptive, EU Says*, The Wall Street Journal (Nov. 8, 2000), available at http://legacy.library.ucsf.edu/tid/tze92c00/pdf.

[26] *Id.*

[27] Center for Science in the Public Interest, *Alcohol Warning Labels Go Unnoticed, Poll Finds* (Aug. 17, 2001), available at http://www.cspinet.org/booze/batf_labels2001_press.htm; J. Craig Andrews, Richard G. Netemeyer & Srinivas Durvasula, *Believability and Attitudes Toward Alcohol Warning Label Information: The Role of Persuasive Communications Theory* 9 J. Public Policy & Marketing 1, 1 (1990).

[28] WHO, *International Code of Marketing of Breast Milk Substitutes* (WHO 1981), available at http://www.who.int/nutrition/publications/code_english.pdf.

[29] Hubert Barennes et al., *Misperceptions and Misuse of Bear Brand Coffee Creamer as Infant Food: National Cross Sectional Survey of Consumers and Paediatricians in Laos*, 337 British Medical J. a1379 (2008).

[30] Surendra J. Patel, *Trademarks and the Third World*, 7 World Development 653, 653 (1979).

[31] Shawn Baldwin, *"To Promote the Progress of Science and Useful Arts": A Role for Federal Regulation of Intellectual Property as Collateral*, 143 U. Penn. L. Rev. 1701, 1704 (1995).

[32] David Jernigan, Thirsting for markets: The global impact of corporate alcohol 9 (1997).

There is a close relationship between many public health burdens – cancer, chronic obstructive pulmonary disease, diabetes, heart disease, hypertension, obesity, stroke, vehicular accidents – and the products associated with some of the most valuable and well-known trademarks, including alcohol, processed food, and tobacco. Tobacco consumption, which each year kills approximately five million people worldwide, represents the main preventable threat to individual and public health in both developed and developing countries.[33] Alcohol consumption harms more third parties relative to other drugs like cocaine and heroin, and also has substantial deleterious effects on users (such as increased risks of cancer and heart disease) and plays a significant causal role in traffic accidents, burns, poisonings, falls, and drownings.[34] Obesity levels, which are on the rise in both developed and developing countries, play a causal role in heart disease, diabetes, certain cancers, osteoarthritis, and strokes.[35]

Despite the individual and public health issues strong trademark protections implicate, in recent decades trademark protective law has expanded in developed, wealthy countries from its historical focus on protecting consumers' expectations to protecting firms' investments in the creation, advertising, and marketing of goods.[36] This expansion ranges from the incremental to the sweeping.[37] In the United States, the Lanham Act has historically provided injunctive and monetary relief for firms able to prove that a competitor's mark created a "likelihood of confusion" as to the source of trademarked goods or services.[38] In 1995 and 2006, Congress strengthened protections for well-known marks through the Federal Trademark Dilution Act and the Trademark Dilution Revision Act, which enabled trademark holders to enjoin activities that damaged certain trademarks, even absent a "likelihood of confusion."[39] German trademark law offered relatively modest protections based on consumer expectations in brands before 1979, when the German Federal Constitutional Court concluded that trademarks constituted

33 Theodore Tulchinsky & Elena Varavikova, The New Global Public Health 23 (2008).

34 David Nutt et al., *Drug Harms in the UK: A Multicriteria Decision Analysis* 376 The Lancet 1558, 1560–61 (2010); Charles Parry, *Alcohol Problems in Developing Countries: Challenges for the New Millennium*, 2 SuchtMedizin in Forschung und Praxis 216, 217–18 (2000).

35 Franco Sassi, Obesity and the Economics of Prevention: Fit Not Fat 15 (2010); WHO, WHO Technical Report Series No 916, Diet, Nutrition and the Prevention of Chronic Diseases 64–66 (2003).

36 WC Howarth, *Are* Trademarks Necessary? 60 Trademark Rep. 228, 228–29 (1970). The Campbell Soup Company, for example, knows that "the average shopper views its red and white cans in supermarkets 76 times a year ... making the well-known name and package equivalent" to millions in advertising dollars. Dorothy Cohen, *Trademark Strategy* 50 J. Marketing 61 (1986).

37 Graeme Austin, *Trademarks and the Burdened Imagination* 69 Brooklyn L. Rev. 827, 829–31 (2004).

38 Lanham Act 1946 (US) § 32, 43.

39 Federal Trademark Dilution Act of 1995 (US); Trademark Dilution Revision Act of 2006 (US).

"property" under the Constitution of Germany.[40] As "expression[s] of an entrepreneur's achievement motivation," German law protects as trademark holders artists, holding companies, and advertising firms.[41] The evolution in German law is broadly reflective of movements in EU law, "i.e., de-emphasizing the traditional source identifying function and emphasizing the trademark owner's rights."[42] Under French law, trademarks are protected as strongly as copyrights and patents (although French courts have carved out exceptions for satire and humor).[43]

As with patents and copyrights, wealthy countries included strong trademark protection in bilateral, regional, and multilateral investment and trade agreements.[44] TRIPS, for example, requires members to define minimum criteria for trademark registrability and resulting rights of use; limits the exceptions governments may impose; and establishes an enforcement regime that encourages strong judicial measures to protect intellectual property.[45] TRIPS grants trademark holders rights to prevent confusing uses of an identical or similar mark on identical or similar goods and limits conditions and special requirements states may impose on trademark rights.[46] TRIPS also allows trademark holders to sell and share their trademarks with greater ease than international standards had theretofore allowed.[47] Member states may adopt protections greater than those detailed in TRIPS. Most WTO member states have done so. Regional integration instruments like NAFTA and EU Council Directives have similarly broadened the protections trademark proprietors may use against commercial competitors and regulators.[48] The protective

40 Rudolf Rayle, *The Trend Towards Enhancing Trademark Owners' Rights—A Comparative Study of U.S. and German Trademark Law* 7 J. INTELLECTUAL PROPERTY L. 227, 235–36, fn 40 (2000).

41 *Id.* at 270.

42 First Council Directive 89/104/EEC of 21 December 1988 to approximate the laws of the member states relating to trademarks [1989] OJ L40/1.

43 Annette Kur, *Fundamental Concerns in the Harmonization of (European) Trademark Law in* Graeme Dinwoodie & Mark Janis (eds), TRADEMARK LAW AND THEORY: A HANDBOOK OF CONTEMPORARY RESEARCH 151 (2008).

44 Burton Ong, *The Trademark Law Provisions of Bilateral Free Trade Agreements, in* Graeme B. Dinwoodie & Mark D. Janis (eds), TRADEMARK LAW AND THEORY: A HANDBOOK OF CONTEMPORARY RESEARCH 229–30 (2008).

45 TRIPS art. 41–45; United Nations Conference on Trade and Development and the International Center for Trade and Sustainable Development (UNCTAD-ICTSD), RESOURCE BOOK ON TRIPS AND DEVELOPMENT 739, 748 (2005).

46 TRIPS art. 16(1). Owners of well-known marks receive additional protection against uses of their marks on dissimilar goods. ibid, arts 16(2)–(3). Article 20 limits the encumbrances that can be placed on trademarks. According to Nuno Pires de Carvalho, Article 20 did not contemplate restrictions on health, food, or security measures; rather, restrictions specifically related to a course of trade required, for example, that a foreign trademark be associated with a domestic licensee. Nuno Pires de Carvalho, THE TRIPS REGIME OF TRADEMARKS AND DESIGNS 331 (2006).

47 TRIPS Agreement, art. 21.

48 North American Free Trade Agreement (US–Canada–Mexico) (adopted Dec. 17, 1992, entered into force Jan. 1, 1994) (1993) 32 ILM 289 (NAFTA) art. 1708; Council Directive

scope of trademarks under NAFTA, for example, is significantly wider than TRIPS.[49] Bilateral investment and trade treaties have further augmented these protections by equating trademarks with more secure forms of property and enabling foreign trademark holders to (1) demand that governments justify to international arbitrators the soundness of their regulatory measures and (2) demand compensation for direct and indirect expropriations resulting from regulatory measures.[50]

Interventions that seek to address these health threats create at least two significant conflicts with trademark protection. First, prohibiting or restricting certain word or stylistic trademarks that convey or shape perceptions of products' health risks conflicts generally with trademarks' purpose of source identification. Second, large or graphic warnings, especially if required on packaging and labeling, may distort trademarks' appearance. Prohibitions on tobacco trademarks that create false impressions are now common, as are graphic warnings. In 2010, Thailand proposed regulatory measures that would require that graphic warning labels cover thirty percent of the surface of beer, wine, and spirits containers.[51] Kenya adopted a similar law requiring thirty percent coverage for written warnings.[52]

The risk that trademark holders will imply health or other product attributes across product lines increases as global consolidation accelerates.[53] Consumers use the semiotic information of a package to establish expectations about the product, often in reference to similar products.[54] Concerning the product package, consumers mainly use package shape and package color to match the design of a product or package, with the characteristics of the product itself.[55] Tobacco manufacturers, for example, created perceptions that "light" and "low" labeled cigarettes by adapting colors and tones from a reference product. For example, Marlboro "Light" packaging featured more white space and softer tones than Marlboro "Reds" to imply that the former is less risky than the latter.[56] A 1999 internal memorandum detailed the ways the brands interacted:

2004/48/EC of 29 April 2004 on the enforcement of intellectual property rights [2004] OJ L157/45, 61.

49 Compare NAFTA, art. 1708 with TRIPS Agreement, art. 16.

50 United Nations Conference on Trade and Development, *Intellectual Property Provisions in International Investment Arrangements* 5 (2007).

51 Patrick Barta & Christina Passariello, *Global Liquor Makers Fight Graphic Labels in Thailand*, The Wall St. J. B1 (Sept. 17, 2010) B1; WTO Committee on Technical Barriers to Trade, 'Notification' (21 Jan. 2010) G/TBT/N/THA/332; WTO, *Tobacco and Alcohol Technical Barriers Among Members' Trade Concerns* (Mar. 24–25, 2010), available at http://www.wto.org/english/news_e/news10_e/tbt_24mar10_e.htm.

52 Alcoholic Drinks Control Act 2010 (Kenya).

53 Hanson & Kysar, *supra* note 21, at 1552.

54 P. H. Bloch, *Seeking the Ideal Form: Product Design and Consumer Response*, 59(3) J. Marketing 16–29 (1995).

55 G. J. F. Smets & C. J. Overbeeke, *Expressing Tastes in Packages*, 16 Design Studies 349–65 (1995).

56 Melanie Wakefield et al., *The Cigarette Pack as Image: New Evidence from Tobacco Industry Documents*, 11 (Supp. I) Tobacco Control i73, i77 (2002).

> Marlboro Red continues to maintain the strongest and most consistent brand essences alive today. The image of the cowboy is one that is respected by smokers everywhere, with its enduring brand equity as one who commands respect, is not easily dismissed, and is willing to take a stand. The loner/less social equities – even though less intense than in the past – may have implications for relevance and frequency of use for those YAMS [young adult male smokers] who want to tap into the more outgoing aspects of their own personality. Because Marlboro Red does not have an inclusive feel, it may struggle to fit into a YAMS world that is more interactive, more open, and highly social. Though the Marlboro imagery may not always be seen as a relevant, aspirational image for these respondents, its underlying values are probably timeless. Marlboro Light enjoys the halo effect of Marlboro Red, albeit with a softer bent. It successfully borrows the confidence of its parent brand, overlaying it with its own more feminine elements of being playful, light-hearted, and approachable.[57]

Similarly, the adaptation of "heritage" brands of beer depended on the careful imaging that went into products so that "Miller Lite" could be perceived as less caloric, even though it ultimately delivered the same amount of alcohol per volume as its anchor products.[58]

Indeed, in consumer product sectors closely tied to individual and public health, only a few industry players dominate.[59] In the beer market, before 2016, SABMiller controlled roughly 15 percent of global volume and was once the largest brewer in the world, until 2008 when second-place InBev acquired third-place Anheuser-Busch to control about one fourth to one-third of global volume.[60] Six of SABMiller's brands are among the top fifty in the world, and the firm has the number-one or number-two spot in more than 90 percent of the markets in which it competes, including China, India, the United States, and South Africa.[61] In 2016, SABMiller and InBev merged, creating a brand giant controlling seven of the top ten global beer brands and eighteen brands that generate more than $1 billion in retail sales.[62]

57 The Golden Door, A Look at the Smoking Behavior of Young Adult Males: Presented to Philip Morris – USA 1999 10 (1999), available at https://www.industrydocumentslibrary.ucsf.edu/tobacco/docs/hhyn0013.

58 IPA, The Launch of Miller Lite (1988), available at https://www.industrydocumentslibrary.ucsf.edu/tobacco/docs/#id=qtmh0213.

59 David H. Jernigan, *The Global Industry: An Overview*, 104 Addiction 6, 7, 10 (2004).

60 Trefis Team, *Anheuser-Busch InBev: What the SABMiller Acquisition Could Mean*, Forbes (Sept. 18, 2014), available at https://www.forbes.com/sites/greatspeculations/2014/09/18/anheuser-busch-inbev-what-the-sabmiller-acquisition-could-mean/#1ab2a1b43c49.

61 Ann Gilpin, *SABMiller and A-B InBev Can Coexist*, Morningstar (July 10, 2009), available at http://www.morningstar.hu/hu/news/articles/82999/sabmiller-and-a-b-inbev-can-coexist.aspx.

62 Bradley Gerrard, *ABInBev to Squeeze Even More Drops out of SAB Miller Deal*, Telegraph (Mar. 2, 2017), available at http://www.telegraph.co.uk/business/2017/03/02/ab-inbev-squeeze-even-drops-sabmiller-deal/.

In the global packaged- and processed-foods market, giants such as Nestlé, Danone, Unilever, Pepsi, and Kraft dominate.[63] Ultra-processed foods including candy, salty snacks, processed meats, and soft drinks now dominate the food systems of high-income countries.[64] For example, 61 percent of energy in purchases by households in the United States comes from such foods. Similar patterns are emerging in developing countries.[65] "The trend for the largest firms to focus and acquire brands in core categories has contributed to higher firm concentration among certain high-margin products with globally recognized premium brands."[66] For example, the markets for soups, breakfast cereals, and baby food are heavily concentrated, with the top four firms accounting for more than 50 percent of global sales.[67] Nestlé alone accounts for 26 percent of global baby food sales.[68] Similarly, Campbell's, Knorr, and Maggi brands together account for nearly 50 percent of global soup sales.[69]

Concentration has also been under way for some time with respect to the global tobacco industry. In 2001, a little more than 50 percent of global market sales were controlled by transnational tobacco companies.[70] Over the last decade, the international cigarette market has been dominated by five companies: China National Tobacco Corporation, Philip Morris International, British American Tobacco, Japan Tobacco International, and Imperial Tobacco. These companies plus Philip Morris USA control 81 percent of the global tobacco market.[71] These industries are not always distinct. Until 2007, Kraft shared its ownership structure with Philip Morris.[72]

Market pressures ensure that consolidation is likely to reduce the extent to which these firms compete on the basis of price, and increase the extent to which they compete on the basis of branding, advertising, and marketing, ultimately distilled

63 Anita Regmi & Mark Gehlhar (eds), New Directions in Global Food Markets (2005), available at http://ageconsearch.umn.edu/bitstream/33751/1/ai050794.pdf.

64 Jennifer Poti, Michelle Mendez, Shu Wen Ng & Barry Popkin, *Is the Degree of Food Processing and Convenience Linked with the Nutritional Quality of Foods Purchased by US Households?* 101 (6) Am. J. Clin. Nutr. 1251–62 (2015).

65 David Stuckler, Martin McKee, Shah Ebrahim & Sanjay Basu, *Manufacturing Epidemics: The Role of Global Producers in Increased Consumption of Unhealthy Commodities Including Processed Foods, Alcohol, and Tobacco* 9(6) PLoS Med. e100123 (2012).

66 https://www.ers.usda.gov/webdocs/publications/42581/30123_aib794g_002.pdf?v=42487

67 *Id.*; Anning Wei & Joyce Cacho, *Competition Among Foreign and Chinese Agro-Food Enterprises in the Process of Globalization*, 2(3/4) Int'l Food and Agribusiness Management Rev. 437–51 (2001).

68 http://www.reuters.com/article/us-Nestlé-babymilk-idUSBRE83N0PD20120424.

69 https://www.ers.usda.gov/webdocs/publications/42581/30123_aib794g_002.pdf?v=42487.

70 Euromonitor International [database on the Internet]. Cigarettes: Global. Euromonitor International. ca. 2015.

71 Nnamdie Madichie & Abdullah Opute, *Consumer Protection in Sub-Saharan Africa: An Exploration of "Big Tobacco" Marketing Practices* in Ayuntunji Gbadamosi (ed), Handbook of Research and Buying Behavior in Developing Nations 315 (2016).

72 Michael Arndt, *It Just Got Hotter in Kraft's Kitchen*, Business Week (Feb. 12, 2007).

into trademarks shaping consumer perceptions at the point of sale (where 70 percent of consumers make their decisions). To be sure, some of the marketing promotional activities may be aimed at mature consumers who may have developed brand loyalties trademark law theoretically protects. Contesting trademark restrictions proposed by Santa Fe province in Argentina, one South American trademark holder posed its position this way:

> Products known as "mature" are those with a long trajectory on the market. These are products known by the general public and especially by those consuming them. They are products that do not need advertising to be known ... Clear examples of this class of products are coffee, chocolate, wine, perfumes, soda beverages and beer, among many others.
>
> *For these products, as opposed to for new or nontraditional products, the function of advertising does not include making them known or increasing their overall consumption*, which is mainly influenced by seasonal, distribution or pricing issues. *The importance of advertising, in this type of products, stems from the distinguishing of the brand itself from that of the competitor. The purpose of such distinction is to attract to the brand clients that already consume the products of the competition, while at the same time maintaining the clients that use their own products.*[73]

But, especially in the tobacco context, those activities in the past have been aimed at both those too young to be legal consumers of certain products as well as those who are not currently consumers of certain products. Belying the frequently asserted "brand-switching" purpose articulated in the quoted passage above, alcohol, food, and tobacco industries have all used as trademarks various cartoon characters and color schemes intended to appeal to children and adolescents.[74]

Trademarks have caused disputes between low- and middle-income countries and firms with steep investments in symbols, logos, and distinguishing marks that may mislead or deceive consumers in those states, many of which suffer high rates of illiteracy. As a result of the conditions prevailing in many low- and middle-income countries, product image and visuals around point of sale are critical for both commercial and regulatory objectives.[75] Trademark holders have asserted

[73] Unconstitutionality Claim Brief for Nobleza Piccardo S.A.I.C. Y F. ¶ VII., Nobleza Piccardo S.A.I.C. Y F. v. Provincia de Santa Fe, 188/2006, Corte Suprema de Justicia de la Nación [Supreme Court] (Arg.) (emphasis in original).

[74] Aron M. Levin & Irwin P. Levin, *Packaging of Healthy and Unhealthy Food Products for Children and Parents: The Relative Influence of Licensed Characters and Brand Names*, 9 J. Consumer Behaviour 393, 393–94 (2010); Joseph R. DiFranza et. al., *Tobacco Promotion and the Initiation of Tobacco Use: Assessing the Evidence for Causality* 117 Pediatrics e1237, e1238–45 (2006). The overwhelming majority of adolescents who smoke prefer the most heavily advertised brands. Centers for Disease Control, *Changes in the Cigarette Brand Preference of Adolescent Smokers – United States, 1989–1993*, 43 Morbidity & Mortality Weekly Rep. 577 (1994).

[75] Rochelle Cooper Dreyfuss, *Expressive Genericity: Trademarks as Language in the Pepsi Generation*, 65 Notre Dame L. Rev. 397, 399 (1990).

international protections for their colors, logos, images, symbols, and words to thwart regulatory efforts to use graphic warnings to inform consumers about the risks of alcohol and tobacco consumption, fight child malnutrition through promotion of breastfeeding, and protect consumers from packaging and labeling tactics that hide health risks.

While trademarks in many consumer product sectors may ultimately affect individual and public health in developing countries in more pernicious ways than in wealthy countries, two product sectors – infant foods and tobacco – have particular relevance for the protection of development based on basic human needs.

INFANT FORMULA

The medical basis for encouraging exclusive breastfeeding in the first six months of life was set forth in Chapter 5. The World Health Organization estimates that 13 percent of the 10.9 million deaths of children younger than five years could be prevented every year if universal protection, promotion, and support of breastfeeding were achieved.[76] In low- and middle-income countries, failure to breastfeed has relevant health effects on infants, mothers, and families [Figure 8.2].[77] Breastfeeding also plays a role in spacing pregnancies where contraception is unavailable or contraception failures are common.[78] Proper mixing of formula often fails in areas with low levels of education and, even when done correctly, may introduce contaminants from nearby water sources.[79]

Trademarks used as part of the marketing and promotion of breastmilk substitutes, including infant formula, add another layer of risks to those that would obtain even in benignly labeled, plain formula containers. The iconic Gerber baby, for example, implies that use of the product will result in a healthy, happy baby. But other trademarks may be dangerous beyond simply encouraging the premature or inappropriate use of the product. In one tragic episode, parents in Laos confused a red label Bear Brand coffee creamer (a Nestlé trademark), the logo of which features a mother bear holding her cub in the nursing position, for a breastmilk substitute, notwithstanding written warnings that the product was not

[76] Gareth Jones et al., *How Many Child Deaths Can We Prevent This Year?* 362 The Lancet 65 (2003).

[77] Resolution WHA27.43, Handbook of Resolutions and Decisions of the World Health Assembly and the Executive Board, Volume II, 58 (1981).

[78] R. Saadeh and D. Benbouzid, *Breast-feeding and Child-Spacing: Importance of Information Collection for Public Health Policy*, 68 Bulletin of the World Health Organization 625 (1990).

[79] Marketing and Promotion of Infant Formula In the Developing Nations, 1978: Hearings Before the Subcomm. on Health and Scientific Research of the Comm. on Human Resources, 95th Cong., 2d Sess. 1-2 (1978) (statement of Sen. Kennedy).

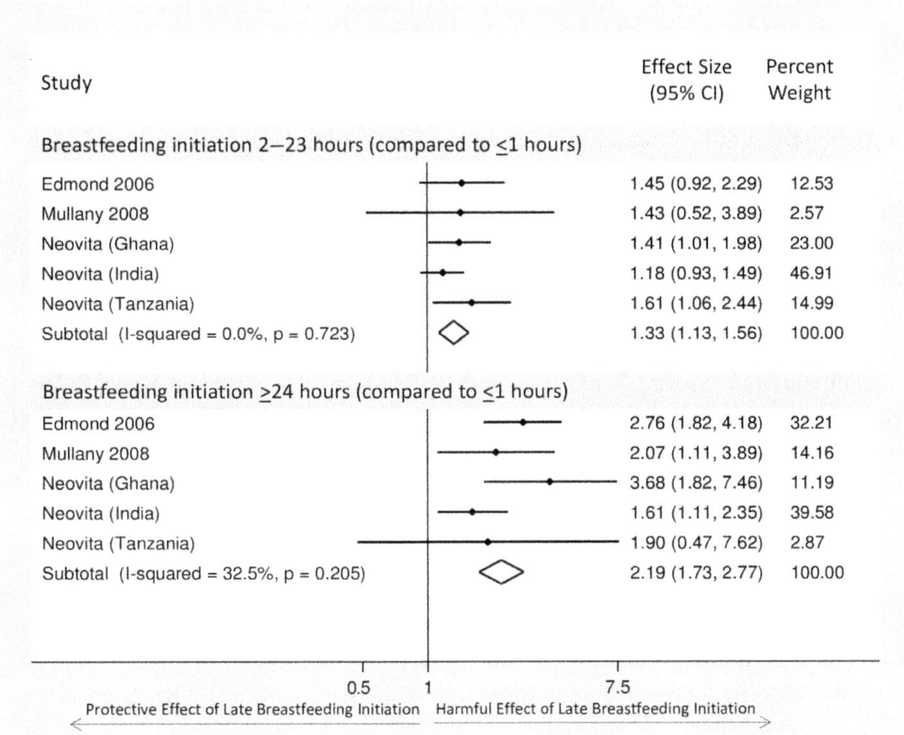

FIGURE 8.2 Forest Plot of the relative risk of neonatal mortality[80]

intended for infants for any reason.[81] The confusion resulted in cases of both malnutrition and death.[82]

Over the course of the 1970s and 1980s, breastfeeding rates in low- and middle-income countries declined, attributable by the World Health Organization and governments in those countries to food firms' marketing of infant formula, other milk products, cereals for infants, vegetable mixes, and baby teas and juices.[83] Those firms' marketing practices explicitly asserted or implied nutritional and other health equivalencies with, or superiority to, breastfeeding.[84] Many low- and middle-income countries adopted national measures to control the marketing of breastmilk

[80] http://journals.plos.org/plosone/article?id=10.1371/journal.pone.0180722. Forest Plot of the relative risk of neonatal mortality (excluding deaths in the first 2–4 days) for infants who initiated breastfeeding 2–23 hours or >24 hours after birth, compared to those who initiated breastfeeding early (<1 hour).

[81] http://www.bmj.com/rapid-response/2011/11/02/misuse-coffee-creamer-breast-milk-substitute-lethal-case-revealing-high-us.

[82] *Id.*

[83] See International Code of Marketing of Breast Milk Substitutes, available at http://www.who.int/nutrition/publications/code_english.pdf.

[84] *Id.* at 4 fn. 2.

substitutes, including the use of images and brands to confuse the health-related attributes of breastmilk substitute products.[85]

Firms resisted those measures based on their trademark investments. In 1983, Guatemala adopted law 66–83, Law on the Protection of Breastfeeding, which restricted the ability of breastmilk substitute manufacturers to display images, brands, or trademarks that might lead its substantially illiterate population to believe that breastmilk substitutes provided an adequate and effective alternative to breastfeeding during the first six months of infants' lives.[86] In 1987, the Ministry of Health implemented the law through Governmental Order No. 847–87. In 1992, Gerber, which products carry one of the most recognizable trademarks worldwide – a healthy smiling baby – applied to introduce a new "step-by-step" product line in Guatemala and requested that the products be registered with the Food & Drugs Registration and Control Division, an equivalent of the US FDA.[87] The FDRC required that Gerber remove its famous infant image, include a notice that "breast-milk is the best for baby," as required under the law, and further specify the age of the child for which the products were intended.[88]

Gerber pursued a three-pronged strategy in response: asserting the products were "complementary" foods under Guatemalan law and therefore not covered by 66–83 and 841–87; bringing a statutory action under US law to eliminate Guatemala's trading preferences for effectively "nationalizing" its trademark; and, threatening Guatemala's compliance with (still pending) TRIPS provisions. Gerber argued that:

> Article 15 of [TRIPS] states that "The nature of the goods or services to which a trademark is to be applied shall in no case form an obstacle to registration of the trademark" In addition, Article 20 of the proposed agreement provides in relevant part that "The use of a trademark in the course of trade shall not be unjustifiably encumbered by special requirements, such as . . . use in a special form or use in a manner detrimental to its capability to distinguish the goods."[89]

Guatemala's food regulatory authority lost in the Guatemala Supreme Court of Justice when, applying a strained interpretation of "complementary foods," it determined that 66–83 and 841–87 applied only to locally prepared foods, not to imported

[85] Gillian Lester, The International Code of Marketing of Breast-milk Substitutes: Survey of National Legislation and Other Measures Adopted (1981–1991) 12 (1992), available at http://apps.who.int/iris/bitstream/10665/61628/1/WHO_HLE_NUT_92.1.pdf.

[86] *Id.* at 12.

[87] Sam Foster Halabi, *Multipolarity, Intellectual Property, and the Internationalization of Public Health Law*, 35 Mich. J. Int'l. L. 715 (2014).

[88] *Id.*

[89] Letter from Mario Permuth to Gustavo Hernandez, Ministry of Pub. Health (Feb. 16, 1994) (on file with author) ("The Gerber Executive explained that they will fight with all their strength for the application and enforcement of their industrial property rights in Guatemala and, at this moment, the major damages affecting them derive from the fact that they have not been able to sell the [infant image-labeled] product in Guatemala.").

goods. Without explicitly acknowledging the role that the trade-based agreements played in their construction of the law, the case "shows . . . that raising the spectre of the new WTO can be an effective pressure tool against small countries that want to implement strong health regulations that may also have negative impacts on commercial interests."[90]

The Pharmaceutical and Health Care Association of the Philippines successfully delayed and then earned relief from comprehensive breastmilk labeling restrictions through similar arguments based in part on the trade-restrictive effect of warnings on formula containers.[91] Even in countries that have more successfully regulated the marketing of breastmilk substitutes, like India, food firms exploit ambiguities in statutory and regulatory language to continue practices meant to imply superiority of substitutes over breastmilk.[92]

TOBACCO

Tobacco consumption annually kills approximately seven million people worldwide, and represents the principal preventable threat to individual and public health worldwide. While direct consumption of tobacco products causes various cancers as well as cardiovascular disease and chronic obstructive pulmonary disease, secondhand smoke increases these risks in nonsmokers as well.[93] The burden of smoking-related morbidity and mortality has shifted dramatically to low- and middle-income countries as global tobacco firms move to less taxed and less regulated countries. Nearly 80 percent of the more than one billion smokers worldwide live in low- and middle-income countries, where the burden of tobacco-related illness and death is heaviest [Figure 8.3].[94] Tobacco consumption is, among other things, an economic and development issue.[95] Tobacco users who die prematurely deprive their families of income, raise the cost of health care, and hinder economic development.[96]

[90] Barbara Feinig, The Position of the International Code on Babyfood Marketing in the WTO, available at http://www.ibfan-alc.org/nuestro_trabajo/archivo/codex/artwemos.pdf.
[91] Rene Raya, *The Philippine Breastfeeding Struggle Continues*, 371(9615) The Lancet 794–95 (2008).
[92] http://www.dairyreporter.com/Regulation-Safety/Nestlé-India-faces-charge-for-alleged-infant-formula-labelling-law-violations.
[93] Gro Harlem Brundtland, Director General, World Health Organization, Burden of Disease and Best Practices: High-level Roundtable on Tobacco Control & Development Policy (Feb. 3, 2003), available at http://www.who.int/dg/speeches/2003/brussels/en/.
[94] WHO, Tobacco, available at http://www.who.int/mediacentre/factsheets/fs339/en/.
[95] Generic Packaging, Supplementary Submission to Senate Comm.; Submission to the Industry Inquiry from W.D. & H.O. Wills (Aust.) Ltd., The Tobacco Growing and Manufacturing Industries 32 (Jan. 1994), available at http://legacy.library.ucsf.edu/tid/kpk33a99/pdf.
[96] *Id.*

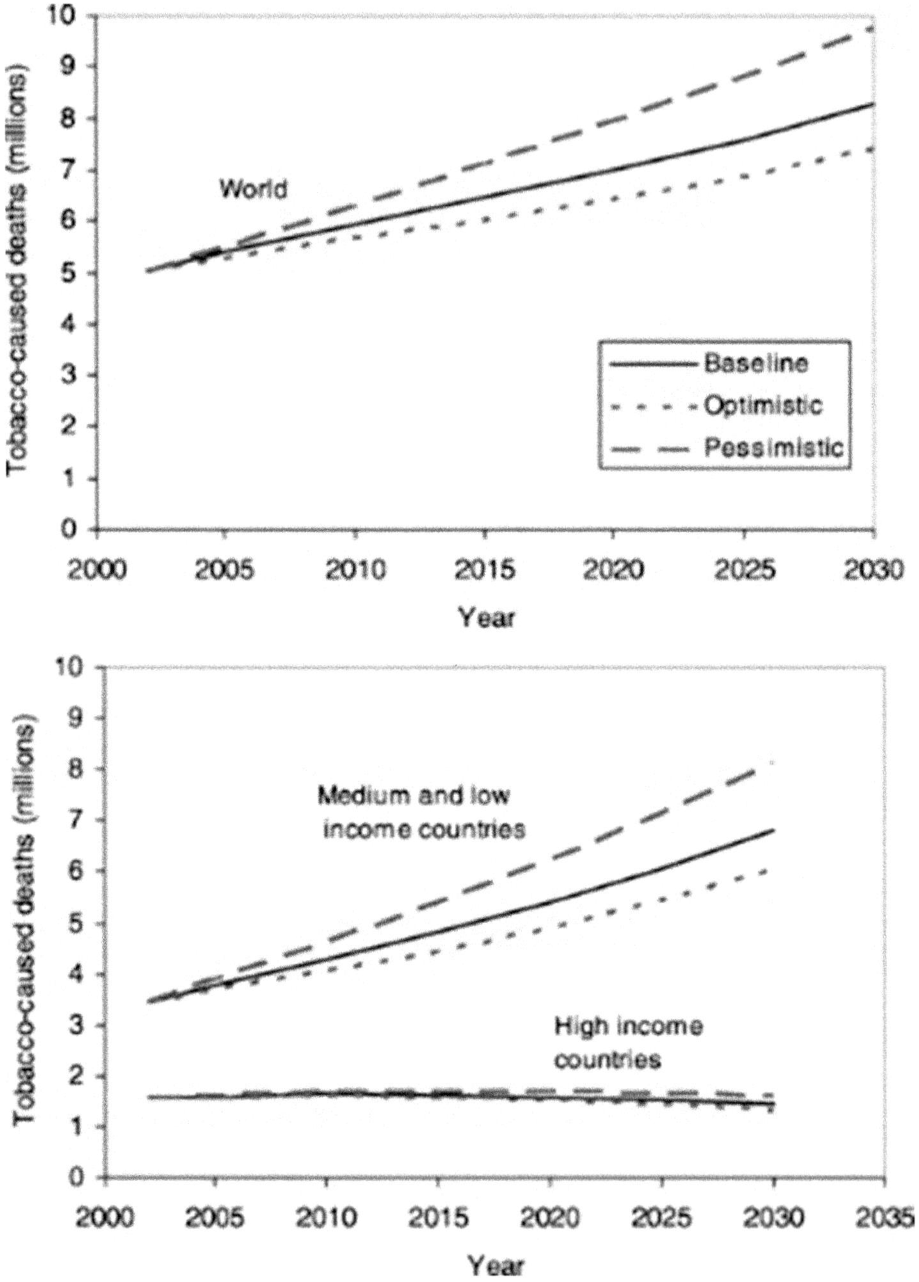

FIGURE 8.3 Projections of global mortality of disease from tobacco consumption in developing countries[97]

[97] Colin Mathers & Dejan Loncar, *Projections of Global Mortality and Burden of Disease from 2002 to 2030*, 3(11) PLoS MED. E442 (2006).

The value of tobacco firms is located almost entirely in their trademarks, which is why they spend billions developing and policing them.[98] A 1987 survey conducted by *Forbes* showed that when offered Marlboro cigarettes in a plain brown package at half the cost of a branded package, only 21 percent of regular Marlboro smokers would purchase them.[99] In 1995, British American Tobacco established an entirely separate entity, BATMark, "to protect the [global] trademarks and other intellectual property assets of the British American Tobacco group and to facilitate their exploitation. Lawyers and Trade Mark Managers advise and handle all trade mark and copyright matters, including anti-counterfeiting the drafting of licenses and other commercial agreements."[100] When Philip Morris's cigarette business overlapped more completely with its parent corporation's alcohol and food businesses, a single trademark-monitoring report from 1999 showed that the manufacturer contended trademark registrations or other actions in Argentina, Ecuador, the EU, France, Germany, Ireland, Japan Peru, the United Kingdom, and the United States and closely monitored actions in Bolivia, Croatia, the Dominican Republic, and Indonesia.[101] Trademark holders, especially of trademarks that represent significant advertising investments, are served by global consultancies that report the (admittedly subjective) value of trademarks as a function of competitors' market share.[102] Trademark monitoring is accompanied by regular quantitative and survey-based research into consumer preferences.[103] Similar infrastructure exists for alcohol and packaged food brands.[104]

[98] U.S. GOV'T ACCOUNTABILITY OFFICE, GAO/GGD-93-38, INTERNATIONAL TRADE: ADVERTISING AND PROMOTING U.S. CIGARETTES IN SELECT ASIAN COUNTRIES (Dec. 1992), available at http://legacy.library.ucsf.edu/tid/yct81f00.

[99] Katherine M. West, *Marlboro Man: The Making of an American Image* (Apr. 3, 1996), available at http://legacy.library.ucsf.edu/tid/rsy97d00.

[100] British American Tobacco Collection, *Effective Trademark Management* 29–06 (Feb. 1998), available at http://legacy.library.ucsf.edu/tid/rcn93a99.

[101] Philip Morris Management Corp., *Inter-Office Correspondence: September – Trademark Activities* (Oct. 11, 1999), available at http://legacy.library.ucsf.edu/tid/rhm62c00.

[102] Alexander Ourusoff, *What's In a Name? (Brand Name Valuation)*, FINANCIAL WORLD PARTNERS (Sept. 1, 1992), available at http://legacy.library.ucsf.edu/tid/xkd42d00.

[103] Kip Reynolds & Adam Adamson, *The Marlboro Trademark Essence Program* (Jan. 13, 1993), available at http://legacy.library.ucsf.edu/tid/ofg89a00.

[104] Philip Morris USA, *Corporate Products Committee Meeting* (Jan. 29, 1996), available at http://legacy.library.ucsf.edu/tid/oxr30h00; Miller Brewing Co., *Five-Year Plan 1992–1996*, available at http://legacy.library.ucsf.edu/tid/psm42e00; Philip Morris Collection, *Beer Operations* (Dec. 7, 1994), available at http://legacy.library.ucsf.edu/tid/ogb72e00; Kraft General Foods International, *Kraft General Foods International: Five Year Plan* (Mar. 4, 1992), available at http://legacy.library.ucsf.edu/tid/dsm42e00; John M. Keenan, *Analysts Presentation Grand Hyatt Hotel, New York City* (Mar. 2, 1995), available at http://legacy.library.ucsf.edu/tid/qrr45c00; Philip Morris Management Corp., *Inter-Office Correspondence: September – Trademark Activities* (Oct. 11, 1999) available at http://legacy.library.ucsf.edu/tid/rhm62c00.

Tobacco manufacturers and their affiliated marketers and advertisers have been shown to frame the information on tobacco product packaging, including the shape and size of the package itself, to increase the likelihood that the product will be purchased and consumed.[105] Medical evidence shows, for example, that many smokers adopted a "light" version of a cigarette as a health measure, often as an alternative to quitting – a decision intentionally shaped by cigarette manufacturers.[106] Tobacco firms now target developing countries far more aggressively than they do wealthy ones.[107]

For this reason, low- and middle-income countries led some of the earliest, strongest challenges to marketing efforts by tobacco firms, which relied heavily on investments in brands, images, and trademarks.[108] In 1994, South Africa introduced "regulations relating to the Labelling, Advertising and Sale of Tobacco Products," which would have required 25 percent of advertisements and 50 percent of the front and back panels of cigarette packs to carry eleven different rotating warnings.[109] The President and CEO of Philip Morris International at the time, William H. Webb, wrote a strongly worded letter implicitly threatening foreign investment in South Africa and detailing the violations the law would cause South Africa under its "internal laws and as a party to the Paris Protection of International Property Rights," including trademark infringement, "assurances to international consumer products companies that their trademark rights will be respected," and outright expropriation.[110] RJR Nabisco focused its lobbying effort "on international trade aspects of the potential trademark infringement the new regulations would create." The final implementing regulations halved the coverage of cigarette packs and reduced the number of rotating warnings.[111]

[105] U.S. Surgeon General, *Reducing Tobacco Use: A Report of the Surgeon General, Chapter 5: Regulatory Efforts* 166–169 (2000), available at: http://www.cdc.gov/tobacco/data_statistics/sgr/2000/complete_report/pdfs/Chapter5.pdf; Joe B. Tye, Kenneth E. Warner & Stanton A. Glantz, *Tobacco Advertising and Consumption: Evidence of a Causal Relationship*, 8(4) J. Pub. Health Pol'y 492, 494 (1987).

[106] J. Etter et al., *What Smokers Believe about Light and Ultra-Light Cigarettes*, 36 Prev. Med. 92 (2003).

[107] http://www.who.int/bulletin/volumes/93/12/15-155846.pdf?ua=1.

[108] Memorandum from M.B. Oglesby, Jr. to Charles M. Harper, Re: RJR Biweekly Status Report, Aug. 26, 1994, available at http://legacy.library.ucsf.edu/tid/ygv66d00.

[109] Draft Letter, President and Chief Executive Officer, of Philip Morris International, Inc. to Director-General, National Health and Population Development of South Africa (Aug. 17, 1994), available at http://legacy.library.ucsf.edu/tid/wdg87e00/pdf?search=%22trademark%20regulation%20warning%20labels%20africa%22.

[110] *Id.* Full letter available at http://legacy.library.ucsf.edu/tid/xot45c00.

[111] Regulations Relating to the Labelling, Advertising and Sale of Tobacco Products, available at http://www.wipo.int/edocs/lexdocs/laws/en/za/za093en.pdf.

A 1995 administrative ruling from the Brazilian Minister of Health mandating 25 percent coverage of cigarette packs with eight rotating warnings was similarly scuttled by industry lobbying on the basis of protected images and brands.[112] In the Philippines, favorable rulings by judges in cases seeking to impose health warning requirements were overturned by legislative actions decreeing that voluntary practices adopted by the tobacco industry satisfied national law.[113]

[112] Letter from James T. Newsome to Gary Morrisroe enclosing two copies of the cases in Argentina and Brazil (Aug. 27, 1997) available at https://www.industrydocumentslibrary.ucsf.edu/tobacco/docs/#id=sxkh0213.

[113] https://www.industrydocumentslibrary.ucsf.edu/tobacco/docs/#id=lhxc0039.

9

Educational and Scientific Printed Works

Along with patent policies, copyright restrictions were viewed as barriers to technology transfer and, relatedly, mass education campaigns over the course of the 1950s and 1960s.[1] The development of local industry, largely without regard to economic sector, required access to scientific and technical materials published in wealthy countries.[2] Similarly, mass education could not be undertaken without access to works overwhelmingly published in Europe and North America.[3] Developing countries have special needs with respect to educational materials: consumptive access for freedom of the press and cultural exchange and bulk access for access to scientific journals, educational texts, and other materials.[4]

Access to these materials was limited because of international copyright restrictions, so that absolutely and relatively poor countries could not afford to purchase but a fraction of what they needed for development purposes. The purchase of foreign works or their translations served as an effective form of wealth transfer from poor countries to rich ones.[5] Even though the internet has changed the role of access to many printed scientific and educational works, the reality is that this makes little difference in many developing countries where access to the internet is not widespread or the efficiencies of using digital platforms cannot be realized.[6]

1 Irwin Olian, *International Copyright and the Needs of Developing Countries: The Awakening at Stockholmn and Paris*, 7(2) Cornell Int'l. L. J. 81, 89 (1974).

2 Jonathan Tennant et al., *The Academic, Economic and Societal Impacts of Open Access: An Evidence-Based Review*, 5 F1000 Res. 632 (2016), available at https://www.ncbi.nlm.nih.gov/pmc/articles/PMC4837983/.

3 Peter Drahos & John Braithwaite, Information Feudalism: Who Owns the Knowledge Economy? 75 (2002).

4 Susan Strba, International Copyright Law and Access to Education in Developing Countries 34 (2012).

5 H. Sacks, *Crisis in International Copyright: The Protocol Regarding Developing Countries*, 128 J. Bus. L., 26 (1969).

6 Adam Taylor, 47 *Percent of the World's Population Now Uses the Internet, Study Says*, Wash. Post (Nov. 22, 2016), available at https://www.washingtonpost.com/news/worldviews/wp/2016/

As Peter Drahos and John Braithwaite have explained, this situation was fundamentally tied to colonialism and imperialism in three ways. First, colonies were used primarily as sources for raw materials, so education was used to create and sustain a class of workers who could manage the bureaucratic aspects of material transfer, not the indigenous creation of scientific or technical knowledge.[7] Second, imperial control was used to mimic the legal order prevailing in European countries:

> In most cases, the transplant of intellectual property laws to developing countries has been the outcome of empire building and colonization. For example, in parts of pre-independent Malaysia, it was English copyright law that applied. When in 1911 the United Kingdom enacted the Copyright Act of 1911, its operation was extended to include "his Majesty's dominions". In the case of pre-independent Malaysia, the 1911 Act was restricted to the Straits Settlement. Later, when British collecting societies began to worry about copying, representations were made to the Colonial Office and to the Board of Trade to have the Federated Malay States, North Borneo and Sarawak enact copyright law based on the 1911 Act. These States passed copyright laws in the 1930s based on the 1911 Act. Copyright policy was firmly in the grip of London, especially London publishers.[8]

"When colonies across the South became formally independent countries, many during the 1950s and 1960s, they increasingly chafed at the imposition of copyright treaty standards that had effectively been imposed on them by a foreign power."[9] Third, the inputs necessary for a publishing industry to exist – paper, ink, presses – were not available in most countries, so domestic publication on a large scale was virtually nonexistent.

Colonialism had created structural barriers to both tangible and intangible means by which to address the severity of the educational and literacy problems facing developing countries.[10] The extent of book publishing in developing countries is negligible and was even less robust in the post-decolonization period.[11] There were few books, and those that were available for sale were unaffordable.[12] The most straightforward way to undertake mass education campaigns was to use the already

11/22/47-percent-of-the-worlds-population-now-use-the-internet-users-study-says/?utm_term=.e9ad535b2601.

7 William Culbertson, *The "Open Door" and Colonial Policy*, 9(1) AM. ECON. REV. 325–40 (1919).

8 Peter Drahos, *Developing Countries and International Intellectual Property Standard-Setting* 5 (5) J. WIPO 765–89 (2002), available at https://www.anu.edu.au/fellows/pdrahos/articles/pdfs/2002devcountriesandipstandards.pdf.

9 PAUL GOLDSTEIN, INTERNATIONAL COPYRIGHT: PRINCIPLES, LAW, AND PRACTICE 22 (2001).

10 Kingsley Banya, *Illiteracy, Colonial Legacy, and Education: The Case of Modern Sierra Leone* 29(2) COMP. ED. 159–70 (1993).

11 UNCTAD/ICTSD, INTELLECTUAL PROPERTY RIGHTS: IMPLICATIONS FOR DEVELOPMENT 129 (2003).

12 Strba, *supra* note 4.

available textbooks from wealthier countries.[13] But from the 1960s onward, developing countries could not reach reasonable terms for the importation of foreign educational materials.[14] "[T]he high production costs of scientific and technical books standing in the way of their dissemination in developing countries could be substantially reduced if the advanced countries would freely allow their books to be reprinted and translated by underdeveloped countries."[15]

Indeed, for many developing countries, the problem remains as severe in 2017 as it was fifty years ago. The costs of importation and royalties comprise a substantial part of the price for educational materials in developing countries, so much so that many texts cost far more on a relative basis than if the material were purchased in a wealthier country.[16] "As an example, the price of a book in Thailand typically consists of: direct costs like paper and ink – 30%; royalty – 10%–15%; labor cost – 15%; and distribution costs 25%–40%."[17]

The relationship between access to educational material and the development of scientific or industrial sectors is clear. "For example, a student in Indonesia paying $81.70 for Goodman and Gilman's *The Pharmacological Basis for Therapeutics* is equal to a U.S. student paying $3,170.97.[18]

Copyright standards in wealthy countries also have impeded development of a wide range of light industries as well as the progress of developing channels for the preservation and propagation of cultures in developing countries into the wide range of media enjoyed in Europe and North America:

> The Director of the Department of Cultural Activities emphasized the need for the newly-independent states of Africa to develop national consciousness to rediscover their national heritage. He indicated the means made available by UNESCO for this purpose; i.e., equipment for audio-visual recordings, fellowships for training of specialists in human scientific research techniques, the loan of experts from libraries and museums, the aid toward the organization of symposia.[19]

Even today, the use of open-source technological know-how remains low in developing countries, emphasizing again the limited access people in developing countries have to web-based resources, even if they had obtained adequate education to take advantage of them.[20] The limitation for educational materials and

[13] Margaret Chon, *Intellectual Property "from Below": Copyright and Capability for Education*, 40 U.C. Davis L. Rev. 803 (2007).

[14] Barbara Ringer, The Role of the United States in International Copyright – Past, Present and Future, 1050 (1968).

[15] C. F. Johnson, *The Origins of the Stockholm Protocol*, 18 Bull. Copyright Soc. USA (1970).

[16] Susan Strba, *supra* note 4, at 31.

[17] *Id.*

[18] *Id.*

[19] Records of the Unesco General Conference, 11th session, Report of the Working Party on the Development of Unesco's Activities in Tropical Africa, Paris (1960).

[20] Information Resources Management Association, Open Source Technology: Concepts, Methodologies, Tools, and Applications 146–47 (2015).

means for technology transfer have an inevitable effect on the human capital reservoir in developing countries as well. Deficits in research and teaching facilities led to a massive flight of those most able to become the next generation of engineers, scientists, and medical researchers.[21]

Just as the revision of the Paris Convention became a focus of developing world because of patent and industrial property barriers to technology transfer, revision of the Berne Convention (and to a lesser extent Universal Copyright Convention) became a priority for developing countries as part of the New International Economic Order.[22] Berne represented the "foreign" law in many newly independent states. It did not allow for "reservations" (an international legal doctrine under which countries may choose not to have certain provisions of treaties apply to them), it was by design principally focused on the rights of authors (rather than, of course, the right to development), and it contained narrow provisions for limitations and exceptions that might accommodate developing countries' demands.[23]

Before TRIPS (which incorporated it), the Berne Convention had been the "primary treaty underlying international copyright law."[24] The Convention afforded authors exclusive rights of reproduction, translation, and creation of derivative works in regard to their respective copyrighted works.[25] The treaty allows members to create limitations and exceptions to authors' rights so long as they are compliant with a three-step test. The test requires that exceptions are afforded only when (1) the work in question is needed for a "certain special case," (2) reproduction would not "conflict with the normal exploitation of the work," and (3) reproduction would not "unreasonably prejudice the legitimate interest of the author."[26]

Because the Berne Convention operated with the primary objective of protecting "the rights of authors in literary and artistic works," it never explicitly sought that member countries enforce a balanced intellectual property legal regime.[27] The Convention has often been interpreted as authorizing the enactment of "more stringent copyright laws," restricting limitations and exceptions to the conditions of the three-step test.[28] Indeed, the stringency of the treaty is one of the reasons the

[21] UNESCO, TOWARDS KNOWLEDGE SOCIETIES 107, available at http://unesdoc.unesco.org/images/0014/001418/141843e.pdf.

[22] Sam Ricketson & Jane Ginsburg, *The Berne Convention: Historical and Institutional Aspects*, in Daniel Gervais (ed), INTELLECTUAL PROPERTY: A HANDBOOK OF CONTEMPORARY RESEARCH 36 (2013).

[23] Peter Burger, *The Berne Convention Its History and Its Key Role in the Future*, 3 J. L. & TECH. 1, 39 (1988).

[24] Sean Williams, *Closing in on the Light at WIPO Movement towards a Copyright Treaty for Visually Impaired Persons and Intellectual Property Movements*, 33 U. PA. J. INT. L. 1035, 1054 (2014).

[25] Melville Nimmer, *Implications of the Prospective Revisions of the Berne Convention and United States Copyright Law*, 19(3) STAN. L. REV. 499–54 (1967).

[26] *Id.*

[27] Williams, *supra* note 24, at 1039–40.

[28] *Id.*

United States avoided it until 1989 and, even after it acceded (and joined TRIPS), was found in violation of its terms for adopting a copyright exception for certain kinds of broadcasts of otherwise copyrighted works.[29]

Before 1967, the latest revision to Berne had been at Brussels in 1948, before dozens of newly independent states joined. From the beginning of the 1960s, preparation for the next round of revisions focused on the demands developing countries planned on making.[30] UNESCO became the primary voice for developing countries' copyright concerns.[31] Beginning in 1963, developing countries, led by India, called for explicit exceptions in Berne for the compulsory licensing of published works for educational purposes as well as translation provisions in the (less author-friendly) Universal Copyright Convention.[32] A proposed Article 25*bis* to Berne expanded those exceptions to translation, (shorter) terms of protection, and regional blocs that might vary Berne's protective terms.[33]

British, French, and U.S. publishers strongly resisted the proposed changes.[34] The objections ran to the core of developing countries' demands. The British delegation, rejecting the exception for access to educational or scientific works, responded that there were few things that are not in one sense "educational or scientific."[35] Sir Alan Herbert, chairman of the British Copyright Council, called the Protocol "a delayed action bomb of dangerous principle into the flagship of copyright; a tunnel under the walls of the copyright fortress."[36] As with the Berne and Paris Conventions' origins, nongovernmental groups representing major publishers weighed in heavily against the proposed accommodations.[37] When the Stockholm revision of Berne finally occurred in 1967, the disagreements boiled over into the main meeting sessions "into a political debate in which ringing anti-colonialist declarations alternated with ingratiating descriptions of the needs of the Third World."[38]

The proposed exceptions failed at Stockholm, and the final set of copyright proposals aimed at meeting the needs of developing countries became the 1971 Appendix to the Berne Convention.[39] The Appendix contained no exceptions

[29] Panel Rep. of 15 June 2000, United States – Article 110(5) of the U.S. Copyright Act, WT/DS160/R.
[30] Johnson, *supra* note 15.
[31] Benedict Atkinson & Brian Fitzgerald (eds), Copyright Law Volume III: Copyright and the 21st Century xiii (2016).
[32] Johnson, *supra* note 15, at 116.
[33] Daniel Gervais, (Re)Structuring Copyright: A Comprehensive Path to International Copyright Reform 2.5 (2013).
[34] Johnson, *supra* note 15, at 142–43.
[35] *Id.*
[36] *Id.*
[37] Rosemary Mokia, *Publishers, United States Foreign Policy and the Third World, 1960–67*, 11(2) Pub. Res. Quarterly 36–51 (1995).
[38] Johnson, *supra* note 15, at 181.
[39] Alberto Cerda Silva, Beyond the Unrealistic Solution for Development Provided by the Appendix of the Berne Convention on Copyright (2012).

for free educational use or for shortening the duration of copyright protection.[40] It authorized the possibility of compulsory licensing of works if voluntary negotiations over translations and reproduction terms could not be reached, although under qualified conditions. Few countries have used the Appendix since it was added to the treaty.[41] With small exceptions, the Berne Convention has mostly continued to "eschew[] facilitation of any additional copyright balance," more so after its incorporation into TRIPS.[42]

With respect to the transition from Berne to TRIPS, in contrast with patents (particularly agrochemical and pharmaceutical patents) and trademarks (particularly tobacco trademarks), there were fewer abrupt, noteworthy episodes between firms and developing countries (although several between their governments).[43] Rather, the conduct of publishers was consistent before and after Berne was incorporated into TRIPS, and as a result, publishers' and authors' rights became enhanced. In the United States, the adoption of legislation bringing its copyright law into compliance caused thousands of works to be removed from the public domain.[44]

In developing countries, litigation was used to deter infringements of copyright even for basic educational purposes. In Uganda, John Murray Ltd. (now an imprint of publishing giant Hachette) sued a Kampala bookshop for selling counterfeit copies of D. G. MacKean's *Introduction to Biology – Third Tropical Edition*.[45] The court determined that knowledge of the books' unauthorized status was irrelevant under Ugandan copyright law, imposing a monetary penalty for the loss of profits on the 765 issues sold. The judgment, according to the African Copyright & Access to Knowledge Project, put Kampala Newstyles, which was at the time the biggest bookshop in Uganda, out of business.[46] While the explosion of the HIV/AIDS epidemic forced changes in the international patent regime under TRIPS (especially for pharmaceutical patents), access to educational and scientific materials related to HIV/AIDS care for health care workers came under no such corresponding pressure.[47] In Thailand, publishers have appeared alongside governmental prosecutors in cases alleging copyright infringement even for protected research purposes. As Susan Strba has noted,

40 David Nimmer, *Nation, Duration, Violation, Harmonization: An International Copyright Proposal for the United States* 55 LAW & CONTEMP. PROB. 211 (1992).

41 SAM RICKETSON, THE BERNE CONVENTION FOR THE PROTECTION OF LITERARY AND ARTISTIC WORKS: 1886–1986 (1987).

42 Williams, *supra* note 24, at 1039–40.

43 Patricia Judd, *Toward a TRIPS Truce*, 32 MICH. J. INT'L. L. 626 (2011).

44 Golan v. Holder, 132 S.Ct. 873 (2012).

45 John Murray (Publishers) Ltd and Others v. George William Senkindu and Another, HCCS 1018 of 1997 (unreported).

46 http://www.aca2k.org/attachments/154_ACA2K%20UGANDA%20COUNTRY%20REPORT%20WEB.pdf.

47 Strba, supra note 4, at 30.

even if the uses of copyrighted material are protected, the threat of lawsuits has a strong deterrent effect.[48]

As with pharmaceuticals, specific consumer goods sectors, and tobacco, the publishing industry – especially medical, scientific, and technical knowledge – has become concentrated, with a corresponding upward pressure on global prices with little relief for developing countries [Figure 9.1].[49]

> In terms of numbers of papers published, the five major publishers in [Natural and Medical Sciences], accounted, in 1973, for little more than 20% of all papers published. This share increased to 30% in 1996, and to 50% in 2006, the level at which it remained until 2013 when it increased again to 53%. In this domain, three publishers account for more than 47% of all papers in 2013: Reed-Elsevier (24.1%; 1.5 fold increase since 1990), Springer (11.9%; 2.9 fold increase), and Wiley-Blackwell (11.3%; 2.2 fold increase).[50]

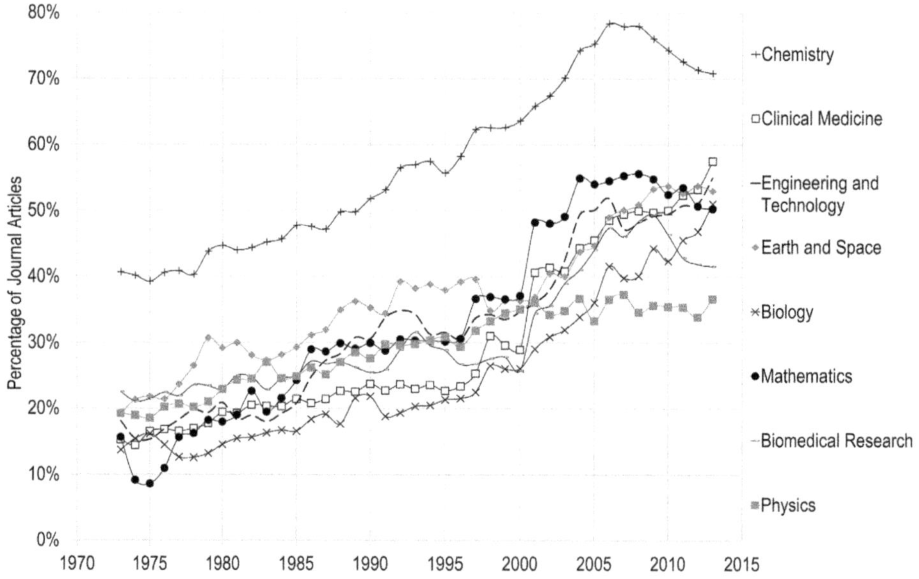

FIGURE 9.1 Concentration in the academic publishing industry[51]

[48] *Id.* at 32.

[49] Carolyn Lipscomb, *Mergers in the Publishing Industry*, 89(3) BULL. MED. LIBR. ASSOC. 307–08 (2001).

[50] Vincent Lariviere, Stefanie Haustein & Philippe Mongeon, *The Oligopoly of Academic Publishers in the Digital Era*, PLoS ONE (June 10, 2015), available at http://journals.plos.org/plosone/article?id=10.1371/journal.pone.0127502.

[51] *Id.*

This is similarly true of the global market for textbooks.[52] The effects of consolidation are clear both in terms of the pricing of scientific articles as well as access to educational materials in the developing world.[53] Even in wealthier countries, research libraries have had to reduce subscriptions and pay more for those they have.[54] Between 2003 and 2012, major research universities threatened to cancel subscriptions and encouraged faculty to publish in open-access journals (and refuse to undertake peer review services for those that charged) as a result of price increases by the small number of academic and scientific publishers.[55] Over the same period, universities in developing countries were forced to make sometimes drastic reductions. "The universities of Addis Ababa (Ethiopia), Nigeria, and Yaounde (Cameroon) had to cancel subscriptions for 1200, 824, and 107 journals respectively."[56]

As with patents, copyright law is generally characterized by a doctrine of "exhaustion" whereby the first sale of a copyrighted work extinguishes most of the rights held.[57] Theoretically, exhaustion should allow third-party countries to import books from countries where they are priced more affordably.[58] Copyrighted material imported from a country where the right has been exhausted, "parallel imports" or "gray market" materials, are therefore not counterfeit goods because they have been produced by, for, or under license from the owner.[59]

As a practical matter, populations in the poorest countries are unlikely to benefit from parallel imports. The incentive is to legally purchase copyrighted materials in countries where the price is lower and sell them where the price is higher.[60] For a large number of countries, the expense of purchase, export, and distribution outstrips the opportunity for arbitrage. Moreover, publishers impose contractual

[52] James Koch, Turning the Page: an Economic Analysis of the Market for Textbooks: Current Conditions, New Developments and Policy Options 5 (2013).

[53] Helmut Anheier & Yudhishthir Raj Isar, Cultures and Globalization: the Cultures Economy 465 (2007).

[54] D. Malakoff, *Librarians Seek to Block Merger of Scientific Publishing Giants*, 290 Science. 910–11 (2000).

[55] Ian Sample, *Harvard University Says It Can't Afford Journal Publishers' Prices*, The Guardian (Apr. 24, 2012), available at https://www.theguardian.com/science/2012/apr/24/harvard-university-journal-publishers-prices.

[56] Strba, *supra* note 4, at 30.

[57] Kirtsaeng v. Wiley, 568 U.S. 519, 133 S. Ct. 1351 (2013); Jason Schultz & Aaron Perzanowski, *Copyright Exhaustion and the Personal Use Dilemma*, 96 Minn. L. Rev. 2112–13 (2012).

[58] Mary LaFrance, *Wag the Dog: Using Incidental Intellectual Property Rights to Block Parallel Imports*, 20 Mich. Telecomm. & Tech. L. Rev. 45, 63 (2013); Mary LaFrance, A *Material World: Using Trademark Law to Override Copyright's First Sale Rule for Imported Copies*, 21(1) Mich. Telecomm. & Tech. L. Rev. 43 (2014).

[59] Michael B. Weicher, *K Mart Corp. v. Cartier, Inc.: A Black Decision for the Gray Market*, 38 Am. U. L. Rev. 463, 463–64 (1989); C. Fink, *Entering the Jungle of Intellectual Property Rights Exhaustion and Parallel Importation*, in C. Fink & K. E. Maskus (eds), Intellectual Property and Development – Lessons from Recent Economic Research, 173 (2005).

[60] E. Bonadio, *Parallel Imports in a Global Market: Should a Generalised International Exhaustion be the Next Step?*, 33(3) Euro. Intel. Prop. Rev. 153–61 (2011).

conditions prohibiting the importation of books from cheaper countries like China or India.[61] Parallel imports are not now, nor under current conditions promise to be, a solution for access to educational and technological copyrighted works in developing countries.[62]

Although developing countries did not achieve their objectives for the revision of Berne (just as they did not achieve a Code of Conduct on Technology Transfer or the revision of the Paris Convention), changes to the treaty in 1967 established alternative channels for developing countries to adapt their national intellectual property laws toward development objectives. In the context of Berne, the primary channel was the introduction of Article 9(2) and the aforementioned three-part test for limitations and exceptions to authors' right to authorize the reproduction of their works.[63] The basic purpose of Article 9(2) was to make the right to reproduce explicit in the treaty; the difficulty was drafting the provision in such a way as to not interrupt the various limitations and exceptions that already existed under national law.[64] The result was a provision that authorized then-acknowledged exceptions, some of which clearly mattered most in wealthy countries ("private use" or "the composer's need for texts"), whereas others, even if originating in wealthy countries, clearly impacted developing countries more ("the interests of the blind").[65] In South Africa, "nursing teachers, public health nurses, and other medical personnel who wish to distribute copyrighted materials about HIV/AIDS to students and patients are required to pay copyright royalty fees. As a result, circulation of information is seriously restricted."[66]

In 1981, the UN General Assembly declared an "International Year of the Disabled," prompting the governing bodies of UNESCO and WIPO to establish a working group to examine the use of Article 9(2) for purposes of creating broader access for the visually and audio impaired.[67] Those populations then, as now, lived overwhelmingly in developing countries. In 2013, there were approximately 285 million visually impaired individuals in the world, with 39 million blind individuals and 246 million dealing with low vision.[68] Roughly 90 percent of this visually impaired population lives in developing countries and regions.[69] The World Blind Union (WBU) estimates that less than 5 percent of the roughly one million books published

61 Strba, *supra* note 4, at 30.

62 Shamnad Basheer, Debanshu Khettry, Shambo Nandy & Sree Mitra, *Exhausting Copyrights and Promoting Access to Education: An Empirical Take*, 17 J. Intell. Prop. Rights 335–47 (2012).

63 Stavroula Karapapa, Private Copying 99 (2012).

64 Justin Hughes, *Fair Use and Its Politics – At Home and Abroad*, in Ruth Okediji (ed.) Copyright Law in an Age of Limitations and Exceptions 245 (2017).

65 *Id.*

66 Strba, *supra* note 4, at 30.

67 http://unesdoc.unesco.org/images/0005/000507/050758eb.pdf; http://unesdoc.unesco.org/images/0005/000539/053955eb.pdf

68 World Health Organization, *Visual Impairment and Blindness* (2014), available at http://www.who.int/mediacentre/factsheets/fs282/en/.

69 *Id.*

every year get made into "formats accessible to visually impaired persons," a number that drops to less than 1 percent in developing nations.[70]

The establishment of the working group led to technical studies identifying legal mechanisms by which access to copyrighted works could be facilitated. A 1982 study by Wanda Noel noted that while compulsory licenses – the circumscribed and underused mechanism of the 1971 Annex – did not get rid of the problem of remuneration, exceptions did.[71] Additional studies into the issue followed.[72] A WIPO report from 1985 highlighted two integral issues that were acting as barriers to providing access to persons with audio and visual impairment.[73] First, it noted that the lack of exceptions or limitations in domestic laws prevented reproduction of works.[74] Second, it found that states were in need of a "mechanism to distribute accessible works across borders."[75] Because of these barriers, there was effectively a "book famine" for people with audio and visual impairment:

> There is a global book famine. It is a huge problem. Without books, journals and magazines, people are cut off from life. They cannot gain an education or participate fully in society. They cannot realize their full potential. That is not just a loss to them – it is also a serious loss to the economies and societies they live in.[76]

Developing countries relied on "downstream intellectual property benefits" to generate the necessary economic development to address the needs of their visually impaired populations.[77] The barriers for this population are in many ways not different than for the sighted: adapted works are published mainly in wealthy countries, importation is costly, and therefore vulnerable populations go without access to educational or technological material.[78] Productions cost are driven higher by the need for entities in each country to individually undertake the task of providing works in accessible formats.[79] Often, "market factors [that] limit the creation and distribution of accessible formats" can further inhibit the ability for these populations to access information.[80]

70 Denise R. Nicholson, Treaty for Visually Impaired Persons (TVI) and Treaty Proposal on Copyright Limitations and Exceptions for Libraries and Archives (TLIB): Implications for the Developing World, 3–4 (2013), available at http://library.ifla.org/239/1/209-nicholson-en.pdf.

71 http://unesdoc.unesco.org/images/0005/000507/050758eb.pdf, at 26.

72 Neil Yap, *Fitting Marrakesh into a Consequentialist Copyright Framework*, 6 N.Y.U. *J. Int. Prop. & Ent. L.* 351, 360 (2017).

73 *The Marrakesh Treaty*, Study, Directorate General for Internal Policies, Policy Department C: Citizens' Rights and Constitutional Affairs *11 (2016).

74 *Id.*

75 *Id.*

76 http://www.wipo.int/edocs/pubdocs/en/wipo_pub_marrakesh_overview.pdf.

77 Shae Fitzpatrick, *Setting Its Sights on the Marrakesh Treaty: The U.S. Role in Alleviating the Book Famine for Persons with Print Disabilities*, 37 B.C. Int. & Comp. L. R. 147 (2014).

78 *Id.* at 158.

79 *Id.*

80 *Id.* at 143.

Out of some 125 developed and developing countries examined in a 2012 survey, only 70 afforded blind and disabled people any limitations or exceptions to facilitate access and use to materials, and the remaining 55 provide zero specific limitations for people with sensory disabilities.[81] "Fair use" and "fair dealing" principles provided little protection, as many of the access barriers involve format shifting and the creation of adaptations, or incorporate licensing and technological protections.[82] There existed no international standard for copyright limitations and exceptions, and the "territorial nature of copyright law" prevented any attempts at cross-border sharing of accessible materials between countries.[83]

Authors and publishers tended to view the market of visually impaired persons as an "'orphan market' that was not economically worthwhile, and sometimes refused to grant licenses, making their works unavailable in accessible formats."[84] Innovation by those within the industry was often discouraged by the high cost of production associated with the market, while limited capital and inadequate production models made it difficult for businesses to increase the availability of accessible works.[85] These costs can then be passed down to visually impaired consumers, "limiting the demand for and distribution of accessible works."[86] These dynamics have caused the visually impaired market to be served primary by non-profit, charitable, and governmental organizations who often suffer from "limited resources [that] constrain the number of accessible works that are produced and distributed."[87]

81 Of the African nations surveyed, four had copyright law provisions specific to people with sensory disabilities. Nigeria, Cameroon, and Rwanda allowed exceptions for only blind persons, and Uganda made provisions for both blind and deaf persons. Malawi had yet to passed proposed legislation providing blind-only exemptions. *Id.* at 4.

82 *Id.*

83 *Id.*

84 Marc Maurer, Nat'l Fed'n of the Blind, Comments on the Topic of Facilitating Access to Copyrighted Works for the Blind or Other Persons with Disabilities 3 (2009), available at http://www.copyright.gov/docs/sccr/comments/2009/maurer.pdf; Tania Sebastian, *'Copyright World' and Access to Information: Conjoined via the Internet*, 17 J. Intell. Prop. Rts. 235, 238 (2012); *Reply Comments of Library Copyright Alliance, the Electronic Frontier Foundation, the Internet Archive, and the Chief Officers of State Library Agencies* 12–13 (2009), available at http://www.librarycopyrightalliance; Allan Adler, *Am. Ass'n of Publishers, Comments in Response to Notice of Inquiry on Facilitating Access to Copyrighted Works for the Blind or Other Persons with Disabilities* 7 (2009), available at http://www.copyright.gov/docs/sccr/comments/2009/adler.pdf.

85 *Id.*

86 *Id.*

87 *Id.* http://www.wipo.int/edocs/mdocs/copyright/en/sccr_18/sccr_18_5.pdf

PART III

International Intellectual Property Shelters

Redistributing Wealth and Regulating Oligopolies

The foregoing chapters have argued that the post-decolonization conflict between wealthy and poor countries has shifted, as did the prevailing conceptions of the conditions necessary for wealth creation. When development was viewed as contingent upon access to modern technology, diversification of mono- or dual-commodity-export economies, control of volatile capital flows, and the rule of law, the "new international economic order" called for technology transfer, globally coordinated control of commodity markets, sovereign debt relief, and the establishment of internal institutions and external controls (mainly of foreign-owned firms) to create the conditions for that development to occur. As conceptions of development began to focus on basic human needs eventually enshrined in the Millennium Development Goals (this movement slightly predated but was nevertheless coincident with the growing influence of "human capital" as a critical factor in development), the "new international economic order" agenda shifted to calls for support for basic access to education, medicine and essential health services, and nutrition.

Where these policy priorities were obstructed or thwarted by foreign firms, there was a corresponding call for those firms' activities to be regulated, just as they were when technology transfer was deemed a priority for development. The evolution of firms' value from tangible to intangible sources replaced the dynamic that prevailed in the 1950s, 1960s, and 1970s with a new one that pitted the extraction of value from intellectual property sources against the basic human needs approach to economic growth adopted conscientiously in many countries and foisted on others by public health or nutrition emergencies. In either set of circumstances, the underlying effort by developing countries was to stanch the flow of wealth from their populations to firms' managers and shareholders located overwhelmingly in already wealthy countries.

These calls for regulation and redistribution occurred both within the agreements establishing heightened levels of intellectual property and outside of them. While scholars have been keenly attentive to the former, they have tended to view the latter only on an issue-by-issue or treaty-by-treaty basis, rather than as a comprehensive contemporaneous response to the dynamics of wealth transfer or as a continuous phenomenon of resistance that originally took shape as the New International Economic Order.

Some of the measures advocated by low- and middle-income countries or scholars writing in sympathy for their position have advocated a number of measures to address the perceived imbalance rendered by the structure of existing agreements, some more practical than others. Kojo Yelpaala has written a searing indictment of the international intellectual property regime beginning with TRIPS and has implicitly called for its ouster:

> It is now widely acknowledged by most observers that TRIPS is a serious threat to human health security . . . Before TRIPS, over forty countries offered no patent protection for pharmaceutical inventions. Such sovereign authority of states has been compromised by TRIPS as part of the WTO system of agreements . . . This exploitation of the inequalities of bargaining power was undertaken at a time when many developing countries were ill equipped or unprepared to appreciate all the implications of TRIPS.[1]

In 2004, Argentina and Brazil sponsored a resolution at the World Intellectual Property Organization calling for a "development agenda" to guide WIPO's activities, a moratorium on new international agreements that "expand and strengthen monopolies and further restrict access to knowledge," and for the formation of a "Treaty on Access to Knowledge and Technology" that would essentially roll back expansive protections for copyrights, patents, and trademarks.[2]

While the more sweeping proposals have not gained much ground, there are movements across certain kinds of treaties or mechanisms within treaties that reflect a consensus that international intellectual property law has overreached. Some states are revising or withdrawing from agreements with strong intellectual property protections.[3] Other solutions involve explicit limitations on the adjudicatory rights private parties enjoy under bilateral or multilateral instruments.[4]

Low- and middle-income states have also started to press for specific intellectual-property regimes in discrete issue areas such as seeds and agricultural technology, vaccines and other medicines, and product sectors such as alcohol, infant formula,

1 Kojo Yelpaala, *Quo Vadis WTO? The Threat of TRIPS and the Biodiversity Convention to Human Health and Food Security*, 30 B.U. Int'l L. J. 55, 63 (2012).

2 Carlos M. Correa, Implications of the Doha Declaration on the TRIPS Agreement and Public Health 13–18 (2002); Carlos M. Correa, Integrating Public Health Concerns into Patent Legislation in Developing Countries 22 (2000).

3 Mercedes Alvaro, *Ecuador Plans to Audit Bilateral Investment Treaties*, Wall Street Journal (Mar. 11, 2013), available at http://online.wsj.com/article/BT-CO-20130311–708469.html; Investment Treaty News, *South Africa Begins Withdrawing from EU-Member BITs* (Oct. 30, 2012), available at http://www.iisd.org/itn/2012/10/30/news-in-brief-90.

4 Daniela Caruso, *Private Law and State-Making in the Age of Globalization*, 39 N.Y.U. J. Int'l L. & Pol. 1 (2006).

and tobacco. Within these issue areas, what this book terms "International Intellectual Property Shelters" are changing or eliminating strong intellectual property rights guaranteed under other international agreements. They are also establishing mechanisms by which benefits derived from intellectual property–protected assets are redistributed to poorer countries. From access to medicines to the protection of biological resources (including seeds) to protection of populations from tobacco advertising and other health threats, a set of international agreements has emerged, which have either jettisoned intellectual property rights in specific issue areas or reengineered the way intellectual property protection incentives function.

10

Medicines and Vaccines

As Chapter 6 elaborated, the international protections for patents established in 1994 had an immediate, debilitating effect on the capacity of developing countries to respond to the HIV/AIDS epidemic. Burroughs Wellcome, a predecessor firm to GlaxoSmithKline, patented azidothymidine (a repurposed cancer drug) for HIV treatment in 1985.[1] The US Food and Drug Administration approved azidothymidine (AZT), marketed as Retrovir, in 1987.[2] In 1991, the FDA approved a second HIV drug; new drugs were approved on a regular basis thereafter.[3] In 1995, the AIDS drug "cocktail," or highly active antiretroviral therapy (HAART), was introduced with dramatic results.[4] By 1997, the number of AIDS deaths in the United States had nearly halved.[5]

The situation could not have been more different in developing countries, especially in sub-Saharan Africa. By 2004, the World Health Organization estimated that five to six million people in low- and middle-income countries needed antiretroviral treatment immediately.[6] However, only 400,000 people had access to it.[7]

The losses caused by HIV/AIDS affected the broader, more fragile food and social safety systems in high-prevalence countries:

1 Teresa Riordan, *Patents: A Court Ruling Extends Burroughs-Wellcome's Monopoly on the AIDS Drug AZT*, N.Y. Times (Nov. 28, 1994), available at http://www.nytimes.com/1994/11/28/business/patents-court-ruling-extends-burroughs-wellcome-s-monopoly-aids-drug-azt.html.

2 *Id.*

3 UCSF, HIV InSite: Didanosine (Videx), available at http://hivinsite.ucsf.edu/InSite?page=ar-01-02.

4 U.S. FDA, *Attacking AIDS with a Cocktail Therapy: Drug Combo Sends Deaths Plummeting*, AIDS Info (July 1, 1999), available at https://aidsinfo.nih.gov/news/493/attacking-aids-with-a-cocktail-therapy–drug-combo-sends-deaths-plummeting.

5 *Id.*

6 WHO, World Health Report 21 (2004); UNAIDS, 2004 Report on the global AIDS epidemic 101–02 (2004).

7 *Id.*

> A vicious cycle exists between food shortages, malnutrition and AIDS. In Zimbabwe, adult HIV prevalence is around 25%. By 2000, AIDS had robbed the country of between 5%–10% of its agricultural workforce. By 2020, FAO projects farm labor losses will approach 25%. In Malawi, households that lost females under age 60 were twice as likely to experience a food deficit as households in which men in the same age bracket had died. In Uganda, 1990s research demonstrated food insecurity and malnutrition were the most serious problems for many female-headed AIDS-affected households.[8]

Households became poorer as a result of the illness and death of members, and in many cases the adults with the highest incomes fell ill or died first. The result was "an erosion of social capital and socially reproductive labor."[9]

Chapter 6 outlined measures taken by Brazil and South Africa to facilitate access to HIV/AIDS drugs. Brazil imposed a requirement that patented medicines be manufactured there, the "local working requirement," while South Africa authorized the importation of drugs from countries where they cost less, or parallel imports. Both governments asserted the necessity for their measures as part of their responses to national public health emergencies.

In both cases, pharmaceutical firms mobilized their respective governments in Europe and North America to bring disputes based on the TRIPS agreement. They also directly challenged the measures in Brazilian and South African courts. South Africa was added to the US Special 301 list, the 1999 report asserting that "South Africa's Medicines Act appears to grant the Health Minister ill-defined authority to issue compulsory licenses, authorize parallel imports, and potentially otherwise abrogate patent rights."[10]

> In February 1998, forty-seven members of Congress sent a letter to the USTR calling for a response to the [South African law], stating that Section 15C permitted parallel importation and allowed for the "administrative expropriation of patented technology," both of which would violate the TRIPS Agreement. In July 1998, pending adequate progress on intellectual property rights protection in South Africa, the USTR used its discretion to withhold trade benefits for a range of South African products that had previously been approved under the Generalized System of Preferences (GSP) program. Furthermore, a provision was inserted into an omnibus appropriations act in October 1998 that conditioned U.S. development assistance to South Africa on the Secretary of State's written report on the steps being taken by the U.S. government to work with South Africa "to negotiate the repeal, suspension, or termination" of Section 15C. The Department of State submitted this report in February 1999, stating that all relevant agencies of the U.S. government "have been engaged in an assiduous, concerted campaign" to

8 *Id.* at 46.

9 Tony Barnett & Alan Whiteside, *Poverty and HIV/AIDS: Impact, Coping and Mitigation Policy*, in G. A. Cornia (ed), AIDS, PUBLIC POLICY AND CHILD WELL-BEING 209–44 (2006).

10 1999 USTR Special 301 Report.

> persuade South Africa to withdraw or modify Section 15C which the State Department believed was "inconsistent" with South Africa's obligations and commitments under TRIPS ... which mirrored statements made by PhRMA.[11]

The European Commission joined the United States in pressuring South Africa to repeal the legislation.[12]

In February 2000, William Daley, the US Secretary of Commerce, traveled to Brazil and Argentina with Raymond Gilmartin, the CEO of Merck, as well as a Pfizer executive to communicate "serious concerns [US] companies have" with medical patent laws. In Argentina, he threatened trade sanctions over the issue.[13] The US government launched an official action against Brazil at the World Trade Organization in June.[14]

Then as now, the number of manufacturers of HIV/AIDS medications was small. Between 1987 and 1990, GSK was the only manufacturer of an approved medication, and by 1995, there were only three.[15] Generics entered the global market after 2000. It was the highly concentrated nature of the sector that allowed the first steps toward discounted pricing of HIV/AIDS drugs. In May 2000, five UN organizations, including WHO and UNICEF, entered into an agreement with five pharmaceutical firms to implement the Accelerating Access Initiative, which offered ARVs at about 10 percent of the commercial price to the public-sector and nongovernmental organizations. The program imposed limiting conditions, but nevertheless showed the possibility of firm–to–international organization negotiation that led to increasing regulation of oligopolistic players whose products disproportionately affected basic human needs.[16]

The real changes to the international pharmaceutical patent regime occurred because of the same kinds of pressures exerted by developing countries during the 1970s. William Fisher and Cyril Rigamonti argue that the position of wealthy countries changed because "developing countries were united and acted as one group," as well as the potential necessity for Canada and the United States to use compulsory licenses during the anthrax scare of 2001 and the mobilization of the AIDS community.[17]

[11] William Fisher & Cyrill Rigamonti, *The South Africa AIDS Controversy: A Case Study in Patent Law and Policy* (Feb. 10, 2005), available at http://cyber.law.harvard.edu/people/tfisher/South%20Africa.pdf.

[12] Letter from Sir Leon Brittan, Vice-President of the European Commission, to Thabo Mbeki, Vice-President of South Africa (Mar. 23, 1998).

[13] Tina Rosenberg, *Look at Brazil,* N.Y. TIMES (Jan. 28, 2001), available at http://www.nytimes.com/2001/01/28/magazine/look-at-brazil.html.

[14] U.S. Request for Consultations, WT/DS199/1 (June 8, 2000).

[15] Joan-Ramone Borrell, *Pricing and Patents of HIV/AIDS Drugs in Developing Countries,* 39 APPLIED ECONOMICS 508 (2009).

[16] IFPMA, *Accelerating Access Initiative (AAI) Factsheet* (2007), available at www.ifpma.org/site_docs/Health/AAI_Factsheet_Jan_07_Q3_2006.pdf.

[17] Fisher & Rigamonti, *supra* note 15, at 15.

In response to the US complaint against Brazil at the WTO, Brazil raised issues of US patent policy that provided allegedly discriminatory support for its pharmaceutical industry.[18] At the WTO, the African Group raised the issues of the HIV/AIDS epidemic, parallel imports, and compulsory licenses at the Fourth Ministerial Conference, held in Doha, Qatar, in November 2001. As a result of the conference, the WTO Member States adopted the Declaration on the TRIPS Agreement and Public Health ("Doha Declaration").[19]

The Doha Declaration on TRIPS and Public Health remains the most famous international intellectual property shelter.[20] Formed to safeguard low- and middle-income countries' access to medicines for HIV/AIDS, tuberculosis, malaria, and "other epidemics," the Doha Declaration established that treatments for diseases affecting low- and middle-income countries deserved different treatment than the typical intellectual property–based exclusivity/price structure characteristic of the regime favored by TRIPS.[21] Instead, afflicted countries should, and ultimately did, enjoy greater flexibility to control monopoly prices strong intellectual property rights caused.[22] The Declaration was specific as to the "commitment of developed-country members to provide incentives to their enterprises and institutions to promote and encourage technology transfer to least-developed country members."[23] Least developed countries now have until 2033 to comply with TRIPS.[24]

The Doha Declaration essentially created a TRIPS-free zone for government policies aimed at assuring access to medicines for the three designated diseases and perhaps other "epidemics":

5. . . .

a. In applying the customary rules of interpretation of public international law, each provision of the TRIPS Agreement shall be read in the light of the object and purpose of the Agreement as expressed, in particular, in its objectives and principles.
b. Each member has the right to grant compulsory licences and the freedom to determine the grounds upon which such licences are granted.
c. Each member has the right to determine what constitutes a national emergency or other circumstances of extreme urgency, it being understood that public health crises, including those relating to HIV/AIDS, tuberculosis,

18 35 U.S.C. §§ 204, 209 (2004).
19 https://www.wto.org/english/thewto_e/minist_e/min01_e/mindecl_trips_e.htm.
20 Sam Halabi, *International Intellectual Property Shelters*, 90(4) Tulane L. Rev. 903 (2016).
21 Elizabeth Chien-Hale & Fred Abbott, *Intellectual Property Rights in Global Trade Framework: IP Trends in Developing Countries*, 98 Proceedings of the Annual Meeting (American Society of International Law) 95–99 (2004).
22 TRIPS art. 31.
23 James Gathi, *The Legal Status of the Doha Declaration under the Vienna Convention on the Law of Treaties*, 15 Harv. J. L. & Tech. 291, 295 (2002).
24 https://www.wto.org/english/news_e/news15_e/trip_06nov15_e.htm.

> malaria and other epidemics, can represent a national emergency or other circumstances of extreme urgency . . .[25]

Wealthy countries also established global financing mechanisms for purposes of facilitating interventions to address diseases that disproportionately affected poorer countries. Contemporaneously with the Doha Declaration, Japan introduced the idea of a global fund for the treatment of HIV/AIDS, tuberculosis, and malaria (Global Fund), which materialized in 2003. The Global Fund is a public–private partnership dedicated to collecting/allocating resources and funds for interventions aimed at the "burden of AIDS, [TB] and malaria."[26] Each developing country has control over its own implementation of measures to prevent the spread of these diseases and is provided funding based on the effectiveness of the measures used.[27] In May 2003, the US Congress enacted and US President George W. Bush signed the "U.S. Leadership Against AIDS, Tuberculosis and Malaria Act of 2003" (P.L. 108–25) (PEPFAR). The law authorized spending of up to $15 billion over five years and created the Office of the Global AIDS Coordinator (OGAC) to manage and coordinate US government–supported HIV/AIDS programs in developing countries.[28]

The market share, by volume, of generic manufacturers in developing countries consequently increased, from virtually none in 2001 to more than 98 percent in 2012.[29] The competition between manufacturers, coupled with high-volume purchases by Global Fund and PEPFAR, has brought the annual cost of AIDS medicines to less than 1 percent of the price in 2000.[30] The rents pharmaceutical patent holders would have obtained under the old system have been partially replaced by the incentive to win opportunities through international funding mechanisms. Indeed, the entire global market has been restructured so that there are a small number of generics manufacturers that sell to a small number of large purchasers.[31]

The Doha Declaration by its terms carved out HIV/AIDS, tuberculosis, and malaria as diseases for which the rewards for medical and research and innovation could be expected to function differently than the patent-and-reward system

[25] Declaration on the TRIPS Agreement and Public Health (Doha Agreement) available at http://www.wto.org/english/thewto_e/minist_e/min01_e/mindecl_trips_e.htm.

[26] *Who We Are*, The Global Fund to Fight AIDS, Tuberculosis, and Malaria, available at http://www.theglobalfund.org/en/about/whoweare/.

[27] *Id.*

[28] Center for Global Development, Overview of the President's Emergency Plan for AIDS Relief (PEPFAR), available at https://www.cgdev.org/page/overview-president%E2%80%99s-emergency-plan-aids-relief-pepfar.

[29] UNITAID, HIV Medicines Technology and Market Landscape 46 (2014), available at https://unitaid.eu/assets/HIV-Meds-Landscape-March2014.pdf.

[30] WHO, Access to Retroviral Drugs in Low- and Middle-Income Countries (2014), available at http://apps.who.int/medicinedocs/documents/s21630en/s21630en.pdf.

[31] *Id.*

pharmaceutical firms envisioned when challenging Brazil's and South Africa's measures to reduce antiretroviral drug prices. Together with international financing mechanisms, the Doha Declaration redistributed default monopoly rents pharmaceutical patents previously directed to the major pharmaceutical firms to (largely Indian) generics firms.[32] Since 1995, Brazil, India, South Africa, and Thailand have led in using parallel imports, TRIPS flexibilities, and compulsory licenses to expand access to medicines for their own populations as well as to obtain collective gains for developing countries generally.[33]

It was and is conceivable that the Doha Declaration may have energized more aggressive compulsory licensing activity outside of the diseases explicitly named in the agreement. In 2007, Thailand granted a compulsory license for the heart disease medication marketed as Plavix. Thailand also issued compulsory licenses for four cancer drugs, the disease burden of which is heavier than HIV/AIDS.[34] In 2012, India granted a compulsory license for kidney and liver cancer medications.[35] Since 1995, "more than half the compulsory licensing episodes occurred in upper middle income countries (including Brazil and Thailand)."[36] Retaliatory measures by both governments and manufacturers have pushed innovators and governments to the bargaining table. Compulsory license activity has abated since Doha, with the enhanced bargaining power of developing states leading to more effective direct negotiations between manufacturers and governments.[37]

So what did Doha do?[38] Between 1998 and 2001, when it was adopted, it caused the fundamental restructuring of global markets for antiretroviral drugs. It did so through the effective regulation of then-dominant pharmaceutical firms, the dilution of theretofore strong patent rights on HIV/AIDS drugs, and the transfer of the industrial centers of production to middle-income countries. Throughout that process, Brazil, India, South Africa, and Thailand emphasized the unique development situations they faced and the challenges disease burdens posed for development.

32 UNITAID, *supra* note 33.

33 Read Beall & Randall Kuhn, *Trends in Trends in Compulsory Licensing of Pharmaceuticals since the Doha Declaration: A Database Analysis*, available at http://www.plosmedicine.org/article/info%3Adoi%2F10.1371%2Fjournal.pmed.1001154.

34 Toni Johnson, *The Debate Over Generic Drug Trade*, Council on Foreign Relations Backgrounder, available at http://www.cfr.org/drugs/debate-over-generic-drug-trade/p18055.

35 Vikas Bajaj & Andrew Pollack, *India Orders Bayer to License a Patented Drug*, N.Y. Times (Mar. 12, 2012), available at http://www.nytimes.com/2012/03/13/business/global/india-overrules-bayer-allowing-generic-drug.html?_r=0.

36 Beall & Kuhn, supra note 47.

37 A. Nunn, E. Da Fonsecab & S. Gruskind, *Changing Global Essential Medicines Norms to Improve Access to AIDS Treatment: Lessons from Brazil*, 4 Global Public Health 131–49 (2009); K. Lee, L. C. Chagas & T. E. Novotny: *Brazil and the Framework Convention on Tobacco Control: Global Health Diplomacy as Soft Power*, 7 PLoS Med. 1–5 (2010).

38 *Id.*

THE MEDICAL RESEARCH AND INNOVATION TREATY

The controversies leading up to the Doha Declaration prompted a broader movement supporting an international agreement to restructure intellectual property incentives in the access-to-medicines context. To be sure, part of the larger problem was that monopoly rents supported by patents, trademarks, trade dress, and data exclusivity meant medicines like antiretrovirals, cancer treatments, and diabetes control drugs would lie out of reach for low- and middle-income countries.[39] But a similar if not larger part of the problem was that drug innovation and development did not occur for Type II and Type III diseases that primarily afflicted low- and middle-income countries.[40] The diseases for which the market would likely be paltry attracted little research-and-development funding.[41]

In 2005, Kenya submitted a resolution to the World Health Organization's Executive Board requesting the creation of a group of member states to discuss a new global framework on medical research and development. In January 2006, Brazil joined the resolution as a co-sponsor. Brazil then requested that a committee of the Executive Board contemplate a framework convention on medical research and development. In May 2006, the World Health Assembly adopted resolution 59.24, *Public Health, Innovation, Essential Health Research and Intellectual Property Rights*, which called for an intergovernmental working group to study the relationship between intellectual property rights, other forms of financing, and the global problem of diseases unlikely to attract purely private-sector attention.[42] In 2012, the WHO's Consultative Expert Working Group published *Research and Development to Meet Health Needs in Developing Countries: Strengthening Global Financing and Coordination*, in which it called for a binding framework treaty to address innovation and research capacity in developing countries and to design a system to promote development of treatments through incentive and other financing mechanisms.[43]

39 Multiple theories of intellectual property protection might apply to the same good. For example, a pharmaceutical patent might apply to a given compound, while trademark or trade dress protection might apply to the appearance of a given pill. Jeremy A. Greene & Aaron S. Kesselheim, *Why Do the Same Drugs Look Different? Pills, Trade Dress, and Public Health*, 365 New Engl. J. Med. 83 (2011).

40 WHO, Defining Disease Types I, II, and III (2012), available at http://www.who.int/phi/3-background_cewg_agenda_item5_disease_types_final.pdf.

41 WHO, Consultative Expert Working Group, Research and Development to Meet Health Needs in Developing Countries: Strengthening Global Financing and Coordination 1–2, available at http://www.who.int/phi/CEWG_Report_5_April_2012.pdf.

42 *Public Health, Innovation and Intellectual Property Rights: Report of the Commission on Intellectual Property Rights, Innovation and Public Health* available at http://apps.who.int/medicinedocs/en/d/Js21428en/.

43 The proposed treaty has been variously called the Essential Health and Biomedical R&D treaty, the Medical Research and Development treaty, the Biomedical R&D treaty, etc.

The CEWG's report extensively covered the obstacles strong IP protections pose for addressing medical research and development needs in developing countries. The report addressed existing IP instruments viewing a medical research and innovation "convention not as a replacement for the existing intellectual property rights system but as a supplementary instrument where the current system does not function" and emphasizing the need for research and development breakthroughs to be shared with other researchers free from the constraints intellectual property protections normally impose.[44]

For example, for Type II and Type III diseases, which disproportionately affect populations in developing countries, the CEWG recommends a binding international treaty that provides for open innovation models where research and development costs are covered by public or philanthropic sources and research results are made available in the public domain; licensing conditions imposed by funders or research organizations that permit nonexclusive licensing or prescribe a low target price for a product; advance market commitments or prize funds that involve separate payments to compensate for the costs of R&D and prescribe either predetermined product prices at a low level or permit competitive manufacture of developed products; and more comprehensive schemes that envisage wholesale replacement of the intellectual property innovation and exclusivity system.[45]

The separation of compensation for research and development from end-user price aims at the core of how intellectual property-intensive industries have achieved their large scale. "Prizes," for example, may impose voluntary or non-voluntary terms on biomedical innovators. Voluntary prize systems offer an option between a specified prize amount for a given medical breakthrough and the default patent exclusivities and may work best where the market for a given therapy is likely to be small.[46] Non-voluntary prizes replace the monopoly system entirely and address the pricing abuses and access problems caused by election of patent exclusivities.[47]

"Advance purchase commitments"("APCs") or advance market commitments ("AMCs") are legally-binding agreements for an amount to subsidize the purchase, at a specified price, of an as yet unavailable therapy against a specific disease causing high morbidity and mortality in developing countries."[48] Theoretically, AMCs should encourage the development of next-generation medicines and vaccines

[44] Report, *supra* note 42, at 122, 147.

[45] Jean-Paul Chretien, Caitlin M. Rivers & Michael A. Johansson, *Make Data Sharing Routine to Prepare forPublic Health Emergencies*, 13(8) PLoS (Aug. 16, 2016), http://journals.plos.org/plosmedicine/article/asset?id=10.1371%2Fjournal.pmed.1002109.PDF.

[46] James Love & Tim Hubbard, *The Big Idea: Prizes to Stimulate R&D for New* Medicines, 82 Chi-Kent L. Rev. 1519, 1522 (2007).

[47] *Id.*

[48] World Health Organization, *Advanced Market Commitments for Vaccines*, available at http://www.who.int/immunization/newsroom/amcs/en/.

and accelerate the development and availability of these products to poor countries.[49] Governments or donors may spend estimable, if large, sums of money to buy products at high prices and then deliver them to the populations in developing countries.[50]

Other possibilities in the framework treaty may be pricing terms whereby developing countries pay only for the marginal production and distribution costs of new drugs or vaccines.[51] Under this system, "the relevant production and marketing costs would be covered in each market regardless of its average income level, while research and development cost would be paid only in the industrialized countries."[52] The core CEWG recommendations call for delinking research and development costs from ultimate profits as well as encouraging more unobstructed sharing of information for diseases that specially affect developing countries.[53]

Deep divides still stand in the way of the formation of the agreement. The idea of the treaty, whatever its exact origin, has become a cause supported in large part by Brazil and Kenya and the many low- and middle-income countries that stand to gain from a treaty that allocates more resources to research into neglected diseases and dilutes intellectual property rights in general. European countries, especially those with large pharmaceutical firm operations, have overwhelmingly opposed the treaty.

In 2013, the United States proposed the use of a series of demonstration projects that might bridge the current deep divides between member states over the treaty's terms.[54] Those demonstration projects, which feature openly available research findings, are as of this writing under way.[55] In 2016, the World Health Organization also created an analytic tool elaborating seven implementation scenarios for a new financing mechanism and estimated how many products, either new or repurposed, might be developed under such a mechanism.[56] The scenarios range from WHO acting primarily as a convener to set priorities to the management of a pooled fund of various sizes (from US$15 million to US$500 million annually) to finance development of needed health products, diagnostics, vaccines, and treatments, from promising leads through to the launch of a new product.[57]

49 Donald Light, *Saving the Pneumococcal AMC and GAVI*, 7 Human Vaccines 138 (2011), available at http://www.landesbioscience.com/journals/vaccines/News-HV7-2-policy.pdf.

50 *Id.*

51 Stuart O. Schweitzer & William S. Comanor, *Prices of Pharmaceuticals in Poor Countries Are Much Lower Than in Wealthy Countries*, Heath Aff. (Aug. 2011), http://content.healthaffairs.org/content/30/8/1553.full.

52 *Id.*

53 WHO, Movement for Open Data during Emergencies Intensifies as Zika Spreads (2016), available at http://www.who.int/csr/research-and-development/open_data_zika_emergencie/en/.

54 Halabi, supra note 24.

55 WHO, Progress Report, available at http://apps.who.int/gb/CEWG/pdf_files/A_RDMCF_2-en.pdf.

56 *Id.*

57 *Id.*

THE PANDEMIC INFLUENZA PREPAREDNESS FRAMEWORK

When Indonesia refused to share H5N1 influenza samples in 2006, it invoked both legal and redistributional justifications.[58] Legally, Indonesia cited Article 15 of the Convention on Biological Diversity, which recognized the "sovereign rights of States over their natural resources, the authority to determine access to genetic resources" and the ability to do so "with the aim of sharing in a fair and equitable way the results of research and development and the benefits arising from the commercial and other utilization of genetic resources."[59] While it remains controversial, Indonesia's assertion that the treaty's use of "genetic resources" included human pathogens caused a fundamental rethinking of how and why global research into infectious diseases was undertaken.[60] This was related to Indonesia's redistributional demand: the long-term observable effect of Indonesia's participation in the theretofore uninterrupted global influenza surveillance system administered by the World Health Organization was the patenting of viral components, subsequent vaccines, and other components like adjuvants by pharmaceutical firms in wealthy countries.[61] Priced out of the reach of ordinary Indonesians or the government on their behalf, the system seemed like an instrument of exploitation.[62] Indonesia claimed that it should not have to share if the viruses were going to be used to create vaccines it could not afford.[63]

Following an interim agreement for Indonesia to resume sharing influenza virus samples with WHO, health ministers of eighteen Asia-Pacific countries called upon WHO to "convene the necessary meetings, initiate the critical processes and obtain the essential commitment of all stakeholders to establish the mechanisms for more open virus and information sharing and accessibility to avian influenza and other potential pandemic influenza vaccines for developing countries."[64] Several developing countries, including Brazil and Thailand, supported the Indonesian decision.[65]

58 Laurie Garrett & David Fidler, *Sharing H5N1 Viruses to Stop a Global Influenza Pandemic*, 4 (11) PLoS MED. E330 (2007), available at http://journals.plos.org/plosmedicine/article?id=10.1371/journal.pmed.0040330.

59 Convention on Biological Diversity art. 15.

60 David P. Fidler & Lawrence O. Gostin, *The WHO Pandemic Influenza Preparedness Framework: A Milestone in Global Governance for Health*, 306 J. AM. MED. ASS'N 200, 200 (2011).

61 World Intellectual Property Organization, *An Update on Intellectual Property Claims Related to Global Pandemic Influenza Preparedness* (Apr. 2011), available http://apps.who.int/medicinedocs/en/d/Js21426en/.

62 Stefan Elbe, *Haggling Over Viruses: The Downside Risks of Securitizing Infectious Disease*, 25 HEALTH POL'Y & PLAN. 476, 477 (2010).

63 Jason Carter, *Who's Virus Is It Anyway? How the World Health Organization Can Protect Against Claims of "Viral Sovereignty,"* 38 GA. J. INT'L & COMP. L. 717, 729 (2010).

64 Jakarta Declaration (2007).

65 Sangeeta Shashikant, *Milestone Virus/Benefit-Sharing Agreement with Shortcomings*, GLOBAL HEALTH WATCH (May 6, 2011), available at www.ghwatch.org/sites/www.ghwatch.org/files/PIP_sangeeta.doc.

Two years later, when Mexico acted quickly, diligently, and in accordance with its obligations to detect, report, and respond to pandemic H1N1 influenza, it nevertheless experienced substantial difficulty in obtaining vaccines.[66] This was so even though the United States was a major source of pandemic vaccine.[67] The experience with H1N1 was broadly shared across the world, as wealthy countries were able to achieve wide immunization coverage for their populations while those in developing countries waited for months and, in many cases, only received vaccines after it was clear that the strain was not particularly severe.[68]

At the 2009 World Health Assembly, countries acknowledged that "member states have a commitment to share, on an equal footing, H5N1 and other influenza viruses of human pandemic potential and the benefits, considering these as equally important parts of the collective action for global public health."[69] The resolution resurrected, in the context of pandemic disease, the fundamental redistributional problems intellectual property protections posed. Wealthy countries with strong pharmaceutical industries opposed a formal relationship between virus sharing and resulting benefits, preferring "market-based" arrangements that might proceed on a country-to-country or country-to-firm basis. As one EU delegate quipped, "We need their virus, they need our vaccine, nobody needs this framework."[70]

Developing countries, on the other hand, demanded a formal link between virus sharing and biomedical products resulting from research on the viruses. This link would be achieved through a binding agreement, enforceable in a neutral forum, that designated benefits for developing countries. Not only governments but also firms would be party to these agreements.[71] This type of "benefit sharing," developing countries argued, would be essential to properly manage global disease threats.[72]

66 Richard Knox, *WHO Resolves Impasse over Sharing of Flu Viruses, Access to Medicines*, NPR (Apr. 18, 2011), available at http://www.npr.org/blogs/health/2011/04/18/135519592/who-resolves-impasse-over-sharing-of-flu-viruses-access-to-vaccines.

67 David P. Fidler, *Negotiating Equitable Access to Influenza Vaccines: Global Health Diplomacy and the Controversies Surrounding Avian Influenza H5N1 and Pandemic Influenza H1NI*, 7(5) PLoS Med. 1 (2010), available at http://www.plosmedicine.org/article/info%3Adoi%2F10.1371%2Fjournal.pmed.1000247.

68 Sam Halabi, *Obstacles to pH1N1 Vaccine Availability: The Complex Contracting Relationship between Vaccine Manufacturers, WHO, Donor and Beneficiary Governments*, in M. A. Stoto & M. Higdon (eds), The Public Health Response to H1N1: A Systems Perspective 203–16 (2015).

69 World Health Assembly Resolution 60.28 (2009).

70 Florian Rabitz, The Global Governance of Genetic Resources: Institutional Change and Structural Constraints 112 (2017).

71 Harvey V. Fineberg, *Pandemic Preparedness and Response — Lessons from the H1N1 Influenza of 2009*, 370 New Engl. J. Med. 1335 (2014).

72 *Interim ECDC Scientific and Public Health Briefing: Updated December 2008 Sharing Influenza Virus Samples & Influenza Vaccine Benefit Sharing*, Executive Summary Only, ECDC (Dec. 2008), available at http://ecdc.europa.eu/en/healthtopics/Documents/2012_ECDC_EU_Briefing_Influenza_Virus_Sharing_200812_Final_ES_Dec4th.pdf.

After four years of negotiations, the result was the Pandemic Influenza Preparedness Framework (PIP).[73] The PIP was explicitly committed to "increase[ing] the access of developing countries to vaccines and other pandemic related supplies."[74] Under the Framework, major pharmaceutical manufacturers retain their ability to access samples shared through the World Health Organization's Global Influenza Surveillance and Response System, but now firms using the system must contribute toward half the cost of its maintenance (approximately $30 million annually).[75] During the 2009–10 H1N1 pandemic, the World Health Organization negotiated with four major influenza vaccine manufacturers (CSL [Seqirus], GSK, AstraZeneca (MedImmune), and Novartis) and in 2015 CSL acquired Novartis's influenza vaccine business.[76] Four firms now control 80 percent of the global influenza vaccine market.[77] Three of them entered into agreements with WHO for access to influenza samples, while Merck holds licensing arrangements with CSL and did with Sanofi (for Europe) until 2017.[78]

Firms must promise to share either intellectual property, products developed through use of the system, or other medical countermeasures critical to pandemic response:

> For manufacturers of vaccines and/or antivirals, the recipient shall commit to at least two of the following options:
>
> A1. Donate at least 10 percent of real time pandemic vaccine production to WHO
>
> A2. Reserve at least 10 percent of real time pandemic vaccine production at affordable prices to WHO.
>
> A3. Donate at least X treatment courses of needed antiviral medicine for the pandemic to WHO.
>
> A4. Reserve at least X treatment courses of needed antiviral medicine for the pandemic at affordable prices.
>
> A5. Grant to manufacturers in developing countries licenses on mutually agreed terms that should be fair and reasonable including in respect of affordable royalties, taking into account development levels in the country of end use of the products, on technology, know-how, products and processes for which it

[73] *Pandemic Influenza Preparedness: In Search of a Global Ethos*, http://www.ghwatch.org/sites/www.ghwatch.org/files/B8.pdf, 149–50 (2011).

[74] WHO, *Pandemic Preparedness Framework* (2011) available at http://www.who.int/influenza/pip/en/.

[75] Lawrence O. Gostin et al., *Virus Sharing, Genetic Sequencing, and Global Health Security*, 345 SCIENCE 1295, 1296 (Sep. 12, 2014).

[76] Halabi, *supra* note 72.

[77] Global Vaccine Market Features and Trends (2010) available at http://who.int/influenza_vaccines_plan/resources/session_10_kaddar.pdf.

[78] Pharmaceutical Technology Editors, *Merck and CSL Sign Vaccine Pact*, PHARMTECH (Oct. 5, 2009), available at http://www.pharmtech.com/week-oct-5-2009-merck-and-csl-sign-flu-vaccine-pact-cardinal-health-names-vp-more; Sy Mukherjee, *Sanofi and Merck Are Ditching 22-Year-Old Joint Venture*, FORTUNE (Mar. 8, 2016), available at http://fortune.com/2016/03/08/sanofi-merck-joint-venture/.

holds IPR for the production of (i) influenza vaccines, (ii) adjuvants, (iii) antivirals and/or (iv) diagnostics.

A6. Grant royalty-free licenses to manufacturers in developing countries or grant to WHO royalty-free, non-exclusive licenses on IPR, which can be sublicensed, for the production of pandemic influenza vaccines, adjuvants, antivirals products and diagnostics needed in a pandemic. WHO may sublicense these licenses to manufacturers in developing countries on appropriate terms and conditions and in accordance with sound public health principles.[79]

Although the framework is specific to pandemic influenza, the outbreak of Ebola in West Africa and more general calls for equitable sharing of benefits using genetic resources from developing countries have made it a preliminary model for redistributing wealth from richer countries to poorer ones.[80] The UN review panel convened in the wake of the Ebola crisis called explicitly for the agreement to be extended to "other novel pathogens, making it legally binding, and achieving an appropriate balance between obligations and benefits, in accordance with the principles of the 2010 Nagoya Protocol to the Convention on Biological Diversity" (discussed in Chapter 11).[81] The PIP framework can be plausibly understood to be the result of low- and middle-income countries changing the international intellectual property regime both ex ante (access to materials for research and development) and ex post (sharing of intellectual property-generated products).[82]

79 WHO, PANDEMIC INFLUENZA PREPAREDNESS FRAMEWORK 34 (2011), available at http://apps.who.int/gb/pip/pdf_files/pandemic-influenza-preparedness-en.pdf.

80 *Id.*

81 *Protecting Humanity from Future Health Crisis, Report of the High level Panel on the Global Response to Health Crises*, http://www.un.org/News/dh/infocus/HLP/2016-02-05_Final_Report_Global_Response_to_Health_Crises.pdf.

82 Suerie Moon et al., *Will Ebola Change the Game? Ten Essential Reforms before the Next Pandemic. The Report of the Harvard-LSHTM Independent Panel on the Global Response to Ebola*, LANCET (Nov. 22, 2015), http://www.who.int/about/who_reform/emergency-capacities/advisory-group/Report-Harvard-LSHTM.pdf.

11

Biological and Plant Genetic Resources for Agriculture

In Chapter 5, the process leading to the Convention on Biological Diversity was elaborated as fundamentally embodying the principles of the New International Economic Order. Its final text was opened for signature at the 1992 Earth Summit in Rio de Janeiro (its sibling treaties are the U.N. Framework Convention on Climate Change and the U.N. Convention to Combat Desertification), although it was drafted before then.[1] The Conference for the Adoption of the Agreed Text of the CBD met at the headquarters of the U.N. Environmental Programme in Nairobi in May 1992. The CBD process unfolded parallel to TRIPS, so that the two treaties established, in some contexts, principles inevitably in tension with one another. The CBD has been a significant source of international agreements that change or jettison the intellectual property rules that would otherwise prevail under TRIPS regimes.

In some cases, the CBD's influence has been indirect, as it was leading to the Pandemic Influenza Preparedness Framework. In other circumstances, such as those related to plant genetic resources for agriculture, its text has served as the foundation for the establishment of additional international intellectual property shelters for seeds and farmers. Although the CBD codified the decades-old principle of "technology transfer" in Article 16, it was Article 15's and Article 19's provisions for sharing benefits on mutually agreed terms and direct participation by developing countries that opened windows for national and international supervision of global agrochemical firms.[2]

[1] H. David Cooper, *The Int'l Treaty on Plant Genetic Resources for Food and Agriculture*, *RECIEL* 11 (1) 1 (2002).

[2] Shailaja Fennell, Law, Institutions and International Development: The Interrelations between Legal Reform and International Development 152 (2010).

THE CONVENTION ON BIOLOGICAL DIVERSITY

The Convention on Biological Diversity (CBD) descended directly from the 1962 UN General Assembly's Declaration on Permanent Sovereignty over Natural Resources, which asserted that it was the inalienable right of each state to handle natural resources as they saw fit and that any profits resulting from the use of these resources should be shared "between investors and the recipient state," as well as the UN's 1972 Stockholm Declaration that highlighted the "importance of scientific research in the context of environmental problems" and sought to establish the "free flow of up-to-date scientific information" as a possible solution.[3] As a result of these declarations and the New International Economic Order generally, developing nations sought to exercise sovereign control over genetic resources. Some governments made it more difficult for foreign scientists and bio-prospectors to obtain resources from their territories.[4] Other governments began to limit or question their participation in one of the critical hubs of the Green Revolution, the Consultative Group for International Agricultural Research (CGIAR).[5]

Alongside the environmental developments described in Chapter 5, countries sought formal international regulation, via a binding international treaty, that would address the exploitation of genetic resources for agriculture, food, and medicine. The CBD resulted, codifying in a legal instrument that developing countries should not only control access to genetic resources but also benefit from any commercial value generated from their utilization.[6] The CBD adopted as one of its objectives the promotion of conservation, and sustainable use, of biological diversity while seeking "fair and equitable" sharing of benefit derived.[7] The CBD's goal of "access and benefit sharing" includes both plant genetic resources as well as the relevant technology associated with their development.[8] It also codified the protection of indigenous peoples and the traditional knowledge they had developed especially for medical and agricultural applications, including a principle of compensation when firms or others commercialized that knowledge.[9] The CBD created a legal zone in

3 Permanent Sovereignty over Natural Resources, G.A. Res. 1803, U.N. GAOR, 17th Sess. Supp. No. 17. U.N. Soc. A/5127, 15 (1962); Stockholm Declaration, G.A. Res. 2998, U.N. Doc. A/CONF/48/14 (Dec. 15, 1972).

4 Jerome H. Reichman, Paul Uhlir & Tom Dedeurwaerdere, Governing Digitally Integrated Genetic Resources, Data, and Literature: Global Intellectual Property Strategies for a Redesigned Microbial Research Commons, 89–90 (2016).

5 Some countries began to demand the return of resources that they feared would be the subject of attempts at patenting or obtaining other intellectual property rights. *Id.* at 90.

6 Convention on Biological Diversity, *open for signature* June 5, 1992, 1760 U.N.T.S. 79. There are 198 states party to the CBD. The United States is not a party.

7 CBD art. 1.

8 Jonathan Carr, *Agreements That Divide: TRIPS vs. CBD and Proposals for Mandatory Disclosure of Source and Origin of Genetic Resources in Patent Applications*, 18 J. of Transnat'l Law and Policy 131, 133 (2008).

9 CBD art. 8.

which biodiverse-rich countries could set terms for exploitation and the protection of their citizens to share in the benefits of any commercialization of their resources.[10] More than sixty nations have created Access and Benefit Sharing (ABS) regimes via their domestic laws, with particular activity from biodiverse-rich states such as Brazil, China, Costa Rica, Kenya, the Philippines, and South Africa.[11]

Article 2 of the CBD defines "genetic resources" as "genetic materials of actual or potential value," which includes "any material of plant, animal, microbial, or other origin containing functional units of heredity."[12] Subsequent agreements, especially the Nagoya Protocol, expanded this definition. Even then, the broadness of "actual or potential value" allows consideration of "nonmonetary benefits" into benefit-sharing alternatives. Article 15 incorporates prior informed consent (PIC) and mutually agreed terms (MAT) as conditions for both access and use of resources.[13] Article 16 incorporates the New International Economic Order demand for technology transfer as a form of benefit that could be available to provider countries.[14] It specifically ties terms of access to intellectual property rights providing that "patents and other intellectual property rights may have an influence on the implementation of [the Biodiversity Convention], [so Parties] shall cooperate in this regard subject to national legislation and international law in order to ensure that such rights are supportive of and do not run counter to its objectives."[15]

While the CBD permits the possibility of regional and multilateral approaches to the issues the treaty covers, it implies by its terms prior informed consent and an agreement be negotiated with every provider/user transaction.[16] The bilateral approach, if implemented effectively, potentially provides an enormous amount of control over intellectual property rights asserted over genetic resources in developing countries.[17] Article 15's requirement for informed consent for access presumes the commercial potential of all research efforts.[18]

As detailed in Chapter 5, in the early 1980s, the expanding protections for patents on agrochemical products and plant breeders' rights led developing countries to mistrust the *ex situ* sharing system characterized by CGIAR, believe the open sharing of materials and information system was under threat, and then take measures to attempt to protect that system from intellectual property claims by firms

10 Michiel Korthals & Bram De Jonge, *Two Different Ethical Notions of Benefit Sharing of Genetic Resources and Their Implications for Global Development*, 28 New Genetics and Society 87, 89 (2009).

11 Nicolas Pauchard, *Access and Benefit Sharing under the Convention on Biological Diversity and Its Protocol: What Can Some Numbers Tell Us about the Effectiveness of the Regulatory Regime?*, 6 Resources 1–15 (2017).

12 CBD art. 2.

13 CBD art. 15(2).

14 CBD art. 16(1).

15 CBD art. 16(5).

16 Reichman et. al., *supra* note 4, at 96.

17 *Id.* at 106.

18 *Id.* at 109.

in Europe and North America.[19] The CBD itself endeavored to balance "open-exchange" policies that were typical with CGIAR repositories and other seed banks with the interests of states with substantial reservoirs of genetic resources.[20] In addition, the Convention encourages parties disclose the country of origin of plant genetic resources in applications for intellectual property rights.[21]

The CGIAR played a vital role in allowing countries to utilize genetic resources that had been developed, often in other countries, to allow sustainable agricultural development.[22] Yet, the proliferation of patents and plant breeder's rights made these countries more eager to pursue claims of biopiracy, making the CGIAR a target from some of those governments.[23] The CGIAR sought protection from FAO's Commission on Plant Genetic Resources, which led to resolutions during the 1990s that "recognized both claims of national sovereignty over genetic resources" and a farmer's and intellectual property rights holders "rights ... to share in the benefits of commercial applications of those resources."[24] In 1994, twelve CGIAR Research Centers signed agreements with the FAO that placed their *ex situ* seed banks within an FAO international network.[25] The agreement allowed the CGIAR to maintain its *ex situ* collections through the continued germplasm contributions of International Agricultural Research Centers, while the FAO recognized the IARCs as "'trustees' of the international community," unable to make ownership claims or seek intellectual property rights for resources.[26]

THE INTERNATIONAL TREATY ON PLANT GENETIC RESOURCES FOR FOOD AND AGRICULTURE (INTERNATIONAL SEED TREATY)

The resolution to the CBD's ambiguity with respect to *ex situ* plant genetic resources for agriculture, plant breeders' rights, farmers' rights, and the interests of developing countries was the International Treaty on Plant Genetic Resources for

[19] Christine Godt, Networks of Ex Situ Collections of Genetic Resources, Common Pools of Genetic Resources (2013).

[20] In one case entomologists studying the Western Ghats in India were forced to abort their project by local authorities due to biopiracy fears. K. S. Jayaraman, *Entomologist Stifled by Indian Bureaucracy*, 452 Nature 7 (Mar. 5, 2008), available at http://www.nature.com/news/2008/080305/full/452007a.html.

[21] Cary Fowler & Toby Hodgkin, *Plant Genetic Resources for Food and Agriculture: Assessing Global Availability*, 29 Annu. Rev. Environ. Resour. 143, 154 (2004).

[22] Reichman et al., *supra* note 4 at 115.

[23] In Mexico, a major bioprospecting project failed to take off because it could not obtain the unanimous consent of the villages involved. Sabina Safrin, *Hyperownership in a Time of Biotechnology Promises: The International Conflicts to Control the Building Blocks of Life*, 98 Am. J. Int'l L. 641, 656 (2004).

[24] *Id.* at 116.

[25] *Id.*

[26] *Id.* at 117.

Food and Agriculture (International Seed Treaty).[27] It is in many ways the embodiment of a disagreement between North American, European, and Japanese governments and low- and middle-income countries that begins with Article 27 of TRIPS. Low- and middle-income countries always maintained that Article 27 was inconsistent with the Convention on Biological Diversity, and the International Seed Treaty achieved, in part, a mechanism under which developing countries could adopt national legislation that effected some of their desired changes under Article 27. The treaty was adopted on November 3, 2001, after a seven-year negotiation process, and entered into force in 2004.[28] The International Seed Treaty was adopted pursuant to the Convention on Biological Diversity and updated the International Undertaking on Plant Genetic Resources.[29]

While the International Seed Treaty was adopted in "harmony" with the CBD, it actually originated with the International Undertaking detailed in Chapter 5.[30] The 1983 Undertaking advocated the view that plant genetic resources are a common heritage of humanity and should be freely available without restriction.[31] This view was later qualified by several FAO resolutions. Resolution 4/89 recognized plant breeders' rights and farmers' rights, subjecting free availability to property rights.[32] Resolution 3/91 went a step further by recognizing the sovereign rights of nations over plant genetic resources within their territories, effectively abrogating the "common heritage" standard and aligning developing countries' interests with the position ultimately taken in Article 15 of the CBD.[33]

The International Seed Treaty created a multilaterally governed gene pool with facilitated access to selected plant genetic resources, which would be publicly available in *ex situ* and *in situ* collections.[34] Parties using the system agree to the fair and equitable sharing of benefits.[35] Articles 5 and 6 of the Treaty oblige parties to

27 H. David Cooper, *The Int'l Treaty on Plant Genetic Resources for Food and Agriculture*, *RECIEL* 11 (1) 1 (2002).

28 *The FAO Seed Treaty from Farmers' Rights to Breeders' Privileges*, SEEDLING 21, 21 (Oct. 2005).

29 Lauren Winter, *Cultivating Famers' Rights: Reconciling Food Security, Indigenous Agriculture, and TRIPS*, 43 VAND. J. TRANSNAT'L L. 223, 244 (2010).

30 GERALD MOORE & WITOLD TYMOWSKI, EXPLANATORY GUIDE TO THE INTERNATIONAL TREATY ON PLANT GENETIC RESOURCES FOR FOOD AND AGRICULTURE 4 (2005), available at https://cmsdata.iucn.org/downloads/eplp_057__explanatory_guide_to_the_international_treaty_on_plant_genetic_resources_fo.pdf.

31 Edgar Tabaro, *Food Security and Access to Plant Genetic Resources: An Analysis of the Multilateral System of Access and Benefit Sharing*, 15 MURDOCH UNIV. ELEC. J. OF LAW 212, 214 n.11 (2010).

32 Lauren Winter, *Cultivating Famers' Rights: Reconciling Food Security, Indigenous Agriculture, and TRIPS*, 43 VAND. J. TRANSNAT'L L. 223, 242 (2010).

33 Tabaro, *supra* note 31, at 216.

34 SHAKEEL BHATTI, DESIGNING THE MICROBIAL RESEARCH COMMONS: PROCEEDINGS OF AN INTERNATIONAL SYMPOSIUM 138 (2011).

35 John Linarelli, *Treaty Governance, Intellectual Property and Biodiversity*, 6 ENV. L. REV. 21, 26 (2004).

encourage sustainable use of all crops, not only those subject to the regime.[36] Article 5 specifically requires collective efforts to promote the development of an efficient and sustainable system of *ex situ* conservation.[37] Article 6, in turn, commits parties to the development of polices and legal measures that promote sustainable use of genetic resources.[38]

The treaty sought to promote a multilateral system for access and benefit sharing (ABS) that left room for bilateral negotiations (outside the resources it covered) under the CBD. It expressly emphasized the importance of scientific research while still noting the role of farmers in domesticating wild plants for use in food and agriculture. The primary goal of the multilateral system under the International Seed Treaty was to achieve "facilitated access" to specific seed and germplasm for member states that would allow them to engage in important research, breeding, conservation, and training efforts.[39]

The negotiations as to which crops would be covered by the multilateral system were contentious and protracted. The result was Annex I, which provided a detailed list of thirty-five food crops and twenty-nine forage species accounting for 80 percent of all human consumption.[40] Annex I also included listings of *ex situ* genetic resources held in the International Agricultural Research Centers.[41] Plant genetic resources not included on the Annex 1 list are not covered by the International Seed Treaty and remain under the legal framework of the Convention, as are resources, even those on the Annex 1 list, accessed for nonagricultural purposes.[42]

Member nations are expected to provide *in situ* and *ex situ* samples of crops under their control and are encouraged to voluntarily contribute genetic resources outside of the Annex and the public domain. Facilitated access is subject to both intellectual property rights and plant breeders' rights, and access to material under development

[36] Reichman et al., *supra* note 4, at 118–19. Apart from European gene banks, however, member states have been reluctant to provide new germplasm and share information about their available materials.

[37] Bernard Le Buanec, *Plant Genetic Resources and Freedom to Operate*, 146 EUPHYTICA 1, 3 (2005).

[38] ITPGRA art. 6.

[39] Reichman et al., *supra* note 4, at 123. With restrictions on chemical, pharmaceutical, and other non-food uses and requirements for "fair and equitable" sharing of derived benefits.

[40] E. C. Kamau, *The Multilateral of the International Treaty on Plant Genetic Resources for Food and Agriculture: Lessons and Room for Further Development*. In COMMON POOLS OF GENETIC RESOURCES: EQUITY AND INNVATION IN INTERNATIONAL BIODIVERSITY LAW (2013).

[41] Gerald Moore & Emile Frison, *International Research Centres The Consultative Group on International Agricultural Research and the International Treaty on Plant Genetic Resources for Food and Agriculture* in Christine Frison, Francisco Lopez & Jose Esquinas-Alcazar (eds), PLANT GENETIC RESOURCES AND FOOD SECURITY: STAKEHOLDER PERSPECTIVES ON THE INTERNATIONAL TREAT ON PLANT GENETIC RESOURCES FOR FOOD AND AGRICULTURE 151 (2011).

[42] Cary Fowler & Toby Hodgkin, *Plant Genetic Resources for Food and Agriculture: Assessing Global Availability*, 29 ANNU. REV. ENVIRON. RESOUR. 143, 167 (2004).

remains under the discretion of the developer.[43] In exchange for facilitated access, recipients are prohibited from seeking intellectual property rights on plant genetic resources in the form received from the multilateral system, including parts and components of such resources.

The system shares many features with the Pandemic Influenza Preparedness Framework. Access and benefit sharing are accomplished through standard material transfer agreements (SMTAs).[44] In 2006, the International Seed Treaty's Governing Body adopted the SMTA that established terms and conditions guiding the transfer of materials between providers and recipient institutions, as opposed to the contracting countries themselves.[45] Parties to the agreement must notify the Secretariat of the Treaty regarding the genetic diversity that is under their control and accessible. The SMTA further requires recipients of genetic resources to impose the SMTA's conditions on any downstream transferees. The FAO administers the treaty (like WHO does for the PIP Framework), and there is a clear legal administrative structure to resolve disputes.

The SMTA's primary purpose is to oblige the sharing of monetary and other commercial benefits that arise due to specificied acts of access or transfer. This duty to pay is conditioned on the extent to which a license restricts access to, or use of, the end product of commercialization.[46] As a result, if a user imposes no restriction on use of their product for additional research or breeding, no duty to pay will apply. Those who adopt restrictions must choose between two mandatory payments options involving net royalties on gross sales or a discounted rate on aggregate sales. The SMTA also includes a provision for notification to the Governing Body of the materials covered by a SMTA and its terms. A similar duty also exists to report uses and sales by the recipients of materials from the system who seek to develop commercial applications.[47] All funds accrued are to be allocated toward managing farms, sustaining genetic resource use, and exchange/transfer of information or technology.[48]

After the expiration of any intellectual property rights, recipients are encouraged to place a sample of their products into a collection that is part of the multilateral system.[49] In addition, they are also required to share all nonconfidential information about the improved plant genetic resources that result from the recipient's research

[43] Cooper, *supra* note 27, at 7.
[44] Standard Material Transfer Agreement, Annex 2, Jun. 16, 2006.
[45] In countries where the Treaty has been ratified, SMTAs are mandatory for any crops listed in Annex I.
[46] Standard Material Transfer Agreement, Preamble, Jun. 16, 2006.
[47] Downstream commercial users may avoid royalties by invoking the research exemption. Reichman et al., *supra* note 4, at 139.
[48] *Id.* at 130.
[49] Standard Material Transfer Agreement, art. 6.9, Jun. 16, 2006.

and development processes.[50] These measures are intended to establish and strengthen conservation and scientific research in developing countries.[51]

Aside from the multilateral sharing system, the International Seed Treaty also influences intellectual property claims through its recognition of farmers' rights.[52] Article 9 of the treaty enumerates three elements of farmers' rights: (1) protection of relevant traditional knowledge, (2) the right of farmers to participate equitably in sharing benefits arising from the utilization of plant genetic resources, and (3) the right of farmers to participate in making decision at national levels. It also states that "nothing in this Article shall be interpreted to limit any rights that farmers have to save, use, exchange and sell farm-saved seed/propagating material, subject to national law and as appropriate."[53]

Unlike the Pandemic Influenza Preparedness Framework, the International Seed Treaty depends in substantial part on implementation at the national level. Developing countries have used the International Seed Treaty to establish heretofore non-existent farmers' and indigenous peoples' rights. They have also used legislation adopted pursuant to the treaty to limit the intellectual property rights asserted by large agrochemical firms based in Europe and North America.[54]

African Model Legislation suggests that countries recognize and protect farmers' varieties and breeds that need not meet the criteria of distinction, uniformity, and stability traditionally required for intellectual property protections such as plant breeders' rights.[55] It also provides farmers with the right to participate in making decisions on matters related to conservation and sustainable use of plant genetic resources; save, use, exchange, and sell farm-saved seed both individually and collectively; and use protected breeders' varieties to develop new farmers' varieties.[56] While farmers may still not commercially sell farm-saved seed of a breeders' protected variety under the model law, they are nevertheless authorized to undertake a number of actions over which TRIPS and UPOV cast a long shadow.[57] While the PIP Framework was adopted by the World Health Assembly, the International Seed Treaty requires ratification by states; several of the world's largest holders of plant

[50] *Id.*

[51] Cooper, *supra* note 27, at 9.

[52] Xiaoyong Zhang, *Access to Plant Genetic Resources for Food and Agriculture and Benefit-Sharing in China: Legal Framework, Current Practices, and Future Developments*, RECIEL 21 (2) 137, 137 (2012).

[53] ITPGRA art. 9(3).

[54] Mohamed Ali Mekouar, *Treaty Agreed on Agrobiodiversity: The International Treaty on Plant Genetic Resources for Food and Agriculture*, 32 Envtl. Policy and Law 20, 23–24 (2001).

[55] Lauren Winter, *Cultivating Famers' Rights: Reconciling Food Security, Indigenous Agriculture, and TRIPS*, 43 Vand. J. Transnat'l L. 223, 231 (2010).

[56] Mohamed Ali Mekouar, *Treaty Agreed on Agrobiodiversity: The International Treaty on Plant Genetic Resources for Food and Agriculture*, 32 Envtl. Policy and Law 20, 23–24 (2001).

[57] *Id.* at 24.

genetic resources, such as the United States, China, Russia, and Japan, have not ratified the Treaty.[58]

India has likewise developed liberal legislation protecting farmers' rights.[59] The Protection of Plant Varieties and Farmers' Rights Act was adopted in 2001.[60] This act permits farmers to protect and recognize farmers' varieties which are defined broadly as "ha[ving] been traditionally cultivated and evolved by the farmers in their fields; or is a wild relative or land race of a variety about which farmers possess common knowledge."[61] As with the African Model Legislation, farmers are permitted to save, use, sow, re-sow, exchange, share, or sell farm produce and protected varieties of seeds as long as the seeds are not sold commercially.[62] These provisions allow such countries as Zambia to protect farmers commercially by granting them intellectual property rights, promote conservation and stewardship by the farming community, and limit the power of intellectual property rights held by third parties.[63]

Other countries have failed to implement legislation that adequately protects farmers or implements the Treaty.[64] The provision prohibiting recipients from taking out intellectual property rights on plant genetic resources in the form received from the multilateral system fails to define what "in the form received" means or what the degree of alteration or change is required to allow recipients to seek intellectual property rights.[65] Some countries interpret it to mean that the Treaty will not impinge on national intellectual property rights, laws, or policies.[66] The European Union asserts that parts and components that are subject to innovation can be protected by intellectual property rights.[67] Developing countries, on the other hand, interpret this provision to mean that applications for intellectual property rights that could restrict access to plant genetic resources are per se disfavored.[68] The SMTA fails to provide criteria or definitions for confidentiality and what may or may not be deemed confidential information.[69]

58 Zhang, *supra* note 52, at 13.
59 Mekouar, *supra* note 56.
60 *Id.* at 23.
61 *Id.* at 24.
62 *Id.*
63 Lauren Winter, *Cultivating Famers' Rights: Reconciling Food Security, Indigenous Agriculture, and TRIPS*, 43 Vand. J. Transnat'l L. 223, 249–50 (2010).
64 Nurcan Atalan-Helicke & Becky Mansfield, *Seed Governance at the Intersection of Multiple Global and Nation-State Priorities: Modernizing Seeds in Turkey*, 12 Global Envtl. Politics 125 (2012).
65 Laurence R. Helfer, *Intellectual Property Rights and the International Treaty on Plant Genetic Resources for Food and Agriculture*, ASIL Proceedings 33, 35 (2003).
66 *Id.*
67 Bernard Le Buanec, *Plant Genetic Resources and Freedom to Operate*, 146 Euphytica 1, 3 (2005).
68 H. David Cooper, *The Int'l Treaty on Plant Genetic Resources for Food and Agriculture*, *RECIEL* 11 (1) 1, 8–9 (2002).
69 *Id.*

Nevertheless, in the nineteen months following the 2006 Agreements, IARCs distributed some 550,000 samples of genetic resource materials under the International Seed Treaty's SMTAs.[70] Various agricultural research institutes not affiliated with the CGIAR have also engaged with the multilateral system, adding 30,000 *ex situ* materials to the international network, even though only about one-quarter of parties have made notifications regarding their genetic resources.[71] Over half of all notified collections are those found in CGIAR's IARCs.[72]

THE NAGOYA PROTOCOL ON ACCESS TO GENETIC RESOURCES AND THE FAIR AND EQUITABLE SHARING OF BENEFITS ARISING FROM THEIR UTILIZATION

While the Pandemic Influenza Preparedness Framework and the International Seed Treaty have carved out specific areas of basic human needs for which intellectual property rights are altered in favor of developing countries, the Nagoya Protocol on Access to Genetic Resources and the Fair and Equitable Sharing of Benefits Arising from Their Utilization (Nagoya Protocol) aimed to encompass the broader universe of drugs, medical therapies, agrochemical products, vaccines, and other products derived from genetic resources not regulated by other international instruments (although its relationship with the WHO Pandemic Influenza Preparedness Framework is disputed).[73] The Nagoya Protocol, formed to give specific content to Article 15 of the Convention on Biological Diversity, regulates access to genetic resources in party states and establishes mechanisms for "fair and equitable sharing of benefits arising out of the utilization of genetic resources."[74] It portends potentially drastic changes to the distribution of wealth arising from agricultural, nutritional, and biomedical research undertaken on genetic resources located in developing countries.[75]

Countries adopting legislation or regulation pursuant to the treaty ensure that any genetic resources within the territory of that country condition access to those materials on prior informed consent not only of the country of origin but also "in

[70] Nearly three-quarters of which had been improved in some form by the IARC and most of which was provided to developing nations. Reichman et al., *supra* note 4, at 132.

[71] *Id.* at 135.

[72] Accounting for some 1.3 million specimens. *Id.*

[73] Nagoya Protocol on Access to Genetic Resources and the Fair and Equitable Sharing of Benefits Arising from their Utilization to the Convention on Biological Diversity, Oct. 29, 2010, UNEP/CBD/COP/DEC/X/1 of 29. COP 10 Decision X/1: X/1. Access to genetic resources and the fair and equitable sharing of benefits arising from their utilization, Convention on Biological Diversity, http://www.cbd.int/decision/cop/?id=12267.

[74] Thomas Kursar, *What Are the Implications of the Nagoya Protocol for Research on Biodiversity?* 61(4) BIOSCIENCE 256–57 (2011).

[75] Evanson Chege Kamau, Bevis Fedder, & Gerd Winter, *The Nagoya Protocol on Access to Genetic Resources and Benefit Sharing: What Is New and What Are the Implications for Provider and User Countries and the Scientific Community?* 6(3) L. ENV'T & DEV. J. 246 (2010).

accordance with domestic law," the consent of indigenous and local communities.[76] Moreover, once access to genetic resources results in a commercially viable product, "benefits arising from the utilization of genetic resources as well as subsequent applications and commercialization shall be shared in a fair and equitable way with the Party providing such resources that is the country of origin of such resources or a Party that has acquired the genetic resources in accordance with the Convention."[77] The precise nature of benefit sharing, both monetary and nonmonetary, is left to the states themselves to negotiate with those who generate commercialized products.

The economic purpose of the Nagoya Protocol was explicit. The CBD as it was originally formed lacked an agreed-on legal framework for cross-border enforcement of its international regime, diminishing the ability for providers subjected to misappropriation of their resources to seek adequate redress. Additionally, user country governments were in no way obligated to address complaints or assist with providing redress. After six years of negotiations, the Nagoya Protocol brought "greater legal certainty and transparency" regarding the exchange of genetic resources while "reaffirm[ing] and clarif[ying] the [CBD's] broad economic scope."[78] It further addressed issues concerning scientific research, also neglected by the CBD, and created new enforcement provisions for user and provider nations to implement within their respective national legal systems.[79]

Before the Nagoya Protocol, implementation of CBD Article 15 had been largely guided by the nonbinding Bonn Guidelines on Access to Genetic Resources and Fair and Equitable Sharing of the Benefits Arising Out of Their Utilization, a set of voluntary guidelines issued subsequent to the Convention on Biological Diversity but before Nagoya, which recommended the following provisions for contracts between sovereign states and commercial entities:

(a) Regulating the use of resources in order to take into account ethical concerns of the particular Parties and stakeholders, in particular indigenous and local communities concerned.
(b) Making provision to ensure the continued customary use of genetic resources and related knowledge.
(c) Provision for the use of intellectual property rights include joint research, obligation to implement rights on inventions obtained and to provide licences by common consent.
(d) The possibility of joint ownership of intellectual property rights according to the degree of contribution.[80]

[76] Nagoya Protocol art. 7.
[77] Nagoya Protocol art. 5.
[78] *Id.*
[79] *Id.*
[80] Bonn Guidelines para. 43.

The guidelines similarly suggested that parties might condition transfer of material on a promise not to seek intellectual property rights at all.

Article 2 of the Nagoya Protocol provides definitions that expand the economic scope of the CBD and address some of its ambiguities, while Article 5 makes benefit sharing legally binding. The "functional units of hereditary" language of the CBD is expanded to include applications of biotechnology in the definition of "utilization of genetic resources," bringing biochemical compounds encoded by genes into the scope of its regime.[81] The Protocol is also applicable to naturally occurring biochemical compounds often utilized by the pharmaceutical industry as well as "traditional knowledge associated with genetic resources."[82] Further, Article 2 made utilization coextensive with research and development. Article 8 requires Contracting Parties to create and implement ABS legislation and regulation that seek to "create conditions to promote and encourage scientific research" via "simplified measures" on research oriented access while also addressing the tendency for noncommercial research to become commercial.[83] The Protocol allows individual scientist to exchange nonmonetary benefits for their noncommercial research and afford providers freedom to negotiate nonmonetary benefits in their agreements.

Article 4 established in broad strokes the relationship between the Nagoya Protocol and other international agreements "relevant" to it, implying but not stating TRIPS and other international intellectual property agreements.[84] Article 4 does not affect rights and obligations under those agreements, "except where the exercise of those rights and obligations would cause a serious damage or threat to biological diversity," and parties may engage in "other relevant international agreements" so long as they "do not run counter to the objectives of the [CBD and the Protocol]".[85] Article 4 also allows for specialized instruments – such as the Pandemic Influenza Preparedness Framework – that regulate access and benefit sharing in particular areas of genetic resources.

Articles 5 through 18 of the Nagoya Protocol provide for the specific mechanisms by which prior informed consent for access to genetic resources may be obtained, the protection of traditional knowledge and indigenous communities, and the mutually agreed terms for benefit sharing. Contracting Parties are required to "take legislative, administrative, or policy measures" to enforce benefit sharing.[86] Provider countries are specifically required to give prospective users "clear and transparent written decision[s]" regarding use of resources that come from a "competent national authority," along with the issuance of a permit or some equivalent to

81 Gerd Winter, Knowledge Commons, Intellectual Property, and the ABS Regime, Common Pools of Genetic Resources (2013).
82 Nagoya Protocol, Preamble (2010).
83 Nagoya Protocol, art. 8.
84 Nagoya Protocol, art. 4.
85 *Id.*
86 Nagoya Protocol, art. 6.

approved users.[87] In fact, all Contracting Parties must designate national focal points by which applicants can find necessary information on PIC and MATs, complete with one or more "designated national authorities."[88] Article 15 specifically required Parties to engage in measures designed to address noncompliance and to cooperate with alleged cases of violation of legislative and regulatory requirements regarding access and benefit sharing.[89] Article 15 and 16 together create liability for member states when violations occur within their territories and require Parties to monitor genetic resource use within their jurisdictions, providing regular updates on overall compliance.[90]

The Nagoya Protocol is notable for its protection of traditional knowledge, indigenous peoples, and farmers, none of which was explicitly covered by the CBD. Traditional knowledge (TK) is a "living body of knowledge that is developed, sustained and passed on" between generations within a larger community.[91] The medicinal and agricultural applications of many forms of traditional knowledge make it of substantial interest for the commercial efforts of agrochemical and pharmaceutical companies.[92] Further, 80 percent of the world population utilizes traditional medicine as the primary source of health care.[93]

Interest in traditional medicines has grown as these indigenous forms of knowledge are recognized as "relatively safe" and widely used.[94] Indigenous pharmacology is the "medicinal knowledge of plants roots, barks, animal products, and other naturally occurring substances, together with the knowledge of its application in the treatment of diseases."[95] In 2009, the United Nations reported that more than 130 patents were obtained for clinically useful therapeutic drugs derived from plants," 70 percent of which were discovered by pharmaceutical companies through their use by indigenous communities.[96] The same report highlighted that

[87] Jerome H. Reichman, Paul Uhlir & Tom Dedeurwaerdere, Governing Digitally Integrated Genetic Resources, Data, and Literature: Global Intellectual Property Strategies for a Redesigned Microbial Research Commons 157–59 (2016). The permits act as "internationally recognized certificate[s] of compliance" to show that genetic resources used have been accessed via PIC and MATs.

[88] Nagoya Protocol, art. 14.

[89] Nagoya Protocol, art. 15.

[90] *Id.*

[91] WIPO, *Traditional Knowledge*, available at http://www.wipo.int/tk/en/.

[92] *Id.*

[93] Jay Erstling, *Using Patents to Protect Traditional Knowledge*, 15 Tex. Wesleyan L. Rev. 295, 297 (2009).

[94] Kwang Kuk Goh, Case Study on Intellectual Property Rights in Establishing a Traditional Knowledge Database in Korea 127, 133 (2010).

[95] Chika A. Ezeanya. *Contending Issues of Intellectual Property Rights Protection and Indigenous Knowledge of Pharmacology in Africa South of the Sahara*, 6 Journal of Pan African Studies 24, 28 (2013).

[96] R. Laskshmi Poorna, M. Mymoon & A. Hariharan, *Preservation and Protection of Traditional Knowledge – Diverse Documentation Initiatives across The Globe*, 107 Current Science 1240, 1241 (2014).

more than 7,000 patents were granted for "unauthorized use of [traditional knowledge] or the misappropriated use of indigenous medicines derived from plants."[97] Herbal medicines, for example, command a $60 billion global market.[98] Market advantages such as the opportunity to avoid the types of side effects typical in drugs and medicines has encouraged these companies to explore traditional remedies that may be patented and commercialized.[99]

Traditional knowledge in the agricultural context is similar to other forms of traditional knowledge, including its own set of potential obstacles and challenges to affording appropriate protection.[100] Agricultural traditional knowledge "comprise[s] [] numerous substantive domains ... as well as management domains," complicating efforts to achieve its protection.[101] As the International Seed Treaty acknowledged, the relationship between agricultural traditional knowledge and intellectual property will likely focus on the generational farming through communities develop shared knowledge on aspects of farming including specific crop traits.[102] This practice has been used by farmers for much of history and continues to be the "dominant approach to seed management for the large majority of farmers around the world."[103]

The Nagoya Protocol endeavors to promote both "defensive" protection of traditional knowledge – preventing those outside a community from obtaining intellectual property rights to that communities traditional knowledge – and "positive protection" – granting proprietary rights to communities in order to "promote their traditional knowledge, control its uses and benefit from its commercial exploitation."[104] The treaty's flexibility allows it to accommodate regimes similar to the PIP Framework and the International Seed Treaty.[105] Moreover, even under systems with robust patent protection, the Nagoya Protocol encourages developing countries to adopt policies that allow patents or new variety claims to be challenged.

97 *Id.*

98 Murat Kartal, *Intellectual Property Protection in the Natural Product Drug Discovery, Traditional Herbal Medicine and Herbal Medicinal Products*, 21 PHYTOTHER. RES. 113, 113 (2006).

99 Ryan Levy & Spencer Green, *Pharmaceuticals and Biopiracy: How The America Invents Act May Reduce the Misappropriation of Traditional Medicine*, 23 U. MIAMI BUS. L. REV. 401, 406 (2015).

100 Stephen B. Brush, *Farmers' Rights and Protection of Traditional Agricultural Knowledge*, 35 WORLD DEVELOPMENT 1499, 1502 (2007).

101 Substantive domains include aspects such as soil types, pests, pathogens, crop genotypes, and environmental conditions while management domains refers to irrigation techniques, planting patterns, pest control, and crop selection. *Id.*

102 *Id.* at 1499.

103 Stephen B. Brush, *Protecting Traditional Agricultural Knowledge*, 17 WASH. U. J.L. & POL'Y 59, 67 (2005).

104 WIPO, *Traditional Knowledge and Intellectual Property*, available at http://www.wipo.int/pressroom/en/briefs/tk_ip.html.

105 2.3 Bioprospecting, Trips, CBD and Traditional Medicines: Concepts and Questions. Report of an ASEAN Workshop on the TRIPS Agreement and Traditional Medicine, Jakarta, (Feb. 2001) available at http://apps.who.int/medicinedocs/en/d/Jh2996e/6.3.html.

Bolivia, Brazil, Colombia, Costa Rica, Ecuador, Peru, South Africa, and Venezuela, for example, have adopted strong laws regulating access to genetic material from their territories.[106] South Africa's Regulations on Bio-Prospecting, Access and Benefit-Sharing, for example, require firms to obtain a permit from the government if they intend to use South African genetic resources for research or patenting. These permits may only be obtained with a benefit-sharing agreement with relevant stakeholders. South Africa integrates this system with its patent application system as well, so that patent applications must identify indigenous biological resources or forms of traditional knowledge leading to the patentable subject matter.[107]

India has similarly used its Traditional Knowledge Digital Library both to gather enormous amounts of information held by indigenous communities and to challenge efforts to patent uses of that knowledge.[108] The Government of India has made the TKDL, which stores traditional medicine treatments from Ayurveda, Siddha, Unani, and Yoga, accessible to patent offices around the world.[109] The database is designed to be easily utilized by patent examiners with information in five different foreign languages and precise information on the time, place, and medium of its publications.[110] The TKDL affords protection to more than 2.9 million medicinal formulations.

The India-based TKDL was an explicit measure to combat patent efforts by major pharmaceuticals in regards to several specific resources within the traditional knowledge of the Indian people.[111] Turmeric is a plant common throughout India and Pakistan that, when boiled into a spice powder, has been traditionally used in India to treat wounds via its natural antibacterial agents.[112] In 1995, the United Stated Patent Office (USPTO) granted a patent on the use of turmeric for healing wounds to two University of Mississippi scientists.[113] Following challenges to the scientists' patent by India's Council of Scientific and Industrial Research, the USPTO

106 Rachel Wynberg, Doris Schroeder & Roger Chennells, Indigenous Peoples, Consent and Benefit Sharing: Lessons from the San Hoodia Case (2009).

107 Neil R. Crouch, Errol Douwes, Maureen M. Wolfson, Gideon F. Smith and Trevor J. Edwards, *South Africa's Bioprospecting, Access and Benefit-Sharing Legislation: Current Realities, Future Complications, and a Proposed Alternative*, 104 South African Journal of Science 355 available at http://www.biopirateria.org/download/documentos/otros-documentos/sistema-abs-convenio-diversidad-biologica/Crouch%20et%20al.pdf.

108 Indian patent examiners now uses a searchable database of traditional medicine to establish prior art when assessing patent applications. http://www.wipo.int/pressroom/en/briefs/tk_ip.html.

109 TKDL, 2011. Traditional knowledge digital library, about TKDL. www.tkdl.res.in/ tkdl/langdefault/common/Abouttkdl.asp?GL=Eng.

110 *Id.*

111 Daniel F. Robinson, Confronting Biopiracy: Challenges, Cases and International Debates 151 (2010).

112 Shubha Ghosh, *Globalization, Patents, and Traditional Knowledge*, 17 Colum. J. Asian L. 73, 93 (2003); Robinson, *supra* note 111, at 71.

113 Shahid Alikhan & R. A. Mashelkar, Intellectual Property and Competitive Strategies in the 21st Century 77 (2004).

canceled all six claims within the patent that referenced the healing capabilities of turmeric for failure to satisfy the novelty requirement.[114]

In the case of the neem tree, two patents were granted to a prominent owner of a pharmaceutical and chemical company for the process of extracting from the tree's seeds to create a "pesticide, medicine, and fertilizer."[115] Again following a challenge on the patent by the Indian government, European courts decided to withdraw the patents previously awarded, but US patent officials determined that the process invented was not based on any traditional Indian knowledge, and continued to award neem patents.[116] The Indian government found better success in their work to prevent a Texas-based company from obtaining what they perceived as an "outright monopoly" on ancient Indian dietary staple, basmati rice. The company sought patents on breeding methods, cooking and preparation of the rice, and even on the actual grain.[117] Plagued by "overly broad wording and scope," the USPTO rejected several of the patent claims.[118] It is the explicit objective of the Indian government to challenge patents worldwide that involve traditional knowledge practices in India.[119] Following the advent of the TKDL, patent claims filed on traditional Indian medicine practices declined by 44 percent.[120] Peru's National Commission against Biopiracy has similarly used its database records to oppose the grant of patents containing Peruvian traditional knowledge.[121]

The Chinese traditional medicine database system is that country's traditional knowledge protection scheme achieved via an online catalog.[122] As its name indicates, the database focuses on Chinese traditional medicine, much of which, although based in ancient traditions, has already been written down in Chinese, making the information within "widespread and highly accessible."[123] The databases itself is demarcated into more individualized databases, around fifty total, with

[114] *Id.*

[115] Ghosh, *supra* note 112, at 106; Robinson, *supra* note 111, at 71.

[116] *Id.*

[117] Ghosh, *supra* note 112, at 105–06; Robinson, *supra* note 111, at 47.

[118] *Id.*

[119] Alikhan & Mashelkar, *supra* note 113, at 78.

[120] R. Laskshmi Poorna, M. Mymoon & A. Hariharan, *Preservation and Protection of Traditional Knowledge – Diverse Documentation Initiatives across the Globe*, 107 CURRENT SCIENCE 1240, 1241 (2014).

[121] WIPO, *Intergovernmental Committee on Intellectual Property and Genetic Resources, Traditional Knowledge and Folklore, Eleventh Session, Geneva, July 3 to 12, 2007: Combating Biopiracy — the Peruvian Experience (2007)*, available at www.wipo.int/edocs/mdocs/tk/en/wipo_grtkf_ic_11/wipo_grtkf_ic_11_13. doc.

[122] Poorna et al., *supra* note 120, at 1242.

[123] This traditional Chinese medicine is also found in neighboring countries such as Korea and Japan, making "legal protection in one country … ineffective." *Id.*; KWANG KUK GOH, CASE STUDY ON INTELLECTUAL PROPERTY RIGHTS IN ESTABLISHING A TRADITIONAL KNOWLEDGE DATABASE IN KOREA 127, 131 (2010).

specific emphasis on varied aspects of tradition Chinese medicine.[124] For example, a database exists for medical literature on traditional Chinese medicine with more than 6 million reference and abstracts that explore qigong, acupuncture, and more.[125] A drug-specific database has 11,000 records each with information on "a single herb, or mineral drug, other natural medicine."[126] Another database focuses on recording medical formulae derived from more than 700 ancient medical books, while another database focuses on news stories relating to the topic of Chinese medicine.[127] One noteworthy database is the Traditional Chinese Medicine Patent Database. This specific database explores the more than 22,000 patents based on traditional Chinese medicine, as well as the 40,000 patented formulae.[128]

While the aforementioned traditional knowledge databases are based primarily on the already codified knowledge systems of the respective indigenous peoples, other countries have also initiated programs to compile databases of noncodified, often orally based, traditional knowledge.[129] In Venezuela, the BioZulua project documented medicinal plants and food crops of the country's twenty-four Amazonian ethnic groups.[130] This database, with genetic profiles of each plant as well as GPS coordination of specific plant locations, is a distinguishable example of noncodified traditional knowledge preservation. Venezuela's database, however, is not made available to the public in an effort to discourage commercialization of knowledge.[131]

Similar efforts have been undertaken in South Africa via the Ulwazi program, an online traditional knowledge database focused on the indigenous knowledge of local communities in Durban, South Africa.[132] The database collects traditional knowledge such as "clothing, [] proverbs, folk tales, spiritual herbs, and traditional agricultural methods in a wiki-style website that allows contributions and modifications from a variety of users.[133] The program is a part of the community's public library network, and any content within is owned by the communities themselves, with the libraries acting as "moderator[s] and custodians of [the] knowledge."[134]

In response to the continued profiting on Amazonian frog skin secretions by American chemical companies (Abbott Laboratories in this specific case), the government of Ecuador and other developing nations began to "restrict[] the freedom of scientist to collect biological samples and demand[] compensation in

[124] Poorna et al., *supra* note 120, at 1243.
[125] An English version also exists with more than 1.2 million references and abstracts. *Id.*
[126] The English version of this database contains 545 records. *Id.*
[127] *Id.*
[128] *Id.*
[129] Stephen B. Brush, *Farmers' Rights and Protection of Traditional Agricultural Knowledge*, 35 World Development 1499, 1510 (2007).
[130] *Id.* at 1243.
[131] *Id.*
[132] *Id.* at 1244.
[133] *Id.*
[134] *Id.*

exchange for permits."[135] After the CBD went into force, the Philippines, Costa Rica, and nations in the Andean Pact (Bolivia, Colombia, Ecuador, Peru, and Venezuela) adopted laws that control access to genetic resources and require compensation. The Philippines was the first country to enact laws responding to the CBD, passing legislation that required compensation and collaboration with local scientists along with the informed consent of local tribes from the areas where resources were being sampled.[136] Andes Pharmaceutical's attempt to form a joint venture with local citizens was rejected four times by the Colombian government who alleged that their "application was not specific enough" on what species were to be sampled or how much would be paid.[137] Other developing nations have even "becom[e] directly involved in the commercialization of their genetic resources."[138] Brazil, hesitant to allow plant samples to be taken out of the country, allows the National Cancer Institute to engage in drug screening there in Brazil.[139] The Sarawak state government in Malaysia formed a joint venture company with the National Cancer Institute and Medichem, a US biotechnology firm, pursuant to an ABS agreement.[140]

Early experience suggests that the Nagoya Protocol shares weaknesses and lacunae with the International Seed Treaty. For example, in 2010, a subsidiary of Nestlé filed international patent applications for therapeutic derivatives of rooibos and honeybush, plants indigenous to South Africa and obtained without the permits required under South Africa's bioprospecting law. Nestlé responded that it had neither sourced the plants in South Africa nor researched them there (they were provided by South African suppliers of other goods), that it had not yet commercialized any products (although that was not relevant under South African law), and that it would comply with the law when or if it became necessary. The case highlights the ambiguities in the treaty text not only over what constitutes covered material and conduct regulated by the treaty, but what relationship third parties may play in evading the treaty's reach.

As of 2015, thirteen countries had submitted legislative, administrative, or policy measures in furtherance of the Nagoya Protocol, and many of the sixty or so countries that have adopted ABS measures pursuant to the CBD are updating those laws. The result is that many of the measures taken to limit intellectual property

[135] Andrew Pollack, *Biological Products Raise Genetic Ownership Issues*, N.Y. TIMES (Nov. 26, 1999), available at http://www.nytimes.com/1999/11/26/business/patenting-life-special-report-biological-products-raise-genetic-ownership-issues.html.

[136] K. N. NINAN, CONSERVING AND VALUING ECOSYSTEM SERVICES AND BIODIVERSITY: ECONOMIC, INSTITUTIONAL AND SOCIAL CHALLENGES 300–01 (2009).

[137] Pollack, *supra* note 135.

[138] *Id.*

[139] *Id.*

[140] Ranjan Gupta, Bjarne Gabrielsen & Steven M. Ferguson, *Nature's Medicines: Traditional Knowledge and Intellectual Property Management. Case Studies from the National Institutes of Health (NIH), USA* 2(4) CURR. DRUG DISCOV. TECHNOL. 203–19 (2005).

rights over genetic resources, protect traditional knowledge, and challenge intellectual property rights claims asserted in wealthy countries will become stronger. Indeed, in the context of Zika and MERS-CoV, Brazil and Saudi Arabia, respectively, have taken preliminary positions as to their ownership of potential therapeutics developed through viruses taken from their territories. As Brendan Coolsaet, Tom Dedeurwaerdere, and John Pitseys have noted,

> The [Nagoya Protocol's] redistribution of resources among the stakeholders allows the state to level the playing field, thereby strengthening weaker actors and, thus, fostering fairer agreements. This latter goal might, for instance, be met through the possible role that international development cooperation could play in developing specific capacity building projects in developing countries and/or for indigenous and local communities.[141]

[141] Brendan Coolsaet, Tom Dedeurwaerdere & John Pitseys, *The Challenges for Implementing the Nagoya Protocol in a Multi-Level Governance Context: Lessons from the Belgian Case*, 2(4) RESOURCES 555–80 (2013).

12

Food and Tobacco Trademarks

The efforts to limit intellectual property rights and redistribute the benefits arising from (primarily) patents in the medicines and agrochemical contexts involved visceral, sometimes shocking depictions of inequality. For HIV-positive patients in Europe and North America, who enjoyed wider access to current therapies, they more-or-less lived with a chronic condition.[1] In sub-Saharan Africa, the devastation of the workforce and lack of access to medications multiplied the burden on families and governments. During the H1N1 influenza pandemic, populations in wealthy countries received vaccines easily while those in developing countries waited for months for vaccines as firms negotiated with WHO and wealthy governments over terms of sale.[2] The growth in size and profits of major agrochemical firms based in Europe and North America contrasted with the declining economic situation of already impoverished farmers in Africa, Asia, and Latin America.[3]

As Amy Kapczynski has argued, these images have almost certainly played a role in "framing" the intellectual property debate in wealthier countries.[4] Over larger populations over the longer term, however, subtler and more attenuated effects of oligopoly and intellectual property have exerted a larger adverse effect. In developing countries, aggressive marketing of infant foods by primarily five global food firms has played a substantial role in the low (only 24–32 percent) rate of infants exclusively breastfed at six months on average. Developing countries "bear more than

[1] Steven Deeks, Sharon Lewin & Diane Havlir, *The End of AIDS: HIV Infection as a Chronic Disease*, 382(9903) LANCET 1525–33 (2013).

[2] Sam Halabi, *Obstacles to pH1N1 Vaccine Availability: The Complex Contracting Relationship between Vaccine Manufacturers, WHO, Donor and Beneficiary Governments*, in M. A. Stoto & M. Higdon (eds), THE PUBLIC HEALTH RESPONSE TO H1N1: A SYSTEMS PERSPECTIVE 203–16 (2015).

[3] FAO & OECD, OECD-FAO AGRICULTURAL OUTLOOK 2016–2025 29 (2016), available at http://www.fao.org/3/a-i5778e.pdf.

[4] Amy Kapczynski, *The Access to Knowledge Mobilization and the New Politics of Intellectual Property*, 117 YALE L.J. 804, 832 (2008).

99% of the burden of suboptimal breastfeeding. Suboptimal breastfeeding is responsible for 45% of neonatal infectious deaths, 30% of diarrheal deaths and 18% of acute respiratory deaths in children under 5 years."[5] Under current trends, tobacco consumption – the market for which is also largely controlled by five global tobacco firms – will kill more than 8 million people worldwide annually by the year 2030, with 80 percent of these deaths in low- and middle-income countries.

While the primary intellectual properties at issue with these consumer products are trademarks, broader policies aimed at advertising, marketing, and promotion for which trademarks are crucial have been the vehicle by which developing countries protect individual and population health. Because product packaging is the most important influence on consumers at the point of sale, limitation of trademarks on packaging has a disproportionately larger effect than other measures to limit advertising, marketing, and promotion.[6] Developing countries have, in product sectors affecting individual and public health, formed international agreements that authorize the limitation of trademarks that promote consumption of potentially or actually hazardous products. While there are now only international agreements for infant foods and tobacco, there are also movements for similar agreements in the alcohol and processed foods sectors as well.

THE INTERNATIONAL CODE OF MARKETING OF BREASTMILK SUBSTITUTES

In Chapter 5, the International Code of Marketing of Breastmilk Substitutes was introduced as a forerunner of developing countries' efforts to regulate global firms in sectors that particularly affected basic human needs. Chapter 8 provided additional detail to both the relationship between exclusive breastfeeding in the first six months of life as well as firms' use of international intellectual property law to thwart measures aimed at ensuring new mothers did so. Based on the medical evidence, the *Lancet* was emphatic in its conclusion about the relationship between exclusive breastfeeding and basic human needs:

> If a new vaccine became available that could prevent one million or more child deaths a year, and that was moreover cheap, safe, administered orally, and required no cold chain, it would become an immediate public health imperative. Breastfeeding could do all this and more.[7]

The International Code of Marketing of Breastmilk Substitutes (International Code), adopted through the same legal mechanism as the World Health

[5] WHO, GLOBAL HEALTH RISKS 15, available at http://www.who.int/healthinfo/global_burden_disease/GlobalHealthRisks_report_part2.pdf.

[6] Pinya Silayoi & Mark Speece, *Packaging and Purchase Decisions: An Exploratory Study on the Impact of Involvement Level and Time Pressure* 106(8) BRITISH FOOD J. 607–28 (2004).

[7] *Editorial, A Warm Chain for Breastfeeding*, 344(8932) LANCET 1239 (1994).

Organization's Pandemic Influenza Preparedness Framework, is technically a recommendation adopted under Article 23 of the WHO Constitution rather than a more formally binding treaty or international agreement such as the CBD or the International Seed Treaty.[8] However, as the following section details, the recommendation is an evidence-based standard adopted by national governments and protecting their decisions to do so through its incorporation into international food safety bodies.[9] Those bodies have decisive influence in cases where measures to protect individual or public health are challenged under TRIPS or other WTO agreements.

The International Code is specific to a "corporation" or "any other entity" in the business of breastmilk substitutes and covers not only infant formula but also "cow's milk, fruit juices, cereals, vegetables, or any other fluid, solid or semisolid food intended for infants" when those foods are marketed or "otherwise represented to be suitable" as a substitute.[10] The Code seeks to prevent firms from advertising; implement strict labeling requirements including a proscription on infant images or other pictures that idealize breastmilk substitutes; limit influence on health care workers; and prohibit distribution of free samples of breast milk substitutes.[11] The Code prohibits "pictures of infants ... [and] other pictures or text which may idealize the use of infant formula."[12]

Eighty-four states have passed legislation enacting all or some aspects of the International Code while another fourteen have such legislation pending.[13] Major infant formula markets such as Brazil, China, and India have banned the use of images on infant formula containers, while a growing number of developing and wealthy countries are considering stronger measures toward limiting the appearance or use of trademarks in connection with infant formula.[14] Kenyan law effectively

8 U.N. Committee on the Rights of the Child General Comment No. 15 (2013) on the Right of the Child to the Highest Attainable Standard of Health ¶ 44 (17 Apr. 2013). Generally, World Health Assembly's (WHA) recommendations are not binding, but they "carry moral or political weight, as they constitute the judgment on a health issue of the collective membership of the highest international body in the field of health." Sami Shubber, *The International Code*, 36(4) Digest of Health Legislation 884 (1985).

9 U.N. Committee on the Rights of the Child General Comment No. 15 (2013) on the Right of the Child to the Highest Attainable Standard of Health ¶ 44 (17 Apr. 2013); 2008 Lancet Series, Maternal and Child Undernutrition, *What Works? Interventions for Maternal and Child Undernutrition and Survival*, 371(9610) The Lancet 417–40 (2008).

10 International Code art. 2, art. 3.

11 *Id.*

12 International Code art. 9.2.

13 UNICEF, International Code of Marketing of Breast Milk Substitutes (2005), available at http://www.unicef.org/nutrition/index_24805.html.

14 Jessica Samakow, *Baby Formula Ads in Sweden May Soon Be Banned from Featuring Babies*, Huffington Post (Nov. 8, 2012), available at http://www.huffingtonpost.com/2012/11/08/baby-formula-ads-sweden-_n_2092920.html; Aideen Sheehan, *EU Bans Photos of Babies on Formula Milk*, Irish News (June 12, 2013), available at http://www.independent.ie/irish-news/eu-bans-photos-of-babies-on-formula-milk-29337896.html.

extends the reach and scope of the International Code by applying prohibitions on pictures, colors, and models to packaging for foods intended to be marketed to infants aged six months to two years.[15]

Measures implementing the International Code are, moreover, protected from the World Trade Organization's dispute settlement mechanism, so challenges under TRIPS would be unusually difficult. When the WTO was established, as well as the TRIPS Agreement, countries needed an efficient mechanism by which to evaluate whether public health and regulatory measures that already existed, and those that might be adopted in the future, appropriately served regulatory purposes, rather than serving as hidden means to discriminate against foreign goods. For example, if France adopted a safety standard for tomatoes that French or European farmers found easy to meet, but would impose enormous cost for Mexican farmers (thereby discouraging the importation of Mexican tomatoes), there needed to be a way to assess whether the French measure was unfairly discriminatory.

The answer, for food and plant safety in any case, was the list of standards already adopted by the Codex Alimentarius Commission, an international organization jointly run by the Food and Agricultural Organization and the World Health Organization. Since 1963, it had adopted standards on food quality, and safety, including food commodity standards and codes of hygienic or technological practice, in an effort to "ensure fair practices in food trade and protect[ion of] the health of consumers."[16] Codex was designated the official standard reference body for the WTO when food safety or labeling measures are challenged as burdening free trade according to its Sanitary and Phytosanitary (SPS) Agreement.[17] It plays a similar, although not dominant, role for the WTO's Technical Barriers to Trade (TBT) Agreement. All countries that agreed to the creation of the WTO in 1994 may be bound by WTO panel decisions regarding SPS and TBT issues; therefore, these countries may be constrained by Codex standards.[18] The Agreement instructs its Members "to base their sanitary or phytosanitary measures on international standards" (Article 3.1.) and presumes those international standards to 'be consistent with

[15] Republic of Kenya Breast Milk Substitutes (Regulation and Control) Act No. 34 of 2012.

[16] Sam Halabi, *The Codex Alimentarius Commission, Corporate Influence and International Trade*, 41 AM. J. LAW & MED. 406–21 (2015).

[17] *Id.* The WTO's SPS Agreement was established in 1995 to regulate food, plant, and animal safety and health regulations. The adjudicatory arm of the WTO resolves trade disputes regarding such issues, and can impose or permit trade-based punitive measures for violations of the SPS Agreement.

[18] Michael A. Livermore, *Authority and Legitimacy in Global Governance: Deliberation, Institutional Differentiation, and the Codex Alimentarius*, 81 N.Y.U. L. REV. 766, 768–70 (2006). The WTO's near-codification of Codex Alimentarius standards regarding sanitary and phytosanitary measures likely casts Codex's SPS-related actions as the organization's most significant activity. A. W. Randell & A. J. Whitehead, *Codex Alimentarius: Food Quality and Safety Standards for International Trade*, 16 REV. SCI. TECH. OFF. 313, 316 (1997).

the relevant portions of this Agreement and of GATT [General Agreement on Tariffs and Trade] 1994" (Article 3.2).[19]

By 1994, Codex had already adopted the relevant trademark restricting provisions of the International Code into its "Standard for Infant Formula and Formulas for Special Medical Purposes Intended for Infants" allowing states, within their food safety regulations, to require that infant formula "label[s] shall have no pictures of infants and women nor any other picture or text which idealizes the use of infant formula."[20] The adoption of the standard means that parties to the WTO may ban images of infants and women without concern that such a measure inappropriately burdens trade. While the Codex standard operates separately from measures sanctioned by TRIPS, the standard effectively creates a safe harbor for banning trademarks on infant formula products. Indeed, despite industry protest against states and other political entities, such as Hong Kong, that have restricted or banned trademarks on infant formula, no state has brought a challenge to those restrictions at the WTO, nor has any of the major food firms made use of the strong enforcement mechanisms available through bilateral investment treaties to protest prohibitions on infant images.

THE FRAMEWORK CONVENTION ON TOBACCO CONTROL

Since tobacco consumption has declined in Europe and North America as a result of strong public health measures and taxation policies, the global tobacco industry has focused on low- and middle-income countries as key targets in sustaining demand for conventional cigarettes.[21] In developing and wealthy markets, tobacco trademarks play a critical role in the broader advertising, promotion, and marketing efforts that go into persuading young men and women to commit to and identify with a specific brand of cigarette with the aim that such identification continues through the individual's adult life.[22] "Tobacco use is growing fastest in low-income countries, due to steady population growth coupled with tobacco industry targeting ... More than 80% of the world's tobacco-related deaths will be in low and middle-income countries by 2030."[23]

While many European and North American countries have prohibited descriptors in trademarks such as "mild," "light," and "ultra-light," many developing countries have not. Firms also shape cigarette containers – or trade dress – to mimic

19 David A. Wirth, *The Transatlantic GMO Dispute against the European Communities*, in Marc Pallemaerts (ed), EU AND WTO LAW: HOW TIGHT IS THE STRAIGHTJACKET 183 (2006).

20 CODEX STAN 72 – 1981 at 9.6.2.

21 VAUGHAN LYON, POWER SHIFT: FROM PARTY ELITES TO INFORMED CITIZENS 147 (2011).

22 WHO, BREAK THE TOBACCO MARKETING NET 1–16 (2008), available at http://www.who.int/tobacco/wntd/2008/wntd_2008_brochure.pdf.

23 http://www.who.int/tobacco/mpower/mpower_report_tobacco_crisis_2008.pdf.

famous perfume or other product packaging, to appeal to target populations.[24] Cigarette manufacturers also use package colors and images to shape health perceptions.[157] Two aspects of trademarks magnify these public health problems in low- and middle-income countries. First, low- and middle-income countries have larger populations that lack functional literacy necessary for written warnings to communicate product risks. Second, trademarks in the cigarette context are explicitly tied to the rise of middle-income classes in wealthier countries.[25]

Motivated by the public health burden imposed by tobacco products and the success of the industry in thwarting regulation, frequently on intellectual property grounds, Canada, Finland, Mexico, and Tanzania sponsored the idea of an international agreement[26] to regulate tobacco at the WHA in 1995.[27] In 1998, Member States established a WHO FCTC Working Group to draft core treaty elements and an Intergovernmental Negotiating Body to develop the treaty text.[28] The FCTC was adopted by Member States in 2003 and entered into force on February 27, 2005.[29] One hundred and eighty-one parties have ratified or acceded to the FCTC as of March 2015.[30]

While the FCTC covers a wide range of supply-and-demand factors affecting tobacco consumption, core aspects of its non-price provisions are aimed at eliminating or limiting trademark protection in the tobacco context. Article 11 (packaging and labeling) and Article 13 (promotion) include provisions curtailing trademark rights.[31] The governing body of the treaty has elaborated additional guidelines that go even further in eroding international protections for tobacco trademarks.[32]

24 E. C. Etzel et al., *Consumer Research Proposal: Camel Filter Revised Packaging Test Study* 5 (1979), available at http://legacy.library.ucsf.edu/tid/qxb79d00. For example, cigarette manufacturers first marketed menthol cigarettes as a remedy for a cold or flu, and the green color of menthol-flavored cigarette packs preserved the original association. Melanie Wakefield et al., *The Cigarette Pack as Image: New Evidence from Tobacco Industry Documents*, 11 Tobacco Control 173, 177 (Supp. I 2002).

25 Sam Foster Halabi, *The World Health Organization's Framework Convention on Tobacco Control: An Analysis of Guidelines Adopted by the Conference of the Parties*, 39 Ga. J. Int'l. & Comp. L. 121, 129–32 (2010).

26 WHO, Director General, *The Feasibility of Developing an International Instrument for Tobacco Control*, EM97/INF.Doc./4 (Nov. 30, 1995).

27 WHA, *An International Strategy for Tobacco Control*, EB95.R9, WHA48.11, WHO PSA/96.6 (May 12, 1995), available at http://www.who.int/tobacco/framework/wha_eb/wha48_11/en.

28 Working Group Preceding the Intergovernmental Negotiating Body on the WHO FCTC (1999–2000), FCTC: WHO Framework Convention on Tobacco Control, available at http://www.who.int/fctc/about/pre_neg_working_group/en/index.html.

29 *Foreword to* WHO Framework Convention on Tobacco Control, at v, May 21, 2003–June 29, 2004, WHA56.1, 2302 U.N.T.S. 166, 42 I.L.M. 518, available at http://www.who.int/tobacco/framework/WHO_FCTC_english.pdf.

30 http://www.who.int/fctc/signatories_parties/en/index.html.

31 WHO Framework Convention on Tobacco Control, arts. 11, 13, Feb. 27, 2005.

32 Sam F. Halabi, *The World Health Organization's Framework Convetion on Tobacco Control: An Analysis of Guidelines Adopted by the Conference of the Parties*, Ga. J. Int'l. & Comp. L. (2010).

Section 1(a) of Article 11 regulating packaging and labeling provides that each party will take measures to ensure that

> tobacco product packaging and labelling do not promote a tobacco product by any means that are false, misleading, deceptive or likely to create an erroneous impression about its characteristics, health effects, hazards or emissions, including any term, descriptor, trademark, figurative or any other sign that directly or indirectly creates the false impression that a particular tobacco product is less harmful than other tobacco products.[33]

In addition, § 1(b) requires that packages carry health warnings describing the harmful effects of tobacco use, which shall cover no less than 30 percent of the principal display area but recommends the coverage of 50 percent or more of the display area.[34]

The Article 11 guidelines elaborate the regulatory measures parties should consider that effectively eliminate the use or effectiveness of trademarks.[35] Paragraph 7 recommends large, graphic health warnings because they are more noticeable, better communicate health risks, provoke a greater emotional response, and increase motivation to quit or decrease tobacco consumption.[36] Paragraph 8 provides that health warnings should be located on both the front and back of the package, at the top of all principal display areas.[37] Paragraph 9 suggests that health warnings should also be located on all sides of the package, inserts, and onserts.[38] Referencing Article 11.1(b)(v), Paragraph 12 of the Guidelines encourages Parties to require health warnings that cover more than 50 percent of the principal display areas, and Paragraph 16 recommends that these warnings should be pictorial because they will "disrupt the impact of brand imagery" and the overall attractiveness of the package.[39]

Paragraph 43 affects words and phrases that would normally be subject to trademark protection. It provides a nonexhaustive list of terms, as mentioned in Article 11.1(a), which "create a false impression that a particular tobacco product is less harmful than others."[40] Paragraphs 8, 10, and 54 address obstruction of warnings by other elements of packaging or trade dress.[41] Paragraph 8 states that health warnings should not be damaged or concealed by the normal opening of the package. Paragraph 10 reiterates the need for warnings to remain unobstructed by other

33 WHO Framework Convention on Tobacco Control, art. 11(1)(a), Feb. 27, 2005.
34 *Id.* at § 11(1)(b).
35 Guidelines for Implementation of Article 11 of the WHO Framework Convention on Tobacco Control, available at http://www.who.int/fctc/guidelines/article_11.pdf.
36 *Id.* at ¶ 7.
37 *Id.* at ¶ 8.
38 *Id.* at ¶ 9.
39 *Id.* at ¶ 16.
40 *Id.* at ¶ 43.
41 *Id.* at ¶¶ 8, 10, 54.

elements of the packaging such as labeling markings, inserts, and onserts.[42] Finally, Paragraph 54 indicates that warnings should not be obscured, obliterated, or undermined by extraneous adhesive labels, stickers, cases, covers, sleeves, and wrappings.[43] Paragraph 46 addresses plain packaging:[44]

> Parties should consider adopting measures to restrict or prohibit the use of logos, colours, brand images or promotional information on packaging other than brand names and product names displayed in a standard colour and font style (plain packaging). This may increase the noticeability and effectiveness of health warnings and messages, prevent the package from detracting attention from them, and address industry package design techniques that may suggest that some products are less harmful than others.[45]

Article 13 on advertising, promotion, and sponsorship also affects trademark rights.[46] Sections 2 and 3 require a party, subject to its constitutional principles, to either ban or apply restrictions on tobacco advertising, promotion, and sponsorship.[47] Section 4 sets minimum standards, subject to the national constitution, for restrictions on tobacco advertising.[48] It requires a prohibition on all forms of advertising, promotion, and sponsorship that promote tobacco by means that are false, misleading, deceptive, or likely to create an erroneous impression about its characteristics, health effects, hazards, or emissions; that health warnings accompany all tobacco advertising; a ban or restrictions on tobacco advertising, promotion, or sponsorship on radio, television, print media, and other media as appropriate; and a prohibition or restriction on tobacco sponsorship of international events, activities, or participants.[49]

Several countries have either implemented or have introduced legislation to implement plain packaging or similar restrictions on tobacco products.[50] Between 2008 and 2010, Uruguay implemented a number of tobacco control measures including two that addressed the manipulation of packaging and labeling to shape health perceptions of tobacco products.[51] First, the state required that pictorial

[42] *Id.* at ¶ 10.
[43] *Id.* at ¶ 54.
[44] *Id.* at ¶ 46.
[45] *Id.* at ¶¶ 7–10, 12, 16.
[46] WHO Framework Convention on Tobacco Control, art. 13, Feb. 27, 2005.
[47] *Id.* at § 13(2), (3).
[48] *Id.* at § 13(4).
[49] *Id.* at § 13(4).
[50] Prathana Knapp & Nutthakarn Phongphunpunya, *Striking a Balance: Public Health vs IP Rights in Thailand's Cigarette Package Rules*, available at http://gip-asean.com/information/newsletter201404th.pdf; *UP Court Recommends Plain Packaging for Cigarettes*, Hindustan Times, Jul. 25, 2014.
[51] Susy Frankel & Daniel Gervais, *Plain Packaging and the Interpretation of the TRIPS Agreement*, 46 Vand. J. Transnat'l L. 1149, 1158 n. 31 (Nov. 2013), available at http://www.vanderbilt.edu/jotl/manage/wp-content/uploads/Gervais-Final-Review.pdf.

warnings cover 80 percent of a cigarette pack's surface. Second, the Ministry of Health limited the sale of cigarettes to only one variety per brand, the so-called single presentation requirement.[52] That part of the law prevented a firm from selling multiple varieties of cigarette under a single trademark. For example, Philip Morris International (PMI), whose most important asset is the Marlboro brand, could no longer sell Marlboro "Reds," Marlboro "Greens," and Marlboro "Blues," leaving "Marlboros" as its only authorized variety.[53] At the time the measures were adopted, Uruguay had one of Latin America's highest smoking rates.[54] As of 2009, more than 5,000 Uruguayans died each year from diseases linked to tobacco consumption, mainly due to cardiovascular diseases and cancer.[55]

The FCTC effectively protected Uruguay's measures from what would have, prior to the FCTC's existence, been strong claims for expropriation of trademarks. PMI first challenged the regulations in Uruguayan courts, seeking an injunction based in part on Uruguay's revised, TRIPS-compliant trademark law. Unsuccessful in Uruguayan courts, PMI initiated (through entities it controlled) arbitration proceedings under Switzerland's BIT with Uruguay. That treaty not only included broad definitions of "investor" and "investment"; it also established narrow exceptions for public health regulation and required even laws passed with that justification and according to due process to compensate an investor for an "indirect" expropriation.[56]

The arbitration panel hearing the dispute determined that Uruguay's measures fell within its obligations under the FCTC, which itself provided an independent basis that Uruguay's measures were evidence based and in the public interest. Citing Articles 2, 4, 11, and 13 of the FCTC (the trademark relevant provisions of which have been discussed earlier here), the arbitration panel concluded that

[52] Uru. Ministry of Public Health Ordinance No. 514 (Feb. 14, 2009); Uru. Presidential Decree No. 287/009 (Dec. 2, 2009).

[53] FTR Holding S.A. v. Uruguay, ICSID Case No. APRB/10/17, Feb. 19, 2011, ¶¶ 45, 89 ("As of 31 December 2009, Article 3 of Ordinance 514 has resulted in an approximately 15 per cent decrease in Abal's sales. The hardest hit brand has been 'Marlboro,' of which the discontinued 'Marlboro Gold,' 'Marlboro Blue' and 'Marlboro Green (Fresh Mint)' varieties represent 40.5 per cent of total sales in 2008 ... It should be noted that Philip Morris affiliates worldwide have invested significant amounts of time and money in developing a revision of the three sub-brands of the Marlboro family. As a result of Ordinance 514, Philip Morris has been prevented from introducing these innovations in Uruguay and accordingly has been deprived of the use of its intellectual property."), available at http://www.smoke-free.ca/eng_home/2010/PMIvsUruguay/PMI-Uruguay%20complaint0001.pdf.

[54] Pan American Health Organization (PAHO) & World Health Organization (WHO) Tobacco Control Report for the Region of the Americas (2013) (R-267), Chart 2.

[55] Pan American Health Organization (PAHO), Global Adult Tobacco Survey (GATS): Uruguay '09 15, 22 (2011).

[56] Agreement between the Swiss Confederation and the Oriental Republic of Uruguay on the Reciprocal Promotion and Protection of Investments, Switz.-Uru., art. 5, Apr. 22, 1991, 575 U.N.T.S. 159, available at http://untreaty.un.org/unts/120001_144071/26/2/00021341.pdf.

> [The single presentation requirement] is part of Uruguay's comprehensive tobacco control policies and is in line with WHO Recommendations and Uruguay's express obligations under Article 11 of the FCTC as well as in accordance with Art. 8 of Law 18,256.485 The SPR thus draws upon the scientific evidence of the FCTC and its implementation guidelines, and constitutes a sound policy that advances important public health objectives.[57]

Similarly, the panel cited Article 11 of the FCTC for support for larger graphic warnings. After the adoption of Uruguay's measures, other developing countries followed: Namibia (55%), Turkey (65%), Ecuador (60%), Burkina Faso (60%), Chad (70%), Uganda (65%), Moldova (65%), Brunei (75%), Sri Lanka (80%), Thailand (85%), Pakistan, and India (85% each) now require warning labels that cover significantly more than half of the front and back of cigarette packs. Nepal has recently increased its warning from 75% of the front and back to 90%.[58]

The contrast with earlier episodes of pressure from tobacco firms could not be more stark. In addition to the measures proposed by Brazil, the Philippines, and South Africa in the 1990s to challenge tobacco firms' practices (detailed in Chapter 8), those firms also attacked measures in wealthy countries. Contesting Australia's 1992 effort to require that cigarettes be sold in plain packaging, British American Tobacco argued in front of an Australian Senate inquiry that the Paris Convention for the Protection of Industrial Property and Australian law would require compensation for the fair market value of its cigarette brands.[59] The Australian government was persuaded. Upon rejecting the proposed regulations, the Ministry of Health announced: "Unfortunately, [the proposal] is just not feasible ... We would have to buy the tobacco companies' trademarks, and that would cost us hundreds of millions of dollars."[60] In 1994, Philip Morris and RJR Reynolds engaged former US and Canadian trade negotiators to argue to Canadian legislators that the "unlawful expropriation" of their trademarks under plain packaging would amount to hundreds of millions of dollars in compensation under a NAFTA Chapter 11 proceeding.

57 ICSID, Award, PHILIP MORRIS BRANDS SÀRL, PHILIP MORRIS PRODUCTS S.A. and ABAL HERMANOS S.A. (THE CLAIMANTS) and ORIENTAL REPUBLIC OF URUGUAY (THE RESPONDENT) (ICSID Case No. ARB/10/7) (July 8, 2016) paragraph 371.

58 *Id.* at paragraph 519.

59 WILLS: WD & HO Wills (Australia) Limited, *Generic Packaging: Supplementary Submission to Senate Community Affairs References Committee*, Bates 800145087 (Feb. 1995) (arguing that the proposals would lead to substantial claims for compensation); WILLS: WD & HO Wills (Australia) Limited, *Submission to the Industry Inquiry: The Tobacco Growing and Manufacturing Industries*, Bates 503950973 (Jan. 1994) available at http://bat.library.ucsf.edu/tid/kpk33a99 (noting that the proposed packaging regulations "amount to a severe infringement of internationally-registered intellectual property rights.").

60 Martin Riordan, *Generics Rejected by Australian Health*, BATES 800190580 (July 24, 1995), available at http://bat.library.ucsf.edu/tid/mrb81a99.

In addition to influencing developing countries, Uruguay's measures encouraged stronger action in wealthy countries as well.[61] Australia introduced plain packaging in December 2013.[62] Under Australia's legislation, packs must be a standard, dark brown color and comply with the following structural aspects: no decorative ridges, embossing, bulges, or irregularities in shape or texture; edges must be ridged, straight, and not beveled or otherwise shaped or embellished in any way; may not make a noise or produce a scent that could be construed as advertising or promotion; may not include features intended to change after sale, such as heat-activated inks or inks that are visible only in certain light; and may not include inserts or onserts.[63] Packs may only state the brand and variant name in a font, size, and color that is uniform across all brands, and may not display any trademarks or other identifying marks[64] In addition, packs are required to display large health warnings with graphics and explanatory messages over at least 75 percent of the front surface of tobacco packaging and 75–90 percent of the back surface.[65] The paper casings of cigarettes are also regulated; they must either be white or white with an imitation cork tip.[66] Australia's law withstood a similar challenge as Uruguay's under a bilateral investment treaty as well as, at least preliminarily, the World Trade Organization.[67]

The Framework Convention on Tobacco Control has so far proved effective at creating a safe regulatory space for the modification or elimination of tobacco trademarks.[68] Given that developing countries led the movement to establish an international instrument for this protection, the disease burden of tobacco disproportionately falls on their populations, and trademarks play a critical role in the advertising, marketing, and promotion of tobacco undertaken by a small number of global firms, the FCTC is, like the International Code, the CBD the International

[61] http://www.nam.org/Advocacy/The-Center-for-Legal-Action/Briefs-Online/2014/LWTOplain packaging-614/.

[62] Jamie Smyth, *Australia Smoking Rates Tumble After Plain Packaging Shift*, Fin. Times (Jul. 17, 2014), available at http://www.ft.com/intl/cms/s/0/c4016952-0d4a-11e4-bcb2-00144feabdco .html#axzz3ELxi9XFb.

[63] Jonathan Liberman, *Plainly Constitutional: The Upholding of Plain Tobacco Packaging by the High Court of Australia*, 39 Am. J.L. & Med. 361, 361 (2013).

[64] *Id.* at 364.

[65] *Id.*

[66] *Id.*

[67] http://www.reuters.com/article/us-wto-tobacco-australia/australia-wins-landmark-wto-tobacco-pack aging-case-bloomberg-idUSKBN1801S9.

[68] Prathana Knapp & Nutthakarn Phongphunpunya, *Striking a Balance: Public Health vs IP Rights in Thailand's Cigarette Package Rules*, 2, available at http://gip-asean.com/information/ newsletter201404th.pdf. Matthew C. Porterfield & Christopher R. Byrnes, *Philip Morris v. Uruguay: Will Investor-State Arbitration Send Restrictions on Tobacco Up in Smoke?*, Int'l Inst. for Sustainable Dev. (Jul. 12, 2011), available at http://www.iisd.org/itn/2011/07/12/ philip-morris-v-uruguay-will-investor-state-arbitration-send-restrictions-on-tobacco-marketing-up-in-smoke/.

Seed Treaty, and the Nagoya Protocol, effectively an instrument of redistribution from wealthier to poorer countries.

While there are only international intellectual property shelters for infant foods and tobacco, the conditions are such that an international agreement on alcohol may also emerge. Alcohol consumption not only results in greater harm to third parties relative to other drugs, but also has substantial deleterious effects on users, such as increased risks of cancer and heart disease, traffic accidents, burns, poisonings, and drownings.[69] Additionally, alcohol consumption facilitates risky sexual behavior, contributing to the spread of HIV/AIDS and other sexually transmitted diseases.[70] All of these burdens are heavier in developing countries.

In 2010, WHO published a report titled "Global Strategy to Reduce the Harmful Use of Alcohol" in which it concluded that "2.5 million people worldwide died of alcohol-related causes in 2004, including 320,000 young people between 15 and 29 years of age."[71] WHO recommended a number of interventions consistent with analogous FCTC mandates including: educating people on the consequences of alcohol abuse; restricting the sale of alcohol to minors; implementing comprehensive marketing restrictions; increasing taxes on alcohol products; and addressing illicit or informally produced alcohol. The report is not binding; it merely serves as a guide for member nations when adopting their own alcohol control laws. Organizations like the American Public Health Association, the American Society of Addiction Medicine, the World Medical Association, as well as leading medical journals advocated an international alcohol control treaty based in significant part on the FCTC and WHO recommendations.[72] Editors of one of these journals, the *Lancet*, has also posed the question as to the desirability of a Framework Convention on Obesity Control based in part on WHO's Global Strategy for Diet, Physical Activity and Health.[73]

The global structure of the market is similar to tobacco as are the use of trademarks for purposes of shaping product risk. Among others, brewers introduced "Ice," "Select," "Lite," and "Light" versions of their beer product lines to implicitly convey product qualities. In North America, consumers associate "Ice" with a beer that might taste better when served particularly cold, although the real intent is to

[69] WHO, Alcohol and Injuries: Emergency Department Studies in an International Perspective, iv (2009), available at http://www.who.int/substance_abuse/publications/alcohol/en/.

[70] Lori A. J. Scott-Shelden et al., *Alcohol Consumption, Drug Use and Condom Use among STD Clinic Patients,* 70 J. Studs. on Alcohol & Drugs 762, 762–63 (2009).

[71] WHO, Global Strategy to Reduce the Harmful Use of Alcohol 3 (2010), available at http://www.who.int/substance_abuse/msbalcstragegy.pdf.

[72] Allyn L. Taylor & Ibadat S. Dhillon, *An International Legal Strategy for Alcohol Control: Not a Framework Convention – At Least Not Yet,* Addiction (June 20, 2012), available at http://www.asam.org/advocacy/find-a-policy-statement/view-policy-statement/public-policy-statements/2011/12/16/establishment-of-a-framework-convention-on-alcohol-control-and-the-exclusion-of-tobacco-and-alcohol-from-trade-agreements.

[73] See http://www.thelancet.com/journals/lancet/article/PIIS0140-6736(11)61356-1/fulltext.

offer product lines with significantly higher alcohol content.[74] Consumers may intuit that Bud Light® has fewer calories and lower alcohol content than Budweiser®, but may not guess that Bud Select® has fewer calories but higher alcohol content than Bud Light®.[75] In 2010, Thailand introduced large graphic warning labels for alcohol containers, prompting threatening responses at the Committee on Technical Barriers to Trade at the World Trade Organization.

[74] Miller Brewing, *Miller Brewing Company Five-Year Plan* 10 (1992), available at http://legacy.library.ucsf.edu/tid/hyi95g00.

[75] *How Many Calories in Beer?*, available at http://www.beer100.com/beercalories.htm.

13

Limiting Copyright

As detailed in Chapter 9, TRIPS and the Berne Convention generally favor protection of authors' rights in national copyright regimes.[1] Librarians, educators, archivists and researchers in developing countries must often circumnavigate "copyright laws that benefit net exporters of intellectual property, rather than addressing their own domestic conditions."[2] While countries in the developed world had already taken to codifying their own limitations and exceptions, many in the developing world have not taken such steps for a variety of often case-specific reasons.[3] Global publishing interests have even lobbied for stricter laws in developing countries than those in wealthier ones, with longer terms of protection but no limitations or exceptions.[4] Specific programs, such as those for technical assistance under WIPO, historically focused on the importance of stricter intellectual property for economic growth and development, disfavoring limitations and exceptions that would apply to the situation of developing countries.[5]

Chapter 9 also provided a brief history of Article 9 of the Berne Convention, which, while introducing a right to reproduce, also articulated an exception for that right. Article 9(2)'s exception became codified in TRIPS Article 13: "Members shall confine limitations or exceptions to exclusive [copy]rights to certain special cases

[1] Denise R. Nicholson, *Treaty for Visually Impaired Persons (TVI) and Treaty Proposal on Copyright Limitations and Exceptions for Libraries and Archives (TLIB): Implications for the Developing World*, IFLA World Library and Information Congress in Singapore (2013), available at http://library.ifla.org/239/1/209-nicholson-en.pdf.

[2] *Id.*

[3] Shae Fitzpatrick, *Setting Its Sights on the Marrakesh Treaty: The U.S. Role in Alleviating the Book Famine for Persons with Print Disabilities*, 37 B.C. Int. & Comp. L. R. 147 (2014).

[4] Margaret Chon, *Copyright and Capability for Education: An Approach from Below*, in Tzen Wong and Graham Dutfield (eds), Intellectual Property and Human Development: Current Trends and Future Scenarios 229 (2011).

[5] WIPO, The Economics of Intellectual Property: Suggestions for Further Research in Developing Countries and Countries with Economies in Transition, Publication No 1012 (2009).

which do not conflict with a normal exploitation of the work and do not unreasonably prejudice the legitimate interests of the right holder."[6] The drafting history of Berne suggests that those limitations and exceptions did not have as their principal aim access to literary works or textbooks for developing countries.[7] Article 9(2) of Berne did, however, create a specific area that would disproportionately benefit developing countries: protecting the interests of the blind and visually impaired (and the accessible formats serving their interests would facilitate). Despite the longstanding acknowledgment of the issue (one of the first suggestions for a new international instrument "that could harmonize the existing patchwork of copyright laws" was made by a WIPO Intergovernmental Committee in 1985), there was little movement at the international level until 2004.[8]

Of the 285 million people the World Health Organization estimates are blind or visually impaired, 39 million are blind and 246 million are visually impaired or have "low vision."[9] The latter category ranges from only light impairment to the inability to read without assistance.[10] The category of "print disabled" or "people with a print disability" includes those who may have other disabilities that preclude holding a book, for example. There are other visual disabilities that may require alternate formats, such as highlighted letters or text written with certain contrasts. The vast majority of people, 90 percent or more, needing alternative formats, live in developing countries.[11]

The availability of books in formats that are available to print-disabled persons is estimated between 7 percent and 20 percent out of an estimated 2.2 million books published per year, leaving blind and visually impaired people in a state of what has become known as a "book famine."[12] Accessible formats include, but are not limited to, Braille, large print, ebooks and audio books with special navigation, audio description, and radio broadcasts. As discussed in Chapter 9, national copyright laws made it difficult to reproduce copies in accessible formats while *international* copyright law erected barriers to sharing accessible formats across borders.[13] National laws were (and to a large extent still are) characterized by a lack of exceptions or

6 TRIPS art. 13.

7 Pamela Samuelson, *Justifications for Copyright Limitations and Exceptions*, in Ruth Okediji (ed), Copyright Law in an Age of Limitations and Exceptions 12–59 (2017).

8 Neil Yap, *Fitting Marrakesh into a Consequentialist Copyright Framework*, 6 N.Y.U. J. Int. Prop. & Ent. L. 351, 360 (2017).

9 World Health Organization, *Visual Impairment and Blindness* (2014), available at http://www.who.int/mediacentre/factsheets/fs282/en/.

10 *Id.*

11 Barry Youngermen, Pandemics and Global Health 239 (2008).

12 European Parliament, The Marrakesh Treaty: Study for the PETI Committee 9 (2016).

13 Judith Sullivan, Study on Copyright Exceptions and Limitations for the Visually Impaired 28–63 (2006), available at www.wipo.int/edocs/mdocs/copyright/en/sccr_15/sccr_15_7.doc.

limitations for reproduction of works.[14] Second, even where countries included such limitations and exceptions, they lacked a mechanism to distribute accessible works across borders.[15] A study commissioned by WIPO in 2006 analyzed the "diverse nature of limitation and exceptions for the visually impaired in national copyright laws."[16] For example, when previously illegal cross-border sharing prevented the visually impaired from benefiting from a variety of works, books would need to undergo conversion in each country individually, duplicating the cost and efforts of making accessible formats.

THE MARRAKESH TREATY TO FACILITATE ACCESS TO PUBLISHED WORKS BY VISUALLY IMPAIRED PERSONS AND PERSONS WITH PRINT DISABILITIES

Unlike the other international intellectual property shelters formed through the FAO, the World Health Organization, or UNICEF, the international agreement to facilitate access to alternative-format books was achieved through the World Intellectual Property Organization, which had with only limited success bridged the rich–poor divide in the context of the Berne Convention and was ultimately marginalized in the process leading to TRIPS.[17] WIPO became active on the alternative formats issue after Argentina and Brazil introduced the concept of a "development agenda" for WIPO, which called for the organization to reform its mandate to de-emphasize promotion and expansion of intellectual property rights and to emphasize development objectives.[18] By 2007, WIPO had created areas in which development priorities might shape its action.

In 2009, Brazil, Ecuador, and Paraguay introduced a treaty drafted by the World Blind Union for a "WIPO Treaty for Improved Access for Blind, Visually Impaired and other Reading Disabled Persons."[19] The treaty was explicit both as to the disproportionate need for access to works in developing countries as well as its relationship to the development agenda.[20]

The negotiations were protracted, with EU and US delegations arguing for nonbinding instruments that emphasized the rights of publishers (indeed, that may ultimately impede rather than expand access).[21] The African proposal, on the

14 Jukka Liedes, *Copyright: Evolution, Not Revolution*, 276 (5310) SCIENCE 223–25 (1997).
15 Sullivan, *supra* note 13.
16 *Id.*
17 Peter Yu, *Déjà vu in the Intellectual Property Regime*, in Matthew David & Debra Halbert (eds), The SAGE HANDBOOK OF INTELLECTUAL PROPERTY 123 (2015).
18 J. Boyle, A *Manifesto on WIPO and the Future of Intellectual Property* 9 DUKE LAW & TECHNOLOGY REV 1 (2004).
19 http://www.wipo.int/meetings/en/doc_details.jsp?doc_id=122732.
20 *Id.*
21 Margot E. Kaminski & Schlomit Yanisky-Ravid, *The Marrakesh Treaty for Visually Impaired Persons: Why a Treaty was Preferable to Soft Law*, 75 U. PITT. L. REV. 255 (2014).

other hand, sought "Exceptions and Limitations for the Persons with Disabilities, Educational and Research Institutions, Libraries and Archives," thus seeking to use the treaty to open access to a far wider range of instituitons.[22] Interest groups representing authors and publishers became suspicious that the treaty would act as a "Trojan Horse" that would allow for copyrights protections to be weakened through future treaties.[23] Copyright owners were afraid the precedent set by the treaty would result in "a series of treaties that specifically focus on trying to set forth minimal limitations and exceptions to [their] right[s]."[24]

The African proposal effectively created a broader class of beneficiaries that included educational and research institutions, libraries, and archives in addition to persons.[25] The proposal attempted to adopt a more "'holistic approach' to the proper recognition of the public interest within the international copyright system." It featured "the most expansive definition" of visually impaired persons (VIPs), one that "conceivably extend[ed] to those possessing the 'disability' of illiteracy."[26] In fact, the African Group's proposal was the only proposal that "*overtly* propose[d] copyright exceptions beyond visually impaired persons."[27] African countries sought a treaty that allowed member states to undertake additional efforts in order to "achieve greater equality of access to knowledge and communications" and "*guarantee[]* that developing countries enjoy [continued] ... access to flexibilities and exceptions without any legal or technical hindrances."[28]

The compromise was a binding instrument that acknowledged "the need to maintain a balance between the effective protection of the right of authors and the larger public interest." It further allowed *voluntary* "commercial availability" provisions. Commercial availability provisions require that prior to the making of an alternative format book accessible, commercial availability of the book on the local market at reasonable conditions be considered.

The ultimate text clearly authorizes the dissemination of accessible works beyond only the populations considered. Article 2 defines "works" so that the Marrakesh

[22] WIPO, SCCR 22th Sess, Proposal by the African Group for a 'Draft WIPO Treaty on Exceptions and Limitations for the Persons with Disabilities, Educational and Research Institutions, Libraries and Archives, SSCR/22/12, June 3, 2011, available at http://www.wipo.int/edocs/mdocs/copyright/en/sccr_22/sccr_22_12.pdf.

[23] Tatiana Synodinou, *On Copyright and Rights of Persons with Disabilities: WIPO Treaty for the Blind* (Apr. 13, 2009), available at http://copyrightblog.kluweriplaw.com/2013/04/19/on-copyright-and-rights-of-persons-with-disabilities-wipo-treaty-for-the-blind.

[24] Yap, *supra* note 8, at 361–62.

[25] Tshimanga Kongolo, African Contributions in Shaping the Worldwide Intellectual Property System 316 (2016).

[26] Sean Williams, *Closing in on the Light at WIPO Movement towards a Copyright Treaty for Visually Impaired Persons and Intellectual Property Movements*, 33 U. Pa. J. Int. L. 1035, 1054 (2014).

[27] *Id.*

[28] *Id.*

Treaty applies to a broad category of copyrighted materials also covered under Berne:

> books, pamphlets and other writings; lectures, addresses, sermons and other works of the same nature; dramatic or dramatico-musical works; choreographic works and entertainments in dumb show; musical compositions with or without words; cinematographic works to which are assimilated works expressed by a process analogous to cinematography; works of drawing, painting, architecture, sculpture, engraving and lithography; photographic works to which are assimilated works expressed by a process analogous to photography; works of applied art; illustrations, maps, plans, sketches and three-dimensional works relative to geography, topography, architecture or science.[29]

Art.2(a) further states that the works covered may be expressed "in the form of text, notation and/or related illustrations" and "whether published or otherwise made publicly available in any media." So, the treaty applies to all technologies, any new forms of digital formats to be covered, whether or not published. Article 22 extends this coverage to audiobooks.[30] Article 2(b) requires that the "accessible format copy" give beneficiaries under the treaty "access to the work, including to permit that person to have access as feasibly and comfortably" as a person who is not visually impaired.[31]

The treaty is similarly expansive as to the persons, charities, and entities that may disseminate accessible works. Under Article 2(3), an "authorized entity" means an entity that is authorized or recognized by the government to provide education, instructional training, adaptive reading, or information access to beneficiary persons on a nonprofit basis.[32] It also includes official institutions or organizations that provide services to beneficiary persons as one of its primary activities or institutional obligations, so libraries, schools, and civil society groups may disseminate accessible works. Authorized entities may also transmit, through whatever means, copies to other authorized entities without the permission of the copyright holder.

Authorized entities must take measures to "establish that the persons it serves" qualify under the treaty, limit its activities to those persons or other authorized entities, discourage unauthorized copies, and "maintain due care" in "and records of" its handling of copies.[33] But these measures are up to the authorized entities themselves, subject only to good-faith implementation.[34] The Marrakesh Treaty lays

29 Berne Convention art. 2.

30 Marrakesh Treaty to Facilitate Access to Published Works for Persons Who Are Blind, Visually Impaired, or Otherwise Print Disabled, June 27, 2013, https://perma.cc/BF8Y-VG2U [hereinafter "Marrakesh Treaty"] art. 22.

31 Marrakesh Treaty art. 2.

32 Marrakesh Treaty art. 2(3).

33 Marrakesh Treaty art. 4.

34 Jingyi Li & Niloufer Selvadurai, *Reconciling the Enforcement of Copyright with the Upholding of Human Rights: A Consideration of the Marrakesh Treaty to Facilitate Access to Published*

out no requirements for national governments to impose on authorized entities, or specifics for approval of those entities. A national system of registration is a possibility under Article 9, but emphasizes its purpose for "the voluntary sharing of information to assist authorized entities in identifying one another."[35]

In addition to the "blind," Article 3(b) defines beneficiary persons as those having "a visual impairment or a perceptual or reading disability which cannot be improved to give visual function substantially equivalent to that of a person who has no such impairment" and so is "unable to read printed works to substantially the same degree as a person without an impairment."[36] This definition is more expansive than the definitions used by the World Health Organization or the World Blind Union to characterize the number of blind or "low vision" people worldwide. The World Health Organization, for example, defines "low vision" as a "one who has impairment of visual functioning even after treatment and/or standard refractive correction, and has a visual acuity of less than 6/18 to light perception, or a visual field less than 10 degrees from the point of fixation."[37]

National legislation under the Marrakesh Treaty must permit the direct supply of an accessible copy to a beneficiary person by "non-commercial lending or by electronic communication."[38] Under the treaty, countries must therefore allow the distribution and sharing of accessible copies over the internet or any lending system.[39] There is a permissive recommendation for implementation of this provision that subjects availability to four conditions in changes to national copyright law:

(i) the authorized entity has lawful access to the work;
(ii) the work is converted into accessible format (including changes needed to navigate information in the copy), provided the conversion does not introduce change to the work other than those that are necessary to make it accessible;
(iii) the accessible format copies are supplied exclusively to be used by beneficiary persons; and
(iv) the activity is undertaken on a nonprofit basis.

Article 5, which addresses the historical barriers that international copyright law posed for the import and export of protected work, requires the cross-border distribution of accessible format copies provided that they are made under an exception

Works for the Blind, Visually Impaired and Print Disabled, 36 EUR. INTELL. PROP. REV. 653 (2014).

35 Marrakesh Treaty art. 9.

36 Marrakesh Treaty art. 3(b).

37 Ramachandra Pararajasegaram, *Low Vision Care: The Need to Maximise Visual Potential*, 17 (49) COMMUNITY EYE HEALTH 1–2 (2004).

38 Marrakesh Treaty art. 4(2).

39 Pradip Ninan Thomas, *Copyright and Copyleft in India: Between Global Agendas and Local Interests*, in Matthew David & Debra Halbert (eds), The SAGE HANDBOOK OF INTELLECTUAL PROPERTY 361–62 (2015).

or pursuant to operation of law.[40] The mandatory right to export obtains when (1) an authorized entity distributes or "makes available" an accessible work directly to a beneficiary person, or (2) when an authorized entity does so to another authorized entity in another country that has ratified the Marrakesh Treaty.[41]

The Treaty was signed in Marrakesh, Morocco, on June 28, 2013 and has reached some sixty signatures to date.[42] It only took the Treaty three months to reach twenty ratifying members, entering into effect on September 30, 2016; it has gone on to be ratified by thirty nations, allowing the citizens of these countries to "benefit from the increase in accessible materials through cross-border sharing and the increased productions of books."[43]

The Marrakesh Treaty seeks that member states establish exceptions and limitations to the exclusive rights of copyright holders within their own legal frameworks that would allow unauthorized transformation into accessible formats and afford persons with visual disabilities a "free flow of accessible copies for use."[44]The Treaty removes administrative burdens to allow for legal and cost-effective cross-border shipment of resources.[45] Despite the expansive scope it gives to beneficiaries, covered works, and international sharing, it does not prevent countries from requiring that reasonable royalties are paid to the copyright holders for any such conversion.[46]

The treaty has already had a substantial effect. Several Latin American countries adopted broad definitions of a "visually impaired person."[47] Indeed, these definitions are drawn not only from the treaty but from the objectives those countries sponsored in the negotiations leading to the treaty. There, they sought a more development focused treaty that would "account for developmental disparities," and wished to address inequality through "more flexible and accommodating copyright laws."[48] These countries were focused on enriching their region and its people by "ensuring the opportunity to develop and utilize their creative, artistic and intellectual

[40] Marrakesh Treaty art. 5.
[41] *Id.*
[42] http://www.wipo.int/edocs/mdocs/govbody/en/mvt_a_1/mvt_a_1_2_rev.pdf.
[43] Thus far Sri Lanka, India, El Salvador, United Arab Emirates, Uruguay, Mali, Paraguay, Singapore, Argentina, Mexico, Mongolia, the Republic of Korea, Australia, Brazil, Peru, the Democratic People's Republic of Korea, Israel, Chile, Ecuador, Guatemala, Canada, St. Vincent and the Grenadines, Tunisia, Botswana, Liberia, Panama, Honduras, Kyrgyzstan, Kenya, and Malawi. *Id.*
[44] Nicholson, *supra* note 1, at 5.
[45] IFLA, *The Treaty of Marrakesh*, available at https://www.ifla.org/DE/node/10916.
[46] Aaron Scheinwald, *Who Could Possibly Be against a Treaty for the Blind?*, 22 Fordham Intell. Prop. Media & Ent. L. J. 445 (2012).
[47] Sean Williams, *Closing in on the Light at WIPO Movement towards a Copyright Treaty for Visually Impaired Persons and Intellectual Property Movements*, 33 U. Pa. J. Int. L. 1035, 1053 (2014).
[48] *Id.*

potential," and proposed that any resulting treaty provided the necessary measures "needed to publish and distribute works in formats that are accessible for [VIPs]."[49]

After the Marrakesh Treaty entered into force, developing countries have implemented the treaty to obtain and then share access to materials they had sought through other mechanisms, including the Berne Convention.[50] These efforts include international networks, such as the collaboration of regional libraries under the International Federation of Library Associations, or critical bilateral, multilateral, or centralized exchanges.[51] Before the Marrakesh Treaty, these exchanges required cooperative agreements between libraries, in addition to permissions for each title involved.[52] Some more prominent centralized exchanges have been the Global Accessible Library (GAL), Trusted Intermediaries Global Accessible Resources (TIGAR), and the most recent Accessible Books Consortium (ABC), which focuses on book exchanges, capacity development, and inclusive publishing.[53] The Consortium acts as a shared digital book catalog that utilizes permissions management systems and secured facilities for "requesting, uploading and downloading files."[54] The ABC is currently comprised of 18 countries and features more than 350,000 items in 35 different languages, serving more than 100,000 beneficiaries.[55]

In Argentina, local nonprofit Tiflonexos has collaborated with the ABC to host a digital library comprised of more than 50,000 Spanish-language materials for the blind and visually impaired.[56] The organization now hopes to take advantage of funding and training from the ABC to reproduce books in the EPUB3 format standard.[57] The "flexible, digital format" affords the print disabled more autonomy and choice between accessing materials "to read with audio, refreshable braille or large print."[58] As of recent, Tiflonexos has plans of reproduce 800 educational books in the EPUB3 format, an effort that has received crucial support from various "publishers who have provided the original electronic files of these 800 books."[59] The books will then be reproduced into a text-based format that allows users to take

49 *Id.*

50 Lida Ayoubi, *The Marrakesh Treaty: Fixing International Copyright Law for the Benefit of the* Visually Impaired *Persons*, 13 N.Z. J. of Pub. & Int'l Law 255 (2015).

51 Victoria Owen, Margaret Ann Wilkinson & Margaret Williams, *Managing in Light of Marrakesh: Making Materials Available to Canadians with Print Disabilities*, OLA Superconference (Toronto), available at http://accessola2.com/superconference2017/Sessions/ThursFeb2/Managing_in_Light_of_Marrakesh_OLA_2017_Final_Version.pdf.

52 *Id.*

53 *Id.*

54 *Id.*

55 *Id.*

56 Capacity Building, Accessible Books Consortium (Aug. 21, 2017), available at http://www.accessiblebooksconsortium.org/capacity_building/en.

57 *Id.*

58 *Id.*

59 *Id.*

advantage of "text to speech" software found in reading devices and refreshable Braille readers.[60]

In a similar vein, the DAISY Lanka Foundation (DLF) in Sri Lanka has also begun to take comparable steps toward implementation of the Marrakesh Treaty.[61] Following support from the ABC, the DLF converted more than 1,000 educational books into accessible formats over the course of a year.[62] Prior to this collaboration, nonprofits and other NGOs would "have had to scan every page of hard copy books using OCR technology" and then edited the scans into an accessible format.[63] Some organizations had also taken to employing human narrators to record audiobooks.[64] Both practices were particularly "resource intensive," whereas the collaborative efforts recently implemented have been notably "more efficient[] and economical[]."[65]

Latin American nations have been particularly active in post-Marrakesh implementation with libraries from eight Latin nations receiving roughly 120 accessible format works from Latin American authors not long after the Treaty was ratified.[66] On September 30, 2016, the "first international exchange of accessible formats under the Marrakesh Treaty" was conducted in Santiago, Chile between the governments of Brazil, Chile, and Argentina.[67] The exchange was organized by the Latinoamerican Union for the Blind (ULAC) Innovarte, TifloLibros, and the Chilean Union of Blind Institutions.[68] Other civil society groups were also in attendance, such as the Chilean Library Association, and the Chilean Biblioteca Central de Ciegos even provided audio books for the exchange.[69]

60 *Id.*
61 *Id.*
62 Previously, the DLF was only able to reproduce 100–200 books over a similar period of time. *Id.*
63 *Id.*
64 *Id.*
65 *Id.*
66 William New, *Big Week for WIPO Marrakesh Treaty on Access for Visually Impaired Human Rights Side Under Focus*, Intellectual Property Watch (Oct. 10, 2016), available at https://www.ip-watch.org/2016/10/03/big-week-for-wipo-marrakesh-treaty-on-access-for-visually-impaired-human-rights-side-under-focus/.
67 *Id.*
68 *Id.*
69 *Id.*

PART IV

International Intellectual Property Shelters, Wealth Redistribution, and the Supranational Regulation of Global Firms

14

International Intellectual Property Shelters as Mechanisms of Redistribution

As Chapters 10 through 13 have argued, the New International Economic Order, especially its explicit calls for the redistribution of wealth and the facilitation of technology transfer, did not fade with the debt crises and structural adjustment reforms undertaken in the 1980s.[1] Indeed, the New International Economic Order was preoccupied with the "regulation and supervision of the activities of transnational corporations" and especially their effect on the economies of developing countries. According to the NIEO, global firms siphoned off wealth from already poor countries and channeled it back to wealthy ones; imposed inappropriate and growth-stunting conditions on technology transfer; and, in extreme cases, interfered with rights normally accorded public authorities under principles of sovereignty.[2] The New International Economic Order sought to reverse these trends, especially with respect to wealth redistribution and regulation of global firms.[3]

That is precisely what international intellectual property shelters have accomplished, or helped accomplish, especially since 2001. In the pharmaceutical context, the Doha Declaration and the Pandemic Influenza Preparedness Framework have not only resulted in the redistribution of wealth from firms in wealthy countries to poor populations in developing countries; they have also facilitated the migration of manufacturing and technology centers to Brazil, India, Indonesia, Malaysia, Mexico, the Philippines, South Africa, Thailand, and Turkey.[4]

1 Jeffrey Cason, *Whatever Happened to the New International Economic Order?*, in Andrew Valls (ed), Ethics in International Affairs, 201–13 (2000).
2 Nils Gilman, *The New International Economic Order: A Reintroduction* 6(1) Humanity 1 (2015).
3 Hans W. Singer, *The New International Economic Order: An Overview*, 16(4) J. Mod. African St. 539–48 (1978).
4 United Nations Economic and Social Council, Commission for Asia and the Pacific, Development of Health Systems in the Context of Enhancing Economic Growth Towards Achieving the Millennium Development Goals in Asia and the Pacific 116 (2007).

To be sure, there are a number of contributing factors to the decrease in the price of medicines that disproportionately matter for developing countries. After the Doha Declaration, the price of HIV/AIDS medications fell by 95 percent or more.[5] This was certainly due in part to the formation of international financing organizations (and the terms they could demand) such as PEPFAR or Global Fund, but those organizations, in turn, represented a new financial commitment from wealthier countries to poorer ones.[6] Just as or more influential were the creations of legal zones where developing countries, especially India and China, could play theretofore unprecedented roles in international markets.

> In 2001, India's Cipla introduced the world's first 3-in-1 fixed dose combination (Stavudine, Lamivudine, and Nevirapine). Now, a third of people living with HIV in 115 countries are taking a Cipla drug ... In addition to offering low cost drugs directly to consumers, Cipla offers free antiretroviral technology to any African nation looking to produce their own drugs. Cipla has done the same for malaria, and is now trying to produce cancer treatments with the same prescriptions for pennies philosophy.[7]

South Africa's Department of Health is now manufacturing its own antiretroviral drugs.[8]

India's pharmaceutical industry is now not only participating in the generics business but undertaking independent research and development. By volume, India's drug industry is the world's fourth largest, producing approximately 20 percent of active pharmaceutical ingredients.[9] Traditionally, Indian firms spent little revenue on research and development, and most drug discovery research was supported by publicly funded research institutes. In 2006, more than 175 firms had established research-and-development centers and approximately 15 firms engage in discovery research, spending around 10 percent of revenue on research and development.[10] "The industry's total annual R&D investment is estimated at around US

[5] Donald McNeil, *Indian Company Offers to Supply AIDS Drugs at Low Cost in Africa*, N.Y. Times (Feb. 7, 2001), available at http://www.nytimes.com/2001/02/07/health/07AIDS.html.

[6] Kevin Klock, *International Public-Private Partnerships as Part of the Solution to Infectious Disease Threats: Operational, Legal, and Governance Implications*, in Sam Halabi, Lawrence Gostin & Jeffrey Crowley (eds), Global Management of Infectious Disease after Ebola 157–78 (2017).

[7] Jacob Anderson-Minshall, *Fortune's Change the World List*, Plus (Sep. 1, 2016), available at https://www.hivplusmag.com/treatment/2016/9/01/these-hiv-pharmaceutical-companies-made-fortunes-change-world-list.

[8] *First ARVs from State-Owned Pharmaceutical Company Expected by 2017*, Health 24 (Mar. 29, 2016), available at http://www.health24.com/Medical/Meds-and-you/Medication/first-arvs-from-state-owned-pharmaceutical-company-expected-by-2017-20160324.

[9] Dipika Jain & Rachel Stephens, The Struggle for Access to Treatment for HIV/AIDS in India 115 (2008).

[10] Hans Löfgren, *The Global Biopharma Industry and the Rise of Indian Drug Multinationals: Implications for Australian Generics Policy*, Australia and New Zealand Health Policy 4 (2007).

$170 million, which is minuscule compared to that of "big pharma," though this expenditure 'buys' more R&D in India than in North America or Europe due to lower labor costs."[11]

There is a similar dynamic in the influenza context, where the Pandemic Influenza Framework Process was accompanied by technology transfer agreements between the World Health Organization, the US government, and facilities in Brazil, Egypt, India, Indonesia, Kazakhstan, Thailand, and Vietnam, which together have an estimated capacity of 200 million doses of influenza vaccine.[12] There are now 13 influenza vaccine manufacturers in low-income countries and 4 in upper-middle-income countries with a capacity to produce 450 million doses.[13] "In addition, several manufactures, including some in developing countries, are establishing adjuvant production and the use of these dose-sparing technologies is anticipated to become more common within the next several years, doubling their current pandemic capacity."[14] In the case of pandemic influenza, the redistribution of wealth is even more direct. Wealthier firms pay proportionately more to make the Framework operate.[15]

Similar redistributive mechanisms now function under the International Seed Treaty. Between 2008 and 2012, the US Congress authorized contributions of $60 million to the Global Crop Diversity Trust.[16] While firms' contributions are voluntary, DuPont and Syngenta have contributed $250,000 and $1 million, respectively.[17]

The more influential redistributive aspects of the International Seed Treaty will be how legislation applies the treaty's principles to use farmers' rights to benefit from the activities of agrochemical firms their territories. Farmers' rights include

> customary rights that farmers have had as stewards of agro-biodiversity since the dawn of agriculture to save, grow, share, develop and maintain plant varieties, of their legitimate right to be rewarded and supported for their contribution to the global pool of genetic resources as well as to the development of commercial

[11] *Id.* at 11.

[12] Martin Friede, Snapshot of Current Influenza Vaccine Manufacturing Capacity Worldwide and Summary of WHO-HHS Activities to Promote Technology Transfer (July 2011), available at http://www.who.int/phi/Session1B_Current_Manufacturing_Capacity_Worldwide_Friede.pdf.

[13] Kenneth A. McLean, Shoshanna Goldin, Claudia Nannei, Erin Sparrow & Guido Torelli, *The 2015 Global Production Capacity of Seasonal and Pandemic Influenza Vaccine*, 34(45) Vaccine 5410–13 (2016).

[14] *Id.*

[15] World Health Organization, *2015 PIP Partnership Contribution Collection*, available at http://www.who.int/influenza/pip/benefit_sharing/2015PCCollectionResults1APR2016.pdf.

[16] Melissa Ho, *International Treaty on Plant Genetic Resources for Food and Agriculture*, Congressional Research Service (Mar. 1, 2010), available at http://nationalaglawcenter.org/wp-content/uploads/assets/crs/R41091.pdf.

[17] Deniza Gertsberg, *Controversy with the Doomsday Vault*, GMO J. (Mar. 22, 2012), available at http://gmo-journal.com/2012/03/22/controversy-with-the-doomsday-vault/.

> varieties of plants, and to participate in decision-making on issues that may affect these rights.[18]

Countries may accomplish these objectives through legislation specific to the treaty, as have Brazil and India, or through other mechanisms such as the Convention on Biological Diversity, as has Peru. In Brazil, the percentage of seeds sourced from local, informal networks varies from 15 percent for maize to 50 percent for soybeans and as high as 85 percent for beans.[19] Small farmers meet the majority of internal food demand.[20]

Brazil's revised Seed Act recognizes plant varieties cultivated by family farmers, land reform settlers, and indigenous peoples.[21] These farmers who multiply seeds or seedlings for distribution, exchange, or commercialization among themselves are exempt from registration with the National Registry of Seeds and Seedlings (RENASEM) (Art. 8.3), as well as with the National Registry of Cultivars (RNC) (Art. 11.6). Brazilian law also forbids restrictions on the use of local, traditional, and creole cultivars in public seed exchanges and family-based distributive systems.[22] At the same time, the Brazilian government has established internal, federally funded agencies that support the seed exchanges authorized under its seed law.[23]

The law has become the basis for increasingly successful legal challenges to practices by large agrochemical firms. In 2013, farmers successfully challenged Monsanto's contracting practices for soybeans as violations of farmers' rights under the law.[24] Because farmer-exchanged soybean varieties became inevitably affected by the "drift" of Monsanto varieties, the court decision effectively gave Brazilian farmers a royalty-free use of a small threshold of Monsanto-protected seed.[25]

[18] Regina Andersen, Realising Farmers' Rights under the International Treaty on Plant Genetic Resources for Food and Agriculture. Summary of Findings from the Farmers' Rights Project, Phase 1. Lysaker, Norway: The Fridtjof Nansen Institute 5 (2006), available at https://www.fni.no/getfile.php/132005/Filer/Publikasjoner/FNI-R1106.pdf

[19] Karine Peschard, *Seed Wars and Farmers' Rights: Comparative Perspectives from Brazil and India*, 44(1) The Journal of Peasant Studies, 144–68 (2017).

[20] *Id.*

[21] *Id.*

[22] *Id.*

[23] Maria Laura da Rocha, *Brazil 's Experiences on Agroecology: Enhancing Family Farming and Promoting Sustainable Rural Development* (June 1, 2016), available at http://www.fao.org/fileadmin/user_upload/bodies/CL_154/Agroecoloby/Perm_Rep_Brazil_-_Maria_Laura_da_Rocha_-_Speech.pdf.

[24] *Brazil Soy Group Says to End Legal Dispute with Monsanto*, Reuters (Aug. 9, 2013), available at http://www.reuters.com/article/monsanto-brazil-lawsuit/brazil-soy-group-says-to-end-legal-dispute-with-monsanto-idUSL1N0GA00720130809.

[25] *Brazilian Judge Rules in Favor of Farmers Against Monsanto*, GM Watch (Oct. 13, 2013), available at http://www.gmwatch.org/en/bills-test/15107-brazilian-judge-rules-in-favour-of-farmers-against-monsanto.

In India, approximately 80 percent of the seed market is met by the "unorganized sector," primarily farm-saved seeds.[26] This market is protected by the Indian Protection of Plant Varieties and Farmers' Rights Act, which protects farmers and creates systems to redistribute wealth from agrochemical farms to farmers. Farmers are recognized as breeders and generally have the same rights guaranteed to public and private breeders.[27] Farmers may register varieties and are entitled to intellectual property protection. Farmers' varieties are defined as (1) those that have been traditionally cultivated and developed by farmers in their fields or (2) those that are wild relatives or landraces.[28] Wild relatives are wild plant species closely related to crops; landraces are genetically diverse varieties, adapted locally by farmers in traditional farming systems in the absence of formal plant breeding.[29] Farmers' varieties enjoy heightened protection because they do not need to meet "novelty" criteria applied to commercial varieties. The system is subsidized by larger agrochemical firms; they must pay a processing fee for registration, while farmers do not. Moreover, farmers may "save, use, sow, re-sow, exchange, share or sell seeds, including from protected varieties," as well as harvested materials, "in the same manner as he was entitled before the coming into force of this Act."[30] The law defines a "farmer" as "any person who cultivates crops himself or herself, or through direct supervision; or who conserves and adds value to wild species or traditional varieties through the selection and identification of their useful properties."[31] Farmers may therefore sell protected varieties' seeds as long as they do so under generic rather than branded labels.[32] Like the interpretation of Brazilian law (although statutorily protected) farmers may not be liable for infringing plant breeders' rights if they demonstrate they did not do so knowingly.[33] Farmers have a right to know expected yields of protected varieties, and to compensation if the seeds underperform.[34]

> The PPV&FR Act also includes provisions for benefit-sharing. Farmers who are engaged in the conservation of genetic resources and their improvement through selection are entitled to receive benefits through the National Gene Fund. Upon registering varieties, private and public breeders must declare if they have used

[26] Sujith Koonan, India's Sui Generis System of Plant Variety Protection 2 (2014), available at http://www.ielrc.org/content/f1401.pdf.

[27] GoI–Government of India. 2001. The Protection of Plant Varieties and Farmers' Rights Act, 2001. Act No. 53.

[28] Peschard, *supra* note 19.

[29] *Id.*

[30] The Protection of Plant Varieties and Farmers' Rights Act, 2001. Act No. 53., Art. 39 iv.

[31] *Id.* at art. 2k.

[32] Marc Cohen & Anitha Ramanna, *Public Access to Seeds and the Human Right to Adequate Food*, in George Kent (ed), Global Obligations for the Human Right to Food 161–90 (2007).

[33] Peschard, *supra* note 28.

[34] *Id.*

> genetic resources maintained by [i]ndigenous people or farmers' communities. Indigenous and farmers' communities are entitled to benefits, and can file claims to the National Gene Fund when they believe that genetic resources from their communities have been used without their authorization.[35]

Applications for variety protection are available on a public website, which also serves as a forum where applications may be challenged.[36]

Peruvian law applicable to plant genetic resources for use in food and agriculture draws from implementation of the CBD constitutional principles protecting indigenous knowledge and practices, as well as application of the International Seed Treaty. The so-called farmers' exception for exchange, selling, and distribution of seeds is protected by Law 27811 for the Protection of Collective Knowledge of Indigenous People.[37] The right to participate in the fair and equitable sharing of benefits derived from access to and use of plant genetic resources for food and agriculture has been recognized in a series of laws and regulations in Peru.[38]

The redistributive effect of limitations on trademarks in specific product sectors is less direct than the sharing mechanisms in place for medicines, vaccines, and seeds, but may in fact have just as great of an effect. Philip Morris International and its subsidiaries claimed that Uruguay's trademark-limiting measures caused it $22.267 million in lost sales.[39] As a result of Uruguay's tobacco control regulations and policies, smoking rates declined from approximately 35 percent to approximately 23 percent of the adult population between 2005 and 2014. Youth rates fell notably, to 8.2 percent as of 2014.[40] While there has been no systematic effort to attribute the declines to the specific trademark-restrictive measures, whatever reduction was thereby caused represents a reduction in the transfer of wealth from the Uruguayan state (which, of course, must bear the costs of smoking to individual and public health) to PMI's corporate entities. As Cynthia Callard has argued, the global tobacco market represents a large redistribution of wealth from poorer countries to richer ones.[41]

35 *Id.*

36 Protection of Plant Varieties and Farmers' Rights Authority, India, available at http://www.plantauthority.gov.in/publications.htm.

37 Law No. 27811, *Law Introducing a Protection Regime for the Collective Knowledge of Indigenous Peoples Derived from Biological Resources*, El Peruano (Aug. 10, 2002), available at http://www.wipo.int/edocs/lexdocs/laws/en/pe/pe011en.pdf.

38 Manuel Ruiz Muller, Farmers' Rights in Peru: A Case Study (2006).

39 International Centre for the Settlement of Investment Disputes, Award, Philip Morris Brands, SARL, Philip Morris Products, SA, and Abal Hermanos SA v. Oriental Republic of Uruguay, ICSID Case No. ARB/10/7 ¶12 (July 8, 2016).

40 Winston Abascal et al., *Tobacco Control Campaign in Uruguay: A Population Based Trend*, PubMed (Sept. 14, 2012).

41 Cynthia Callard, *Follow the Money: How the Billions of Dollars That Flow from Smokers in Poor Nations to Companies in Rich Nations Greatly Exceed Funding for Global Tobacco Control and What Might Be Done about It*, 19(4) Tobacco Control 285–90 (2010).

A similar dynamic applies to countries that adopt the International Code of Marketing of Breastmilk Substitutes'proscription on images of infants that imply the superiority of formula over exclusive breastfeeding for the first six months of life. Brazil fully incorporated the International Code into law in 1988, embedded subsequent World Health Assembly resolutions into administrative regulations, and authorized third-party monitoring. Breastfeeding rates have risen steadily as a result.[42] According to India's National Family Health Survey (NFHS)-4, 41.6% children under 3 years of age were breastfed within one hour of birth in 2015–16 as compared to 23.4% in 2005–06.[43] Approximately 55% of India's children are exclusively breastfed, which was nearly 10% more than the decade before. Like Brazil, India has adopted prohibitions of pictures that imply or state superiority of infant formula over breastfeeding for the first six months of life.

Unlike the indirect redistribution accomplished through trademark restriction, the Marrakesh Treaty is explicit in its redistributive objectives and its purpose of fulfilling development priorities of poorer countries. The treaty acknowledges that the "majority of persons with visual impairments or with other print disabilities live in developing and least-developed countries," attributes the lack of access for poorer countries to a global market failure ("the market is unable to provide such access"), and asserts a "balance" between the rights of authors and the public interest, even though the ultimate effect of the treaty is to diminish theretofore protected authors' (publishers') rights to reproduction.[44] On September 30, 2016, the day that the treaty entered into force, libraries in Argentina, Chile, Ecuador, El Salvador, Guatemala, Paraguay, Peru, and Uruguay began sharing accessible copies in ways that international intellectual property law would have previously rendered impossibly expensive.[45]

Generally, scholars of international intellectual property law highlight it as a unidirectional redistribution of wealth from poorer countries to richer ones.[46] That is a fair characterization of the changes made to the international intellectual property regime that unfolded between 1967 and 1995. Yet there have also been, especially since 2001, counterredistributive movements under way. In the areas of basic human needs as would have been understood by Robert McNamara, as well as

[42] See M. F. Rea, *Rethinking Breastfeeding in Brazil: How We Reached 10 Months of Duration*. 19 Cadernos de Saude Publica suppl.1: 37–45 (2003).

[43] Rhythma Kaul, *World Breastfeeding Week: More Women in India Are Breastfeeding than Before*, Hindustan Times (Aug. 4, 2017).

[44] Marrakesh Treaty, Preamble (2013).

[45] La Asociación Tiflonexos, Press Release (Sept. 30, 2016), available at https://www.facebook.com/tiflonexos/posts/1659624707687376:0.

[46] Vandana Shiva, Biopiracy: the Plunder of Nature and Knowledge (1999); Vandana Shiva, Monocultures of the Mind: Perspectives on Biodiversity and Biotechnology (1993); Peter Drahos & Ruth Mayne (eds), Global Intellectual Property Rights: Knowledge, Access, and Development (2002); Mario Cimoli, Giovanni Dosi, Keith Maskus, Ruth Okediji, Jerome Reichman & Joseph Stiglitz (eds), Intellectual Property Rights: Legal and Economic Challenges for Development (2014).

the leadership of most specialized UN agencies, a number of treaties have emerged or are in the process of emerging that either stymie otherwise strong intellectual property protections or allow them their anticipated force but redistribute the resulting benefits. As the next chapter describes, these countermovements have also erected international or supranational regulatory structures that either substitute for a lack of regulatory capacity at the national level or impose regulatory regimes that are less feasible at the national level. These structures, it is argued, have the substantial potential to implement the kinds of oversight, at least in industries with small numbers of firms whose activities have a disproportionate effect on the interests of low-income countries and their populations, that the New International Economic Order always sought.

15

International Intellectual Property Shelters and Supranational Regulation

Oligopolies are not unique to the sectors playing crucial roles in developing countries' technology transfer and growth objectives. Indeed, oligopoly characterizes not only the sectors of the global economy analyzed in the foregoing chapters but many national economies as well, including the United States. As Derek Thompson summarized,

> To comprehend the scope of corporate consolidation, imagine a day in the life of a typical American and ask: How long does it take for her to interact with a market that isn't nearly monopolized? She wakes up to browse the internet, access to which is sold through a local monopoly. She stocks up on food at a superstore such as Walmart, which owns a quarter of the grocery market. If she gets indigestion, she might go to a pharmacy, likely owned by one of three companies controlling 99 percent of that market. If she's stressed and wants to relax outside the shadow of an oligopoly, she'll have to stay away from ebooks, music, and beer; two companies control more than half of all sales in each of these markets. There is no escape – literally. She can try boarding an airplane, but four corporations control 80 percent of the seats on domestic flights.[1]

Even at the global level, the trend is in many industries not necessarily affecting basic human needs.[2] The European Aeronautic Defense and Space Company and Boeing control more than 50 percent market share within the global civil aerospace products manufacturing industry.[3] In certain product sectors, it is essentially a

[1] Derek Thompson, *America's Monopoly Problem*, The Atlantic (2016), available at https://www.theatlantic.com/magazine/archive/2016/10/americas-monopoly-problem/497549/.

[2] Alexander Ovodenko, *Governing Oligopolies: Global Regimes and Market Structure* 16(3) Global Environmental Politics 106–26 (2016).

[3] Glennon Harrison, Challenge to Boeing-Airbus Duopoly in Civil Aircraft: Issues for Competitiveness (2011), available at https://fas.org/sgp/crs/misc/R41925.pdf.

duopoly.[4] DHL, Fedex, and UPS control roughly 50 percent of the global logistics/courier market.[5] Global energy firms and smartphone operating systems are similarly concentrated.

As this book has argued, what distinguishes global oligopolies in pharmaceuticals, agrochemicals, specific consumer products sectors, and academic publishing are their relationship with the basic human needs approach to development adopted by many, if not all (in some form), poorer countries. Traditionally, at least since the end of the nineteenth century, the normal regulatory approach applied to oligopolies (in collusive oligopolies sometimes stronger laws are applied) has been antitrust or competition law. Under that law, monopolies, duopolies, and oligopolies are, depending on certain circumstances, subjected to regulatory review before they materialize (for example, pre-merger) and, after they do, challenged by consumers adversely affected by their conduct (conventionally identified through abnormally high prices but which may involve a number of practices that aim to restrict competition), governments acting in consumers' interests for similar reasons and other competitors or potential competitors. Competition law is, at its core, motivated by the idea that public authorities may create, construct, define, and limit markets.

The idea that planners may so structure markets is controversial. Friedrich Hayek accused antitrust laws of destroying competition by creating market winners and losers conscientiously or inadvertently favored by the state.[6] Monopolies, according to Hayek, were natural and permissible except in rare cases such as a monopoly over "essential commodities" like water.[7] Influential organizational theorists such as Ronald Coase and Oliver Williamson argued over the course of the 1960s and 1970s that market behavior that appeared anticompetitive really served efficiency purposes that would enhance overall social welfare.[8] As noted in the introduction, Schumpeter famously argued that in research and development intensive sectors, concentration was necessary for the next, steep investments in innovation. Antitrust law in some countries, notably the United States, has endeavored to accommodate this possibility. The questions surrounding competition law's nature and reach remain disputed in both the economic and legal literature.

4 Tim Hepher & Cyril Altmeyer, *Boeing Overtakes Airbus in Annual Sales Race*, REUTERS (Jan. 17, 2013), available at http://www.reuters.com/article/us-airbus-orders/boeing-overtakes-airbus-in-annual-sales-race-idUSBRE90G0CF20130117.

5 Nick Carey, *Fedex Just Scored a Major Victory against UPS*, BUSINESS INSIDER (Apr. 7, 2015), available at http://www.businessinsider.com/fedex-just-scored-a-major-victory-against-ups-2015-4; *And Then There Were Three*, ECONOMIST (Sept. 2012), available at http://www.economist.com/node/21561894.

6 Friedrich Hayek, *"Free" Enterprise and Competitive Order*, in INDIVIDUALISM AND ECONOMIC ORDER 107–18 (1948).

7 FRIEDRICH HAYEK, THE CONSTITUTION OF LIBERTY 136 (1960).

8 Oliver Williamson, *The Vertical Integration of Production: Market Failure Considerations*, 61 AM. ECON. REV. 112–23 (1971); RONALD COASE, THE FIRM, THE MARKET, AND THE LAW 6 (1988).

What is generally not disputed is that antitrust or competition law *is or should be* the applicable body of regulation. Even if consumers or patients ultimately challenge monopolistic or oligopolistic conduct they view as injurious (rather than other market competitors or public authorities), the normal relief afforded them is money in the form of recompense for the higher prices they paid; decrees from courts or regulators that specific anticompetitive conduct cease; and, breakups or forced sales of firms deemed too large for society's good.[9] In one of the largest illegal cartel arrangements in recent history that affected human health and nutrition – vitamins – the overwhelmingly largest relief given to consumers was money.[10]

International intellectual property shelters, the areas of international intellectual property law carved out in the interests of poorer countries' development, should be understood as regulatory alternatives to antitrust or competition law. While the background principles are similar – concentrated markets with adverse effects on consumers – the regulatory objectives differ. Rather than redistribute abnormally high monopoly or oligopoly prices through courts or public authorities, international intellectual property shelters redistribute those prices through other mechanisms. That is, oligopolists share anticompetitively produced goods with those adversely affected: medicines, vaccines, books, seeds, and other products similarly regulated. As Chapter 14 analyzed, sometimes that redistribution is in favor of market competitors like technology necessary to manufacture medicines and vaccines or low-cost or royalty-free use of proprietary seed varieties.

With respect to trademarks, this mechanism works slightly differently. Under optimal conditions, as Chapter 8 analyzed, trademarks serve two purposes. First, they protect a firm from competitors "free riding" on the investments the firm has made in producing a high-quality good or service.[11] Second, trademarks provide a low-cost source of product information for consumers, who may quickly identify the good or service they prefer.[12] In the context of the product areas analyzed in Chapters 8 and 12 – infant foods and tobacco – international intellectual property shelters eliminate or authorize the obfuscation of trademarks that *do not and cannot* serve a consumer information cost-reducing purpose. Indeed, in those cases, trademarks targeted under the International Code of Marketing of Breastmilk Substitutes and the Framework Convention on Tobacco Control actually *raise* the cost of consumer information.

9 Frank H. Easterbrook, *Workable Antitrust Policy*, 84 Mich. L. Rev. 1696, 1701 (1986); Herbert Hovenkamp, The Antitrust Enterprise: Principle And Execution 297–302 (2006).

10 Mitsuru Igami & Takuo Sagaya, *Measuring the Incentive to Collude: The Vitamin Cartels 1990–99*, available at http://economics.yale.edu/sites/default/files/igamisugaya_170309_vitamin cartels.pdf.

11 Apostolos Chronopolous, *Legal and Economic Arguments for the Protection of Advertising Value through Trademark*, 4(4) Queen Mary Journal of Intellectual Property 256–76 (2014).

12 William M. Landes & Richard Posner, *Trademark Law: An Economic Perspective*, 30 J. Law Econ. 265 (1987).

To be sure, most countries maintain laws that prohibit product packaging and labeling, especially trademarks, that assert "false" or "misleading" statements.[13] But these prohibitions rarely reach the subtle forms of communication mediated by trademarks. The image of a healthy, smiling baby on an infant formula container is by its nature at odds with medical evidence that "exclusive breastfeeding is best for the first six months of life," but it is difficult to argue that the image, out of context, is "false."[14] Similarly, light-blue packaging of branded cigarettes is perceived by consumers to be less hazardous than a bright-red or black package of the same brand, but without seeing those packages against one another, it would be difficult to say one or the other "misled" a consumer.[15]

That the international intellectual property shelters described in Chapters 10 through 13 are effectively supranational forms of regulation is borne out by the perceptions of the regulated firms themselves. The global pharmaceutical industry has tended to discuss broad access-to-medicines agreements and frameworks in terms of their regulatory nature. Reacting to the ways in which the Doha Declaration altered the global landscape of pharmaceutical patents, the IFPMA, the global pharmaceutical trade group, argued that compulsory licenses "should be seen as a final option" and that "frequent use of them could discourage introduction of new medicines . . . and . . . undermine the system that underpins the ability of the private sector to undertake essential R&D."[16] The negotiations over the establishment of the WHO Pandemic Influenza Preparedness Framework Agreement were viewed, at least by the IFPMA, as fundamentally about what level of supranational regulation would be imposed for them to participate in the Global Influenza Surveillance and Response System for virus samples with pandemic potential.

The 1981 International Code of Marketing of Breastmilk Substitutes is effectively a Nestlé-specific treaty that, even in 1981, controlled 50 percent of the global infant formula market.[17] Between 1979 and 1981, negotiations over the International Code's scope potentially affected each of Nestlé's markets differently. Each had a strong position that it first urged its host country to support. Efforts to thwart or manage

13 Paris Convention art. 6 *quinquies(B)(iii)*; G. H. C. Bodenhausen, Guide to the Application of the Paris Convention for the Protection of Industrial Property 70, 116 (1968).

14 UNICEF, *Protecting Breastfeeding in West and Central Africa*, available at http://www.unicef.org/wcaro/WCARO_Pub_Breastfeeding.pdf.

15 E. C. Etzel et al., *Consumer Research Proposal: Camel Filter Revised Packaging Test Study* (Legacy Tobacco Documents Library, Mar. 2, 1979), available at http://legacy.library.ucsf.edu/tid/qxb79d00.

16 Manisha Desai, *Compulsory Licensing: Procedural Requirements under the TRIPS Agreement*, in J. L. Valverde & Eduardo Pisani (eds), *The Globalisation of the Pharmaceutical Industry*, 18 Pharmaceutical Policy and the Law 31–44 (2016), available at https://www.ifpma.org/wp-content/uploads/2016/11/The-Globalisation-of-the-Pharmaceutical-Industry-Monograph.pdf.

17 Mongoven, Biscoe, and Duchin, Inc., An Analysis of the International Framework Convention Process 3 (1997), available at https://www.industrydocumentslibrary.ucsf.edu/tobacco/docs/gkyk0061.

global regulation at the national market level, according to Nestlé internal analysis, "were canceling each other out."[18] When momentum picked up for the establishment of an international agreement regulating the use of infant images and other visuals to promote breastmilk substitutes, Nestlé established a central office under the control of its Chief Operating Officer to coordinate the responses of each global market.[19]

When Canada, Finland, Tanzania, and Mexico introduced the idea of a global tobacco control treaty at the World Health Organization, four corporations controlled 75 percent of the global market and had already demonstrated a strong ability to shape health perceptions of their products through the use of their trademarks.[20] The global tobacco industry put the conceptual notion of supranational regulation at the core of its fierce resistance to the Framework Convention on Tobacco Control. In one of its many communications regarding the treaty, BAT argued that supranational regulation was warranted "only if and insofar as the objectives of the proposed action cannot be sufficiently achieved by individual countries," a line echoed in submissions by Brown & Williamson to the US Department of Health and Human Services.[21] Because tobacco control measures could be adopted at the national level, the argument went, there was no need for an international instrument.[22] Philip Morris endeavored generally to discredit the WHO as a tobacco regulatory body and sought to weaken the treaty through its influence on national delegations.[23]

Attorneys for major publishing and copyright-holding constituencies have similarly tended to view the Marrakesh Treaty and similar developing countries' efforts at the World Intellectual Property Organization as thinly veiled attempts to create a new kind of supranational regulatory regime over publishing interests.

> Not surprisingly, the debates and controversies percolating in the United States are not unlike those occurring in international fora. One example is the call for an extreme make-over of copyright law by the adoption of broad mandatory collective licensing schemes for on-line music (and other media) services - perhaps even cross-border services ... these broader notions of mandatory collective licensing are far

[18] *Id.*

[19] *Id.*

[20] *The WHO FCTC and the Tobacco Free Initiative*, in Mitchell and Voon (eds), THE GLOBAL TOBACCO EPIDEMIC AND THE LAW 13 (2014), available at https://www.theatlantic.com/health/archive/2015/02/has-a-global-tobacco-treaty-made-a-difference/386399/.

[21] Comments of Brown & Williamson Tobacco Corporation on the World Health Organization Framework Convention on Tobacco Control, Mar. 29, 2000, available at http://legacy.library.ucsf.edu/tid/uri45a99.

[22] Comments of British American Tobacco Corporation on the World Health Organization Framework Convention on Tobacco Control, Oct. 2000, http://legacy.library.ucsf.edu/tid/kwc65a99.

[23] H. M. Mamudu & Stanton Glantz, *Civil Society and the Negotiation of the Framework Convention on Tobacco Control*, 4(2) GLOBAL PUBLIC HEALTH 150–68 (2010).

> afield of the treaty limitations and the confines of the three-step test . . . As another example, there are some countries within the WIPO (including Brazil, Ecuador and Paraguay) calling for broader exceptions, and perhaps even new treaties, for particular uses and users . . . [The] call for new – broad – exceptions, understandings among nations (such as "best practices" for fair use or fair dealing), or even a treaty, has raised serious and legitimate concerns for developed countries and rightsholders, given the ease of copying and the dissemination across borders of works in the digital era.[24]

In its implementation guide, the International Publishers Association refers to "the potential for harm to result from unintended consequences of implementation" of Marrakesh and recommends that it, and its constituent groups, be the "natural stakeholder" to coordinate between WIPO, the World Blind Union, and libraries making accessible copies available, so as to "monitor the correct implementation of" the treaty's provisions.[25] Berne's and TRIPS's three-step test are asserted to be the prevailing international regulatory standard and the IPA is clearly concerned that under Marrakesh "there is a risk that the conditions of the Three-Step Test [may not be] met," in which case "the implementation regulations must be adapted. In that sense, they may not be interpreted too broadly."[26] The alternatives, of course, represent regulatory interests that might, as Chapter 14 detailed, authorize or facilitate additional redistributive channels.

The purpose of understanding the international intellectual property shelters described and analyzed in Chapters 10 through 13 as forms of industry regulation is to better understand how regulation adapts (if at all) when it is formed at the supranational level as well as, in understanding that adaptation, what lessons to date about regulation mean for the future of supranational mechanisms aimed at supporting developing countries' objectives. There remains a fairly identifiable division in the literature generated by economists, international relations theorists, political scientists, and sociologists that regulation is either a commodity driven by industry demand or a political response that emerges to protect the public interest from pernicious firm behavior, including monopolies and oligopolies.[27] At the international level, there is far less agreement as to the contexts, industrial sectors, or international organizations in which governments, firms, or other groups may exercise greatest influence.[28] International intellectual property shelters may enrich

[24] Eric Schwartz, *An Overview of the International Treatment of Exceptions*, 57(3) JOURNAL OF THE COPYRIGHT SOCIETY 473, 495–96 (2010).

[25] International Publishers Association, *IPA Guide to the Marrakesh Treaty* (2013), available at https://www.internationalpublishers.org/images/Accessibility/IPA_Guide_to_the_Marrakesh_Treaty.pdf.

[26] *Id.*

[27] Ernest Dal Bo, *Regulatory Capture: A Review*, 22(2) OXFORD REV. OF ECON. POLICY 203 (2006).

[28] Walter Mattli and Ngaire Woods, *In Whose Benefit? Explaining Regulatory Change in Global Politics* in Walter Mattli and Ngaire Woods (eds) THE POLITICS OF GLOBAL REGULATION 1–43 (2010).

the theoretical debate occupying the middle ground between these positions, as well as offer pragmatic insights as to how supranational regulatory mechanisms may work, when they do, differently than national-level analogs.

Orthodox economic criticisms of regulation (which arose primarily in the context of utility regulation) have tended to focus on the tendency of regulatory structures to ultimately benefit the targeted industry or to "capture" those structures.[29] As with the regulatory structures analyzed herein, the normative desire behind a regulatory regime may commence with an objective to protect the public interest from monopolistic abuse, but end up adversely distorting markets by creating barriers to entry for new participants, ensuring special privileges, or effectively fixing high prices.[30] The mechanisms of capture are less clear, although the "revolving door" between regulatory bodies and regulated firms features prominently in many analyses.[31] There is at least preliminary, anecdotal evidence to suggest that the regulatory regimes analyzed above are subject to the same industry pressures and interests that have characterized national regulatory regimes.

The mechanisms of the International Seed Treaty have exposed its potential use to exacerbate rather than ameliorate global concentration and related practices of large agrochemical firms. Under the terms of the treaty, large agrochemical firms are by right empowered to request access to all seeds deposited, "splice in [genetic modifications] then patent and sell the seed."[32] According to the Center for Food Safety, the agreements governing deposits into seed banks are opaque and complicated, inherently favoring wealthier parties seeking to acquire seeds for patenting and marketing purposes rather than farmers in developing countries seeking to create new varieties.[33]

In the context of the Framework Convention on Tobacco Control, Philip Morris International, like other tobacco giants, initially opposed the treaty precisely because of its likely effect of reducing smoking rates globally.[34] However, the firm began to

[29] George Priest, *The Origins of Utility Regulation and the "Theories of Regulation" Debate*, 36(1) J. OF LAW AND ECON. 289–323 (1993).

[30] George Stigler, *The Theory of Economic Regulation*, 2(1) BELL JOURNAL OF ECONOMICS AND MANAGEMENT SCIENCE 3–21 (1971).

[31] B. Meehan & B. L. Benson, *The Occupations of Regulators Influence Occupational Regulation: Evidence from the US Private Security Industry*, 162(1–2) PUBLIC CHOICE 97–117 (2015); D. Coen & M. Vannoni, *Sliding Doors in Brussels: A Career Path Analysis of EU Affairs Managers*, 55(4) EUR. J. POL. RES. 811–26 (2016); S. Hong & J. Lim, *Capture and the Bureaucratic Mafia: Does the Revolving Door Erode Bureaucratic Integrity?*, 166(1–2) PUBLIC CHOICE 69–86 (2016).

[32] Kent Whealy, *Svalbard Doomsday Vault: Biopiracy by UN Treaty* (Oct. 2010), in Catherine Phillips (ed), SAVING MORE THAN SEEDS: PRACTICES AND POLITICS OF SEED SAVING 263 (2016).

[33] Andrew Kimbrell, *Seed Banks*, available at https://www.centerforfoodsafety.org/issues/303/seeds/seed-banks.

[34] Ruth Roemer, Allyn Taylor & Jean Lariviere, *Origins of the WHO Framework Convention on Tobacco Control*, 95(6) AM. J. PUB. HEALTH 936 (2003), available at http://ajph.aphapublications.org/doi/pdf/10.2105/AJPH.2003.025908.

view the treaty as a way to establish international standards that would fix its position as the global premium cigarette maker (the state-owned China National Tobacco Corporation with its enormous internal market technically has the largest global market share) and to adopt measures that would disadvantage potential or actual competitors.[35] Since expressing support, the tobacco giant has devoted substantial resources to undermining aspects of the treaty that disfavor it, labeling it a "regulatory runaway train."[36]

International intellectual property shelters also suggest structural or policy alternatives that may be more likely to create organizational incentives for public interest protection. Regulation at the supranational level may allow for explicit acknowledgment of capture risks and measures to address those risks more difficult under national frameworks. Within the shelters identified above, some entirely barred participation by regulated firms while others included them as integral parts of the negotiation process. The World Health Organization allowed participation by "representatives of non-Member States, of liberation movements referred to in resolution WHA27.37, of organizations of the United Nations system, of intergovernmental organizations with which WHO has established effective relations, and of nongovernmental organizations in official relations with WHO," effectively cutting global tobacco firms out of the official treaty-drafting process (although they could and did participate as part of national delegations). This norm was codified in the treaty itself in Article 5.3, which required parties to protect their health policies from tobacco industry interests, made even stronger in guidelines issued by the Conference of the Parties, which declared a "fundamental and irreconcilable conflict between tobacco industry interests" and public health and set forth recommendations that, at their strongest, quashed tobacco company participation in the policy-making process altogether.[37]

The International Code of Marketing of Breastmilk Substitutes, by contrast, involved regulated firms from its first draft. Not only were infant formula company representatives from nine countries consulted by WHO drafters but also the global trade group, the International Council of Infant Food Industries.[38] Similarly, the WHO's Pandemic Influenza Preparedness Framework could not have materialized, at least in its present form, without the participation of the major global pharmaceutical firms, as they not only promise to share benefits of participation in the Global Influenza Surveillance and Response System; they fund its operation.

[35] Skip Wollenberg, *Philip Morris: Could OK Regs*, Wash. Post (Aug. 31, 2000), available at http://www.washingtonpost.com/wp-srv/aponline/20000831/aponline000101_000.htm.

[36] Aditya Kalra, Paritosh Bansal, Duff Wilson & Tom Lassetter, *Inside Philip Morris' Campaign to Subvert the Global Anti-Smoking Treaty*, Reuters (July 13, 2017), available at https://www.reuters.com/investigates/special-report/pmi-who-fctc/.

[37] FCTC Article 5.3.

[38] Sami Shubber, The International Code of Marketing of Breastmilk Substitutes 11 (1998).

Between full participation and prohibition of formal participation exist a number of possibilities including participation as part of national delegations, the forms of influence firms may exercise through each channel, and what role, if any, direct financial support for negotiations or shelter mechanisms may be. Each of these factors may influence the extent to which a given regulatory regime effectively reorients intellectual property rights from private wealth accumulation to redistribution or furtherance of global population health and nutrition outcomes.

Similarly, the access and benefit-sharing mechanisms prompted by the Convention on Biological Diversity and the Nagoya Protocol open possibilities for regulating in favor of end-users (other than market structure or price) in ways less frequently adopted in national frameworks. Whatever unintended effects regulation renders on target firms in the national context, there is wide agreement that the purpose of regulation is rule making, rule monitoring, and rule enforcement.[39] Typically those rules are developed by an administrative agency, another specific focus of regulatory theory. Even under the modified term of "governance" by which a broader set of stakeholders, institutions, and policies over a given subject area is analyzed, the typical models include hybrids of already existing regulatory mechanisms, stakeholder forums, and public-private dialogues.

International intellectual property shelters lie outside regimes with those characteristics. They are certainly regulatory in nature but do little in the way of rule making or "governance." The WHO Pandemic Influenza Preparedness Framework Standard Material Transfer Agreements, for example, condition access to biological materials collected through the Global Influenza Surveillance and Response System on promises to provide pandemic vaccines, share intellectual property, or share doses of antiviral medicines as well as requiring pharmaceutical, medical device, and diagnostic firms to pay for half of the GISRS system. There is otherwise no effort to condition the behavior of regulated firms.

The International Code of Marketing of Breastmilk Substitutes and the Framework Convention on Tobacco Control are more typical of regulatory efforts: prescribing rules, best practices, and guidelines to achieve a given public interest objective. But that objective itself – maximizing exclusive breastfeeding for the first six months of life – offers a level of specificity, supported by medical evidence, atypical of most regulatory agencies and their mandates. More importantly, in the latter case, the regulatory apparatus operates with the explicit exclusion of the target industry.

Whatever the context, it is clear that international intellectual property shelters are *both* a comprehensive and cohesive response to the international intellectual property exertions made by wealthier countries over the course of the 1980s and 1990s, as well as a *continuation* of New International Economic Order policies that

[39] Christopher Hood, Henry Rothstein & Robert Baldwin, The Government of Risk: Understanding Risk Regulation Regimes (2001).

prioritized the regulation of multinational firms. The emergence of a small number of global firms that dominate knowledge-intensive markets was made possible through the expanding network of trade and investment treaties. Now, those firms directly participate in regulatory regimes that affect the price and availability of their products, require them to directly pay to support international mechanisms that at least partially redistribute their revenues, and, in some cases, prescribe limits on their conduct based on medical or scientific evidence rather than the positions those firms press through participatory channels.

Conclusion

The New International Economic Order reflected the drastic gap between global rich and poor that followed decolonization and, as many poorer countries argued, was directly traceable to distortionary and destructive colonial policies. Focused on global wealth redistribution, technology transfer, and the behavior of global firms based in Europe and North America, the New International Economic Order was channeled into the confrontation between expanding intellectual property rights and the development interests of low- and middle-income states during the 1980s and 1990s.[1] The system of international intellectual property protection that commenced with disputes over technology transfer in the 1970s and morphed into a trade issue after 1986 has attracted a great deal of attention from scholars, some of whom have given the topic extensive, multi-volume treatment.

Many of these analyses tied the establishment of the new international intellectual property regime with the far less extensive literature on the politics of global regulation of private firms.[2] Yet even within this latter literature, the depiction of the current state of intellectual property and development is overwhelmingly focused on the "ratcheting up" of intellectual property to the detriment of developing countries' interests.[3] No doubt, those claims are well supported.But those analyses have missed at least part of the inevitable response undertaken by developing countries.

Agreements and treaties negotiated in contexts as diverse as staple crop seed protection, access to influenza vaccines, and regulation of infant formula trademarks represent a cohesive effort to redistribute intellectual property monopoly rents back to poor populations in poor countries. Moreover, these agreements, termed herein "international intellectual property shelters," emerged not only as

1 Amy Jocelyn Glass, *Costly R&D and Intellectual Property Rights Protection*, 19 Int'l J. of Tech. Management 1 (2000).
2 John Braithwaite & Peter Drahos, Global Business Regulation (2000).
3 *Id.*

geopolitical responses but as regulatory responses, in many cases explicitly so, to market failures in the same way that regulatory structures are understood to emerge in national economies.[4]

As forms of regulation, international intellectual property shelters' design will ultimately determine how well they achieve their objectives, whether those are protection of global public welfare or merely efforts to redistribute wealth from rich to poor or vice versa, and in which contexts additional shelters are likely to emerge. This book has endeavored to take the first of these steps by identifying a heretofore unrecognized phenomenon at work in international economic law.

4 Rahim Moloo & Alex Khachaturian, *The Compliance with the Law Requirement in International Investment Law*, 34 FORDHAM INT'L. L. J. 1473 (2011).

Index

Lightning Source UK Ltd.
Milton Keynes UK
UKHW022354150722
405943UK00004B/42

9 781107 177802